DON BAYLOR

DON BAYLOR

Nothing But the Truth:
A Baseball Life

DON BAYLOR
with Claire Smith

ST. MARTIN'S PRESS/NEW YORK

Design by Glen M. Edelstein

Library of Congress Cataloging-in-Publication Data

Baylor, Don.
    Don Baylor—nothing but the truth: a baseball life / Don
  Baylor with Claire Smith.
      p. cm.
    ISBN 0-312-02906-3
     1. Baylor, Don. 2. Baseball players—United States—Biography.
    3. Baseball—United States—History. I. Smith, Claire. II. Title.
GV865.B334A3   1989
796.357′092′4—dc19
[B]   88-35151
                                          CIP

First Edition

10 9 8 7 6 5 4 3 2 1

This book is dedicated with love to my mother, Lillian; father, George; my son, Don, Jr.; and most of all, my wife, Rebecca, for showing me all the faith and love a heart can hold.

D.B.

To my father, who always sees the beauty in the stars; and my mother, who sees the mystery beyond those stars. To Bill, Bart, Hawk, and Sophia, with love. And to Bob Wright and Jon Pessah—my Frank and Brooks.

And to Don. Thanks, Big Guy.

C.S.

CONTENTS

PART 2

PART 3

FOREWORD

YOU'RE about to read the story of a guy who probably won't show up in a lot of the all-time statistical record books. He's not a publicity seeker and although I find this hard to believe, he's played in only one All-Star Game.

But guess what. He probably has a greater right to be called a "winner" than any player in the major leagues right now. You don't play on three different World Series teams in three straight years by accident.

When told that I've served as Don Baylor's role model, I feel as much pride in that title as I have in any other I've earned over my long career in baseball. Why? Because it's Don who has served as a role model for so many of today's players. His work ethic on and off the field is unsurpassed in the major leagues today, of that I am sure. I've always admired the way he has played the game—his enthusiasm and pride, no matter what game, or what time of the season.

Don has always played the game a lot like I did, and that isn't an accident, either. We both spent a lot of time helping to build one of the greatest franchises in baseball history—the Baltimore Orioles.

When you think of the Orioles, the names that most often come to mind are Brooks, Frank, Boog, Palmer, McNally, Murray, Ripken, etc. Don's name usually doesn't come as quick. But it should. He's as typical of the old Orioles style as anyone—a classic team player, fundamentally flawless, tough, aggressive, and always willing to listen—characteristics that made the Orioles teams of the sixties, seventies, and early eighties great.

Playing in an Orioles' uniform for six years was a special time for me and Don has made no secret that his tenure with the O's was the best time of his career. It's a proud kinship we share.

As much as we have in common, I've really only worked closely with Don once. And he proved then just how willing he was to listen, learn, and, if necessary, change. It was in 1977, after I had left the Indians and had been hired by Angels manager Dave Garcia as coach for the second half of that season. Don was my main project. He had been struggling through the first half. We looked at videotapes of Don when he was hitting well and noticed that his stance in the batter's box had changed. His hands, too, were in a different position than they normally were. We made the necessary adjustments and just talked hitting all of the time.

I think the main thing I did was to get his head straight. He had just signed a large contract the year before and was pressing, worrying about living up to it. I helped him with his mental approach and his mechanics came along to the point where he was back hitting the way he could. He had an outstanding second half and wound up with 25 home runs. He was a great student and it was rewarding for me to see him turn it around.

I remember the first time I started to take serious note of Don. It was in 1970—Don was on the Orioles' Triple A team while I was with the Orioles. You could tell then he was going to go a long way. The only area he was a little short on was his throwing. Typically, however, in time he made himself better defensively in other ways. He concentrated on getting to the ball quicker and getting rid of the ball faster. He did whatever he had to do to make himself a better outfielder.

As I mentioned, he's played the game hard, aggressively, enthusiastically, just like I did. Off the field, Don and I also share similarities. Tell me something and I believe it, whether it's a teammate, coach, manager, or the ballclub saying it. I believe in people; Don is the same way. In fact, he's been accused by some of his former teammates of trusting people too much. That's not a fault. It's just the way he is.

I know Don will leave his mark on this game. And I know he'll have no problem remaining in the game when he's finished playing. He'll get his offers and he'll have his pick of where he wants to go. It would be great if he ends up in Baltimore, either in the front office or as a coach or in the minor-league/scouting end. Wherever he goes, he has been, and always will be, a tremendous influence on young players and I know he would instill in them the right work ethic and the best way to go about playing this game. When you get right down to it, there's only one way I can describe Don Baylor—he's a winner.

—FRANK ROBINSON
Manager, Baltimore Orioles
November 1988

FOREWORD

ONCE in a great while a major leaguer comes along who recognizes his obligation to past, present, and future players. Don Baylor is one of those special people.

He commands the respect of all. Needless to say, he has done it all.

I have known Don since he was an unassuming, almost shy, youngster working his way though the Baltimore Orioles' system. To be able to see a young player develop and to watch him mature over the years and reach the height of his profession is indeed gratifying.

To this day, I see things in Don no one else sees. I guess it is because I have known him for so long. Don is terribly sentimental, very loyal to his friends, and a man with a wonderful sense of humor. To know Don, one must go beyond the public perception of him as a steely leader who menaces the opposition, although he is very much a leader and a fierce competitor.

Don possesses compassion because he knows what it is to have your heart broken. In my years as a player with the Orioles, I never saw a man more devastated by the news that he had been traded than Don was on April 2, 1976, when he learned he had been dealt to the Oakland A's.

It was a terrible blow for Don and for all of us. We lost a source of strength and of boundless enthusiasm for the game; he lost his innocence. Don grew up in a hurry after that.

So many fond memories flash through my mind whenever I think of Don. Things like his nickname—"Groove"—and how he acquired it.

While standing near the batting cage one day, Don said nonchalantly, "If I get into my groove, I'm gonna play every day."

We never let him forget that and he has carried that tag—"Groove"—throughout his career. He takes a lot of kidding about it, but the fact is that no one in the game could hit a line drive any harder, get any hotter, or be more dangerous than Don Baylor when he was in his "groove."

It has been such a joy to watch Don grow in stature. Don's impact as a player has been well documented. An unprecedented three straight World Series with three different teams says it all. He helps a team just by being there.

I hope Don's life will continue to be baseball, whether it be on the field or in the front office. In either case, success will follow.

—BROOKS ROBINSON
Baltimore Orioles
November 1988

ACKNOWLEDGMENTS

ALL through 1988, Don Baylor and I worked on a book that would cover thirty-nine years of a man's life. In a long and sometimes tedious process, we both came to cherish family and friends who lent unending support and assistance.

Becky Baylor, Don's wife, showed tremendous patience, provided welcome advice. Becky also lent an invaluable assist in helping link Oakland and New York via computer. The words and ideas would have stopped flowing without Becky. Her enthusiasm for the project never waned. For that I am forever grateful.

Sophia Agbaje, my friend and confidante, transcribed hours and hours of tape, writing a book within a book. Her efforts, which included interrupting her life to travel all over the country, will never be forgotten by either Don or myself.

Don's mother and father, Lillian and George Baylor; his sister, Connie Baylor; brother, Doug Baylor; and aunt, Ruth Brown, lent memories and time to reconstruct the Austin years. Frank and Anne Seale also played an integral part in Don's life and in writing this book. Candy and Buzz Saylor and Dwight and Susan Evans provided aid and comfort from beginning to end.

My mother and father, Bernice and William H. Smith, have provided loving support in a most fruitful, but exhausting career. They've also helped dot the *i*'s and cross the *t*'s and have never tired of just being there to listen and provide support.

Jon Pessah, sports editor of the *Hartford Courant* and my friend, helped edit, offered understanding and patience through a long year. Tom Pedulla of Gannett/Westchester Rockland Newspapers offered endless amounts of editing tips, advice, counsel and was a tireless sounding board. My love and appreciation to both.

The support of my peers did not end there. Those who lent advice and counsel:

Murray Chass, George Vescey, Michael Martinez, and Dave Anderson of the *New York Times*; Moss Klein of the *Newark Star Ledger*; Jack O'Connell of the *New York Daily News*; Marty Noble of *Newsday*; Ernie Palladino of *Westchester Rockland*; and Steve Buckley and Greg Garber of the *Hartford Courant*. Also: Larry Whiteside of the *Boston Globe*; Mark Vancil and Howard Sinker of the *Minneapolis Star-Tribune*; Susan Fornoff of the *Sacramento Bee*; Bud Geracie of the *San Jose Mercury*; Ken Picking of *USA Today*; Gerry Fraley of the *Atlanta Constitution Journal*; Mark Hyman, Jim Henneman, Tim Kurkjian, and Ken Rosenthal of the *Baltimore Sun* papers; Tracy Ringolsby of the *Dallas Morning News*; Richard Justice of the *Washington Post*; John Hickey of the *Hayward* (Calif.) *Review*; Peter Gammons of *Sports Illustrated*; Pete Cafone of the *San Francisco Examiner*; Ted Haider of the Rochester *Democrat and Chronicle*; Mike James, Mike Penner, and Ross Newhan of the *Los Angeles Times*; and Vivian Lingard of the *Wall Street Journal*.

It's no coincidence that many of the writers and/or editors listed above work in the cities where Don played. I know he appreciates the respect they've shown him over the years and returns it in kind.

This book could not have been written without the cooperation and assistance of the media-relations departments of the teams for which Don played. Special thanks to Bob Brown of the Baltimore Orioles and Tim Mead of the California Angels. Also: Rick Vaughn, Helen Conklin, and Ken Nigro of the Orioles; Jay Alves and Kathy Jacobson of the Oakland Athletics; John Sevano of the Angels; Harvey Greene and Lou D'Ermilio of the New York Yankees; Dick Bresciani, Josh Spofford, and Jim Samia of the Boston Red Sox; and Tom Mee and Remzi Kiratli of the Minnesota Twins. Thanks also to Mickey Morabito, the traveling secretary of the Athletics.

Frank Robinson, Dwight Evans, Dave Winfield, Brooks Robinson, Phil Niekro, and Davey Johnson provided insights and suggestions as to how to approach not only their friend and peer, but also a ballplayer's autobiography. Steve Garvey and Ken Griffey provided this writer advice and support. A special thanks to Donald Fehr, executive director of the Major League Baseball Players Association, for his insights on labor history.

Ruben Rodriguez, Harlan Frankel, Maria Cicchelli, Ken Kweku, and Tony Lutchman of Tandy, Inc., transcribers Mary Jennings and Barton Smith, and researcher Hawk Smith kept the process from ever stalling out. Photographers Susan Ragan, Susan Grayson, Lou Sauritch, and Mitchell Haddad lent their time and art to these pages. Thanks also to our agent,

Basil Kane; and editor, George Witte, who stuck by the project from beginning to end.

Last, but not least, a special thanks to the person whose very existence, not to mention love and respect for the game of baseball, made this book possible. Don Baylor has provided many memories for millions of baseball fans, touched countless people's lives. It was truly a privilege to work with him. He will forever be my friend—The Big Guy, The Shy Guy, The Funny Guy, The Stubborn Guy, The Sensitive Guy, The Caring Guy.

Thanks, Guy.

—CLAIRE SMITH
November 1988

INTRODUCTION

WE were as close to dead as a team could be.

California led Boston 5–2, in the top of the ninth. It was Game Five of the 1986 American League Championship Series and the Angels led the best-of-seven playoffs, three games to one. If the Angels got three more outs they would win their first American League pennant.

To some people, I was an emerging elder statesman, a future executive, one of the players sought by the media to speak on behalf of black players. To me, I was just a ballplayer. And at that moment, on October 12, 1986, I was dying a little with each out, praying the Red Sox had just one more rally in them.

Jim Rice fouled a pitch straight back. Kneeling in the on-deck circle, I turned and watched as the ball rolled up the screen toward the California Angels' private boxes.

The ball approached the owner's box, heading toward frail, aging Gene Autry, the father of the Angels. Mr. Autry was the first man to sign me to a multimillion-dollar contract. Confined to a wheelchair because of a broken hip, he was surrounded by television cameras. There were still three outs to go, but the TV lights were already on as the technicians prepared to record history.

As the ball rolled back down the net I thought of Mr. Autry, and all the other Angels executives up there. I thought about the general manager's box where Buzzie Bavasi used to sit throughout my playing days in Anaheim.

I turned back to watch Jimmy, but I was thinking of Buzzie. I could not stop myself. His words slammed around in my mind. I could picture his face, so real I could almost touch it.

"What's Don doing in that picture with the two hitters?"

Buzzie sat somewhere in the Big A that warm October day, out of power, but not out of mind. He was the man who'd questioned my right to stand alongside Fred Lynn and Rod Carew in a photo on the cover of an Angels' program years before, the executive whose lack of faith and respect had prompted him to make that statement to reporters. His words, when they were reported in newspapers across Southern California, caused me to unofficially retire for one day in 1981. I didn't "un-retire" until my teammates begged me to forget Buzzie, until my friend and manager, Jim Fregosi, asked me to come back, if only for him, until team consultant Gene Mauch told me, "Little people do little things, big people do big things. You're not a little person."

Buzzie had said he was speaking in jest. I did not believe him and I never have forgotten or forgiven. He was on my mind the day I walked away from Anaheim and headed to New York and George Steinbrenner's Yankees in the winter of 1982. He was on my mind from the moment the 1986 playoffs began.

Now we were all there. Mr. Autry up in his box, Bavasi somewhere in the Big A, and me. Meant to go opposite ways one last time.

Jimmy Rice, one of the most powerful hitters ever to put on a Boston uniform, wanted to put the ball deeper into the orange seats in left than he'd ever done before. But he couldn't pull it all together, not in the playoffs, not in that at-bat. He took strike three.

Two outs left. The Angels stood that close to ending our season. The Red Sox stood that close to writing another devastating chapter in their history, adding to all the negatives New Englanders seem to enjoy. All summer long the Boston media hadn't wondered when we would win, but how and when we would lose it. You could hear it in the stands, on the radio talk shows. Now we were at that moment all the doubters had said we would inevitably reach.

I knew how much the at-bat, the game, meant to Jimmy and the other longtime Red Sox because of that history. I knew how much it all meant to me because of my own past. Boston had no claim on heartbreak in October. This was not the first time I had reached the last painful inning of the last painful playoff game. I had come that close to a World Series four times before only to see the other team end up sipping the champagne.

Twice I had gotten to the same point with the Orioles, in 1973 and '74, only to lose to the rebellious but talented Oakland A's. But when you're a kid, you're just happy to be playing in the postseason. When you're twenty-four, twenty-five, you think you're going to live forever, play forever, be a Baltimore Oriole forever, win pennants forever.

I had also reached the playoffs twice for Mr. Autry, "The Cowboy," the most understanding team owner I'd ever played for. But we could not give him his first Series. Not in 1979, my MVP season that ended so quietly, with just 3 hits and 2 RBI in four games against my friends and ex-teammates—the Orioles. Nor in 1982, when the Angels lost again, to the Milwaukee Brewers, an agonizing defeat for Gene Mauch, whose every move as manager will forever be second-guessed. Everything I had to give, I'd given. Ten RBI in five games, tying or setting three LCS offensive records. Still, there was no World Series.

The moment the '82 Angels lost I had tied another American League Championship Series record, one I had never wanted: most times on a losing club.

So many talented teams, so many chances and still no pennant, no World Series, no championship ring.

Now, on that balmy day in Anaheim, many friends stood on the other side, on the verge of celebration. Bobby Grich. Reggie. Bob Boone. Conditioning coach Jimmy Reese, onetime roommate of Babe Ruth and watcher of all Angels. And Gene, the man who the late Dick Young once wrote had been put on this earth to suffer. It seemed Gene's suffering was about to end. And I was facing a fifth heartbreak.

I was in my sixteenth season and, of all the active players, only the Niekro brothers, my buddies Phil and Joe, had gone longer without making it to the Series. Only Grichie, my first roommate in the minors, and Houston's Jose Cruz had gone as long as I had.

In New York that very day, Jose's Astros were going against the Mets in the National League playoffs and he stood just two victories away. And playing second base that day for the Angels was Grichie, his uniform dirty, his face fiercely determined behind his Fu Manchu mustache. After Mike Witt struck out Rice, Grichie stood just two outs away from realizing his dream. One of us would make it this time. As Jimmy walked by me back to the dugout I could not help but wonder if it would ever be me.

I walked to the plate, past home-plate ump Rocky Roe, past Boonie. Dave Stapleton, a pinch-runner for Bill Buckner, stood there on first. Gene had to be thinking get a grounder, get a double play. End of game, end of season—for the Red Sox.

That's what I didn't want, to be the player whose one swing set off the pandemonium. I had to get by Witt.

A tall, thin right-hander, Mike looked almost anemic out there. But I knew better. I had known Mike since he was a kid. In fact, Mr. Autry had asked me to scout him a few years before, when Mike was even skinnier and still pitching high-school ball in Anaheim. I took one look that afternoon years before, saw all arms and legs, a fastball that was nothing but 90-plus mile-per-hour heat and I thought, *Yep, he looks pretty tough to me.* That opinion hadn't wavered one bit by 1986. And on that October day, Witt was very much the master for eight-plus innings in the most important game of his young career.

I knew what I needed. The same thing I had just told my teammates that we all needed. Told them after Tom Seaver and I had walked up from the clubhouse to meet our fielders in the dugout. Tom and I had watched the bottom of the eighth on the TV in the clubhouse, where I usually get loose for my at-bats as designated hitter. We had watched as television crews set up a platform—the losers' platform—to get our reaction when the Angels clinched. I knew the technicians were just doing their job. Still, I didn't like it. Tom didn't like it, either. But nothing was said. This was not a day to flip over TV stands or pull cables out of cameras. Tom and I had been around too long not to understand that there would always have to be a loser when there was a winner.

So Tom and I had paced quietly, a man who had won 300 games and a man who had hit 300 home runs talking about what the Red Sox needed to do. There was no panic in that clubhouse or in the two of us when we walked to the dugout. We knew we could not afford to find any panic there. When we got outside, though, the dugout was deathly quiet in a stadium gone mad.

We were surrounded by more than 64,000 "laid-back" Southern Californians who were absolutely berserk. I had never heard it so loud in all my years as an Angel. Dwight Evans said that when he was in right field during the eighth the noise hurt his eardrums. Fans were dancing in the aisles. One had climbed the back of the screen behind home plate. Ushers were lining the stands, expecting the worst. All that was missing were the mounted police and German shepherds.

Our teammates were trying to be professional, milling around, grabbing bats and batting gloves. But the silence, in the middle of all the pandemonium, was nerve-racking. In my mind, we were too quiet. Someone had to say something to break the overwhelming silence. So I did.

It was hard for everyone to hear me, even though we were all squeezed into one end of the dugout. The other half had been occupied by California Highway Patrolmen, there to control the fans who would surely spill onto the field if the Angels clinched. The noise was so deafening by the time Witt finished his warmup pitches I had to scream to be heard. "If we're going down, we're going down with quality at-bats. We're going to fight them. If you're going to make an out, make a quality out and then we can live with ourselves the rest of the winter."

I said it to no one in particular, everyone at once.

Pretty corny, I guess. Somewhere there was probably someone who could have been a lot more eloquent. "Quality at-bats" was about the only thing I could come up with. Still, I had said something. There were many players who had been with the Red Sox for years. I'd only been there six months. To this day, though, I don't think anyone expected it to be anyone else. The guys in that dugout knew I had never pretended to be more than their teammate. But they also knew I hadn't run away when John McNamara asked me to talk to a troubled Dennis "Oil Can" Boyd the day after I was traded to the team in March. Nor did I pull away when Dwight—one of the team's senior members—asked me to set up a kangaroo court to instill more discipline and togetherness. I knew what Mac and Dwight were looking for, from the first day until the last.

So I stood there pushing, pleading for quality at-bats.

We were still in need of an Olympian effort, a team desperate for a "10." I remember thinking, *We're like the Bad News Bears, outnumbered, with no expectations.* What did we have to lose? Get a little crazy. Anything can happen. So, as Witt warmed up, everybody in our dugout started yelling, trying to turn it around just one more time. We were a bit desperate, even a little giddy, maybe. It was crazy. But it was special, too. The 1986 Red Sox had never been closer than we were in those few moments.

I was hollering so much I became hoarse. My voice started to go even before Bill Buckner stood in to face Witt. Screaming hard, inside and out, not knowing that the most incredible ninth inning of my life was about to unfold. Things seemed to move in fast-forward, slow motion, and reverse all at once. Buck, our number-three hitter, black and blue and barely able to walk, let alone run, singled. At the time, though, I didn't know how he got on, I was so locked into the first seed of a possible rally and what I would have to do as the third batter due up. All I knew is Buck got his quality at-bat. Jimmy, our cleanup batter, then struck out. *Nobody really ever gets well against Witt,* I thought. Even though Buckner had poked through a hit we were not touching Witt. We were not coming close.

Now it was on me.

Just walking to the plate seemed to take an eternity, although it took just seconds. I thought about Becky, my future wife, sitting in the stands, operating on what I don't know because she had not been able to sleep much the night before. I thought about my mom and dad and my son, Donny Jr., who were all watching on television in Austin, Texas. I knew that Donny, then not yet fourteen years old, must have been dying. My dad, too. I was also thinking, *I don't want to be the one who makes an out here. Not in front of Mr. Autry, not in front of Gene . . . and never, ever in front of Buzzie.*

Witt got the count to 2–and–2. The next pitch, a breaking ball, was a tease, just off the plate.

It was one of those pitches, the split-second-decision kind.

Do I pop up, swing and miss? Or do I take and hope the umpire sees it my way?

I took it for ball three.

By then I didn't know if the crowd was cheering or what. I didn't know what was going on in the stands or the dugouts or if they'd got that guy off the screen behind home plate. . . . I'd *never* seen a guy on the screen in Anaheim Stadium before.

All I knew was that I was ahead of Witt, 3–and–2.

He's got to come to me. The next pitch has got to be a fastball.

Witt threw a breaking ball.

As I looked at it, I was thinking, *There's no way this ball should be hit.*

It was down and away and out of the strike zone, four or five inches off the plate. A pitcher's pitch in layman's terms, a bastard pitch in hitter's terms. Down and away, unhittable.

To this day I know Mike Witt must be asking himself, "How can he hit that pitch?" But I did. A high line drive, toward centerfield.

Gary Pettis, the Angels' centerfielder, turned and gave chase. He was always like Superman to me, the way he used to turn long line drives into miles and miles of outs against the Yankees and Red Sox teams I played on.

Not this time, though. I'd hit enough baseballs in that park to know whether I had gotten one or not. On that one, I knew.

Unless Gary can fly, that ball is out.

The ball went over the centerfield fence, over a photographers' stand, the same stand in front of which our centerfielder, Dave Henderson, had caught a ball hit by Grichie three innings earlier only to have it fall out of his glove and over the fence. Bobby's home run had given the Angels a lead they had yet to give back. And it had ignited Anaheim Stadium. My home run put the Red Sox back in the game and the quiet back in the ballpark.

In what could have been my last at-bat of the season I had finally hit a home run against the Angels, the only American League team that had kept me in the park all year long.

I really believe that Frank Robinson and Brooks Robinson would have appreciated the home run, but would have liked my words more. If I had not said something, Frank probably would have kicked my butt. Brooks, always the Southern gentleman, would not have shown anger, just disappointment. Both, I'm sure, would have thought that if I had said nothing it would have been because I was too concerned about my at-bat and not about the team. They had taught me better than to disappoint them like that. And I hadn't.

Somewhere Earl Weaver probably smiled. As my first major-league manager, Earl had always pushed me to hit home runs. I'd always argue back, "But Earl, I'm a line-drive hitter." I could just imagine Earl's rasping voice saying "I told you so." Well, Earl, I hit a home run. A line-drive home run.

On the other hand I'd probably really ticked off Yankees owner George Steinbrenner and maybe caused Billy Martin to punch out another salesman in some bar. Steinbrenner had said Don Baylor could no longer hit right-handers. I do believe Mike Witt is right-handed, just like Brian Fisher, who'd served up a 3-run double to me upon my return to Yankee Stadium that previous June. Steinbrenner had also said Baylor's bat would be dead by August. Well, the bat and the player were alive and well and heading to the World Series, while his team sat at home.

I thought about Gene Mauch, too. And Reggie, my onetime roommate in Anaheim. Wade Boggs, sitting in our dugout when I'd walked up to the plate, said he saw Reggie in the Angels dugout, smiling, ready to celebrate. Reggie had taken his wire-rimmed glasses off and put them in his pocket. He had walked over to Gene and put his arm around the manager. Later Reggie told me Gene had said, "Not yet, big boy, not yet."

Gene had been right.

Wade kept watching Reggie and Gene as I rounded the bases. He said Reggie took his arm from around Mauch, put his glasses back on, and slowly walked to the other end of the dugout. Reggie—my buddy, "Jack"— always knew where the cameras were. By then the cameras were no longer pointing at the Angels.

We would play late into the afternoon because of that ninth inning. Because, with two outs, Gene would make more moves destined to be second-guessed. And because Dave Henderson, down to the last strike in the ninth, would hit a two-out, 2-run home run to give us the lead. The Angels would tie it in the bottom of the ninth, but would get no more. Two innings later Hendu would deliver again, with a game-winning sacrifice fly.

I scored the game-winner, having reached base at the start of the inning when Donnie Moore hit me with a pitch. He wasn't wild. I had just been crowding the plate, my continuing refusal to concede the inside part of the plate to pitchers. They believe it's theirs. I believe it's mine. So I've been hit by more pitches than any player in history, more than 260 times. Only Nolan Ryan ever hurt me.

An incredible ending to an incredible game was still unfolding when Moore hit me. As I stood on first base, Grichie walked over and asked me, "What do you think?"

"Greatest game I ever played in," I said.

Bobby slapped my hand. "Me, too, partner."

The miraculous ninth, the miracle victory, had taken the heart out of the Angels and put it back in us. Two victories later, the Red Sox, not the Angels, would taste the champagne, would head to the promised land.

The World Series, at last.

When all was said and done, Gene would dwell on the home run that had wiped the smile off Reggie's face and put 64,000 Angels fans back in their seats. Gene told reporters the home run off Witt had merely been hit with Don Baylor's "B" swing. I understood why Gene needed to say that, how much he hurt, how many times he'd had crushing defeats break his heart. Walter Hriniak, the Red Sox hitting instructor and a close friend of Gene's, took exception. "If that was a 'B' swing I'd like to roll into the Hall of Fame with you on that swing," Walter said.

My first World Series would follow because of that game. And with it, more such moments, good and bad, in seven games against the Mets. There would be no championship ring, though, only more heartache because the Red Sox were destined to come within one strike of winning it all only to lose.

But amazingly, a year later, there would be another World Series and, at last, a championship. As a member of the 1987 Minnesota Twins, I would see victories, not defeats, in Games Six and Seven of the Series. I would bat .385 against Whitey Herzog's Cardinals, hit my first World Series home run, drive in 3 runs and score 3 more.

A year later, another pennant, this time with the Oakland Athletics, a talented team filled with the young and powerful, with Jose Canseco and Mark McGwire, the wave of the future. The A's won the pennant by sweeping the Boston Red Sox, two more chapters in my life overlapping. We celebrated as Dwight and Jimmy Rice watched their hopes of avenging the 1986 World Series loss die.

Later, as I walked from our clubhouse at the Oakland Coliseum, I bumped into Bruce Hurst, the Red Sox left-hander Oakland had beaten in the finale.

"Okay, Don," Bruce said in mock resignation, "tell me where you're going to be next year so I know who's going to win."

And it was mindboggling. Bruce was heading home. I was heading to my third straight World Series with three different teams, something no major leaguer had ever accomplished. Only sixteen have ever played in the Series with three different teams, period.

By the end of 1988, after the Athletics lost a frustrating series to the Dodgers, there was much to consider, including where I would be in the eighteenth season of my career. I wanted number eighteen as badly as I had wanted the first, the seventeenth, and all those in between. There was no reason to believe that the odyssey that had brought seven division titles, three pennants, one world championship, and fourteen finishes in the money, had to end. I had not exhausted my search for more special moments.

To me, that's always been where the beauty is found, in those moments, and in the extraordinary people in them. Frank and Brooks. Weaver and Mauch. Grichie and Dwight. Reggie, Steinbrenner, Yogi, and Billy. Dave Winfield and Dave Stewart, Canseco and McGwire.

I will always feel there's something left to prove. That's what's always been important for me, in the proving, when you either come up big or pack and go home. The situations your teammates want you in, situations other teams never want you to see. All the people and places, the heartaches and the moments of sweet deliverance go through your mind on afternoons such as October 12, 1986, and again and again, in all the years left to you.

PART
1

1

"PRESENCE?" WHO ME?

JUST before the first game of the 1987 playoffs, Paul Molitor walked over to me at the batting cage in Minnesota.

"Hey, Don, when are you going to come to Milwaukee?" Paul asked. "We want to win, too."

Paul Molitor knows plenty about winning; he was on the Brewers team that beat the Angels in the 1982 playoffs and is one of the game's most dangerous hitters. Paul was joking around with me, his way of saying congratulations for a second straight playoff appearance. He laughed when Murray Chass of the *New York Times* pointed out that Paul might be out of a job if I did go to the Brewers since we are both designated hitters.

I smiled and turned back to the cage to watch as my Twins teammates, the eventual world champions, continued to get ready for the Tigers.

A few days later, on a frosty day at Tigers Stadium, Richard Justice of the *Washington Post* asked my opinion on the possibility of Frank Robinson becoming Orioles general manager. As Richard and I talked, a small group of reporters gathered around, and the subject eventually turned to minorities in baseball management.

I care greatly about affirmative action, but I never set myself up as a spokesman for black athletes. Nor do I consider myself the ultimate authority on baseball's labor relations or drug policies. I have never walked into a manager's office and demanded to be named captain. No player can ever say I told him to listen to me and only me on how to play the game. Yet, in the last five or six years, I've been sought out by media and management alike to comment on things other than home runs, RBI, and base hits.

I've also heard the questions, the conversations—both serious and humorous—about baseball's "rent-a-leader." Some of the questions are downright mindboggling, like "When did you first start noticing that you stopped following and started leading?" as if I could point to a time and date and say, "Yep, that's it, that's the day Don Baylor, the player, became Don Baylor, the leader."

To me, it's all very flattering, all very mystifying. I wish I could give the answers people are looking for. It would make this all so easy. But I can't.

I have never campaigned for the title of leader. I cannot single out any one point where I purposely established any kind of mystique or hung a sign over my locker that said, "Quiet, please, 'Presence' at work."

In my mind, all I've ever tried to do are the things I've been taught from day one. Call it the Orioles way, the veteran way, or whatever, it's just how I was raised as a major leaguer, just like a lot of other guys. Yet the questions keep coming. Even Paul's funny line at the playoffs set off a new round. Usually I stand there, trying hard to come up with answers. Like I said, it's pretty mystifying.

I don't think any of this happened because of one single incident, or even an appointment to a kangaroo court judgeship. Yogi Berra was the first manager to hand me the gavel, but my Yankees teammates in 1984 and '85 did not fear me. Just because pitcher Joe Cowley nearly had to sign over his Corvette because I assessed so many fines doesn't mean I wasn't fair. Was that intimidation or a supposed "force"? In my mind, no. Phil Niekro—the one-man Supreme Court who presided over the cases of the Yankees who appealed my fines—was a force; he never, ever lost a case and believed in capital punishment. I just took my teammates' money.

Now I know there's one story a lot of reporters would like to hang the leadership tag on. There seems to be a common belief that after the Angels lost the 1982 playoff series, I got mad at Reggie Jackson and decked him, gave him a black eye. There's only one problem with that rumor.

I didn't hit Reggie. Okay? Did not do it. I want to make that clear. I know that such a rumor builds mystique. Look at all the mileage Graig Nettles got out of one little punch, when he decked Reggie after their Yankees team had won the 1981 playoffs. Thing is it just did not happen between Reggie and me.

Even though he's my friend, I sorely wanted to hit Reggie on many occasions because he is one of the most exasperating human beings I have ever met. He's the only guy I know who can make the simplest thing, like going to a restaurant, an adventure in dining and etiquette. I've seen him chase away fans who wanted his autograph and then sulk when people didn't pay him enough attention.

I once spent half a plane trip trying to calm down a flight attendant because Reggie threw a tray of vegetables at her back during an Angels charter in 1982. He did it because she had rejected his overtures and because Reggie is Reggie.

The woman was in tears. We were in shock. Grichie was stunned and the only thing he could think to say was "Is that what's meant by a tossed salad?"

Grichie was trying to break the tension, but it didn't keep the flight attendant from breaking down and crying. Gene Mauch came back from first class to survey the damage. He looked around like he was committing to memory where every carrot stick and radish had landed. I know he must have lightened Reggie's paycheck more than a couple bucks for each vegetable he saw. Reggie later apologized in writing to the flight attendant. On the plane, though, it was I who apologized to her, sat with her until she calmed down.

At times like that it was very easy to think about dismantling Reggie. But, more often than not, "Jack" and I got along. I know that Reggie is not afraid of me. And I certainly am not afraid of him. I also understand Reggie. In this whole wide world, the only person who scares Reggie is Reggie.

I don't know if Reggie ever eased up on his act because I was around. I don't know that Jimmy Rice ever did, either. I do know that Jimmy and I were like oil and water in the clubhouse. And I know that there were times I wanted to just jump him.

I came within an inch of doing that once in 1987. Jimmy had this annoying habit of sitting at his locker criticizing his teammates to clubhouse personnel. To me, that was not something a team captain is supposed to do. I know he never asked for the job of captain, but it was up to Jimmy to do something positive with it. By midseason Red Sox players were saying behind Jimmy's back that he didn't deserve being captain because he was concerned about Jimmy and no one else. I had heard all the stories from years past about how Jimmy was supposed to be a selfish guy; I had not believed them. But when I saw what Jimmy was doing in 1987, even after he was named captain, I wondered.

Maybe I was the one who had the problem, but to me, when you put on the team uniform, you're fighting the enemy together. I ignored his sniping as much as I could, but with Jimmy, the complaining was constant.

Finally, I'd had enough. I went to Dwight Evans and implored him to give me one good reason why I should not go after Jimmy; after all, Dwight had seniority. Dwight asked for a night to sleep on it. The next day he came in with eight Bible passages in hand. Dwight said each passage showed why I shouldn't kill Jimmy, or die trying in a fight.

I couldn't believe it. I carry a Bible with me to this day and I have never read anything in there about not fighting Jim Rice. But there wasn't, or isn't, anyone in uniform I respect more than Dwight. And he believes part of being a team player means not pounding on teammates unless absolutely necessary. So Jimmy and I never went at it. We had an unspoken truce that carried through the remainder of our time together in 1987. And I believe that Jimmy and I worked well together through all of 1986, when he was zoned in during the entire championship season.

Was that initial "understanding" because of the court, or the new emphasis on team, or even the presence of "The Presence"? You have to ask him. All I know is that he and I both were very much aware of where we stood. So the truce lasted. We even joked about it with writers in spring training of 1987 because of some stories that had been written about our alleged problem. We joked that Baylor vs. Rice was nothing more than a college football rivalry in the Southwest Conference. If it had ever developed into more, though, I think we could have sold tickets.

The fact is I never built any kind of reputation by putting a teammate against a wall. I did try to strangle Freddie Patek after a game in the old Met in Minnesota in 1980 when we were both with the Angels. But I don't really think that counts because Freddie is only five-foot-four and it was a definite mismatch. But Freddie was like one of those little dogs that yap at your feet and just won't go away. One day he was in my face pretty bad. "What have you ever done in this league?" Freddie yelled at me. He was angry; some of the guys were hassling him because he was not only short, but overweight. I wasn't bothering the man, but still, he went after me.

"What have I done?" I grabbed a players register off the shelf, opened to my bio, and shoved it in his face. Freddie would not let it go. "What have you done? What have you done?" he kept asking, as if he were one step away from Cooperstown. I just snapped. Before I knew it, I had him up against a wall and was choking the life out of him until Jason Thompson pulled me off.

Probably the only "presence" Freddie cared about that day was the presence of mind I had not to kill him.

It may have been a mismatch but at the time it was fun watching Freddie's feet dangling a half-foot off the ground. The next day, though, I was mad at myself. Freddie had been wrong, but it was an unfair fight. I apologized to Freddie. He apologized to me. I cannot say Freddie and I were ever friends before or after that, but we did respect each other as ballplayers.

Teammates certainly never looked to me to fight them. They never minded the fights I got into for them, though. Like the two-part brawl against Cleveland in 1981, after John Denny started a beanball war. The first brawl took a good ten minutes. After it broke up and the Angels were walking back to the dugout, I saw Indians left-hander Rick Waits standing at home plate. He was staring at me. I was glaring at him.

"Who are you looking for?" I asked him, rather politely, I thought.

Waits said, "I'm looking for you."

My right fist came up, hit him square in the jaw, and dropped him right there, on home plate.

Later on, Waits said that he was stunned by my reaction. "I thought you were a Christian man," he said.

"I am," I told him, "but once you get between the lines it's a different story."

"Well, that's fine," Waits said, "but I was just joking."

I felt bad about that, but at least I didn't break his jaw. I did get kicked out of that game, however. No one else did, not even Denny. When he pitched a complete game and won, Gene Mauch told me I had decked the wrong guy. I guess I was still learning about where to aim all of that aggression.

Billy Martin also probably wondered about where I directed my aggression. Like why I never hung out in hotel bars to fight civilians for him when he was my manager in New York. My philosophy, one I learned from Earl Weaver, was that players don't go into bars in the team hotels. Those bars belong to the coaching staff and management. Besides, you might meet the kind of people you don't want to see. Like Billy. As far as I was concerned, protecting Billy in bars, like some of my Yankees teammates did on occasion, was not in my job description. Billy probably wouldn't vote a leadership award for that attitude. That's fine with me.

The enforcer reputation couldn't have been because Don Baylor seized control of a club with loud words or threatening actions. I've seen veterans take over a team, saw the 1974 Orioles do it because they tired of watching Earl wait for 3-run home runs. Saw Brooks and Mark Belanger and Paul Blair, among many others, decide the players would sacrifice, hit-and-run, steal bases on their own. That team won the American League East. I marveled at those veterans and also at Earl. He knew that we knew that he knew and was still manager enough to take it.

I was just a kid back then, so I didn't say a word when the insurrection took place. That Orioles team certainly did not need to hear from Don Baylor on that day. Not when it had all those future Hall of Famers, Cy Youngs, Cy "Olds," and "Cys of Relief," as Earl once said.

Those years in Baltimore were not the last time I was overshadowed by dominant personalities. My first time through Oakland, the remnants of Charlie Finley's dynasty were still there, stalwarts like Sal Bando and Joe Rudi. In California, Reggie dwarfed every Angel around him when it came to seizing the spotlight. And there were other sure Hall of Famers over the years—Rod Carew, Nolan Ryan, and Tommy John. The Yankee teams I played on had Dave Winfield, Goose Gossage, Lou Piniella, Graig Nettles, Willie Randolph, and Ron Guidry. It was not my place to lay claim to any kind of captaincy there, and I never tried, no matter what Billy Martin thought. In Boston there were also well-established stars, such as Dwight and Jimmy Rice, Wade Boggs and "The Rocket", Roger Clemens. The 1987 Twins had proven winners, guys like Bert Blyleven, Joe Niekro, Jeff Reardon, Roy Smalley, and sure Hall of Famer Steve Carlton. They also had a confident group of youngsters who were making names for themselves, like Tom Brunansky, Greg Gagne, Gary Gaetti, Kirby Puckett, Frank Viola, Kent Hrbek, and Tim Laudner.

I always felt comfortable with almost every teammate, never felt a need to battle anyone of them for headlines. But most times I never even thought of myself as the fifth or sixth most notable guy in any given clubhouse, let alone the first or second. And that was fine with me. Reggie may have needed to throw tantrums to get everyone's attention, but that has never been my thing.

Well, maybe once it was. There was one little tantrum, nothing really. I just kicked over the food table after a tough loss in 1979. And I started screaming a little at the reporters who had just entered the Angels' clubhouse . . . just to get their attention. It was August and the Angels had just dropped out of first place. Shortstop Jim Anderson had committed the error that led to the winning run. After the game Anderson sat at his locker and looked as if he was in a state of shock. The reporters headed right for him, but I could see that the kid was in no shape to answer questions about pennant races or anything else. So I pitched the fit, started yelling, demanding the press show a little ingenuity.

That did it. Good reporters never pass up clubhouse temper tantrums.

They all came over to me. Then I sat down, kind of smiled, and said, "Okay, guys, what do you want to know?"

Tracy Ringolsby of the *Long Beach Independent Press-Telegram* smiled, too. Later on, after a calmer Anderson had talked to reporters, Tracy told me I had not fooled him with my "tantrum."

"I know," I told Tracy, "but what am I supposed to do? Jimmy Anderson isn't the best shortstop in the world, but at least he wants to play." And Jimmy, a backup to Bert Campaneris, had never said "no" when he was handed a start. Campy, on the other hand, seemed to have lost the desire to fight one more pennant race out. He had crawled in the trainer's room a week before and hadn't been seen since. So there was no reason for anyone in that clubhouse to let Jimmy Anderson dangle out there all by himself. I paid the clubhouse guy for the food he lost and the cost of the cleanup. And maybe Anderson got a little of his appetite back in the process.

The media has always understood when I've done things like that and I've always had a pretty decent relationship with writers. One time, though, thirty or so reporters had to go. Chris Knapp had just lost a game to the Royals in Kansas City in the latter stages of the 1979 pennant race. We had been slaughtered. Knapp was the main victim of guys like George Brett and Hal McRae.

The first questions were aimed at Knapp. I walked by and heard the word "choke." That did it. We needed Chris Knapp and I didn't think that it helped one little bit to put negative thoughts in our pitcher's mind. I started toward the pack and told them to clear out.

"What do you mean, 'out'?" one reporter asked.

"I said, 'Out.' Your story is not here. The story's in the other clubhouse. George Brett and McRae had about nine hits between them. You go talk to them. Clubhouse is closed, period. Knapp has nothing to say to you. If you want to talk about choking, go talk to the Royals. If you want to talk about winning, come back and talk to us. Because that's what we're going to do."

Somebody has to stand up not only for Knapp, but for a pitching staff that was giving up almost 5 runs a game. I know we had to score 6 to win, but we did. I don't ordinarily bully writers, don't have much respect for players that do. But on that day, I thought the press was bullying our pitcher. We needed guys like Knapp and Dave Frost. We couldn't pitch Frank Tanana and Nolan Ryan every day.

Is that the moment everyone has been looking for? I would be surprised because, in my mind, I was just doing my job. You have to stand up for certain things. Sometimes such stands are for fun, like some of the trivial fines in the kangaroo courts that bring teams so close together. Sometimes they are more important, such as calling for the basic agreement to be printed in both Spanish and English by the Major League Baseball Players Association. I made that request, which the MLBPA granted, after Campaneris came to me and asked what benefits he was entitled to. Bert, born in Cuba, was having no luck translating a document many English-speaking players can't understand. The bilingual printing was just one small way for the MLBPA to pay back some loyal members for their support.

And sometimes you have to stand up for things that are deadly serious. Protesting the prejudice that keeps minorities out of management positions or publicly objecting to Padres second baseman Juan Bonilla's statement that every major leaguer had either snorted a line of cocaine or smoked marijuana just because he did were things that had to be done. I didn't need to be a team captain to speak out on those issues, nor did I need a captain to tell me to do so.

Maybe that's it. Maybe the same kid who learned not to compromise on the segregated streets of Austin, Texas, and fought back with his fists, just never believed you should stop fighting for things you believe in. There isn't one instance when I stopped being a follower, crossed out "designated hitter" on the job description and wrote in "designated leader."

All I've ever tried to do is be true, to my teammates, to myself. All I've ever asked was a chance to prove my worth. And somewhere along the line maybe teammates, friends, family said, "Yeah, we recognize and appreciate that," people who matter most, people in places like Oakland and Minnesota, Boston and New York, California and Baltimore.

And in places like the Clarksville section of Austin, where my fight first began.

2

CLARKSVILLE

IN the early 1960s, in Austin, Texas, no one had to tell me which water fountain I was or was not supposed to drink from. No one ordered me to sit in the back of the bus. No one had to. It was understood. You knew your place in life. You were a second-class citizen.

In Austin there was a crossroads. On one side, the white world; on the other, Clarksville.

Clarksville, the oldest black section of the city, was home to about seventy-five to a hundred families, including mine. Most were black, some were Mexican, all crammed into an area about a half-mile square. As soon as the white neighborhood stopped and Clarksville began, the asphalt pavements and the sidewalks stopped, too. Our roads, our playgrounds, were black Texas dirt, dust, and weeds.

The only school, Clarksville Elementary, was an old wooden building, with two classrooms and a lunch room, and two teachers for four grades. After that Clarksville kids were bused, not to integrate but to remain segregated.

Schooling continued in predominantly black East Austin, five miles and two bus rides away. To get back and forth across Austin you had to transfer in downtown Austin, at Congress Avenue near the State Capitol. Blacks were bused to East Austin or to Clarksville, Mexicans to South Austin. And you were never allowed to stay where you were not wanted.

As a ten-year-old kid riding in the back of those buses, I never thought it could or would change. Twenty years later, though, things had. Congress Avenue was renamed "Don Baylor Avenue" for a day in honor of the American League Most Valuable Player.

I knew there was a better life. I didn't even have to imagine it. I only needed to walk four blocks to see the paved streets, kids playing on tennis and basketball courts, in playgrounds, on immaculately kept football fields and baseball diamonds. But I could not play on those fields or playgrounds. They were in West Austin, the most affluent white community in the city. The governor's mansion, where John Connolly lived, was in West Austin. University of Texas football coach Darrell Royal lived there, too.

West Austin surrounded Clarksville. I suppose the only reason Clarksville was allowed to exist was that it had long been the quarters for maids and butlers. Both my grandmothers, Eula Baylor and Ellen Brown, who also lived in Clarksville, took in white people's laundry and starched clothes in big black iron kettles in their backyards.

I don't know what people consider being poor, but I don't believe my family was. To me poverty is what I saw later on in life, when I played baseball in Bluefield, West Virginia, for the Orioles in the Appalachian Rookie League. In destitute mountain towns coalminers and their families lived in dirt-floor, tin-roofed shanties, eight to nine in a room. People, both black and white, were hungry, living without electricity, without indoor plumbing. The poverty was so overwhelming it frightened me. That was not the case in Clarksville.

My father, George Baylor, was a baggage handler for the Missouri Pacific Railroad for twenty-five years. My mother, Lillian, worked as a pastry cook at the local white high school, Stephen F. Austin.

My brother, Doug, baby sister, Connie, and I looked clean and presentable every day we went to school. We were never without shoes or shirts. Some kids were.

I must admit I didn't fully understand my parents' sacrifices. Once, when I was fourteen, I used fifteen dollars of my paper-route money to buy a University of Texas football helmet because, like every kid in Austin, I loved the Longhorns. My dad hit the roof. "The helmet has to go back," he said. "It cost too much money." I was angry. I also had spent one dollar more than my parents paid every month to rent the five-room, tin-roofed, wooden house we lived in. That fourteen dollars was about all my parents could afford.

That helmet *did* cost too much.

We were not tied down by excessive rules. Going to church on Sundays was a must, and since I grew up right next to Sweet Home Missionary Baptist Church it was like a second home to me. Mostly my parents allowed us to be kids first. All they asked was that we stay out of trouble.

That was tough for me because of Clarksville.

I wanted to play on those playgrounds. But when my cousins, brother, and I showed up, the West Austin kids would yell, "You niggers don't belong here."

"Hey, we just want to play," we would argue. "It doesn't matter to us. You want to play black against white, or whatever. It doesn't matter."

They didn't want even that. "Go home, niggers." That's all we heard. There were a lot of confrontations, ripped shirts, pushing and shoving. A lot of times they would have to call the cops to get me to go back across the railroad tracks to Clarksville.

When I was fourteen years old a group of my buddies and I were out trick-or-treating on Halloween and we ventured into West Austin. We did not know it but another group of black kids had jumped some white kids and stolen their candy. Suddenly there were cops everywhere. They stopped us and took our names and phone numbers. They only let us go after they called our families and told them we had beaten up and robbed white kids.

My grandmother took the call. She lived right across the street from our home and had the only phone in our immediate family. By the time I got home my dad knew about the phone call. And he was all over me. He didn't believe that I was not involved. To him, I had always been in that kind of trouble. That time, though, I hadn't been involved. Still he punished me, made me sit out the junior-high–school football game the next day. It's the only time I ever told a coach or manager I was hurt when I really wasn't. I couldn't think of any way else to get out of playing without letting my teammates know I was being punished. I walked home from school crying my eyes out.

Between me, my brother, and cousins from both my parents' families, there were about sixteen kids right about my age. We'd form our own teams and during those long hot summers we'd play on the one concrete basketball court in Clarksville or on the dirt baseball field. We also went across town to play against East Austin kids. That's when even more trouble started.

East Austinites thought of Clarksville as the ghetto. They looked down on us although we were all black. So we often ended up going at each other.

People soon realized my cousins and I could play. And fight. And we did.

I did. A lot. When you're the oldest, and you feel outnumbered, you do what you have to do. I just don't like anyone picking on Doug, Connie, or my cousins. You fought for your family. You never backed down.

Not that we didn't fight each other in an instant; once my cousin, Ronnie, hit with me a two-by-four right in the middle of the back because of a hard tackle I'd made. I guess he was upset because we were playing touch football at the time.

But we all banded together when we had to. I fought so much that sometimes I think even my brother was scared to death of me. It never mattered if other kids were bigger than I was; if they were I would bite them. I was also quite a rock thrower; with all the unpaved roads I never ran out of ammunition. Or targets.

Looking back, I guess I was kind of a terror. When I wasn't fighting or throwing rocks I played baseball. Even that got me into trouble.

If people told me I couldn't do something, anything, all it did was make me more determined to do it. And older kids always told me I didn't belong on the same field with them. But I always wanted to go against the ones who were four or five years older because it was a challenge. More often than not I proved I did belong.

Many of the kids who fought me are probably still walking those same Austin streets. They probably never did much outside of that little world. But the competitiveness they brought out in me helped me get out of Austin and survive for seventeen years in the majors. Some guys can't get out of a slump or summon a fight-back attitude when they really need it. Fortunately, I could, more often than not.

I could always hit the ball a little farther than the other kids. Since we played in the streets or anywhere we could, I usually ended up hitting it into someone's yard. I don't remember breaking all that many windows, but people sure got mad. A lot of them wouldn't let us into their yards to get the balls back. They would do everything they could to stop us.

Do you know how hard it was for a kid to get a baseball back then? We couldn't buy new ones, or even used ones. So we had to stand in the runways at Disch Field, where the Braves' minor-league team played. When foul balls or home runs were hit, we'd scramble out to the gravel parking lot to get the balls. Sometimes we'd have to wrestle with the Mexican kids the Braves hired to retrieve the balls. We won most of the time. Then we'd lose the baseballs on one swing, usually mine.

There weren't many ways to get even with the people who kept our baseballs, but I found one. When I was thirteen and delivering the *Austin Statesman* newspaper, I purposely threw the Sunday edition, the heaviest paper of the week, at—and through—certain screen doors.

Perhaps the only relief Clarksville ever knew from such a terror came on Sundays because of Sweet Home Missionary Baptist Church. The ministers, many of whom could have taught Jesse Jackson a thing or two about sermonizing, were like family. It was hard to be a really bad kid living right under their gaze.

As a kid you might have wanted to do something else on Sundays, but when your dad's a deacon and your mother's the church clerk, there was only one place you could be.

When I was seven I officially became a member of Sweet Home. I stood in front of the congregation and told why I wanted to be saved and baptized. My mother recorded the event in the church records. The ceremony took place on Mother's Day. I've always felt that was appropriate because of how important that old church was and still is to my mom.

I liked to go to summer conventions because you could see so many different girls. To go I had to join the choir, which wasn't easy because I couldn't sing. But I always got by, standing in the back and lip-synching. That was good enough to get me to the conventions, important for a guy just discovering why it was better to be where the girls were.

As I got older my religion became more important. As a teenager I was superintendent of the Sunday school, overseeing the other kids. Even after I signed with the Orioles I would go back to Austin in the winters and serve in the same capacity. Sweet Home is still a part of my life, though my days in Austin have long since passed. My dad is in charge of the building fund and he's always known where he could go for a donation. I guess I've rebuilt half of that old church, and bought just about every hymnal with the money I've earned playing baseball. The efforts were worth it. Sweet Home, more than 110 years old, has been declared a historic site. While the home in which I grew up is long gone, my other "home" hopefully will stand for a long time to come.

Sweet Home instilled the belief I should give something back, not only to the church but to the community. While I was growing up, though, I often wondered why the community would not give of itself.

Clarksville had trapped my parents and their parents before them in a vicious cycle and drove home over and over that there was no way out for their generation.

My mom is a strong woman, a pillar of the community, just like her mother before her. My mom rose above being just a pastry cook and, in time, became a cafeteria supervisor at Pierce Junior High School in charge of many workers, both black and white.

Every day, at six-thirty in the morning, she would head off to work. She wouldn't arrive home until just before dusk. She cooked all day, first for the high-school kids, then for her own kids. A quiet woman, she never complained, never took it out on us. When she had to punish us, the spanking she'd give us with a sapling branch hurt her more than it hurt us.

My mom always told me not to fight, but when Doug would run home to tell I was fighting, she would get angry with him. "Why aren't you out there helping him? Get back out there." She just didn't think Doug, who is twenty-two months younger than I am, should have run away. Especially if the fight started because of that one word—"nigger."

My dad had a more difficult time. His family was strict Southern Baptist, and his mother was a strong, domineering woman. All his life he felt like he was being held down by segregation as well as a restrictive lifestyle. He rebelled even after he was married and had kids. He would gamble, shoot dice, lose large parts of his paycheck. My mom would argue with him about the undesirables he ran around with, fights we could hear all over the house.

In a way, I guess my dad felt trapped. My dad and his four brothers had only one escape. They would sneak beer and liquor by my grandmother's house to their own homes. I think that my dad and all my uncles had drinking problems because there was no way out.

Never did my dad take out those problems on his children. For a big man, he was very affectionate, in fact. There was always a hug or a kiss. I knew there was a problem, I knew that my mom was hurting because he was hurting. But I never pulled away from my father because he never pulled away from me. I always knew he loved me.

That doesn't mean he wasn't strict. He could wield a heavy switch. And I felt that he would go harder on me because I was the oldest. But he knew I should have known better than my little brother, or my sister, who was seven years younger. There was a right way and a wrong way to grow up. You respected your elders, did not talk back. My dad was always there to make sure I did what I was told. When I didn't, he'd say "A hard head makes a soft ass," which meant the switch was coming out.

My dad's job was within walking distance of West Austin's playing fields. When the leagues integrated and Doug and I got to play in the Pony League, he would cross the bridge over the Colorado River on his break and watch us play. When I moved up to the Babe Ruth League, my dad couldn't get away so often. When he couldn't take off, he'd stand atop a wooden baggage car to watch us on the lit fields below the train station.

Dad would play catch with us every chance he could. We would also go fishing along the banks of the Colorado or in the Pedernales River. Fishing, more than anything else, brought out the childlike wonder in my dad.

For about six summers he took the family to Laredo, when he was ordered to temporarily work at the railroad station in that border town. We would move in with another family. During the days my brother and I would stand on the banks of the Rio Grande and look into Mexico. Little Mexican kids, with barely a stich of clothing on, would dive into the river to retrieve pennies we threw from the American side of the river. I guess we weren't as poor as some people, after all.

Even though my dad had his problems, he's always been a proud man. He never complained to us, never made us feel that he felt ashamed. All he wanted was something better for us. He never let us stop hoping, even though it seemed he would never get past that railroad station.

A lot of kids say they want to be like their fathers. I wanted something better than what my father had. But what I didn't know is that he gave me something more, taught me to fight to make my life better. What was right and what was wrong were ingrained in me. And I never walked around with a chip on my shoulder. My dad wouldn't let me.

I believe my playing sports drew my dad and me even closer and drew him away from the bad things in his life. The gambling stopped long ago. The arguments with my mom stopped, too. Dad's retired, now, and there are very few things he enjoys more than watching me play ball.

I think my dad knew all along that sports would take me away from Austin and that life. When I signed my first contract with the Orioles, at age seventeen, my dad cosigned. He made sure the contract contained college-tuition clauses so that the Orioles would finance my education.

When we finally agreed on my first professional contract, I signed for $7,500, more money than my mom and dad had ever made in a single year in their lives.

My dad wanted that baseball career for me as badly as I did. Maybe he wanted it too much. Shortly after I signed, he had a nervous breakdown. I know it was because he was so worried about me moving so far away. By the following fall, when I had finished playing in the rookie league in West Virginia, my dad was still sick. I knew my life had to go on. He wanted it that way. Since the idea of going to college was so important to him, I enrolled in Blinn Junior College in Brenham, Texas, fifty miles outside of Houston. I attended school during the week, then went home every weekend. I only spent one weekend on campus.

That Thanksgiving I visited my dad in the Austin Mental Health Hospital. There were a lot of people there worse off than he was. Still, it was painful to see this big, once-powerful man in his weakened condition. He was always the strongest man I knew. I was an outstanding physical specimen, a proven athlete. My mom was healthy. My brother and sister were good athletes, strong and sound. Yet there was my dad, unable to tell the difference between toothpaste and hair cream, hot and cold. Unable to protect himself from the things that could harm him. Seeing my dad in an institution, having to feed him and then leave him there, just tore me apart. It hurt even more to know there was nothing I could do but wait for him to get better. My dad did recover, in a matter of months. But I still remember those frightening days. And I've never been able to look at Thanksgiving the same way again.

Everyone survived and, in a way, had grown closer and stronger. I was a teenager who was scared for his dad, overwhelmed by the changes that were taking me away from the only world I knew. But I had not quit. My dad, my mom had taught me better. Besides, I had worked too hard to make something of my life, work that began a half dozen years before when I first crossed the railroad to stay.

3

CROSSING THE LINE

FOR years, kids from Clarksville had boarded buses to attend Kealing Junior High in East Austin or University Junior High School near the University of Texas. Then, those lucky enough to go on to high school attended Anderson, again in East Austin. For the white kids there was O. Henry Junior High and, after that, Stephen F. Austin High.

After fourth grade, I also boarded the buses for that endless ride away from the white neighborhood next door and followed the same path as my parents and their parents had.

I hated every single minute of that ride. None of it made any sense and no one had any answers for my questions. I thought they could not be answered. Little did I know that there were other people asking the same questions. People like John F. Kennedy and Martin Luther King, Jr. And little did I know that when they forged sweeping civil rights changes, I would be affected.

The greatest of these changes was called integration. And, by 1962, it had reached Austin's public-school system.

Our whole world changed. Suddenly there were options. I was thirteen, about to enter seventh grade and able to attend O. Henry, if I wanted. We all could. Yet all around me, cousins and friends, just could not cross that line. They chose to board one bus, then another, chose to ride anywhere from forty-five minutes to an hour just to go to school.

That wasn't for me. I could finally walk to school. A new world was there, one that offered alternatives other than trade school or a black college, such as Fiske or Texas Southern.

It was my chance and I took it. For me, segregation was over.

Only two other children from Clarksville made that choice: Lewis Chambers and Lenore Higgins.

The first day I walked into O. Henry I really didn't think, *Wow, this is integration!* I didn't see myself knocking down barriers. After all, I was just a kid. Besides, it wasn't dangerous like Little Rock. No one tried to stop us. No one had to call out the National Guard. That first day was rather uneventful. Still, it was strange.

O. Henry was a spacious, modern school with auto-mechanic shops, printing shops, a huge cafeteria, tennis courts, a track that hugged the beautiful grass football field.

Across the street was a gorgeous public golf course, where O. Henry's golf team practiced. It's where one kid two years younger than I built a reputation for not only his golf game but his temper tantrums. That little kid, a noted red-ass because of his hot-headedness, was Ben Crenshaw, who turned out to be some golfer when he grew up.

O. Henry was filled with the children of doctors, car dealers, and bankers. Some of them had been taught all their lives that blacks were not supposed to go to school with them. Blacks were people who cleaned their pools and mowed their lawns. I bet the blacks who had to cater to some of those kids cheered the day Lewis, Lenore, and I walked into O. Henry.

My first encounters with my new classmates were strained. Most of the kids were apprehensive. I was nervous, just like Lewis and Lenore. It was the most difficult thing any of us had ever gone through.

In my homeroom session the first day, I realized just how unnerving the whole experience was going to be. Everybody had to stand and introduce him or herself. I didn't exactly stand up and say "Hi, I'm the black kid who is invading your territory." But this was not like my first day of kindergarten, either. This was like being on trial. If I screwed up so much as my name I knew I would be in trouble. I wanted to show I was not frightened or intimidated.

"My name is Don Baylor," I said. I wasn't feeling real assertive, then, and couldn't think of anything else to say. So I just sat down.

The West Austin kids mostly kept their distance. They were seldom openly hostile, but you'd see huddles and you knew the kids were talking about you. Lewis, Lenore, and I were very rarely in classes together, which made the days long and lonely.

Once, in civics class, I was asked to tell where the 38th Parallel was. I was pretty sure I knew, but I was frightened to death of giving the wrong answer. The teacher, Robert Pennick, figured everyone should know that answer; the Korean War was recent history. When I didn't answer right away he smashed me over the top of the head with a book.

"You'll know where it is tomorrow," he snapped.

In the next three years I never saw or heard of Pennick hitting a white kid. But I couldn't do anything about what happened because I wanted to stay in school. I did try to avoid him, never said a word to him if I didn't have to. Years later, after I had made a name for myself, Pennick asked me to speak to one of his classes. I did. I wanted to show him I was the bigger man. But I didn't have anything to say to him then and don't to this day.

I don't know what most of those kids' parents did to get them ready for Don Baylor, but I do know my mom tried to prepare me. "Don't fight when they call you a nigger," she said and made me give her my word I would not. I made that promise, but I didn't keep it very long.

One day I was on my way to class when a kid walked by and shouted, "Why don't you niggers go back to the other side of town, go to school there!" To me, "nigger" is a fighting word, as bad as if someone said something obscene about my mother. Words like "nigger" just never had a place in my vocabulary and never will. To this day I have trouble saying it, cringe when black guys use the word when speaking among themselves. The kid took off, with me right behind him. He ran into the auditorium, made it all the way up onto the stage before I caught him. I tackled him so hard we both slid across the stage floor and right on under the curtain. I wanted to tear his head off, but before I could get a good punch in the other kids pulled us apart.

I ended up in the principal's office and in trouble, but it was worth it. Word got around. Baylor would fight back. No one ever said that word to my face again at O. Henry. And I never heard of Lewis or Lenore having a problem of that sort, either.

There was more to prove than just the fact that I wouldn't be bullied or scared away. I also wanted to show that I belonged in the same classes with the other kids. I really hit the books. I had to. I was going against kids who'd had the use of encyclopedias and libraries from day one. I had to catch up and I broke my back trying. The courses were basic. But little things, like jumping from arithmetic to algebra, were tough. I had always been a straight-A student. Not that year, but I held my own. Mostly a lot of B's, just a couple of C's. But no D's or F's.

I soon learned I was not hated by every white kid. Some befriended me right away. I know that was awkward for them. It cost them some other friendships. But those few that reached out didn't care about that. Dean Campbell, the son of the local TV cartoon show host, did not care who knew that we were pals. In a lot of ways, Dean was the same kind of friend Brooks Robinson turned out to be in 1971 when he went out of his way to make life easier for a scared kid just up from the minor leagues.

It was Dean who suggested I go out for the football team. Later in high school he made sure I had rides to practice. He had a car; I didn't until after I signed my first professional contract.

Dean was also driven to play sports. I don't think he ever grew to be more than five-foot-five and 155 pounds, but Dean couldn't stand being told he was too small to play sports. He may have been the smallest kid on the block, but he made the junior-high and high-school football teams as a halfback. He was so good, one of his neighbors, Darrell Royal, gave Dean half a scholarship to the University of Texas. Dean ended up starting, as a split end. A five-foot-five split end. Impossible. I was so proud of him when he put on that burnt orange uniform. Dean has since gone on to coach at Texas, the universities of New Mexico and North Carolina, and Texas A & M.

Danny Covert, who was a year behind me, was also a loyal friend. The three of us were inseparable. Danny was the joker and thought Dean and I were too serious. So Danny tried to keep us loose, especially with well-aimed water balloons. By the time we got to high school, Danny got a new car every half-year, courtesy of his dad, who owned the local Buick–Pontiac dealership. Once he had this Super Sport Grand Prix I would have killed for. I used to tease him all the time about maybe buying it from him cheap. Six months later Danny exchanged that car for a brand-new Riviera. I thought I'd die.

Danny was a good ball player and eventually signed with the Cleveland Indians. He didn't make it to the majors; now he runs that dealership and probably still gets himself a new car every six months. For three years, Dean and Danny were the only white kids who ever invited me to their homes. I had other friends, but for some reason, if I visited them, I had to wait outside. Dean and Danny weren't afraid to invite me in. Dean's mother, who was widowed while we were in the eighth grade, was also super. She addressed my mother as Mrs. Baylor. A small thing, but it's hard to describe how much that meant.

I don't know if Danny or Dean ever realized how amazing it was for me to see their lifestyles. Those West Austin houses looked like mansions. The closest a black kid would usually get was to rake leaves or cut the grass on the front lawn. When Dean or Danny invited me inside I thought I was in a museum.

I couldn't even dream of living in such places. I know my parents didn't. But no one should ever stop dreaming. In 1976, after I signed my first million-dollar contract after joining the Angels as a free agent, I took my parents around Austin. "Where do you want to live?" They picked a nice, brand-new three-bedroom house in Northeast Austin. It was theirs. In 1982, I bought them an even larger home in the same neighborhood.

A month or two into my first year at O. Henry, things had become almost normal. There were other kids who became friends. One such friend was Sharon Connolly, the governor's daughter. She and her brother, John Connolly, Jr., and I went through junior high and high school together.

I guess the thing I remember the most about Sharon was how excited she was on November 22, 1963. School was to be let out early because her father was to escort a special visitor to the state capital—President John F. Kennedy. But the President never made it to Austin. The principal announced over the public address system that the President and the governor had been shot in Dallas. He made that announcement before telling Sharon. I could hear her screaming two classrooms away. Years later, when the space shuttle crashed, I remember thinking that it was the second American tragedy in my life, the kind when you'll never forget where you were and what you were doing. I'll never forget President Kennedy, or Sharon's screams, as long as I live.

Mostly, the days at O. Henry were ordinary—to the extent they could have been for Lewis, Lenore, and me. The day we first walked into O. Henry no announcements were made. No "Here come the black kids." That's the way we wanted it. All we wished to do was fit in, do the things that everybody else did without having to think twice.

I wanted at those playing fields. And I spent a lot of time worrying about whether the white kids would let me finally get there. I should have wondered about the coaches. For it soon became obvious that while Lewis *or* I would be tolerated, two of us was one too many.

Lewis could run faster and was considered the perfect size for a running back. I was five-foot-seven, 135 pounds and I felt I could do the same things Lewis could. But he became the chosen one who was given a uniform by O. Henry's coach, Buddy Weise. To me, Weise said no.

He had all sorts of built-in excuses, but I knew that it had to do with race. Parents were having a tough time accepting black kids on the team. It was new to them and football was and still is sacred in Texas. Weise had a hard time accepting it, too.

I could not swallow that kind of rejection. So I asked for a uniform and a tryout.

"Well, I don't have another uniform," Weise would say. Another time he would claim the shoulder pads were missing or that they didn't have the right size. Like I said, he never ran out of excuses.

I asked for that tryout three times before Weise gave in. When he finally gave me that chance, I made the team.

Because of Weise I learned two lessons. I knew that I would have to demand little things, like a uniform or a tryout. I also learned that the natural athletes, like Lewis, turn coaches' heads. That was not me. I would have to work hard. But that was okay. While other kids may have been faster, I knew what I had in my heart.

I never had to ask for a uniform again. For three years I was a starting tight end. The year after Lewis and I first played, other black players came along. I wound up blocking for another slick young runner from Clarksville—my brother, Doug.

By the time I got to Stephen F. Austin High School I decided I wasn't going to play football anymore. I liked the game, never minded the hitting or hard work. But coaches like Weise and his assistant, who happened to be Robert Pennick, had turned me off so much that after I proved I could play, that's all I wanted of organized football.

So I turned to intramural football. One day during a school break, a bunch of us were just messing around with a football. I was all over the place, catching passes over my shoulders with one hand, the whole bit. The high-school coach, Jim Tolbert, was watching. He must have really liked what he saw because the next thing I knew he went to my mom in the cafeteria and asked her if I could come out for the team. Mom said it was up to me. I didn't say yes until a year later, when I was a junior.

I only played two varsity seasons, but started as both tight end and corner safety. Both years I was named All-District in the Austin area. In my senior year I was honorable mention, All-State. By the time I graduated I had received football scholarship offers from the University of Texas, Stanford, the University of Texas, El Paso (then known as Texas Western), Oklahoma, and Sul Ross University in Nagadoches, Texas.

At last, there were a whole bunch of football coaches who wanted to give me a uniform, including Darrell Royal, the most important man in the college game at that time.

But in the one year I'd sat out, another sport recaptured my attention. Stephen F. Austin High School also had a baseball team. No black kid had ever worn that uniform.

In my sophomore year I decided to go out for baseball.

4

LEARNING THE TRADE

FOOTBALL was like a religion in Texas when I was growing up, so much so that baseball was an afterthought for most. Not for me, though. I wanted to play because I was good.

By the time I was a teenager everything I did on a baseball field became easier and easier. In the summer Pony League I hit .550 to .600, pitched, and played shortstop. I even threw a no-hitter. It reminded me of a Joe Cowley no-hitter I saw years later. I won the game, 15–13, because the other coach wouldn't let his guys swing and he kept sending midgets to the plate. They had no strike zone. And if there was a zone, I couldn't find it.

I could run and hit the ball farther than most kids my age. There was never an excuse needed to grab a bat or a ball and join in a pickup game or just play catch with my dad and brother.

By the time I was fifteen, major-league scouts were talking about this kid named Baylor.

None of that mattered to Travis Raven.

Raven, the baseball coach at Stephen F. Austin, was a true Texan, in the cowboy sense, a real traildriver. He barked orders at players instead of talking to them.

Raven was about as ready for me as Weise had been, which was not at all. It was bad enough that Raven had gone through his entire career without ever having coached a black kid. From the way he reacted the first day, I'd be willing to bet that was the first time he had ever come into contact with a black.

So in just three years I'd had white coaches who had made me feel unwanted, made nothing but negative impressions on me. It was like they were doing me a favor just to let me on their teams. And I knew it wasn't because of ability. You could see it in their eyes. With Raven, I could almost read his thoughts. *What's my banker friend gonna say when he sees his kid not playing and this black kid is?*

Raven just did not know what to do with me. All he ever said to me was "Get out to the field," and I would just sort of drift to right field. But he knew he could not turn me away completely. I had made a reputation for myself. There were players on that team who knew I could hit, run, and play the outfield as well as anybody he had. They wanted me there. After the final cuts, I was one of just two sophomores to make the team.

When you are a sophomore on the varsity you don't get a lot of playing time, let alone a regular position. So I played a lot of right field, left field, center, filled in here and there. To this day, I believe if it had not been for Travis Raven, I probably would have started.

In a lot of ways Raven reminded me of Gene Mauch in that he was always thinking, but without anywhere near the success Gene enjoyed. In fact, Raven thought too much. He used to pull one outfielder in to make him a fifth infielder when the team had to prevent the winning run from scoring from third. Just like Mauch. I never saw that play work for Raven. I never saw it work for Mauch, either, come to think of it.

Raven continued to do nothing to make me feel welcome. He really didn't have to talk, though. The walls of the school's old field house talked to you all the time, about Austin High's rich history. Everywhere there were photos of the championship football and baseball teams. Those pictures were filled with the guys who had made Austin a powerhouse. Ray Culp, who later pitched for Gene Mauch's Phillies. Mike Cotton, a University of Texas All-American quarterback, played baseball for Austin High. Their faces stared out at me every day.

I wanted to be a part of that tradition. Even as a little kid I would sit at my home in Clarksville and on Friday evenings listen to the school's marching band at football games, hear the drums and the cheering crowds. I wanted in. I threw myself into sports, especially baseball. I don't know if there are pictures nowadays of the teams I played on. But I do know that when my son, Donny, Jr., walks the hallways of Austin High and plays for the same teams, he gets to pass by the school's Hall of Fame. There he sees the retired numbers of players or plaques honoring great athletes like Ben Crenshaw. He also sees a plaque with a picture of me from my senior season and one from my MVP year as a California Angel.

It was my teammates who made baseball enjoyable. I never had any run-ins or scuffles. Practice was the easy part, because of the guys. The seniors especially reached out to me.

Opposing teams had also started to ignore race, because competition was too great at the high-school level. But I did start hearing things like, "Let's keep this guy off base because he can steal."

I felt good playing the game. Outfield was home. I was as good as any outfielder Raven had. I started measuring myself against other kids. I played against some guys, with some guys, who probably could have played professionally. The level I was reaching for kept getting higher and higher.

There was still Travis Raven. I knew my life could be a lot easier if he weren't there. By my junior year I got my wish. Raven left Stephen Austin to take a job as head football coach at another high school. His old job went to a guy from Bryan, Texas, named Frank Seale.

My baseball education was about to begin.

My first impression of Frank Seale was that drill instructors had nothing on this guy. He was from Texas A&M, a military college, and it showed. He was a strict, no-nonsense guy. Slender, but well-built, Frank looked like a basketball player or pitcher. No one doubted his toughness. He poured a military discipline into everything he did. He believed in fundamentals, guys knowing how to play the game the correct way. For the first time my education was coming from a coach. And the more I wanted to learn the more he wanted to teach.

Frank Seale came along when I really needed something positive in my life. I could talk to him, trust him. I finally had met a coach who believed in me and one that I could believe in, too. Others would follow—Joe Altobelli, Earl Weaver, Gene Mauch, and John McNamara. But Frank was the first.

On the field, Frank was a strict disciplinarian who believed in hard work. Winning was as important to him as it was to any coach, but how we won was even more important. He didn't let us take anything for granted, no matter what the score.

One of Frank's "lessons" involved using the field. Literally. Deep in left field at Stephen Austin there was a hill that rose on a steep grade toward the fence. Chasing a ball meant chasing it uphill. Anyway, after one game we were all pretty happy because we'd won big, real big. Frank wasn't happy, though. He made us hit the hill. "Just keep running until I tell you to stop," he said.

I couldn't believe it. The other team was watching and they were the guys who had just been crushed. Here we were, killing ourselves, our punishment for winning.

If Raven had said that it would have been a personal vendetta. But when Frank said it, deep down inside we knew he was trying to teach us something. I found out later that Frank was angry because he thought we'd let up. Frank never quit and he didn't expect us to, either. He taught me that baseball didn't allow for guys who thought they had something won and then lay back.

Frank stuck up for his players. He thought that we deserved to be treated with respect by other teams and never wanted anyone to get hurt because of poor field conditions. He very rarely got into it with other coaches but when one school in Killeen, Texas, wanted us to play on an infield of muddy, black Texas dirt, Frank blew his stack. "What are we doing here?" he said. "This is like a cow pasture." But Frank never welched on a deal, either. He just told us to be careful and play hard.

Frank had his funny moments, too, sometimes not by design. Once we were in a double-elimination tournament during my junior year. We had to play three games in one day. We won all three. But another school ended up with the same record, so we had to flip a coin for the trophy.

Frank called tails. Nobody ever calls tails. Naturally we lost and the other school walked off with that four-foot trophy. Frank really showed me he was an Aggie by losing that trophy. I don't think a Longhorn would have called tails.

Baseball with Frank was a pleasure. But there were moments when every kid had to question his own sanity. Especially in those long, hot summers.

Sometimes playing in Texas seemed more like survival training than fun. They put that roof on Houston's Astrodome for good reason. Texas has two seasons. Hot and hotter. And sometimes, playing in July and August, you'd feel like you were about to die.

One torrid August night we were in a town called Lamarque, Texas, where Frank had taken our American Legion team for a tournament. Lamarque is right outside of Texas City, and it's probably the hottest, most humid place I have ever been in my life. The air was almost too hot and heavy to breathe and when you did, the pollution almost asphyxiated you. There were gasoline plants all over and no matter where you went you could not escape the smell of formaldehyde.

Our team stayed at Lamarque's American Legion Hall, with about eight other teams. Almost a hundred guys, all thrown together in one gigantic hall, sleeping on folding cots. There was just no way to get a good night's sleep, smelling those smells, hearing kids snoring and tossing and turning. Our team had a catcher who was kind of chubby. He almost expired, the formaldehyde got to him so bad. He couldn't keep his glove up. That's when I learned what a "retriever" was as opposed to a receiver. That poor guy kept having to retrieve the ball from the backstop because he just could not catch a thing. It was killing everybody. We didn't know whether to laugh or cry. That night I vowed if I lived to get out of Lamarque, I would never step into that hellhole again. Lamarque got Doug the next year. Fortunately, he survived, too.

Frank was not only my coach, but my friend. He looked after me and made me feel like I was part of his family. Every kid on the team felt that way. Frank went out of his way to get to know our parents, too. I couldn't imagine that Travis Raven even knew what to say to a black man who handled baggage at the train station. Frank did, treating not only me, but my mom and dad with respect. In fact he and my mom formed an unbeatable alliance. I never could skip lunch, let alone a class. My mom and Frank watched me like hawks. In two years Frank was the biggest buffer I had. He refused to treat me differently; I wasn't his black player, just another one of Austin's athletes. Other coaches did not see it that way. Gay Walker, the basketball coach, and some of the football coaches, would come to me and tell me I shouldn't allow the girls in the Red Jackets drill team to walk me to class or make banners for me. Those were two things the drill team had traditionally done for years for lettermen. Other teachers had told my coaches it didn't look good to see the white girls with a black kid.

Interracial dating was still forbidden and even the thought of it could set off serious repercussions. I felt that tension when I became friendly with Gretchen Morgan, the daughter of a white Southern Baptist minister. We talked on the phone a lot, teenage infatuation. Then one of the coaches probably got wind of it. Suddenly it was "suggested" to her by some coaches and certain administrators that we stop the phone calls. We stopped, just for the sake of avoiding problems for her and for me. My worst nightmare was being kicked off the team because of something like that.

Frank and the principal, W. R. Robbins, had to be under a lot of pressure to stop interracial dating, but neither said a word.

I wish I could say that the only problems I had because of race came from whites, but that was not the case. While it was all right for me to play during the summer or in the Pony League, I found out as soon as I joined the school team that my black schoolmates did not like it one bit. It didn't matter to them if I played football or basketball, both of which I played on the varsity level. But the idea of baseball really burned them up. To them, blacks just didn't play baseball.

I thought that was ridiculous. Jackie Robinson played baseball. Frank Robinson played baseball. I knew about Willie Mays and Henry Aaron. Sometimes I wondered if black kids growing up in Austin knew about them. Looking back, though, I guess I can understand their thinking. We mostly got Yankees games on TV on Saturdays. There were not a lot of black faces on that team.

So there was pressure not to play. But I didn't give in. I was still that same hardheaded kid who used to throw rocks or newspapers through screen doors to prove a point.

In my three years of baseball at Austin High only one other black ever came out for the team. In my senior year I was by myself again. I was also one of only two players who had lettered for three years. Before my senior season, Frank named me captain.

Throughout the years to come, I would read many times that Don Baylor is the "unofficial captain" of this team or that. To this day Frank Seale is the only coach or manager to ever make it official.

Frank Seale, Mr. Robbins, and Marjorie Ball—a counselor who really believed in me—taught me a valuable lesson I would never have found in any textbook. I learned that caring people do not view others in terms of color. Those three were exceptional people.

Mr. Robbins, a real positive guy with a great sense of humor, went out of his way to pump me up. He used to tease me about the pro scouts who were starting to appear more and more. He'd tell me that when I got into the World Series I'd have to get him tickets. Even after he retired he would remind my mom about those tickets. Unfortunately, Mr. Robbins died fifteen years before I faced the Mets' Bob Ojeda and doubled off the Green Monster in Fenway in my first World Series at-bat in 1986. But Frank Seale was there. A year later he was in the Metrodome to see my first Series home run, one that helped the Twins win Game Six and eventually the world championship.

Nothing could have been more fitting. After all, Frank was my first baseball "stepfather."

Unfortunately, Frank, Mr. Robbins, and Miss Ball were exceptions. Many of the other officials had preconceived notions of what the black kids could or should do. To be told by counselors that you should try for a trade or some other nonacademic endeavor after high school was not at all unusual. Most black kids heard that "advice." That was all that was expected of us.

I had good grades, though, and I knew that college would figure in my future, no matter what. And sports offered the ticket out.

In baseball, my averages over three years—.345, .344, and .500— attracted college scouts. In basketball I was a forward but I jumped center because I was better at it than our six-foot-six center. I averaged approximately 15 points and prided myself on being tough under the boards. That kind of play also earned some scholarship offers.

My abilities attracted college scouts from all over Texas. Blacks were just starting to make their way into the Southwest Conference schools. Southern Methodist University's Jerry Levias was the first black to play football in the SWC, integrating the league in 1965. So colleges and universities throughout the region started to come through with scholarships for kids like me.

I received offers from Texas Western (now known as the University of Texas–El Paso), Nagadoches, Stanford, and Oklahoma. I guess the Sooners needed another Texan to go back home to beat on the University of Texas.

I could not imagine being a Sooner, though. Texas U. was still my dream. Darrell Royal wanted me, too, and also offered a scholarship. There was only one problem. I had it in mind that I would play football, baseball, and basketball. Darrell had it in mind that football in Texas was a full-time job. The only way he'd have a baseball player on his squad was if the guy was a pitcher. After I hurt my shoulder playing football in my junior season my pitching career had ended. I guess that's where my dreams of being a Longhorn died, too, because Darrell wouldn't give in and I wouldn't give up baseball.

Ironically, the shoulder injury that kept me off the pitching mound and, therefore, out of the University of Texas, also scared away some pro scouts. Until that time, the Houston Astros had let it be known that I would be their number-one draft choice. No less than Paul Richards, then the general manager, had come to Austin to see this kid named Baylor. I was their first target and then they planned to go after a kid from Detroit named John Mayberry. But when word got out that my shoulder was hurt, Houston switched to Mayberry in the 1967 amateur draft.

Later on, scouts told me that Houston had planned to take me second. In the second round there was still no call from Houston. There was a call from the Orioles, however. The world champions had chosen me. I was second on their list behind a surfer from Long Beach, California, a pretty good shortstop named Bobby Grich.

There was still one last tug to play football in college. Frank Seale thought education was the most important consideration. I was convinced, then, that I should go to Texas Western. But Dee Phillips, the Orioles' scout, asked me the most important question of my life. He asked if I wanted a career or a limp. Baseball would offer an education, too, Phillips argued.

For the second time in my life I chose baseball over football.

I knew then, in my heart, I was going to the major leagues. Here I was, seventeen, not even old enough to sign my contract without my dad's permission. But I knew. And when I signed, I thought about those counselors who'd told me and every other black kid from Clarksville, "Try a trade, try a trade."

I had a trade. Baseball. And I learned it well.

5

BABY BIRDS

I SQUARED and tried to drop a bunt. There was a runner on second and no one out. *Get the runner over,* that's what I was thinking.

Joe Altobelli, manager of the Bluefield Baby Birds, stood there, arms folded, shaking his head.

It was my first game as a professional in the Appalachian Rookie League. Alto had placed me third in the batting order and wanted to see what this strong kid from Austin could do. I struck out.

When I got back to the dugout Alto took me aside. I thought I was going to hear about the strikeout, that maybe guys in the rookie league weren't ever supposed to do that.

"Line drives, that's why you're hitting third, to drive in runs," Alto said quietly. "You're not gonna get a man in like that."

He wasn't talking about the strikeout, but about the bunt attempt.

Alto didn't yell. He was more the arm-around-the-shoulder kind of guy, like your dad and best friend all in one. Alto's job was to teach the Baby

Birds how to be professionals. What he was gently letting me know was that when you're seventeen, you may think you know everything about baseball, but you really know nothing.

I was in a new world, unlike anything I'd ever seen. I knew that the moment I stepped off the plane in the Appalachians to begin my pro career in Bluefield, West Virginia, in June 1967. The day I arrived Alto had just released five guys. I'm thinking *What did I get myself into?* My college eligibility was gone. Now there I was, just like every other Baby Bird. Big on the playing fields back home, three-sport heroes, the whole bit. The guys Alto had cut were from college, older, stronger, more experienced. And they'd just gotten that one little look. Talk about a scared kid. I wasn't even the Orioles' number one pick. That title belonged to the guy from Long Beach, California, the guy who wasn't even in camp. Bobby Grich, who was also being recruited to play quarterback for UCLA, was holding out for every dime he could get.

I remember thinking if he'd only seen those five guys leaving he'd be here in a second. But Bobby wasn't there in a second. He held out for a week. And when he did arrive he had a $35,000 signing bonus. I had gotten a $7,500 bonus, which I thought was very good. So had Frank Seale and Bill Bowers, the assistant secretary of the state of Texas, who was a friend of my dad's. I'd just learned lesson number one. Check with Bobby Grich before signing anything.

My first game was in Johnson City, Tennessee. Ron Blomberg, the number-one pick in the country, was playing there. Bobby and I were in awe when we visited Ron. This was the same Ron Blomberg who had hit a ball over the centerfield fence in a high-school all-star game in Atlanta's Fulton County Stadium. The same kid who was the top pick of the New York Yankees. Ron was living in an air-conditioned hotel room; he'd signed for $90,000. I'd just met my first superstar.

My first game told me just how far I had to go. I went to the plate five times and struck out three times. I don't even know if I got a ball out of the infield. Alto gave me the next day off. I must have looked rattled. Halfway through that second game Alto called on me to pinch-hit. I doubled. I never sat out a game again.

I became Alto's centerfielder and he became my tutor. After almost every game Alto would take me, Bobby, and a kid from California named Stan Martin to Denny's Restaurant in Bluefield and talk baseball. We'd talk far into the night. Alto's philosophies became mine. He took bunting out of my game and put aggressiveness into it. "If I hit in certain parts of the lineup, let me drive the guy in," became my attitude. "Not bunt him over for somebody else to drive in."

Alto taught me the importance of good work habits. He was a tireless worker himself, serving as manager, batting-practice pitcher, third-base coach, and, when you got right down to it, a baby-sitter. He taught us to respect the game. He was a friend and teacher, the kind of person you figure must manage every team in the pros.

Like I said, I still had a lot of growing up to do.

Alto and I went our separate ways a long time ago. We reunited in New York for a while and, in 1983, I was pulling hard for Alto when he managed the Orioles to the world championship. Last summer, before a game, my manager with the A's, Tony La Russa, came over to me in the clubhouse. He had been watching a Cubs broadcast in his office and had seen Alto, the third-base coach for Chicago, interviewed on TV. "Altobelli just paid you one of the highest compliments that you can bestow on a ballplayer," Tony told me. "He said that in thirty years of baseball the players that stick out in his mind the most as real winners are Mattingly and Baylor."

If you measure success by those who respect you, then I guess I had achieved a lot.

Life away from Austin overwhelmed me at first. There were the fringe benefits of being a working man. As soon as I signed I bought my first car, a used 1966 GTO. I also had wanted to give something back to my mom and dad, so I gave them half of my bonus.

After just a short time I realized that the most important day in the minors was payday. I always had to pay the phone company about seventy or eighty dollars. I was homesick and also had a bad case of puppy love.

For the first time I really appreciated mom's cooking. Our meal allowance was two dollars a day. On a five-day road trip they would hand you ten dollars. I couldn't believe it. I have never been able to live on two dollars a day at any time in my life. But I told myself that if I didn't eat right I couldn't play. And I just couldn't eat hamburgers all the time. I was six-foot-one and 195 pounds and still growing. So I cut into the bonus again and fed myself as well as I could.

Between the phone calls and the meals, I was less homesick and not as hungry. I didn't feel that rich anymore, either.

In the minors, players move in with families because they cannot afford apartments or hotel rooms. In Bluefield, there were very few black families and that left the black guys on the team in a bind. So Herman Grant, Lew Beasley, and I decided to share a hotel room, for a hundred dollars a month. One room, three guys, in the middle of God's Little Acre.

Herman was from Newport News, Virginia, and Lew was from Virginia Beach, Virginia. They were a couple of good old country boys. Both were about three or four years older than I, real worldly, in my eyes. Herman had a hot-rod roadrunner, modified for drag-racing, purchased with his bonus money.

I had never thought much about sharing a room with my brother, Doug, but this was different. Herman blasted his tape deck all the time, mostly James Brown. There's only so many times a person can listen to "Poppa's Got a Brand New Bag" before you wish that James Brown had never been born.

There were only two beds. Herman, a pitcher, always got one. The other went to the guy who got the most hits. Get more hits, you get the bed and the box spring. The other guy got the floor and the mattress. Sometimes it went down to the last at-bat. Wanting to get off the floor might have had something to do with my winning the batting title, the only time I ever led a professional league in hitting.

Once, the three of us went into the mountains to visit a black family we had all gotten to know. My first look at life in the Appalachian mountains scared me to death. The hills were riddled with mine shafts. Tiny, dirt-floor, tin-roofed shanties were scattered all over the mountainside. Coal was being taken out of the ground right in front of the grim little homes. Coal-car tracks were everywhere.

Blacks and whites lived up in those hills and we had been told that the people who didn't make their living in the mines made money running moonshine. Moonshiners were mean, not friendly L'il Abner-types in cartoons.

The coalminers were hard people, too. The local folks supported the teams but, in places like Marion, Virginia, and Wytheville, Tennessee, the people were openly hostile.

One day, when I was playing in Wytheville, a beer-bellied hillbilly was all over me. Every time I went to the plate, every time I took the field. He called me everything but a nigger. He probably wanted to but just couldn't pull the trigger. So, over and over, he yelled what he must have thought was an insult. He kept shouting that I was "all meat and no potatoes." To this day I still don't know what he meant. I was what I was, a skinny black kid who didn't look like he was getting enough meat or potatoes on a regular basis.

Just getting from town to town made me fear for my life. Minor-league ballclubs weren't spending large amounts of money on buses. A couple of times on long road trips I thought I wasn't going to live. Bad shocks and hairpin turns turned your stomach inside out. Chugging up the side of mountains in slow motion only to barrel down the other made rollercoasters seem dull. We got to ride those roads twice a day, once in daylight and then, for real fun, in the dark. I used to sit as close to the door as I could, probably figuring I'd jump before the bus hit the bottom of one of those ravines.

I had a good year despite the new environment. One game, against Salem, I accidentally made one of the best catches of my career. I was playing center and at the plate stood Richie Zisk, who would go on to make a name for himself with the Pirates. Richie was leading the Appalachian League that year in hitting, batting around .400. He lined a ball that I thought was veering to right-center. I broke to my left only to realize the ball was hooking back, toward center. I could not recover in time to get my gloved left hand in position. So I skidded and reached back with my bare right hand and caught the ball.

I threw the ball back as if it were nothing. Zisk was dying because his average was dying. That catch made him something like 0–for–30.

There would be many more years of growing ahead. Most of that growing, for the next fifteen or so years, would be done in the company of the surfer from Long Beach.

Right from the start Bobby Grich and I were a little more than curious about each other. Being the Orioles' top two draft picks, I had heard about him and he had heard about me. I'd never met a surfer and beach bum from the Golden State. He'd never met a black cowboy from Texas.

We were a perfect match, if you overlooked the fact that our tempers clashed from day one. We'd holler and scream in a heartbeat. I couldn't believe it, but he was a bigger red-ass than I was.

Bobby and I were roommates on the road. After a tough game Bobby would break things and we'd start screaming. He'd throw something and we'd holler some more. We never fought, although we squared off a couple times.

Bobby loved it. He took after his dad, who was a longshoreman and a professional boxer. Grich, like his dad, was wiry and tall and loved to fight, too.

Bobby could lose it on the baseball field as quickly as anybody I've ever seen. If a guy tried to cheap-shot him at second base on a slide, he would just go crazy. Once he put on his uniform it was kill or be killed.

Bobby was a darned good shortstop, a little slow-footed but he had an arm on him and great range and he just about made all the plays. But the Orioles happened to have a guy at short named Mark Belanger and Mark was the best. No offense to Ozzie Smith, but any guy who was confident enough to play eighteen years and never wear a protective cup, had to not only be the bravest, but the best. So the Orioles made room for Bobby at second, eventually trading Davey Johnson.

Bobby, being a good-looking guy, liked women a lot. He was so smooth he could field a grounder, sneak a look in the stands before he threw, spot a good-looking girl, and then send a note as soon as he left the field.

That's where we differed. I was having a hard enough time keeping my head together and concentrating on baseball. I couldn't walk into bars because I was underage. I didn't have girlfriends in every city. I'm not saying I stayed in my room every night, but there was just no comparison. Bobby was a legend.

Bobby showed me where his priorities were a couple years after I met him. By 1969 we were playing for Alto with Dallas–Fort Worth in the Class AA Texas League. Again the thing to fear most was not a wild pitcher, but a wild bus ride. Mountain road treachery was replaced by the desolateness of the wide-open desert. On one endless trip, from Dallas–Fort Worth to Albuquerque, New Mexico, the bus broke down. Guys were roaming up and down the road. Alto knew the bus was finished and so he told us to get to New Mexico the best way we could. Everybody started thumbing for rides, including the bus driver. Grichie was thumbing, too, but he was also looking for girls. Not until a girl stopped in a convertible did Grich get started for New Mexico.

Just because Bobby made five times as much money didn't mean he flaunted it. He didn't buy televisions. He rented them. Black-and-white, too.

By 1968 the Vietnam War was gearing up; I'd be lying if I said major-league teams didn't use the National Guard or college to keep its prospects stateside.

I did not want to go to Vietnam. It was a war that was chewing up a lot of guys I knew, guys who had the wrong skin color and could not get into the Texas National Guard. I did not understand why Americans were fighting in a civil war 10,000 miles away. I did not want to die in a war no one understood. So I went to school.

I was told that to assure my draft-exempt status, I'd have to maintain eighteen credit hours per semester to classify as a full-time student. That meant going to Blinn Junior College in Brenham, Texas, during the winter and then transferring to Miami Dade-North Community College during the 1968 exhibition season. While I was in school in Florida, I played for the Miami Marlins of the Class A Florida State League.

Bobby was in the Guard by 1968 and his playing time was limited to weekends. His first year was a tough one, so bad the Orioles placed me, but not him, on the protected roster in the expansion draft of winter 1968. Bobby hit about .220, struck out 120 times or more. He was struggling in the field at shortstop, trying too hard in the little time he had. He was still young, not fully developed as a player.

In 1967, though, we had never dreamed of things such as batting slumps, promotions or demotions. We were the Baby Birds and we were about to do what the big club had done the previous fall: win a championship.

Aside from Bobby and myself, Alto had the Orioles' next five draft picks at Bluefield, too. We were kind of cocky. We figured if the Orioles could win a championship, so could we. And we did win the Appalachian League pennant, finishing with a 42–25 record. We all received rings.

I led the Appalachian League in hitting (.346), hits (85 in 67 games), runs scored (50), stolen bases (26), and triples (8) and was named Player of the Year.

The big leagues, the big money, couldn't be that far away, I thought. I looked to improve on a $500 per month salary, which barely kept me from starving. Orioles assistant farm director John Schuerholz offered me twenty-five dollars more a month. I was furious. I had read how Frank Robinson had received his contract from Baltimore after his Triple Crown season, took it out of one envelope, placed it in another, and mailed it back without ever reading it. Whatever the offer was, Frank just knew it was not enough. So I got an envelope and mailed the proposed new contract back, unsigned.

With Frank Seale's help, I was able to talk Schuerholz all the way up to a fifty-dollar-a-month raise. John is now the general manager of the Royals and has a lifetime contract. Too bad. I certainly would have liked to be on the other side of the bargaining table one day to renegotiate his salary. In the winter of 1987, John tried to sign me as a player and then eventually move me into the front office. I'm sure John could show me how to negotiate without giving up a cent.

It was on to California and the Stockton Ports of the Class A California League. There I hit .369 with 7 home runs, 40 RBI, and 14 stolen bases in 68 games. Ports GM Clay Dennis told reporters, "Don could be the Willie Mays of the future."

In 1968 I played at three levels. After starting the season in Stockton and batting .369, I was promoted to Elmira of the Class AA Eastern League. I only stayed a week, moving up to Rochester of the International League after the Orioles called up Merv Rettenmund from the Triple A club.

I was nineteen years old and one step away from the major leagues. Nothing could stand in my way. Or so I thought, until I met Billy DeMars.

Billy wasn't with Rochester when I first arrived because he had suffered a death in his family. Herm Starrette, the interim manager of the Red Wings, put me in the starting lineup right away. I was scared to death, but I got 2 hits my first game. As soon as DeMars came back, I went right to the bench.

Maybe it was because I was just a teenager and Billy didn't want to throw me to the wolves. But I never knew what he was thinking because he hardly ever talked to me. And when he did it was more like a lecture. All I felt was hostility.

Since I had never met the man before I couldn't help but think he disliked me because I was black. Maybe DeMars just hated young players, period. I also noticed that his favorite targets were blacks like Chet Trail, Mickey McGuire, and a guy from Puerto Rico named Rick Delgado. I felt that DeMars did not have my best interests at heart. I was trying very hard to learn, but I got nothing from him.

I started drifting further and further away from DeMars on the bench, to what I started calling the "I-hate-the-manager" corner. Wherever he was in the dugout, I was at the other end. And I was not alone.

Usually, in Triple A, you'll find older players down at that end, guys who probably know they're not going to make it to the bigs, guys like Billy Scripture. He was about twenty-five, from Virginia Beach. He had to be the craziest person I had ever met, a Triple A lifer who no longer had anything to lose. Billy was good with wood; he could carve the prettiest duck decoys you'd ever seen. He also liked to eat wood. One day, in the trainer's room, Billy got down on his hands and knees and took a bite right out of a wooden table. He had to have the strongest teeth around. Later, when Billy became a minor-league coach, he stood in front of a pitching machine and let the balls hit him in the chest just to prove it doesn't hurt to get hit by a pitch. Billy Scripture was a legend. And a psycho. But at least he helped keep me sane.

Under DeMars, I felt frustration for the first time in my pro career. I hit just .217 in 46 at-bats, the first time I'd failed to hit over .300. I knew I was overmatched by Triple A pitchers and that I had gotten there so quickly it was natural that there were guys ahead of me. I wasn't being rushed, surely an organizational decision. But DeMars never told me why I was on the bench. It was a wasted stay and I felt empty by the time the season ended.

I got my confidence back in the Instructional League in Clearwater, Florida, that winter. I just kept in mind what I wanted to accomplish. Frank Seale had told me years before: "Don't get down. The biggest enemy can be yourself."

In the spring of 1969 I was invited to the big-league camp for the first time. There I finally met Frank Robinson, the player whose style I wanted to adopt. First, I adopted something else. Frank used a special bat model, the R161, a 35-ounce, 35-inch beauty from Hillerich and Bradsby, a real Louisville Slugger. I asked Frank what the R161 meant, since players of his stature got to design and name their own bats.

"The 'R' means Robinson," Frank said. "And the number one stands for my first MVP season and sixty-one for the year I won the MVP."

The "R161" not only had one MVP season, but two in it. When you are in the minors, you're looking for anything that feels good in your hands. It did. When the Red Wings played at Louisville, I visited the Hillerich and Bradsby plant, took an R161 with me, and said, "That's the bat I want to use." I've used it ever since.

I had a good season in '69, even though I dropped back to Double A. In a sense, going down one level was a relief because I was back with Alto, someone I knew had my best interests at heart. I was with Bobby and we both thrived in Dallas–Fort Worth. I set career highs in almost every category, including hits (122), doubles (17), triples (10), home runs (11), and RBI (57).

I had a good spring training in 1970 with the big club, a great way to start my first full season of Triple A. Three years after I had signed, I was in Rochester, never to slip lower again.

6

"THE GROOVE"

FRANK Robinson stood in the middle of the Orioles' clubhouse at Miami Stadium in the spring of 1970, a newspaper in his hand.

Frank was reading aloud from an article. He seemed to find it amusing that one of the young spring-training invitees had told writers that if he got hot he didn't care if the Orioles did have Frank Robinson, Paul Blair, Merv Rettenmund, or Don Buford in the outfield. "If I get into my groove, I'm gonna play every day," Frank quoted his new teammate as saying.

If the other Orioles were not certain of the identity of the article's subject, they needed only to look at the one player who seemed like he was about to die. Me.

I had spoken to the press after a particularly good day in a Grapefruit League game. The day those quotes appeared the team was on a road trip to West Palm Beach. Frank had stayed in camp and had seen the article in the Miami papers. He had a whole day to plot his revenge. So, the next day, Frank called everyone to attention and read every single word I had said.

I could have crawled under my locker stool. From that day on, I was no longer known as Don. My teammates called me "The Groove." Mark Belanger teased me, saying, "That's going to stick for a long time." It did. To this day I don't know if Belanger or some of those other guys even remember my real name.

The whole incident was humbling. And, within weeks, I learned I was headed back to Rochester despite a good spring. In my mind, I was ready for the Orioles. They, however, obviously were not ready for me. Frank, Blair, Buford, and Rettenmund could, indeed, get along without "The Groove." And history shows they managed quite well, easily winning the world championship.

Still, I had learned something about myself that day I sat in the clubhouse being razzed by Frank and the others. I learned I had even more determination than I had thought. I had opened my mouth and now it was time to back up those words. If the proving had to be done at Rochester, so be it. I knew I would be back.

Frank had given me the fight to get where he was, to stand next to him and say I belonged. I wanted to prove that to Frank more than anyone else.

The 1970 Red Wings started out strong and so did I, immediately jumping out to the league lead in doubles and triples. I knew I was building a phenomenal year. I felt so good, I thought I was almost invincible. I remember getting hit in the head by Jim Bibby, a wild, hard thrower with the Tidewater Tides. He could have killed me, but he didn't even knock me out of the game. I just bounced up and ran to first. The next time up against Bibby I tripled. I didn't fear anyone.

I batted third and played center for my new manager, Cal Ripken. International League pitchers, who had eaten me alive in 1968, now, more and more, stood no chance in 1970.

Rip told every reporter who would listen about this kid who could run, hit, drive in runs. The thing that pleased me the most was that he also talked about my desire.

In one game, against Louisville, I nearly decapitated the pitcher with a two-out single to start a rally. In the seventh inning I hit a 3-run home run into the wind that carried over the third bank of billboards in left field at Silver Stadium over 430 feet away. The day before, I'd shown power of a different sort. I drove a ball deep to right-center and never stopped running until just before I slid into third, head-first, literally in a cloud of dust. I looked up at Rip, who was also the third-base coach. "Did I get you dirty?" I asked sheepishly, realizing that I'd not picked up his signal to stop at second or keep running. "No," Rip said, "but you didn't even look at me."

But he wasn't angry. He knew that I liked to run the bases even more than I liked hitting home runs. Having the bat in your hand is one thing, but running the bases is a truly special feeling of power.

All that season guys like Grichie and me pushed hard. And as the RBI and home runs and batting averages got better and better, it was hard not to think about moving up. It was also hard not to wonder if anyone was even noticing, as month after month passed.

Bobby could not temper his feelings. After one game, in which the Red Wings stomped Buffalo, 27–4, Bobby looked at his 3 home runs, his 7 RBI, and declared himself ready. "In order to get to the big leagues, I have to move somebody out," Bobby told reporters. "There's a lot of good defensive players up there, but it's hard to find a guy who is both a good hitter and a good defensive player. . . . Belanger is only hitting around .211. He's a guy who can hit .240 and stay up just because of his glove. But I don't know about .211. . . . But you can't second-guess."

I found out later that there *was* some second-guessing going on. In mid-July, after the International League All-Star Game, Cal announced he didn't feel I could play centerfield in the majors. He told reporters he felt I had to play left to make it because of my throwing ability. It was the first time, but not the last, that someone with my fate in his hands would question my arm. Cal had attached a "can't throw" tag that would haunt me throughout my career. Rip told reporters I had started the first 73 games in center "to make sure he got a real test out there." In his eyes I guess I didn't pass. I flip-flopped positions with Tommy Shopay, never to play center full-time again.

I did not agree with Rip any more than I agreed when major-league managers started moving me out of left field to first base and then eventually into the designated hitter's position by the time I was twenty-six. I knew my right shoulder had been badly damaged in a high-school football game. As a safety, I'd used my shoulder to hit runners. Twice in one game I hit thigh pads. The first time I suffered a pinched nerve. The second time I suffered a separated shoulder. Between those injuries and the wear and tear of pitching, my shoulder had taken a severe beating. If those injuries occurred today I'm sure I would have been diagnosed as having a torn rotator cuff. Yet, throughout my career, I always felt that I could make the plays. To me, hitting the cutoff man was what a centerfielder was supposed to do. I did that. But Cal wanted to go in another direction.

If ever a kid needed a vote of confidence, I did. I got it from an unexpected source. "Arms are overrated in the major leagues," Earl Weaver said when asked by reporters about the possible "roadblock" in my career. "I'll bet you don't have five throws all year that decide a ball game. Look at Frank

Robinson. It's no secret . . . his arm has never been as good as Rettenmund's, but it didn't keep him from being the Most Valuable Player in each league."

Earl said he would not compare me to Paul Blair because Paul was in a class by himself. "Merv is a good centerfielder, like Reggie Smith and Mickey Stanley. Put Baylor in that same class," Weaver said.

Something else happened in 1970. The afternoon before a doubleheader I got married. I know now it was based more on loneliness than love. When you're a kid and 2000 miles from home, the minor leagues can be very lonely. I did it so that someone would be there for me, hopefully to share the good times and the bad.

I still hadn't had much exposure to the world outside Austin other than summer months in minor-league towns. She was a home-town girl, someone I could relate to. Maybe if I had known more of the world I would have known it would have been best to wait. From day one it was rough. We had to live on a $1000 a month. We had to move in with her parents in the off-season. Just packing a new family up to go to Puerto Rico for winter ball for the first time was overwhelming.

We just weren't ready for any of it. After all, I was just twenty and she was nineteen. I know for a fact I was too young. I tried to do the right things, like putting my wife through school, my sister, too. It just never seemed to be enough.

An additional stress was my introduction to an unpleasant side of big-city life in the North. The Red Wings front office kept a notebook listing all sorts of houses for rent. My teammate, Elijiah Johnson, his wife, and my wife and I, searched that book for a place large enough for two families; neither Elijiah nor I could afford to rent a house on our own. When we finally found the perfect place we called and made an appointment to meet the owner the next morning.

Bob Turner, the Red Wings' general manager, went with us to look over the house. The five of us arrived a little early, so we stood out on the sidewalk waiting for the owner to arrive. A car drove by very slowly. About twenty minutes later the same car came back. The driver got out, told us he was the owner and said that the house had already been rented.

Turner hit the roof. He said there was no way that place had been rented and told the owner he would hear from the Red Wings and the authorities because he was discriminating against blacks. The club filed a complaint with the city's Fair Housing Board. The owner was fined, plus he was ordered to pay our hotel expenses until we found a place to live. Each couple was awarded $1000.

We ended up living with a black family in a small house that had paper-thin walls. The couple had three or four kids. They also fought a lot. It was not the ideal first home, but there was not much more I could do on $1000 a month.

Rochester was thousands of miles away from Austin. There were never any signs that said outright we were not welcome. But I learned there could be a more subtle kind of racism, the kind you could hardly ever prove, but you knew in your heart existed.

As for my marriage, if the idea was to share the good times and the bad, then there was one good time that I would never give back. On November 20, 1972, my son, Donny, Jr., was born. Twelve years after the marriage, ten years after Donny's birth, we were divorced.

If 1970 was a sobering year personally, it was nothing but fun professionally. Triple A pitching continued to present no problem. I drove in 107 runs in 140 games, batted .327, hit 22 home runs, 15 triples, 34 doubles. I scored 127 runs, collected 166 hits altogether. It wasn't a matter of whether I'd go up to the majors when the rosters expanded in September, but when. And, sure enough, on September 8, I finally got the call, along with catcher Johnny Oates and outfielder Roger Freed.

My first major-league game was in RFK Stadium in Washington, D.C., the home of the Senators. The day before I'd been in Silver Stadium on Norton Street, in Rochester, an eighty-year-old park that stretched the meaning of the word "quaint." Now I was in an arena that had 70,000 seats, where Ted Williams managed, where Frank Howard played.

I watched as Johnny Oates got his first major-league hit. Seeing that, knowing a major-league career had just been born, well, I wanted my chance. I sat on the bench, not knowing what to say, what to do. I got clammy just thinking about my first at-bat, never knowing when or if Earl would ever look my way. I wasn't afraid of failing; I was terrified of that first at-bat, period.

Earl's call did not come for days. Then, on September 18, Earl wrote my name in the lineup against the visiting Cleveland Indians:

No. 5, Don Baylor, right field.

The first time I batted, the bases were loaded. How Indians righthander Steve Hargan managed to get into such a jam in the first inning I didn't even know. When I walked to the plate, my mind was completely jumbled. All I remember thinking is what every kid who steps into the batter's box for the first time remembers.

Scared to death . . . No scouting reports . . . No idea what Hargan throws except what I've seen when I peeked at him warming up on the sidelines . . . Asked the guys what he throws . . . I know they told me, but I'm walking to the plate and I can't remember. . . .

So I swung at the first pitch. It went between first and second and on into center. A base hit. A 2-run single. To this day I don't know how it happened. You always say a prayer on the way to the plate, anyway. That day I was not just praying. I was begging. Someone in the dugout asked the Indians for the ball. It was mine. The one I had wanted just about all my life.

Now, a lot of guys probably get that first hit and thank their high-school coach, then mother, their father, or whatever. I thanked Grichie.

Bobby had been called up about a month before me and had been playing off and on. A few days before he had also been faced with a bases-loaded situation. Earl had the Orioles in first place by a comfortable margin, he really had nothing to lose by letting a kid hit. But Earl had the throttle down. He wanted to obliterate the rest of the AL East. He wanted to win by 20 and right about September his team led the division by about 17, 18 games. So on that particular day, Earl had a chance to blow open the game. Grichie was walking to the plate with the bases loaded when he heard a whistle; it was Weaver. Bobby looked back and saw Brooks Robinson coming out of the dugout to pinch-hit.

Bobby was furious. He went back to the dugout and grabbed Weaver by the throat, started strangling him and screaming. "How do you expect me to hit in this league when you keep pinch-hitting for me all the time?" I couldn't believe my eyes. There he was, a rookie, trying to kill baseball's little genius. Elrod Hendricks had to separate the two. After I got to hit with the bases loaded, I often wondered if Earl thought I would try to kill him, too, if he had sent up a pinch-hitter.

Later, in my first game, I doubled off the top of the wall in right field to drive in the winning run in the bottom of the eleventh inning.

When you're twenty-one years old, and you've just driven in 3 runs in your major-league debut, you're hitting a clean .400 after one game, you start to believe nothing is out of reach.

I did more watching than playing that final month. And I knew I had so much to learn. During one hitters' meeting, I was told that the Indians' Sudden Sam McDowell had two pitches—an outstanding curve and a high-velocity fastball. "He throws gas," Rettenmund and Belanger both told me. I knew I had to jump on one pitch, the fastfall. The only problem was that, on the first pitch, McDowell threw me a straight changeup. I almost fractured my wrist trying to hold up. Later in the dugout, the guys laughed. "Forgot to tell you about that one," Belanger said. "He's got a third pitch. He's crazy. He'll do anything." If I knew then just how crazy Sudden Sam was, because of all the drinking problems he later admitted to, I probably would have tiptoed into the batter's box.

The Orioles veterans and their stamina awed me. In the minors, if you played 140 games, you were dead-tired, could hardly lift a bat. By the time I joined the Orioles they had played at least 130 games and looked to be turning the energy level up another notch. They were just like Earl. They wanted to run away with it all. The Orioles steamrolled the Twins in three straight in the League Championship Series. They then dismantled the Cincinnati Reds in five games to win the World Series.

They were winners. And none were more immense in my eyes than Frank and Brooks.

7

BROOKS AND THE JUDGE

WHEN I first came to the major leagues, Frank Robinson *was* the Baltimore Orioles.

Even though I would only play that one September with him and then for about another week in 1971, Frank made a more lasting impression on me than any teammate I ever had.

I had felt the magnitude of the man three years before I laid eyes on him. It had filtered all the way down to Bluefield because of the Triple Crown he had won and because of the world championship he'd led the Orioles to in 1966. Then, in 1969, I was playing alongside him in spring training. A year later I was watching him play in a September pennant race, in the big leagues.

Everybody, including Brooks, flocked to Frank with his problems. How to run the bases, how to play certain stadium walls, how to hit, or whatever. And the way he played the game was the way it should be taught. He was an intimidating, awesome player and if you couldn't learn from watching him, you couldn't learn anything.

The other players would tell a story about how once Frank beat the Red Sox in Fenway, even though he could not swing the bat. Frank had a real bad back, he'd hurt it when he hit the right-field wall taking away a home run to assure extra innings. Frank did not want to come out of the game. He also did not want the Red Sox pitcher to know he was hurt, not with the bases loaded. So he bunted perfectly for a base hit.

Frank did not solicit the leadership role he eventually assumed, that of unofficial captain. After all, he had his own responsibilities, such as hitting and driving in runs. And the Orioles did have a strong manager in Earl Weaver. Yet guys gravitated to Frank because he had charisma. He was the manager on the field.

If veterans revered Frank, it's not hard to understand what a kid like me thought. I was in awe of him, probably feared him more than anything. With Frank, it was almost like you were in class and had to raise your hand and timidly ask the professor, "Sir, may I say something to you?" I would just say, "Hi, how are you doing?" and keep moving. You had to watch what you said around Frank, something I learned the hard way when I stopped being Don Baylor and became "The Groove."

Frank ran the clubhouse with absolute authority. Third-base coach Billy Hunter had suggested Frank start a kangaroo court when Frank arrived in Baltimore. By the time I arrived, Frank's reputation as judge was well established.

Frank held court after every victory at home. He closed the clubhouse for fifteen minutes or so, letting players relax and talk things over. Then came judgment day. Frank's fine system was a funny, caustic reminder that the game should be played correctly—or else.

Frank did not fine players for physical errors, but fines for mental errors were almost automatic. Such blunders included pitchers giving up home runs on 0–2 counts or baserunners being thrown out trying to stretch a double into a triple with either no outs or two outs in an inning. Such infractions cost players anywhere from five dollars to twenty-five dollars. If Frank ever tried to take a hundred dollars back in those days he would have had a fight on his hands.

Frank handed out his fines in formal court sessions. Frank played his role to the max, wearing a judge's wig he made out of a rag mop. He'd call the court to session using a real gavel. No one spoke unless he raised his hand and Frank called upon him. I never spoke, nor did any other rookie. Mostly, we hid in our lockers and hoped Frank's gaze would not find us. We were young, but we weren't stupid. We knew we had absolutely no chance in Frank's court.

If you made a mistake on the bases you lost more than money. You'd find an old beat-up shoe hanging in your locker, Frank's "base-running" award. Frank had a "long-ball" award, a tattered baseball that he hung in the locker of the pitcher who allowed the longest home run. Then there was the "red-ass" award, a toilet seat that was painted red. It was for hotheads. That toilet seat lived in my locker. I didn't throw helmets or bats on the field, but if I got mad I'd go up the tunnel between the dugout and clubhouse and try to beat the wall to death with my bat. Guys would hear the crashing and know it was me.

Sometimes the guys would goad me and goad me until I'd lose it. Then they'd walk over and put the "prize" in my locker. I'd go crazy again. They loved it.

Frank had spies everywhere and never was there more fun than when we'd nail Earl for mismanaging. The whole team would yell "Guilty"! Earl would shout right along with us.

Many of the Yankees, Red Sox, and A's who paid through the nose in my courts have Frank to thank—or blame. I learned some of my best judicial moves from him.

My relationship with Frank was interesting from the first. He certainly wasn't in awe of me, at least not the way some kids today expect veterans to be in their presence. And yes, he was intimidating. But that was okay. He's Frank Robinson, after all, and as far as I was concerned, I was there to watch and learn, and there was no one I would have rather had teach me than Frank. The more I listened, the more I knew I wanted to model myself after him.

Bobby was never intimidated by Frank. In fact, Bobby and Frank had to be separated in the dugout in the spring of 1971 because Bobby thought Frank was mocking him. Grichie choked up on the bat a lot. Way up on the bat. He also was going through a time when he changed his stance and his bat model every time he batted. One day, Bobby was just choking the bat to death. Bobby heard someone say something about his stance. He thought it was Frank and started hollering. Next thing you know they were screaming at each other in the dugout. Grichie was yelling, "If you don't believe I can hit like this, you just stick around this league for five or ten years and watch me hit!"

I couldn't believe it. I'm going, "Bobby, please . . . Frank's gonna kill you."

He probably would have if other players had not separated them. But Bobby didn't care. He never backed down from anyone.

Bobby had done something I could never see myself doing. But I do think that when Frank looked in the mirror he saw a lot of me in him, a guy who would fight for what he believed in, especially in defense of teammates.

Frank saw that during a game in winter ball in 1972. Doyle Alexander, a pitcher with Santurce, was screaming at shortstop Juan Beniquez. Juan was just a kid and hadn't yet learned to speak English. Doyle was cursing and screaming because Juan had committed an error and then Doyle gave up a 2-run single to the pitcher. Juan was cringing, did not know what this crazy American big-leaguer was saying. Enough was enough. I grabbed Doyle and had him against the dugout wall by the time Frank and Elrod Hendricks pulled me away.

Frank knew I would fight him, if I had to. But Frank and I never had reason to fight. I still considered myself just as big a red-ass as Bobby, but I had more tolerance for the veterans' humor.

Neither of us had to worry about such barbs from the Orioles' other Robinson.

Brooks and Frank were as different as any two players could be, but I came to realize quickly that the Orioles had not one, but two, leaders.

Brooks was more open than Frank. And, surprisingly, even though he was the bigger name in Baltimore, he was easier to talk to than Frank. To this day he's considered one of that city's two living legends, along with Johnny Unitas. Brooks's teammates respected his standing in the city and in baseball because Brooks was so down to earth about it. In fact, he used to joke about it, saying out of the blue sometimes, "Hey, I'm a living legend." Brooks would laugh. So would I. He made me feel welcome, something I'll never forget.

I lockered between Brooks and Paul Blair. It was good for a shy kid from Austin to see that Brooks was still a shy guy from Little Rock. He never talked of himself as the greatest third baseman that ever lived. He did not have to because so many others did. Jimmy Reese, Babe Ruth's roommate who has seen nearly sixty years of major-league baseball, says Brooks and Pie Traynor are the best he's ever seen. Brooks didn't have the strongest arm, but his throws, no matter how difficult, always seemed to be there before the runner. When he had to throw from way down the line, he would leave his feet a lot and his legs and arms always seemed to be going in opposite directions.

General Manager Harry Dalton told me Brooks played bunts as well as anybody who ever lived. Brooks knew, down to the step, how to execute that play. "Within eight or nine," Brooks would say and, sure enough, by the time he took that many steps he had thrown the ball. After he fielded a bunt I never saw him throw side-arm, like most third basemen. Brooks always came over the top.

Graig Nettles and Mike Schmidt, outstanding third basemen, used the more conventional delivery after fielding bunts, since side-arm or down-under throws allow for more accuracy in the short amount of time left to throw out the runner. Those deliveries almost always ensure an arch on the throw so that the ball drops right into the first baseman's glove. Brooks didn't need to rush, however, because he got to bunts so quickly. So coming over the top was the norm for him. I rarely saw him hurry a throw or wind up sprawled on the ground next to the pitcher's mound, a sure sign a desperation play had just unfolded on a bunt play.

It wasn't that Brooks was a superb athletic specimen. He was blessed with quickness, but still, he was an extraordinary talent hidden in a rather ordinary body. Other players lifted weights to build arm strength. Others used aerobics to improve coordination and foot work. Brooks did none of those things. What he did do was spend hours at his craft, taking grounder after grounder, day in and day out. He worked hard to look that smooth. No matter how tired he was, infield practice was the first thing he did.

The magic was in Brooks's dedication, his work ethic and his ability to reach back in order to make the spectacular look routine.

He was simply the best third baseman I've ever seen.

One day I noticed Brooks was signing autographs with his left hand. "What gives?" I asked. After all, by definition being a great third baseman means that you field with a gloved left hand and throw with your right. Brooks also hit right-handed.

"I do everything else left-handed," Brooks said.

It turns out Brooks is a natural left-hander. That's why he could throw so well while running to his left and why he could make brilliant plays with his left hand. He could play the line and still get to balls in the hole between third and short, he was that adroit.

Brooks's fielding overshadowed his clutch hitting. He loved a guy to get on, have him steal a base, and set up an RBI challenge. When I batted in front of Brooks and we needed a big run, Brooks would walk over to me in the on-deck circle and say in that soft Arkansas drawl, "Just get on base and I will get you in somehow." I knew if I got on I could steal a base. And if I did, more often than not he'd keep his word. He was uncanny. And good.

About the only thing Brooks couldn't do is run. That was okay most of the time. After all, I hit fifth and he hit behind me. Except in one game in '72, when Earl dropped me to eighth and hit Brooks seventh in a game against Mel Stottlemyre in Yankee Stadium. Twice Brooks reached base and twice I doubled behind him. Each time Brooks made it to third—barely. He was killing himself on the bases, and killing me in the RBI column.

I would play many games in which Brooks taught me something about being a professional.

Once, after he made three errors in one game, he was devastated. Writers came over to Brooks, knowing he prided himself on his defensive abilities. They wanted to know what happened. Brooks did not hide, but rather answered the questions, mostly saying as good-naturedly as he could that it was "just one of those days." He was always there, for both players and the press, after the good games and the bad. That was a great example for a young player to see because Brooks not only talked about the importance of conducting one's self as a gentleman and a professional, he was a living example of how to do so.

Guys did not go to Brooks the same way they did to Frank, though. He did not go around telling guys how to hit. Brooks did not say much. He was a teacher and stabilizing force because of his actions. All you had to do was watch him.

Frank was the one who taught kids—and other veterans—the nuts and bolts. His National League roots influenced his hitting philosophy and, therefore, influenced me.

Frank taught me that on 2–0 counts, National Leaguers always assume they will get fastballs but American Leaguers assumed they would get anything from a curveball to a knuckler. Frank liked to swing only at the fastball on 2–0 pitches because that pitted strength against strength. If a pitcher came in with a fastball, he'd say, look for it in your power, your extra-base hit zone, from the middle of the plate on in. If the pitcher got you out on such a pitch, tip your hat. If he missed with it, Frank advised, a 3–0 count strengthened the hitter's position even more.

There would be many good years to be shared with Brooks, only a few cherished weeks with Frank. I cannot imagine there was ever a time when more lessons in professionalism flowed from two players into one.

A good winter-ball season would follow that all-too-short September with Frank and Brooks in 1970. I played for Hiram Cuevas's Santurce club in the Puerto Rican League. There I would get to know Frank even better because he was my manager and hitting guru. He taught me how to bring my hands in closer to my body so that I would stop doing my Carl Yastrzemski impersonation with the bat held almost over my head. Mostly he taught me to think while hitting. "A guy pitches inside, hit that ball right down the line," he would say. "Look for certain pitches on certain counts." Frank also wanted me to start using my strength more. Frank knew there was a pull hitter buried somewhere inside me and fought to develop that power.

I started to see past Frank's veil of intimidation and into a very complex man. He wanted to be a manager, the best possible. And his time in Puerto Rico was used to hone his skills as well as his players'. It was fun to watch Frank's focus turn from at-bats to running a team. The majors had never had a black manager. I knew he would be the first. He had to be.

In 1975, Frank did become the first black to manage, when he was hired by the Cleveland Indians. Nearly three decades after Jackie Robinson broke the color barrier for players, another Robinson made history. Last season Frank was named manager of the Orioles, his third managerial position. By the end of the 1988 season Frank was still the only black manager in the majors and one of only three to ever be hired. Frank's Giants came within two games of winning the NL West in 1982. But mostly he's been given second-division teams and neither the time nor authority to really make a difference.

Last season was Frank's toughest challenge. He took over the Orioles after that team had lost its first 6 games under Cal Ripken, Sr. The team would go on to lose a record 21 straight to start the season, as unbelievable a streak as I can imagine. Those were horrible days for the once-proud Orioles and for Frank. He had known that organization in the best of times. Now he watched the results of too many years of bad trades, poor drafts, and just plain bad luck.

Closet bigots wrote to newspapers and magazines and, using the team's record, said Frank was over his head and that he wouldn't have gotten the job if he weren't black and if baseball were not being pressured to hire minorities. I wondered where the bigots were by last August, when Frank's O's overcame that awful start and amazingly caught the Atlanta Braves in winning percentage and then took aim at the Seattle Mariners. I believe Frank showed just how good a manager he can be if given the chance. Baltimore, under Frank's restructuring, looked like a major-league team again. All Frank wants is time to rebuild. There's no one who is better qualified. I know. I watched him teach players how to be winners every day I was around him so many years ago.

In Santurce, Frank worked with me to strengthen my defense and throwing. And, oh yes, my hitting. For most of the winter I hovered around .340, but I wound up hitting .290. I guess I just wore down because, between Rochester, Baltimore, and Puerto Rico, I played more than 230 games. Even so, for most of the winter season I had been in a real "groove." I had played well for the person who had given me the desire to prove myself so many months before.

With everything that had happened, it was all surely enough to convince the Orioles I was ready. They would have to make room in 1971, I told myself again and again. Little did I know.

I was stuck.

8

GRADUATION DAY

"WHAT did they say to Baylor . . . go back and have a good year?"

Brooks spoke to a group of reporters in the visitor's locker room at Fort Lauderdale Stadium. And even the gracious gentleman from Little Rock could not hide the sarcasm in his voice.

It was the last week of March 1971. The Orioles had just cut their roster and informed me I had to go back to Rochester.

It was becoming a nightmare. All I had done in four minor-league seasons was hit .346, .369, .375, and .327. I'd given the organization the stolen bases, the power, the line drives it wanted.

I had understood when Earl shipped me out in 1970; I probably was too young and other players, such as Merv Rettenmund, had paid their dues longer. I did not understand in 1971. Earl had said he didn't want me sitting on the bench taking bits and pieces. "I'll take the two hundred fifty at-bats," I told Earl. "I want to play in the big leagues."

Earl just shook his head. I was gone, the Minor League Player of the Year heading back to Rochester.

It was no better for Bobby. When Orioles general manager Harry Dalton broke the same news to Grichie he had to shout it through a locked hotel-room door because Bobby refused to let Harry in. Bobby was close to losing it. When it happened to me, I just tried to keep up a brave front, telling reporters, "If they tell me to go back to Rochester I'll do the best I can." But I felt like I was falling into the same quagmire in which I had seen other prospects fall. Steve Demeter, a decent third baseman, stayed at Rochester for ten years because the Orioles had Brooks Robinson. Mike Epstein and Roger Freed had won minor-league Player of the Year awards, just like Bobby and I had, but both were traded. A year after Elijiah Johnson drove in 100 runs for Rochester, he gave up his dream of playing for the Orioles and signed with a Japanese team.

Their numbers had been right there. They all felt they were ready. The Orioles obviously disagreed. It was nothing personal, they wanted us to believe. It was just that, in a talent-rich system, the policy was strictly "no room, no need." So Orioles prospects were left down in the minors to become not just qualified, but overqualified. Not like today. The Orioles, who have fallen so low, would kill to have just one prospect like the dozen or so they used to keep stocked in the minors. In 1971, rebuilding wasn't on Earl's mind. So I went back to play for Alto and for the first time ever I was distracted by, of all things, the telephone. Every time the phone rang in the clubhouse I hoped it was the Orioles, looking for me. One day, when I was sitting in the dugout, I heard an announcer on a fan's radio say either Terry Crowley or Don Baylor would be called up after the game. So Terry and I went head-to-head all day. Terry got 4 hits, including 2 home runs. I got 2 hits, one of them a home run. The Orioles called up Terry.

By the end of June, I was batting .324, with 11 home runs and 53 RBI. In my mind there wasn't anything more I could do or any way to improve. I began resenting the excuses about my throwing and believed the extra work I was assigned was just to keep me busy. I knew graduation was long overdue.

I hit .313 that season, led the league in doubles, with 31, had 10 triples, 20 home runs, and 95 RBI in 136 games. By the time Rochester finished winning the Little World Series, the Orioles had scant use for Red Wings; I appeared in just 1 game for Baltimore. Grichie, who led the International League in hitting (.336), appeared in just 7 Orioles games. That winter I again played for Santurce and I won the Puerto Rican League batting championship, hitting .329.

I knew I was going to play somewhere in the majors in 1972. I had already been optioned three times; if a player was optioned four times the team lost rights to him.

The Orioles made room. While I was playing in Puerto Rico, Baltimore traded Frank to the Dodgers.

The Orioles had opened a roster spot for me and a position in right field for Rettenmund, but Earl sounded a cautious note by telling reporters: "If you're talking about talent we have no one player who's going to replace Frank by himself. The others have to be themselves. . . . This allows us to bring Baylor along. Our organization feels Baylor is another Frank Robinson, a guy who, in five years, will be what Frank was."

Another Frank Robinson. That was tough. I knew, in my heart, I was ready for the major leagues. I wasn't ready to be the next Frank Robinson. My emotions were certainly mixed. To this day I don't know why Earl let Frank get away. I would have gotten rid of someone else, even myself. In my mind the trade took the heart out of the team. Besides, I had wanted to play alongside Frank, not replace him.

I tried to put those thoughts out of my head right away. I don't believe Merv could, though. Earl kept telling Merv they traded a guy who drove in more than 100 runs a year and hit 30 home runs. "You can't do that hitting to the opposite field," Earl would say. Merv wasn't a power hitter. He hit for average. Suddenly that was not enough. All he heard was "pull, pull, pull." Merv became a part of Leaper's Row. He jumped at every single pitch. He ended up hitting .233.

It had not helped anyone's outlook that the start of the season was disrupted by the first-ever players strike. For thirteen days that spring, a new name became part of the sports lexicon. Marvin Miller, head of the emerging Major League Baseball Players Association, called a strike to protest the handling of the pension plan. All of baseball came to a halt as the strike wiped thirteen days and 86 games off the major-league calendar before a settlement was reached. I had to live with my in-laws, was worried that the lockout might be permanent or last so long I'd be hurt financially. But I felt the pension fight was a worthy cause. I wanted to know more about the association. Nine years later I would sit beside Marvin in strategy sessions during the fifty-day strike of 1981, as a player representative to the MLBPA.

Once play began in 1972 Earl had his work cut out. Not only was he trying to break in two new outfielders, but also Grichie at second, because Davey Johnson's role had been reduced.

Earl let me play sporadically at the start. I've always been the kind of hitter who gets warmed up after the weather gets hot. That year was no different. I could feel the hits starting to come as April passed. In late May

I faced Ken Brett in Milwaukee. I doubled in my second at-bat, then homered on my next two swings. That gave me 12 hits in just 29 at-bats. Our next game was in Boston and I could not wait for my first crack at the Green Monster in Fenway Park. The way I figured, Earl couldn't wait, either, especially after the way he raved following my game in Milwaukee. He told reporters, "He's as good a low-ball hitter as I've ever seen." And on the letter-high pitches, he said I either swung perfectly level or down on the ball, driving it instead of popping it up.

I should have read between the lines. Earl called me into his office in Boston and told me I was benched because, of all things, I didn't get height on the ball. "Those three balls you hit yesterday would be off the wall for singles here," he said. "You're not playing."

I was stunned. "But Earl," I sputtered. "I'm hot. I'm swinging the bat good."

He just looked at me and said, "You're not playing."

I went to the outfield and sulked. I didn't hit or pick up one ball during batting practice. Some of my teammates mocked me because they thought it was funny—a rookie standing in center, moving to one side or the other in order not to field balls. To me, it was deadly serious. Let the guys who were good enough to play for Earl chase the baseballs.

By the seventh inning we were down 3–1. When we got a runner on, Earl called on me to pinch-hit. I'm boiling, now, thinking, *I can't start against Sonny Siebert, but all of a sudden, I'm Earl's number-one pinch-hitter against him.* I hit Siebert's second pitch into the net over the Green Monster, my third straight home run, my fourth straight extra-base hit.

As I was running around the bases, I was thinking *Earl is gonna be there on the top step to shake my hand. So I'm gonna walk down the middle of the dugout and shake hands with the guys, but not Earl.* Blair had shown me that trick. He could pretend Earl did not exist better than anyone I ever knew. So I ignored Earl, never looked at him. But I could feel the heat from his gaze. That was okay. It was my way of letting him know I wanted to play. So what if he was a legend and I was just a kid . . . an obnoxious kid displaying a ten-year-old mentality?

Earl understood and had more patience with me than I had for him. Besides, there were not a lot of days like that. And I never tried to strangle him like Bobby did.

Earl let me stay in that game against the Red Sox. In my next at-bat Bobby Bolin struck me out to end my home-run streak. Two starts later, in my first at-bat against Marty Pattin, I hit a ball over the fence in center. Four home runs in nine at-bats. Earl let me play steadily after that. For about two whole weeks.

When I wasn't sharing left with Buford I spelled Blair in center and Rettenmund in right. Buford was the veteran most threatened by my presence. It was hard on Don, a proud guy who did not think of himself as a platoon player. Don would walk into the clubhouse and look at the lineup card every day. More and more, his name was not there. One day he snapped. He ripped the lineup off the wall, tore it in half, and threw it on the floor. He never showed any anger toward me. He did not have that kind of meanness in him. He looked out for younger players in a way that you don't see veterans do these days; he helped me immensely.

That season I learned the true meaning of "Gold Glove" and understood why the Orioles could win with pitching, defense, and 3-run home runs. I was surrounded by some of the purest fielders ever to play the game—Brooks, Belanger, and Blair. Those three turned me into somewhat of a spoiled stargazer when I played left. I got to the point where I didn't expect the ball to get by them. I got used to watching Blair take home runs away from hitters that were already over the fence. With Brooksie and Belanger it was just one great play after another. Belanger was like Brooks, not blessed with a great arm. He did not do the acrobatic things Ozzie Smith does. All Mark did was make the plays, the great and the good. He positioned himself as close to perfection as any shortstop I've ever seen.

Impressions were made by someone else too. Me. Chuck Tanner and Gene Mauch would tell me later that I reminded them of the most gifted athlete they'd ever managed—Dick Allen. That was flattering because the Allen I saw play during my rookie season was absolutely awesome. Dick was with the White Sox, playing his best ball ever under Tanner. Once, when the Orioles visited Comiskey Park on a cold, rainy day in April, I figured nobody could hit a ball into the stands under those conditions. Mike Cuellar threw a screwball down around Dick's ankles. It was like he had waited for that pitch all winter long. He jumped all over it and launched it over the roof in left. I looked up, waiting for the ball to bounce off the roof, hoping it would not kill me. But it never came down. It was gone, see you later, out of the ballpark.

Later when the White Sox came into Baltimore, they had a day off before the series began. Allen could not be found on the off-day or game-day. So Chuck put Tony Muser at first base and batted him third. In the top of the first inning, as Muser walked to the plate, Allen walked into the dugout. Chuck saw Dick, turned and whistled for Muser to come back. He pinch-hit for the guy in the first inning. That was how awesome Dick was that MVP year. He did not take batting practice until August and he was beyond compare, winding up with 37 home runs, 113 RBI in 148 games.

The '72 Orioles fell to 80–74 and finished third, a letdown considering the 1971 team had come within a game of winning its second straight world championship. I wound up playing 102 games. Major-league pitchers held me to a .253 average, 11 home runs, and 38 RBI. I did steal 24 bases and showed Earl that his left-fielder could occasionally dazzle with the glove, too.

At season's end I again joined the Santurce team. That winter reminded me once again that things other than baseball also shape a life.

In November 1972 my son, Donny, was born. I was in Santurce when my wife went into labor in Austin. I flew from San Juan to Miami to Atlanta to Dallas and then to Austin, calling the hospital at every stop. But I could not get there in time. He was in the nursery when I arrived. I was a typical first-time dad, thumping the glass, listening to the nurses tell me how much he looked like me. Until that moment I hadn't really been able to visualize a baby; Donny had just been a tiny little kick that would come every once in a while, usually when music was playing. But finally, there he was, tiny hands and feet and a face, a real little person. I felt pride and love of the sort I'd never really known before.

Five days after Donny was born, he arrived in Puerto Rico, his first road trip. Suddenly I was not just a married man, but a father trying to get enough sleep between late-night feedings and trying to understand just how an infant could sense when the sun came up. Donny always knew and as soon as he opened his eyes he would start to cry. I spent many a morning walking him along the beach in front of the condo where we lived, talking to him, trying to soothe him. Soon he would go back to sleep and then I would, too, on the training table at the ballpark.

I learned a lot about baseball in Puerto Rico and also learned about that island. It has a magnificent baseball tradition and the pride increased tenfold in 1971 when Roberto Clemente helped the Pirates to a spectacular World Series victory against the Orioles and was named the Series MVP. When Roberto played in Puerto Rico that winter I got a chance to witness up close what a great player he was.

In a game against Roberto's San Juan team, I tried to score from second base on a hit to right. I know I had the play beat. I ran the bases the right way, made the proper turn, cut the corner well. But by the time I started my fade-away slide catcher Manny Sanguillen had the ball. I couldn't believe it. I was out. There was no question. Never before had I been thrown out at home plate trying to score from second on a hit to right field. But Roberto made a throw that had me talking to myself. *If this guy plays this way in winter ball, what's he like all the time?* I had heard about the great arm. That play made me a believer.

Right around Christmas, 1972, Roberto began an emergency relief effort after a major earthquake nearly destroyed the city of Managua, Nicaragua. Roberto, who had gotten a lot out of his baseball career, never forgot what part of the world he came from. To him, helping Nicaraguans was like helping his brothers, part of his drive to give something back. When Roberto started the relief effort, the whole island mobilized around him.

The relief planes took off around the clock. The American players would stand on the beach and watch the busy airport in nearby Isla Verde. It seemed the plane engines never stopped droning. On New Year's Eve the airlift was still going on. Finally, when it got dark, the decision was made to stop. Later, I heard that Roberto had decided to personally deliver the last New Year's Eve shipment. Apparently it was getting so late they just threw the supplies on board without tying them down. The cargo must have shifted because the plane banked shortly after takeoff and could not right itself. It crashed into the ocean. The next morning it seemed the whole island was down on the beach, hoping the searchers would find Roberto and the crew alive. But reports said the plane had gone into the ocean nose-first and had exploded when it hit. Roberto was never found.

The whole island mourned. Ruben Gomez, one of my teammates, tried to explain the sorrow. "When you talk about Clemente you are talking about a god down here," Ruben said. "Orlando Cepeda, he lived here for years and years. So did Mike Cuellar. But Roberto was special. The whole island feels like it has lost their best friend, their hero."

Manny Sanguillen, Roberto's closest friend, was devastated. Manny kept walking the beach, looking for Roberto. When the other players from Santurce and San Juan tried to talk him into giving up, Manny would just look out at the ocean and tell us, "My best friend in life is out there. I know he is alive, I know he is alive."

Manny walked the beach for three days.

Three Kings Day, a regional religious holiday connected with Christmas, came and went that first week in January. Then we started to play again. So did Manny. Life had to go on.

Roberto's last hit had been his 3000th. He had gotten it on the last day of the 1972 season, off Jon Matlack, to become the first Hispanic player to reach that milestone. In my heart, I now believe that was Providence. God did not want Roberto to fall short. He knew what Roberto would sacrifice that New Year's Eve. He allowed Roberto to achieve that one last dream.

Shortly after the tragedy, major-league baseball renamed its humanitarian award after Clemente. It's given annually to the player who best exemplifies the game on and off the field. In February 1985, I was chosen as the fifteenth recipient, because of my work for the Cystic Fibrosis Foundation and the success of the "65 Roses" clubs.

The name "65 Roses" is derived from the way one child pronounced cystic fibrosis, a genetic disease that kills children and young adults. The idea was to bring athletes and community business leaders together to raise funds for research. Players begin a club by soliciting pledges from sixty-five members of the business community to contribute certain amounts to match specific achievements, such as home runs or strikeouts. I helped establish the first club in southern California when I was with the Angels in 1979, along with Dr. Gene Moses and Joe Beagen of the foundation and Red Patterson of the Angels.

I've always believed that, as players, our career contributions are measured through stats, but our contributions to mankind should last a lifetime. When I first started working with CF not too many people knew about the disease. I hope I have helped increase awareness of cystic fibrosis among athletes. I think I have. There are now "65 Roses" clubs in each major-league city. Many athletes in baseball as well as pro football, hockey, and basketball sponsor clubs. When I received the Roberto Clemente award, over $1.7 million had been raised by "65 Roses" clubs and other events, such as the celebrity golf tournament Grichie and I sponsor each year.

As national sports chairman for CF, I've devoted time, money, and work to this cause. When I think about what Roberto gave up, though, my efforts never seem enough. I think about Roberto every time I look at his award, which stands beside my MVP trophy and all the awards a player collects through the years. In my mind, Roberto's is the most important award I possess because it represents a man who made the ultimate sacrifice. He gave up his life.

Nineteen seventy-two had changed my life forever. I was no longer a kid, but a father with all the responsibilities that entails. For the first time I had tasted union life and labor strife. I had been involved, if only by association, with one of the biggest trades in Orioles history. And I was a major leaguer.

Earl Weaver had said way back in 1970 that Don Baylor could play for him. It had finally happened.

9

EARL

EARL Weaver had this thing about balls being hit over the heads of his outfielders, especially after the seventh inning or if we had a lead. It just drove him crazy. He'd warn outfielders, over and over, "If it goes over your head, make sure it's out of the ballpark. Just make sure."

One day in 1972, Royals shortstop Freddie Patek was batting against big Grant Jackson in Memorial Stadium. Freddie hit a ball off the top of the fence in left. It was my misfortune that it went over my head, but not out of the park. There was no way I could have gotten that ball. Still, it was the seventh inning and Patek's double drove in 2 runs.

I could feel Earl's anger half a field away. Whenever Earl stood in the dugout and glared at you, his hat pushed back on his head, his hands on his hips, you knew you were in trouble. And he had just assumed his classic "I can't wait for you to get in this dugout" stance.

Now, I wasn't one to defy a manager. But I can only run so far and jump so high. Earl expected me to be Superman on that play. As far as I was concerned, I was at the right depth for Patek. Was I going to play him on the track? The guy was the shortest player in the majors. So after the last out was recorded, I sprinted off the field and right over to where Earl was standing. "If you think I could have caught that ball then here is the glove; you go out there and play left field," I said as I towered over him, giving him my best glower.

He did not say one word.

I was learning.

Earl Weaver was an intimidating, gruff, sarcastic little guy. The Orioles' bantam rooster, he could shrink you with his stare, defy logic with his moves. Visiting players ranted and raved about him, umpires set records throwing him out of games. He fought and argued with the Orioles veterans who had egos as big as his and bullied the ones who were quiet and withdrawn. He could make you crazy with his quick temper, with his slow way of breaking a kid into the majors, and with managerial whims no one understood but him.

Earl was the best manager I ever had.

Gene Mauch knows the rule book better than the guy who wrote it. Billy Martin, in his early years, was as good a field manager as anyone this side of Weaver. Watching Billy and Earl was like watching two chess masters. Yogi Berra earned respect instantly from his players because his intentions were always good. You can't get angry at your grandfather. And that was Yogi. But Earl was the best. He made an art out of motivating twenty-five different guys, making you hate him but also making you play harder than you had ever played before. He didn't play favorites or hold grudges. He cared about his players off the field, but tossed aside emotions when it came to winning one game that day. That's all he cared about on the field. His attitude was that of a winner and it rubbed off on almost every player he managed.

When the Orioles were feared in the early 1970s as an American League East power and revered because of their deep organization, Earl deserved a lot of the credit. He was the heart of the whole thing. Earl made it clear not only to kids, but veterans and coaches alike that his way was the only way. Every minor-league manager made sure Orioles prospects knew how to hit the cutoff man, how to bunt, how to run the bases before they got to Earl or there would be hell to pay. So every manager, including Alto and Rip, had the same book as Earl. None of them had his lungs, though. And none of them could scream like he could. He gave young players a figure to fear, but also respect. Because of him you wanted to do things right, you cared how you carried yourself and represented the Orioles.

How to deal with Earl, that was the only question I needed to have answered as soon as I arrived in the majors.

Earl never thought two weeks ahead, even if we had a big series looming. He would think only of that one game, that one day. If his strategy meant benching a hot player, if his desire to win that one game meant upsetting someone, that was fine with him. Every player responded differently to those moves. Mostly, they made me furious. I stopped reacting like a ten-year-old, like I did that day in Fenway in 1972. I started using my bat to get even. "I'll show him" was the attitude that burned inside me every time Earl took me out of the lineup.

And he did bench me at the strangest times. On one road trip, in 1973, I made just 7 outs in 22 at-bats. Nine of the 15 hits were for extra bases. At the last stop, in Texas, I was 9–for–10 in the first 2 games, with 8 straight hits; only one was a single. One of the 2 home runs I hit that weekend, a 3-run shot, came against Sonny Siebert, the former Red Sox pitcher Earl didn't let me face the year before in Fenway. The next day I went 0–for–2 in the finale in Arlington, but all told, it was a major breakthrough for me. I'd never played well in Texas, probably because I tried to do too much in front of my family. I had finally gotten past that and thought maybe I had shown Earl I had matured. But when we returned home, darned if he didn't bench me. His only explanation: "I'm giving you a day off." I pleaded, argued, the whole bit. There was never any changing his mind.

He absolutely infuriated me. I couldn't play against Chicago's Stan Bahnsen, but I could play against Terry Forster the next day. Forster was the left-hander David Letterman made infamous by calling him a "fat tub of goo" on national television when Terry was finishing up his career a few years back. But the Forster I faced in 1973 was younger, definitely thinner, and threw about 94 miles per hour. That didn't matter. I hit a homer the first time up and went 2–for–4.

Again, I chose to ignore Earl in the dugout. I had let him know with my bat that I was a better player than he thought. Or I supposed he thought. I know now that I didn't make Earl mad. He loved it. Earl never minded rebelliousness if it worked. He got more mileage out of some guys, like Dave McNally, Jim Palmer, and Davey Johnson, when they were feuding with him than when everybody got along.

McNally, one of the Orioles' four 20-game winners in 1971, was more stubborn than Earl. And Mac thought nothing of going against Earl if he felt Earl was wrong. Once during a game in the old Met in Minnesota, Mac watched as Earl aired out Paul Blair. Blair had played shallow and a ball was hit over his head and bounced over the fence for a ground-rule double. Paul was the best centerfielder I've ever seen. If the ball was hit over his head it meant that it could not be caught, as far as I was concerned. But after that one play Earl just tore into him. Paul just sat there taking it like a whipped puppy. The next inning Steve Brye hit a ball up the middle for what should have been a routine single. But it wasn't routine because by then Blair was playing on the warning track. Brye stretched the hit into a double.

McNally, who was pitching, was steaming. At the end of that inning, McNally went right to Blair and told him, "The only thing Earl knows about baseball is that it is hard to play. You've won Gold Gloves. You're my centerfielder. You play anywhere you want." McNally was a man of few words, but he knew the game. And Blair knew Mac would back him up again and again if he had to.

Mac never gave in to Earl on any point. When Earl had to take Mac out of a game, Mac would get so mad he never, ever handed the ball to Earl. He'd give it to Elrod Hendricks, Clay Dalrymple, Andy Etchebarren, or whoever was catching. That enraged Earl. But he couldn't get too mad because he needed Mac. Earl's fear of losing Mac showed in 1973. Late in the season Mac was pitching a shutout, one of his last tune-ups before the playoffs. In the seventh, Mac had given up something like 4 hits and looked strong. Mac was winning comfortably, but when he put a runner on, out of the dugout popped Earl.

"That's it," Earl said and asked for the ball.

"If I can't pitch for you now, I ain't pitching for you in the playoffs," Mac said. Then he turned and walked off the field.

Earl couldn't believe it. He quickly gave the ball to the reliever and ran up to the clubhouse to beg Mac to pitch.

Earl came out to the dugout with tears in his eyes. McNally still was saying no. By the time the playoffs rolled around, though, Mac would have killed Earl if he wasn't given the ball.

Davey Johnson made Earl crazy, too. He was one of those thinkers. He kept charts on what hitters hit what pitchers, fed them into computers, the whole bit. He would put printouts together for Earl. I don't know if Earl ever paid one little stat any attention. That never stopped Davey from dropping printouts in Earl's lap, though.

Palmer might have been Earl's prime-time antagonist. Whenever Earl would try to tell guys how to hit, Palmer would butt in and tell Earl the only thing he knew about hitting was that it was hard to do. At other times Palmer would stand behind Earl in the dugout, especially if we had runners on, and have a running debate on strategy that was absolutely hysterical. Earl did not believe in moving runners; the only thing he believed in was the 3-run home run. So Palmer would stand there and shout in Earl's ear, "Bunt! Bunt!" I thought Earl would kill him a couple times. Probably would have if Jim didn't win about 20 games a year for him.

Sometimes it seemed Palmer was about as infuriating as Earl. Every time we opened a series, we'd have meetings on how our pitchers would pitch the other team so that the fielders would know how to shade hitters; Earl was a stickler for setting the defense. Every single time Earl would decide that we'd pitch a hitter a certain way, Palmer would say, "That's not the way I'm going to pitch him." Every single time. And Jimmy meant it.

You did not have to be a veteran to be a Weaver tormentor. In 1974, we got a crazy pitcher from the Reds named Ross Grimsley, known simply as "Scuzzy" because of his long, stringy hair and weird, some say sick, sense of humor. Grimsley always carried very strange paraphernalia to put on display in his locker including a two-foot-long dildo. He's lucky he did not work in the present-day world, with all the women reporters around, because Scuzzy did not have a PG-rated bone in his body. Grimsley taunted Earl openly. Earl never liked to be reminded that he was short, but Scuzzy always managed to arrange the hair dryers so that the only plug available for Earl was the one at the very top of the mirror. Somebody would always have to plug it in for Earl. After he did, Grimsley would come by and pull the plug out of the socket while Earl was still drying his hair. The only way Earl could put it back in himself was if he had his platform shoes on. Grimsley would also move Earl's wallet to the top row of the small lockers where we kept our jewelry and money during games.

Not all of Earl's feuds were so good-natured. He and Earl Williams never did hit it off. Williams had been called "Big Money" in Atlanta because he always got clutch hits, but when he came to Baltimore he struggled so badly he started out hitting about .150, or as players like to say, a buck-fifty. So Rettenmund and Palmer nicknamed him "Small Change." Rettenmund also called Williams "The Retriever" because Earl was not a good defensive catcher and he spent a lot of time chasing passed balls or wild pitches. Earl always looked for any little thing to get after Williams, trying to light a fire under him. Once, in Boston, Williams missed the team bus. When Williams arrived late Weaver went berserk. "You're suspended," he screamed. "Go sit in the stands. Don't even get dressed."

There we were, in Fenway Park, needing all of the right-handed hitting we could get and Weaver suspends a right-hander who was capable of knocking a hole in the Green Monster. But it did not matter. Weaver refused to let Williams back into the clubhouse in Boston.

Earl could singe a player with his language, probably could embarrass a sailor. Cursing is an art form I never wanted to master, but I did not take it personally.

Pat Kelly, an ordained minister, and Earl made a particularly unusual pair. Pat's concern for Earl's soul was great. Earl's concern for baseball was greater. One day, he asked if Pat could hurry the team's chapel service. Pat said, "Earl, you need to walk with the Lord."

Earl replied, "Pat, you need to walk with the bases loaded!"

Earl had more superstitions than any other manager I ever played for. He rivaled Mike Cuellar, who slept with the lights on because he didn't want ghosts to come into his room. Earl had to run off the field, he would never walk. George Bamberger was his good-luck charm and George had to sit in the exact same seat if the team was on a good streak. Poor Bambi could not move. We had a saying, "Get into your offensive seats," because Earl would want everybody in the same position he had held during big rallies.

When it came to umpires Earl was also a little weird. Umpires feared his reputation, but never backed off an argument. And the fights were classics. No matter how angry Earl got, though, he never put his team in jeopardy. He wanted to win too badly. He proved that one day in Baltimore. Nester Chylak, one of the veteran American League umpires, had thrown Earl out, but Earl refused to leave the dugout. So Nester walked over and told Earl he had thirty seconds to get out or the game would be forfeited. Earl said, "I'm not going anywhere." So Nester started counting, "Thirty . . . twenty-five . . . fifteen . . . ten, nine, eight . . ." Chylak got down to about three. Earl jumped up and said, "Okay, okay, I'm leaving." Earl's arguments had a lot of show business in them. Not like Billy Martin's. Billy's had a fury about them that really angered the umpires. When I was with the Yankees in 1983, the feuding between Billy and the umpires got so bad that I felt every close play went against us. Sometimes, a split-second before umpires would make the call, they would look into the Yankees' dugout. I swear they were looking at Billy.

Earl had a little piece of plywood, about four feet wide and five feet high, erected at the end of the Orioles' dugout closest to home plate. You really didn't even notice it unless you knew why it was put there. Earl used the wall to hide behind so that he could holler and not be seen by the home-plate umpire. The only problem was that the third-base umpire could see him; Earl was short, but not that short.

Earl also used the wall to hide the fact that he was a chain-smoker. Earl always smoked in the dugout and umpires did not believe managers should be seen puffing away. One day he was caught and thrown out of the game. The next day, when Earl took the lineup out, he had a candy cigarette dangling from his lips. He got heaved, again, probably the only manager in history ejected for eating candy.

The wall also protected Earl from the opposing players he liked to harass the most. His absolute favorite was Yankees outfielder Lou Piniella, who had played for Earl in the minors. Lou was a red-ass from day one, just like Earl.

Lou always got Weaver going by calling him "Mickey Rooney." Earl would give it right back, shouting the whole time Lou was hitting, "You're gonna pop up like you do all the time! You're gonna pop up!" Lou couldn't see him, but he knew the voice, so he'd start yelling back, right in the middle of his at-bat.

Earl's sense of humor was biting, sparkling, and always kept you guessing. But he had his serious side and that's when his concern and love for his players really came through.

When I started playing left regularly midway through 1973 I became more and more daring. I chased fly ball after fly ball into the corner. I crashed into the wall at Memorial Stadium a lot and wound up jamming my wrist every time I would try to blunt the collision. Finally I told Earl that my wrist was killing me because the outfield fence was not padded. Earl went right to Frank Cashen, the general manager. Next thing I knew the wall was padded. That was the good news. Earl was no where to be found that winter when Cashen started negotiations on my contract by informing my agent, Jerry Kapstein, that he could start the contract talks minus $3,500, the cost of padding in left and right field. Looking back I'm sure he was joking. At the time, though, I couldn't believe it. I wanted to tell Cashen I would pay for my half of the wall if Rettenmund paid for his. Cashen never docked our salaries.

Earl's concern showed in other ways.

When Dick Tidrow beaned me on the next-to-the-last day of the season in 1972, Earl went absolutely crazy. I had hit a 3-run homer against Tidrow in my first at-bat and he drilled me the next time up. Luckily my helmet had a flap or Tidrow would have killed me. I got up and stole second and then third; that was retaliation enough for me. Not for Earl. He was still going crazy by the time I reached third, hollering and screaming at Tidrow. "I hope you get hit by a truck this winter, I hope you get hit!" I thought Earl was going to have a heart attack.

Earl had hard-and-fast rules for us about protocol. He did not want his players hanging out in hotel bars. After a long, tough night game, it's always tempting to have a nightcap and then go up to bed, but we never went behind his back. Looking back, it made sense. His rule helped players avoid arguments or fights with the coaches. Maybe you're not playing or your friend's not playing. Earl felt the hotel and its bar were not the places to work out those problems.

Billy Martin probably agrees. In 1985 Billy had one angry player in Eddie Whitson, a wild-eyed Tennesseean who reminded me of some of those tough mountainmen I had seen in the Appalachian League. Eddie used to refer to the joints he used to hang out in at home as "buckets of blood" because of all the Saturday night fights. Eddie could get a little wild on just a couple drinks. One weekend in Baltimore Eddie had nothing but time to drink; Billy had removed Eddie from the Yankees rotation, said Eddie was hurt when he wasn't. "Go ask Dr. Martin," was all Eddie would say to reporters. Eddie ran into Billy in the hotel bar at the team hotel—the Cross Keys Inn. Before long they were rolling around the barroom floor and then the lobby, trying to kill each other. Eddie was no marshmallow salesman. He kicked Billy and broke his arm. That brawl was played out in front of half of New York's traveling press corps. It was not a proud moment to be a Yankee. If and when I become a manager, my policy will mirror Earl's in one way— the coaches and manager will have their own watering holes and the players will have the hotel bar. The coaching staff can have the rest of the city. It's easier to get four or five coaches safely into cabs and back to the hotel than twenty-four players.

At least it should be. Earl was kind of a problem on the road. Some of his more notorious headlines unfortunately had to do with drinking and driving. One such arrest came after a 1982 game in which I hit a 3-run home run off Palmer to lead the Angels to victory. Earl thought the umpire missed a strike-three call before the home-run pitch. He was fuming during the game, after the game, and apparently fuming when he got pulled over by the police. And not fit to drive, according to the authorities, who charged him with driving while intoxicated. I'm just glad he did not hurt himself or anyone else.

Underneath all of Earl's histrionics and great theater was a baseball mind almost beyond compare. There were times when I needed to call on his wisdom. Not just about balls and strikes, but when I questioned my judgment and tactics. And Earl was there for me at my toughest moment on the field.

It was 1974 and the Orioles were playing the Indians. I loved running the bases, prided myself on hard, clean slides when breaking up double plays. Remember, Frank Robinson was my hero and that's how he played. I was on first base when Brooks grounded to short. Frank Duffy had to go to his right to field the ball. For some reason he used an outfielder's glove with a T-web, I guess so he could see through it. Anyway, the ball got stuck for a split-second, long enough to give me an extra step. I got to second just when Duffy's throw reached second baseman Angel Hermoso.

Hermoso came across the bag and instead of taking the throw and just settling for one out, he still wanted to turn the double play. He gambled and straddled the bag, hoping not to get hit. But I could do all the things needed to take a fielder out at second, no matter how hard they tried to avoid me; that's where my football instincts took over. Some guys slide head-first, my natural slide was feet-first. I slid right into him. It wasn't a cheap hit, no spikes-high kind of thing. But I hit Angel hard. I heard bones shattering as his left leg broke in three places, including the femur.

Angel came down on top of me and, unbelievably, still tried to make the throw. Then he started screaming. I thought I was going to be sick as I watched him roll around on the ground. They strapped him onto a stretcher and carried him away. I didn't need a doctor to tell me he was hurt real bad.

I could not sleep that night. I got dressed at eight the next morning, my head pounding, my stomach still churning. I grabbed the papers to read just how severely Angel was hurt. The report said he would be out for the year; they did not know then that Angel would never play again. I read on and found out what hospital he was in. I jumped into a cab and went right over. Angel was lying in bed, his leg suspended by ropes and pulleys. The huge white cast made him look so small. Angel was talking with his wife when I walked in. "No hard feelings," Angel said quietly. That's all I can remember.

Earl called me into his office as soon as I arrived at Municipal Stadium. "I heard you went to see Angel," he said. "You know there's nothing else you could have done yesterday. It was a clean aggressive play. It's too bad what happened, but don't you let that stop the way you are playing. What happened is a part of the game that you can't do anything about."

I had not even realized it, but Earl told me that shortstops and second basemen had begun to cheat toward second base when I was on first, trying to assure a quick in-and-out before I got to second on double plays. That was an infielder's way of saying he feared the runner. Yankees shortstop Gene Michael told me once that he almost suffered heart failure because of one of my slides. I roll-blocked him during a play at second and then pinned his throwing arm between my arm and body and would not let go. "I thought you wanted to fight," said Gene, known as "Stick" because he is so tall and slender. "I was scared to death. All I was doing was trying to tag you and throw." I laughed. "I wasn't mad," I said. "All I wanted to do was keep you from throwing the ball."

Earl wanted the threat of my aggressiveness to be a part of my game. He felt as badly about Angel as I did. And to this day I wish I could take that one play back. But I know Earl was right. It was a good, clean slide.

I was long gone from Baltimore by the time Earl's era came to an end. He retired once, watched Alto win a world championship in 1983, then came back, for the money, I heard. It was sad for me to see Earl, in 1986, the beginning of the end of the Orioles' dynasty. To look into the dugout and see Earl just sitting there emotionless and listless was tragic. I had seen the fire in this man so many years before, watched him teach so many people how the game should be played. He has seeds all over baseball—players, coaches, other managers. But maybe after twenty-five years of just constant pounding to win, win, win, it just became too much. To see his team beaten, day after day, had to kill him. So maybe Earl just decided he was out of players, out of talent, out of the game, period. It was over.

I won't remember Earl that way, though. To me he'll always be that little guy standing in the dugout, cursing, shouting, and haranguing players and other managers, kicking dirt on umpires. In all, I played for Earl from 1972 through 1975, less than a quarter of my career. But Earl and the Orioles built the foundation for and made possible nearly two decades of major-league baseball. Earl let me know in my first full season what he expected of me. "You could be the Most Valuable Player by 1978," he told me in 1972. "It's up to you."

Earl was off by one season; I won the American League MVP in 1979. Four seasons after I had played my last game for Earl Weaver, he still showed me he could read my pulse better than any person in baseball.

10

A TASTE OF CHAMPAGNE

ON the first day of the 1973 season I went to the plate four times against the Milwaukee Brewers, doubled twice, tripled, and homered, a major-league record for the most extra-base hits in an opening-day game. I knew 1973 was going to be better than 1972.

I did not get another RBI for three weeks.

I thought maybe it was my mustache. I'd never worn one before, but I read where Charlie Finley paid his Athletics $300 each to grow mustaches, so it seemed like a neat idea at the time. After going 0–for–April and –May, though, I shaved the mustache off.

It wasn't the mustache.

By the All-Star break I was hitting just .217. "You're the strongest guy in baseball," Blair kidded me. "You have to be. You're holding up the entire league."

But I started to creep back. In the second half I hit .366, which enabled me to finish the season at .286. It was the year of my 15–for–22 road trip, when I buried pitchers from Minnesota to Texas. I got so hot Brooks started to kid me after almost every hit, saying, "You're really in the 'groove,' now, Groove."

They all knew it. Earl knew it. And most importantly, I knew it. I had shown myself I could come back. Sure, I had been down, but some guys stay down. I learned two things: not to get too excited about a good spring training, which I had, because you cannot bring the palm trees north with you; and secondly, don't retire or let anyone retire you if you go 0–for–April.

When the hits started coming I gained confidence daily. Guys around me were expressing confidence in me, too. I wasn't walking around beating my chest saying, "Listen to me, I'm gonna carry you guys to the promised land." But I was playing every day and finally I felt like I was helping fill the offensive void caused by the Frank Robinson trade.

Pitchers treated me differently. The previous season I saw nothing but fastballs and sliders, pitches most kids can't handle. In 1973, I handled the slider and fastball so much better pitchers started throwing more breaking balls. At first I would chase them or practically break my wrists trying to hold up. Fortunately, I made the adjustment. I started to think along with the pitchers. In the second half, I got going, and it really didn't matter what the pitchers threw. That's how comfortable I felt.

The power output was consistent through the early years; 11 home runs in 1972, 11 in '73, 10 in '74. But the RBI were increasing, from 38 to 51 to 59 by 1974. The strikeout/at-bat ratio actually decreased, from 50 in 320 at-bats in 1972 to 48 in 405 at-bats a year later and 56 in 489 at-bats in 1974. I was having fun at the plate, and on the bases. I stole 32 bases in 1973, tops on the team.

What made 1973 even more fun was the fact that the Orioles finally recovered from the loss of Frank. Al Bumbry and Richie Coggins, a couple of rookie left-handed hitters platooned with Blair, Rettenmund, and I and gave the Orioles a new look with their speed. Billy Martin, the manager of the Tigers, called them Heckel and Jeckel, after the television cartoon characters. Billy will never convince me that that wasn't a racial slur. But that's okay, because Bumbry and Coggins tore up the Tigers and everyone else in the league.

We had another new addition, a veteran from the National League, Tommy Davis, the ex-Dodger and two-time batting champion. Tommy had played a few games here and there for the Orioles in 1972, but in 1973 he found the perfect niche as the Orioles' first "designated hitter." The DH was introduced into the American League to get the bats out of pitchers' hands and get more offense into the game. Tommy was a pure hitter and perfect for the job. He hit .306 and drove in 89 runs.

Tommy invented the art of using the clubhouse between at-bats to relax. The other hitters got to go out on the field, but not DHs. Tommy knew he would go nuts just sitting on the bench. He would stay inside, play a little nerf basketball, usually against Palmer when Jimmy wasn't pitching. Or Tommy would settle in, eat a hot dog or two, then rush off to hit, sometimes coming to the plate with mustard on his mustache or uniform. Tommy also talked on the phone a lot. Instead of hanging up when he had to bat he would just leave the phone dangling, go out, get his single and RBI, then come back and finish his conversation.

I was impressed.

Earl didn't get mad, either. How could he? Tommy drove in more runs than any guy on the team.

Tommy loved to talk hitting. When you are a right-handed hitter you don't run to third base and then to second and then to first, he would tell me again and again. So right-handers should hit the same way, first to third. Tommy's motto was "The field is laidout from right to left, not left to right in RBI situations for right-handers. Advance the runner." If I was hitting with a man on third base, Tommy wanted me to try to hit the ball anywhere from the middle of the field to the right side. Pulling the ball into the defense on the left side was no good, he said, because no one could score.

Tommy practiced what he preached. He was the master of what he called "the ugly hit." Those hits looked as good as the pretty ones in the box score. And they got the runs in.

Tommy, Brooks, and Boog Powell took care of Grich, Bumbry, Coggins, and myself. We were all grown men, but it was still a good feeling to know that Boog or Tommy was over one shoulder and Brooksie was over the other, watching out for us.

We won our division by 8 games. Ahead was the American League Championship Series. There, waiting for the Orioles were the Oakland A's. The Orioles had never lost a playoff game in three series since the inception of division play in 1969. All that stood in the way of a fourth World Series berth in five years were the mustached, rebel forces of Charlie Finley. To get to the Series we had to win the best-of-five American League Championship Series.

Palmer, coming off a 22–9 season and on the verge of winning the Cy Young, started Game One. Elrod Hendricks, who usually warmed up Jimmy, always warned the outfielders if Jimmy said he had great stuff. "Play deep and cut across," Elrod would say. "He's got nothing, so just back up as far as you can." But if Jimmy moaned that he had nothing, Elrod would tell us, "Just throw your gloves down. You won't need them."

That day we could have given our gloves away. Jimmy, cranky and nervous, walked the first two batters he faced, then struck out the side. He went on to strike out 12 A's and pitch a 5–hit shutout to win, 6–0. I started in left field, was 2–for–3 with an RBI single. The Orioles routed Vida Blue, who did not survive the first inning.

We did little against Catfish Hunter the next game. McNally was hit hard, though, touched for 2 home runs by Sal Bando and 1 home run each by Campaneris and Joe Rudi. We lost, 6–3, the Orioles' first LCS loss in 11 games.

We flew off to Oakland and picked up a jinx along the way. Our traveling secretary, Phil Itzoe, placed an envelope with my meal money on my chest while I was asleep. When I moved, it fell on the floor unnoticed. When the airline crew cleaned the plane the envelope mysteriously disappeared. So did my stroke, my concentration, everything. Cuellar was brilliant in Game Three, allowing just 3 hits and 1 run in ten innings. Unfortunately, Ken Holtzman gave up just 1 run and 3 hits in eleven innings. It ended in crushing fashion when Campy stepped in against Cuellar in the bottom of the eleventh and hit Mike's second pitch over the left-field fence into the first row of seats. I would have had to be Superman to get it, but that did not stop Earl from jumping all over me. I felt bad enough that Cuellar had lost a heartbreaker. I didn't need Earl telling me an uncatchable ball should have been caught.

Vida Blue came within three innings of shutting us out in Game Four, but our offense finally, finally exploded. Earl Williams walked to start the seventh. I followed with a single. Brooks then singled in our first run and Andy Etchebarren followed with a 3-run home run. We went into the eighth tied at 4–all, but Grichie took care of that, homering against Rollie Fingers. The LCS was even at two games each. One more victory was all we needed. All we had to do was get by Catfish.

I remember walking through the lobby at our team hotel in Oakland at about eleven the night before the finale and spotting Catfish in the lobby bar, having one drink after another. I was on my way to bed and I wasn't even starting the next game. But here was the starting pitcher for the other side, getting ready—for a day game. I still could not figure out veterans.

The next day Catfish shut us out, 3–0. We couldn't touch him. I watched from the bench as he added another jewel to a Hall of Fame career, limiting the Orioles to 5 hits and 2 walks.

I had never allowed myself to even think about the World Series. All I was thinking was "Don't embarrass yourself against the A's." In four starts I was 3–for–11 with 1 RBI. I felt I had learned about pressure, thought how it would be even smoother, easier the next time around. When you're young you always think like that. But I learned a long time ago there simply is no easy path to the World Series.

In 1974 the road was tougher, not easier, and the only thoughts were of survival, not Series shares.

We floundered up until late August. In a last-ditch effort Brooks and Blair called a team meeting, after a night loss, at Blair's house. We were in the middle of a four-game losing streak that would leave us at 63–65 with 34 games to go, in third place, 8 games behind the first-place Red Sox.

Every veteran spoke at the meeting. Brooks told us we all knew what we had to do, that we all knew how to play the game.

Others chimed in. Have a man on first base and second base with nobody out? Get them over . . . bunt or do whatever you have to do. . . . You look down to third and Billy Hunter gives you the signal to hit away, just use your own discretion.

There it was, the insurrection of 1974. We respected Earl, but he was waiting for 3-run home runs that no longer came. Frank Robinson and Davey Johnson were gone. The power that won games in 1969, '70, and '71 had left us. This was a different club.

We needed to play what Gene Mauch calls "little ball." Bunt, hit-and-run, steal a base or two, things that were not part of Earl's game. We were going without the coaches' consent. So the veterans warned that everybody had to back everybody else. If a guy bunted on his own, everybody was told to be up on the top step cheering when he came back to the dugout. Earl could fight one guy, but not twenty-five.

I didn't feel it was my place to say anything more than "I'm with you guys. . . . Whatever it takes to win." Deep down inside, though, I was scared. There I was, my third year in the big leagues and about to enter into a rebellion against Weaver and take orders from Brooks, Blair, and Palmer. I respected Earl, but I respected my teammates, too, believed they knew how the game should be played. So I did what they wanted, after that first little twinge.

After a couple days Earl was over in his corner, grumbling, "What the hell is going on? That's not the sign I gave." But I don't think he ever asked anybody face-to-face why he was being ignored. I was sure he figured it out. During a game in early September I realized he had.

Facing the Red Sox at Memorial Stadium I stepped in with guys on first and second. I was feeling real good about my swing. When I looked at Billy Hunter in the third-base box for a sign, though, he flashed the bunt sign. I stole a quick look at Brooks in the on-deck circle. Brooks barely nodded. I knew what I had to do. So I swung away and hit the ball off the top of the wall for an RBI double. I didn't feel like a renegade standing out there at second. But I was worried about Earl.

When I got to the dugout, all Earl said was, "You had better be glad you got the hit." That's when I knew he knew. But I also knew that as long as we executed, it was okay. Brooks had been right. Earl wasn't going to jump twenty-five guys. Knowing Earl, he probably thought it was funny. He loved defiance. He probably was saying under his breath, "Those sons of bitches . . . I know what they're doing, but they're winning." And that's the only thing that ever really mattered to Earl, anyway.

We became as united as any team I've ever seen. Our motto became "Who's the hero today?" Everybody started thinking pennant, not individual stats. The competition was fun, with guys saying, "If you get four hits I'll get five."

In one rainy game in Baltimore in early September, Tommy McCraw hit a home run to put the Tribe ahead. It was extremely late because of rain delays; we knew that the league curfew would not permit an inning to start after one A.M. We tied the game exactly at one o'clock and then went ahead. The Indians did not score again and we won, to sweep a doubleheader.

From August 29 to September 7, the Orioles won 10 straight. The Red Sox were in the midst of losing 8 straight and fell out of first place. The Yankees were in the process of winning 11 of 12; we knew who our competition would be going into October. It was a two-team race from then on.

We ended the season in Detroit while the Yankees played in Milwaukee. We won Friday night and then again on Saturday to reduce our magic number to one. A Yankees loss or another Orioles victory Sunday and the division would be ours. We gathered in Earl's room to listen to the Yankees play the Brewers that night. We listened as Milwaukee's George Scott hit a nineteen-hopper up the middle. When "Stick" Michael collided with another infielder the ball trickled through for a game-winning single.

The Orioles, in a bloodless coup, had won 28 of the final 34 games, including the last 9 to finish 2 games ahead of the Yankees. Fifteen of the last 28 victories were won by 1 run. It was the greatest pennant-race stretch run in Orioles history.

The Athletics awaited us again. This time the playoffs would be even more painful than last, however. We were tapped out. It was like the last 34 games had been our playoffs and we had nothing left. The A's took the pennant in just 4 games. I made the final out, striking out against Rollie Fingers with the tying run on third and the go-ahead run on first. I was still a dozen years away from Anaheim and another playoff in which I would start an improbable comeback instead of ending a season. Knowing how it felt in

1974 made the '86 home run against the Angels all the sweeter. But that day in Baltimore was devastating. I watched as the A's mobbed each other on the mound. They were going back to the World Series. We were going home.

The A's may have been the bad boys of baseball, with their long hair, mustaches and beards, their wildly colored gold, green, and white uniforms. Everybody took shots at them because of their image. Everybody tried to beat them. But they had stopped the dominant team of the decade twice, made themselves the first great team ever produced by the AL West. They had won every division flag from 1971 to 1975 and four of the five pennants. When the A's defeated the Dodgers in the '74 World Series, it was their third straight world championship.

I felt more disappointment than I had at the end of the '73 season. It was no longer enough to be a division winner. I'd had more of a hand and had not really contributed, with 4 hits and no RBI in 4 games.

I still had a lot to learn.

But the hurt did not last long. When I finally looked back I realized how a very special team had done something no one thought imaginable. In my heart I knew the Orioles were just as much winners as any team in baseball.

11

GOOD-BYE, BIRDS

I STEPPED to the plate at Fenway Park with two men on in the seventh inning. The Orioles and Red Sox were tied at 6–6 and right-hander Reggie Cleveland was trying to get the Red Sox out of trouble and to the bottom of the inning.

Cleveland threw a pitch that I turned on well and slammed deep toward left field. It did not stop rising until it hit the light transformer high atop the Green Monster in left-center.

The next night at Tiger Stadium I stepped to the plate with two men on in the first inning against right-hander Tom Walker. He threw a perfect slider. Perfect for pulling. I hit the ball midway in the upper deck in left field. In the third inning right-hander Fernando Arroyo tried to come inside with another slider. I turned on it and drove it to within a couple seats of where the first home run had landed. An inning later, right-hander Bob Reynolds threw a fastball in my pull zone. Seconds later it landed a couple of seats away from the spot the other had hit in the third deck.

I had walked in the ninth inning of the game at Fenway. Walks do not count as official at-bats. So I became only the thirteenth player ever to hit home runs in four consecutive at-bats over the course of two games. I fell one home run short of tying the single-game record and also one short of the two-game record.

The home runs had come on the first two days of July 1975, giving me 13 with 87 games to play. I was on my way to a 25-home run season, my best ever. No one was more pleased than Earl. "That's the same guy who said he was only a ten- to fifteen-a-year homer man," he told reporters.

Earl was chiding me, but he was right. I'd always said that I would rather get 3 to 4 hits than go 1–for–4 and hit a home run. Earl insisted I could replace Frank as a power hitter, even said I was the only guy other than Frank strong enough to hit the ball out of Memorial Stadium. For years the Orioles had looked for more than 11, 12 home runs a season from me. Hitting instructor Jim Frey predicted that the home runs would come in my late twenties, as soon as I learned to look for certain pitches and get lift on the ball. Frank, Earl, and Jimmy hammered away at me—*pull, pull, pull.* The other field was for little slap hitters, Frank said, or guys who have to grow into their power. He said the power was already there for me if only I would use it. He said as a right-handed hitter I should use my natural pull field—left.

Finally, after many lectures and arguments, Frank and Earl wore me down. And, in 1975, I finally began to translate theory into fact. I began to follow through on my swing and the power started to flow as I hit 25 home runs, 21 doubles, 6 triples, and drove in 76 runs. All but the doubles set career highs. I did not throw out everything Tommy Davis had taught me. I still tried to hit to the middle-to-right field on pitches away. But the idea, as Frank said over and over, was to think, to hit the ball where it was pitched. "You can't defense that kind of hitter," Frank said. The more I listened, the more complete I felt as a hitter. And my 1975 average, .282, was the second-highest of my career. On one 8-game road trip, I had 19 hits in 33 at-bats, including 5 doubles and a triple. I drove in 7 runs and scored 11. Seven of the hits came in 2 games at Fenway; 8 hits came in 3 games at Tiger Stadium, two parks rapidly becoming sentimental favorites.

The 1975 season had some down moments, from injuries to attacks on my defense. I had tendinitis in my wrist, which cost me eleven days. My shoulder ached, a combination of constantly hitting that outfield wall and the old football injury. I knew the sharks were circling because of my arm. And, at times, it was rough. In one game against the Yankees I was playing left and lost a Terry Whitfield liner in the lights. Both Earl Weaver and Yankees Manager Bill Virdon told the press that every outfielder suffered that fate at one time or another. The next day, though, I picked up the

Baltimore Evening Sun and saw how columnist Bill Tanton used that play as an opportunity to criticize my throwing.

Tanton wrote: "Around the American League, Baylor's arm commands little or no respect. Baserunners don't even hesitate when Don is making the play. They just keep running."

The words hurt. But Earl was right there for me again. His response to Tanton's questions about whether I belonged in the outfield was: "Don Baylor is a future Most Valuable Player in the American League."

Despite the injuries and growing questions about my defense, 1975 proved to be the most satisfying season of my young career. We fell short by 2 games in the AL East, losing to Boston. Still, I felt good about our chances in 1976 and about my future. I had finally done what the Orioles wanted, was finally paying Earl back for the faith he had shown in me. I led the team in home runs, triples, slugging percentage, and stolen bases. It was the fourth straight season I topped the Orioles' list in steals. I was now Earl's full-time leftfielder and believed I would play for Baltimore for the next ten or fifteen years.

On April 2, 1976, about a week before the season was to begin, Earl pulled me out of an exhibition game. I had gotten 2 hits and did not understand what I had done wrong. When he told me to sit beside him I knew something *was* wrong.

"I hate to tell you this," Earl said quietly, "but we just traded you to Oakland for Reggie Jackson."

I looked at Earl, but he could not look at me. I was stunned. If he had stabbed me in the heart, it could not have hurt any more than the words he had just spoken. I started to cry, right there on the bench. I felt like my family had just thrown me out of the house. I could not comprehend, or accept it. I could not let go.

"Earl," I sobbed, "I don't want to go anywhere."

"I don't want you to go, either," said Earl, who, by then, was fighting back tears, too. "But we had to make the deal. We need a power hitter from the left side."

I was a wreck, crying like a baby and not able to stop. Earl took me into his office so that I could get myself together. I felt nothing but agony when the game ended, and I walked into the clubhouse and saw Bobby and Brooks. I started to cry again. Bobby was sobbing, too, and Brooks was close to tears.

"You finally do what they wanted you to do and they trade you," Brooks said angrily.

"I did, I did," I said, still not understanding what had happened or why.

I knew going into the spring of '76 I would have trouble settling on a new contract. I had made $42,500 in 1975 and expected a hundred percent raise. And there had been absolutely no progress in the negotiations over the winter. But I didn't see that as a major obstacle, even though I was still unsigned a week before opening day. There were a lot of others unsigned, including Bumbry, Coggins, Grichie, and pitcher Wayne Garland. So was Mike Torrez, a 20-game winner from the year before who held out and arrived in camp late.

Our new general manager, Hank Peters, assured everyone he could not trade Mike after Torrez signed. I felt everyone would eventually sign, too, including me. The organization had been fair to me. In 1971, then General Manager Harry Dalton gave Bobby and me each $2000 raises to bring us up to the major-league minimum even though there was no room for us on the big-league club. Harry was no longer in charge, though. On April 2, Peters broke his word to Torrez and broke my heart. He traded the two of us, plus right-hander Paul Mitchell for Reggie, left-hander Ken Holtzman, and right-handed prospect Bill Van Bommel.

The toughest thing I ever had to do in baseball was to take off that uniform and walk out of the Orioles' clubhouse forever.

Years later, when I was with the Angels, Elrod told me that things on the other side had not really changed. Earl still held his strategy meetings. And Palmer still refused to go along with anything Earl said. Elrod told me one other thing, that Earl paid me the highest compliment during one of those meetings. He was going over the Angels lineup and when he got to my name he told the pitchers and fielders that if I was hot to just make sure they did not get hurt. Then Earl went to the next guy. "He didn't say how to pitch you, didn't try to set the defense," Elrod said. "And, for once, Palmer didn't disagree."

Looking back, I know now I would not have had the same qualities as a player or person if it hadn't been for the Orioles. Alto and Frank, Brooks and Earl will always have a special place in my heart. What they taught will stay with me for the rest of my life.

The only lesson I wish I never had to learn was the last: baseball is, first and foremost, a business.

Finishing school was over. It was time to get on with my career.

PART

2

12

CHARLIE O.

THE way I figured it, I had nothing to lose, so I wrote a figure on a cocktail napkin and handed the paper to Charlie Finley.

Charlie looked at my note, folded it, and put it in his pocket.

If he was surprised by the message—"one million dollars"—it did not show. Charlie was getting used to the zeroes, the negotiations, the free-agent circus he had helped create in the city by the East Bay. And, in the fall of 1976, after a season of playing for his Oakland A's, I was still trying to get used to Charles O. Finley.

I was just a couple of weeks away from having my name placed in baseball's first-ever free-agent reentry draft. So many decisions would have to be made, so many suitors to consider. The first was Finley. He had just a couple of weeks left until the draft if he wished to re-sign me. I had to decide if I so wished.

To say Charlie was a character, an eccentric, a free spirit, is too easy. He's a complex man who had love-hate relationships with everyone in baseball.

He could be as generous and charming in courting players as he could be tyrannical and cheap once they signed.

I had learned quickly why his A's were renegades. They were locked in a constant battle with Charlie. If Finley had a dress code, the A's players went out of their way to smash it. T-shirts under sports jackets, no socks was typical attire on team charters. Because of Charlie. He fought the players over so many things they replied in kind, rebelling over every little thing.

Sal Bando always had stacks and stacks of fan mail piled in his locker, refusing to waste energy answering the letters. He knew Charlie would not pay the return postage. When the piles got unmanageable, into the trash they went.

Once I walked upstairs at the Coliseum looking for the team offices. I could not find them. I ran into my manager, Chuck Tanner. He was looking for the front office, too. I knew I was in trouble then, because if the manager didn't know where Charlie's forces were hiding no one knew. There wasn't much of a front office by then, anyway, just Charlie's cousin, Carl, and a switchboard operator.

Charlie did not discriminate. He drove managers crazy, too. Before a series in Arlington, Chuck received a call from Charlie. All Finley said was that Billy Williams was to play centerfield and lead off, but then immediately be replaced by Billy North. Charlie ordered the move three straight nights without explanation. I think that's when Chuck realized he was not too long for Oakland. He always had a look on his face that said, "This is not the kind of madness I agreed to when I came over." But he had to know. After all, Chuck was the only manager ever traded for a player, Pirates catcher Manny Sanguillen.

Perhaps the thing that amazed me the most was that despite all the turmoil, the 1976 A's were very good. We had a captain's captain at third in Bando. He ran the infield, which included Bert Campaneris at short and a kid they called "Scrap Iron" at second, Phil Garner. When I arrived the A's moved Joe Rudi from first to left and put me on first. The pitching staff included Mike Norris, Vida Blue, Stan Bahnsen, and Rollie Fingers. But at the center of it all stood Charlie.

As for myself, I had a very difficult time at first, felt like an orphan who knew he had a real family somewhere, but could not find his way home. It had not helped that Charlie cut my salary. I had gone into the spring hoping to gain a hundred percent raise over my 1975 salary of $42,500. After I was traded, Charlie exercised his right under the basic agreement between management and the union to renew my contract without my consent. He also exercised his right to cut my salary the maximum twenty percent. I went from thinking about living on $85,000 to making $34,000. It was nothing personal. Charlie also cut Sal Bando, Gene Tenace, Rollie Fingers, Joe Rudi, and Bert Campaneris—all potential free agents.

We watched as the supposedly conservative Red Sox gave raises to their potential free agents, Fred Lynn, Carlton Fisk, and Rick Burleson. During every negotiating session that winter I kept thinking about that lost year when I had to learn a new position and play under a contract I could do nothing about.

And it *had* been a lost season. Everything, including Oakland's temperature, threw me. The A's played in a ballpark that officially was called the Coliseum. The players from the era of Reggie, Rudi, and Bando called it the "Mausoleum" because it was so cold and drab. It always seemed to be sixty degrees and I always seemed to be shivering.

Fortunately, guys like Rudi, Bando, and Tenace made me feel less like an outcast. I was looking for friends. Looking for base hits, too, because the pressure was instantaneous. I had replaced another legend. First Frank, now Reggie. They'd gotten me to hit home runs, so that's what I was going to have to do. I also wanted to prove I was worth the kind of money I would soon be demanding.

Charlie knew what was coming, too. Even though he was sending me those reduced paychecks he kept telling manager Chuck Tanner that I was his first baseman of the future.

My first encounters with Charlie, however, did not go well.

By June I realized that he was trying to get out before free agency and declining attendance sapped all his money. On June 15, baseball's trading deadline, Finley ignored the fact that we were in a pennant race and tried to sell Fingers and Rudi to the Red Sox and Blue to the Yankees for a total of $3.5 million.

Fingers and Rudi were actually in Boston uniforms when the news came that Commissioner Bowie Kuhn had stopped the deals, ruling they were a detriment to the game.

I could not believe it. First Fingers and Rudi were on one side of the field at Fenway, then they were walking back into our clubhouse. The circus really was on. All Charlie had to do was bring out the elephants.

Fingers dropped every obscenity on Charlie you can imagine. Rollie saw the sale as nothing more than a get-what-you-can-before-they-bolt move. Two days after the trading deadline I realized how they felt. There had been a third sale planned, one Finley either never got to consummate or backed out of at the last moment. Finley had tried to sell me to Texas Rangers owner Brad Corbett for $1 million.

Shortly after, I discussed that situation with Finley. He had called the clubhouse from Chicago to speak to all the potential free agents. It was my first one-on-one with an owner to discuss such a serious matter. I was nervous, remembering what Charlie had done to poor Mike Andrews in the 1973 World Series, trying to remove him from the roster because he committed 2 errors.

Before I picked up the receiver Rudi called me aside. "Any time you hear him clearing his throat he's lying," Joe said. "If you hear him say 'a-hem,' watch out." I listened as Finley said how he understood my position, how we could still work it out. He also cleared his throat about ten or twelve times.

A little while later our conversation appeared almost word-for-word in *Sports Illustrated*. I had learned an important lesson. Private conversations mean nothing in baseball. In my heart I felt Charlie had leaked the details of our talk. I soon learned that Finley knew everything that happened in that clubhouse, which was curious, since he hardly ever left his offices in Chicago and never visited the team, even when we played at Comiskey Park. I felt as if I had bugs crawling over me. Electronic bugs.

After the fire sale, Fingers all but said there was no way he'd be back. I knew the other guys felt the same. There was no collusion, or acting in concert, but there was a general feeling that whether the A's won again, or offered "x" amount of dollars, the free agents were all gone.

That did not stop Charlie. My first serious negotiations with Finley came at the end of the season. Charlie wined and dined me and my first wife all over San Francisco. At a restaurant in Sausalito, Charlie, as bold and brash as ever, tried to impress us. When the owner came around, Charlie said, "Why don't you buy us a drink?" The owner was not impressed. "If you were Al Davis I would because he comes in here all the time," he said.

Charlie explained that he had tried to sell players to remain financially solvent. He said he wanted to keep the team in Oakland and he wanted to keep me. I could not believe him. He had shown me how much he wanted me as a part of his baseball "family" by cutting my salary. I could not do anything about the twenty-percent slash; Charlie had the hammer at the beginning of 1976. But I had it at the end.

Charlie was relentless. He followed us back to Austin in order to meet with my financial advisers. We met at the Headliner's Club, an exclusive, private meeting place for the state capital's power elite. The only other black faces in the restaurant belonged to the waiters and busboys. I knew some of them by sight. And they knew who I was, who Charlie was, and what was going on. After all, the headline that ran above the page-one masthead in the June 17 edition of the *Austin Herald Statesman* had read: FINLEY TURNS DOWN MILLION FOR BAYLOR. Never have water glasses been filled and refilled so quickly; it seemed like every employee tried to listen in.

It was that evening that I asked for a total of $1 million for five years, signing bonus included. Charlie later informed me that his offer was $900,000 and that he did not intend to pay any player a million dollars. It was over.

I had some bargaining chips even though 1976 was a dismal year personally. I stole a career-high 52 bases, including 25 in a row. Both Finley and Tanner said I was the best baserunner they had seen since Dick Allen. That was a big compliment because Dick used to steal bases looking back at the catcher without ever breaking stride, just like Willie Mays. I did not mind the comparison at all.

The stolen bases were important because I ended up hitting just .247, with 15 home runs and 68 RBI. I'd lost the power in my swing the second day of the season, when Dick Drago of the Angels hit me in the left hand with a pitch. I always figured that was retaliation for the opening-day home run I'd hit against Frank Tanana. Drago paid me back, all right. He broke a small bone in the back of my hand, causing me to lose the gripping power in my ring and little fingers. By the middle of May, when I had only 4 home runs, I was tired of being embarrassed and unable to drive the ball. I asked Tanner to place me on the disabled list so I could let the hand heal. Chuck, an easygoing guy, told me even if I didn't hit home runs I could help in other ways, like stealing bases. So I played through it.

When the A's finished second to the Royals, 2.5 games out of first, a very long season had ended. Nineteen seventy-six had started with tears in Florida, had wound up in fog 3000 miles away. Now, after playing through a disabling injury, playing with a salary cut, I knew what baseball's priorities were.

Teams talked about loyalty, but there was no longer any such thing as "family" to me. A year in the zoo by the East Bay reinforced that. I wanted my next contract to take me to the plateaus all players dreamed about in 1976—$100,000 a year, at least $1 million long-term. Charlie Finley was not going to get me there. My road out was through free agency. After all, baseball was a business, that's all. The final lesson learned in Baltimore had taken hold completely.

13

FREE AT LAST

IN my eyes, Jerry Kapstein has a knack of predicting the future. Years before any player ever took a crack at testing his worth on the open market, Jerry, my first and only agent, predicted free agency was the wave of the future. He figured that one day the players would shed the slavelike bonds of the owners.

Jerry was right. Curt Flood's attempt to overturn major league baseball's infamous reserve clause had been rejected by the Supreme Court in 1972. Curt paid the price for fighting for his freedom· by sacrificing his career. But the seeds had been planted.

After the 1975 season, arbitrator Peter Seitz declared pitchers Andy Messersmith and my old teammate, Dave McNally, "free agents." They had not played the 1975 season with signed contracts, but rather had been "renewed." Seitz determined that owners could not control any player indefinitely. If a player forced a team to automatically renew his contract, Seitz ruled that the club could exercise the renewal clause only once. Then, once the "option year" was over, the player was free.

The ruling by Seitz effectively killed the reserve clause, as it had previously been understood. The owners' lifetime stranglehold on players had ended. Clubs would have to "compete" for players' services.

McNally, stubborn to the end, proved his point and promptly retired. But Messersmith jolted the Dodgers and jumped to the Braves, signing a three-year, $1 million contract. Catfish had gone free by way of a technicality the winter before and signed with the Yankees for $3 million over five years. But this was different. Messersmith and McNally had found an avenue of escape for all players.

The owners fired Seitz, but they could not undo his ruling. The courts upheld the decision. When the owners and players failed to negotiate a new collective-bargaining agreement, the owners locked us out of spring training in 1976 until Kuhn, employed by the owners, announced the end of the lockout; part of the dispute had centered on free agency. In July 1976, the two sides reached a new collective-bargaining agreement that set ground rules on free agency. Players who had contracts renewed before August 9, 1976, were allowed to count 1976 as their option year and thus would be eligible for free agency that winter. Anyone who had signed after that date would have to play for six seasons before he became eligible.

If Finley had negotiated with me instead of renewing my contract, I would not have been free. But he was intent on cutting not only me, but Bando, Fingers, Rudi, Campaneris, and Tenace. He lost us, eight players in all. Baltimore was another big loser as Reggie Jackson, Grichie, and Wayne Garland, a 20-game winner, all went free. In all there were twenty-four free agents. Each one knew that what had happened to us would change baseball forever.

We had no idea if the owners were going to bid or if they would act in concert to make us remain with our former clubs. There was reason to fear. After all, they had reacted with hostility to Seitz's ruling. I started feeling like the explorers on the *Nina, Pinta,* and *Santa Maria*, sailing into unchartered waters, praying the earth was round. Little did we know that the owners would not act in concert until nearly a decade later, when they were found to have colluded to kill free agency in the winters of 1985 and 1986 by not bidding on players. That was certainly not the case in 1976. In that first free-agent season, the owners turned absolutely ravenous.

The courtships actually began before the last pitch of '76 was made. In my case it began at Yankee Stadium on Oakland's last trip in.

Elston Howard, once a great Yankees' catcher, was the first-base coach. I was playing first and Elston started to talk to me as I was throwing the ball around the infield between innings. He asked if I would be interested in playing for the Yankees. I started throwing the ball around a little softer, listening to every word he was saying. Before he stepped back into the coach's box he handed me a note. It said. "If you are interested in coming to the Yankees, tell Elston yes or no." There was no name attached.

The note did not say "George Steinbrenner," but in my mind, it did not have to. All I knew was that I was being looked at by the New York Yankees.

Elston talked to me off and on for three days. His sales pitch was good. He told me what a good place it was to play, how the man treated his players well and how they would all like me to be a part of what the Yankees were trying to build. I thought about playing alongside Thurman Munson, someone who always went out of his way to say something nice to me. Little things, like "I would love to play with you someday because you're my kind of player." The feeling was mutual.

I had always been a little in awe of the Yankees, overwhelmed by all that tradition. I had seen old Yankee Stadium, the original monuments. It was kind of scary. Times Square, Broadway, all that was a little too fast for me. I never stopped to think that players lived in New Jersey, not downtown. There was still a lot of that wide-eyed kid from Clarksville left in me.

All these things ran through my mind after Elston delivered his message. I knew the conversations were mostly chitchat. And I knew my job at that moment was to hit against Catfish and Ed Figueroa. But I couldn't help thinking to myself, *The man wants you here.* And I also could not help thinking about the heights to which Steinbrenner was taking free agents. It was all very flattering, all very mindboggling.

By the end of the '76 season the only decision I had made was that I would leave the A's. Then I placed my future completely in the hands of Jerry.

I had met Jerry in 1972 in the old Leamington Hotel in Minneapolis. Jerry had graduated from Harvard and Boston College Law School and had served as a member of the Navy's Judge Advocate Generals Corps. Jerry, who worked in Providence, Rhode Island, had decided to become a player-agent. So he was looking for clients. Neither Bobby Grich nor I had an agent, so we agreed to listen. When we sat down to have lunch we came face-to-face with a Steve Garvey clone who was wearing a corduroy jacket in the middle of summer. I had a feeling a guy who dressed that conservatively and was a former military judge must have his head together financially and every other way.

After Bobby and I huddled for a while, we decided to go with Jerry. I shook hands with Jerry, the only "contract" I ever had with him until California law required that agent-client agreements be put in writing. Little did I know that it would prove the best deal I've ever made in baseball. Four years later Jerry still wore that same corduroy jacket, so I knew he wasn't misspending my money.

Aside from Grichie and myself, Jerry's first clients were Darrell Evans, Garvey, and Dusty Baker. By the time 1976 rolled around, Jerry also represented Tenace, Rudi, Fingers, Campaneris, Goose Gossage, Fred Lynn, Rick Burleson, and Carlton Fisk, among others. Ten of the two dozen players eligible for the first-ever free-agent reentry draft were represented by Jerry. Providence, Rhode Island, became the baseball capital of the world.

The reentry draft took place on November 5, in New York City. Each player could be drafted by a maximum of twelve teams. A player's original club did not have to draft the individual, but had to inform the player whether or not it intended to retain negotiating rights.

Only Tenace was drafted more quickly by the maximum number of clubs than I. I was one of only five players, including Grichie, Rudi, and Reggie Jackson, who were taken by the full quota. The dozen teams that officially opted to bid for my services were, in order, the Rangers, White Sox, Angels, Indians, Yankees, Brewers, Cubs, Orioles, Phillies, Royals, Mets, and Twins.

Finley, who told reporters that the draft was "a den of thieves trying to cut one another's throats," opted to retain bargaining rights for me. That made it a baker's dozen.

The bidding was on.

Some teams only drafted players for the publicity, with no intention of seriously negotiating. And there were teams I knew I had no intention of signing with. Cleveland offered a strange, but interesting contract: $200,000 a year for ten years, plus a $100,000 signing bonus. The only drawback: spending ten years in Cleveland. I had known a lot of players who demanded trades and not one ever asked to go to Cleveland. Drab, rainy Aprils and Septembers in Municipal Stadium—"the mistake by the lake"— did not appeal to me, either. If I wanted to be punished I could go to San Quentin, Attica, or that rock out in the middle of San Francisco Bay.

The National League teams were a curiosity, but not interesting enough to command serious consideration. They felt that they had the best players and their running game was appealing, but the American League was where I wanted to be. So the Cubs, Phillies, and Mets were out.

Tugging at my heart again were the Orioles. They were going to lose Reggie to free agency. Were they willing to go back to 1975, as if the trade had never happened? Orioles superscout Jim Russo called me during the 1976 season and read a hypothetical lineup that included Grichie, Ken Singleton, Bumbry, Powell, Brooks, Belanger, and myself. Just like old times. But Jerry never received a serious overture from Baltimore. And I never interceded because I had put my trust in Jerry.

George Steinbrenner, Gene Autry, and Brad Corbett were the big-money guys and the owners of teams I was certainly considering.

Texas, the team that drafted me first, offered very good money: $200,000 a year for five years, plus a $100,000 signing bonus and a five-year, $100,000-a-year broadcasting contract to kick in when I stopped playing. The Yankees were talking about a five-year, $1.5-million deal with a $400,000 signing bonus. The Angels were offering $1.6 million for six years with a $580,000 signing bonus. The offered signing bonus by California was just $20,000 less than the total of a three-year contract Finley had offered a month earlier.

For a guy who'd made $34,000 the season before, it was heady stuff.

The Rangers' offer showed me Brad Corbett was serious about bringing home a Texas native. But being that close to home was a concern. I had all that family there and it had never been a pleasant place to visit. There were too many relatives and not enough time to spend with them all, so someone's feelings were always hurt. I appreciated Corbett's interest, but living and playing in Texas just did not appeal to me.

I didn't have to be a genius to see George Steinbrenner was prepared to outbid everyone. But I knew in my heart that I was not ready for New York. I did not know the A train from the B train. The city was tough. So was the media, or so everyone told me; only later would I learn that the label New York writers have is unfair.

Still, I was only twenty-seven and I knew I had not gotten where I wanted as far as confidence goes. I was not looking for an easy ride, but I was not ready to stare at all those monuments and all that history every minute. Some day, maybe, but not right then.

I really did not know much about the Angels other than they were a team struggling in the shadow of the Dodgers. But for years I'd been in love with Southern California. Bobby Grich had filled my head with tales of "the land of milk and honey" and from what I saw in my first trips West, I understood his love for that part of the country. The weather, the mountains by the sea, the endless sunshine, all those things appealed to me. Also, there was an old friend there doing the courting. Harry Dalton, the man who signed me to my first Orioles contract, one of my baseball "stepfathers," was the Angels' general manager. I trusted Harry and I had never forgotten that he paid me a big-league salary in my last year in the minors.

I wrestled over the choices. On November 15, I left Austin to join Jerry in negotiations in Providence. When I stepped on the plane I figured that the Yankees would be the team most likely to erase my doubts and change my mind. Steinbrenner was a marvelous salesman and was not yet the overzealous guy who could scare away free agents. When the plane touched down in Dallas for a brief stopover, I phoned Jerry. He said the Rangers were prepared to up their offer. I was even more confused. Yet, by the time I arrived in Providence, I knew in my heart there really was only one choice.

I wanted to play for the Angels.

Mr. Autry was the one owner who had given me the best indication that the family feeling I thought I'd lost forever could be regained. And Bobby's land of milk and honey—that's where I wanted to spend the rest of my life, where I wanted to raise my son.

When the decision was finally made, Jerry started hammering away at the details with Harry, Angels scouting director Walter Shannon—another refugee from the Orioles—and attorney Maurice Angly, my financial adviser from Austin. Jerry wanted to assure that I had veto power over trades in the first three years of the contract. In the fourth and fifth seasons I would have the right to list the only four teams to which I would not agree to accept a trade. After the fifth season I would regain complete veto rights under baseball's basic agreement because I would be a ten-year major-league veteran who'd been with the same team at least five years.

We went at it until three A.M. on the morning of November 16, dotting *i*'s and crossing *t*'s. Then Jerry said, "It's done." I shook hands with Harry. Then, nine years after Harry had handed a seventeen-year-old kid from Clarksville a $7,500 signing bonus, he handed me a check for $580,000. There I stood, at three A.M. in the middle of Providence, holding over a half-million dollars, more money than my parents or their parents ever dreamed of making in their lives. To me, it was all the money in the world.

I thought I was going to pass out. I went right to the front desk and got them to open the safe so I could lock up the check. I could not sleep at all, though, wondering what the Brinks robbers were up to that morning.

A few hours later I walked into the Bank of Boston branch in Providence. Jerry had prepared them for my request in the tiny little bank: $500,000 worth of Treasury bills. When I made the request I saw about twenty heads turn. Little did those bankers know that a day later Joe Rudi would walk in with a million dollars; he had also signed with the Angels. A day after Rudi, the same bank was visited by Grichie, who came in with $600,000; he, too, had signed with California.

Jerry had done well in negotiations. But we were all still learning. A financial adviser would have never suggested I sign that late in the tax year. It was a blow on April 15. Still, I'd seen more money than I'd ever seen in my life. It was always a wonder that someone paid me to play baseball to begin with. Now a generous old cowboy had made me rich beyond my wildest dreams.

On my way home to Texas I wanted to celebrate, shop big-time for

Christmas all over New York, especially in Bloomingdale's. But there was not a room at a civilized hotel to be found. The Orioles' hotel, the A's hotel, every first-rate establishment, was booked. There I was, with financial papers for legal tender worth a half-million dollars, plus a cashier's check, but it did not matter one little bit. I ended up staying at a fleabag hotel, with the ceiling all cracked and the wall paper peeling. Maybe it was New York's revenge. Or George Steinbrenner's. Either way, I came back to earth real fast. It was no more Mr. Bigshot. It was time to earn that money.

14

SECOND-CLASS ANGELS

"I'VE hocked the horse. I've got a saddle left and that's about it."

Gene Autry, Hollywood's legendary Singing Cowboy, spoke in quips to the media on November 18, 1976. One day after Mr. Autry signed me to a $1.6-million contract he had dipped back into the saddle bags for $2.09 million to sign Joe Rudi to a five-year deal.

The amount Mr. Autry agreed to pay Joe was only $10,000 less than he spent to purchase the expansion franchise in 1961. "I still don't believe all this is good for baseball," The Cowboy told reporters. "I'm not happy about it."

He could not have been too upset because on November 19, Mr. Autry signed Grichie to a $1.55-million, five-year contract.

Most teams were limited to signing two free agents. The Angels were allowed to sign three because they had lost three players in the reentry draft: Paul Dade, Tim Nordbrook, and Billy Smith. And Mr. Autry had gone the limit in style.

The Angels, in the biggest week for one team in the still-young era of free agency, had spent $5.2 million in a three-day period, spent enough, everyone figured, to buy a pennant ten times over.

No one was happier than Grichie. He had been driving home from Baltimore to Long Beach when he heard that the Angels had signed me. His first thoughts were of happiness for me even though he still did not know where he might wind up. Then he heard about Rudi. Knowing the Angels had only one more slot available, Grichie immediately called Jerry. As a Long Beach native, Bobby was a lifelong fan of the Angels, who played in nearby Anaheim. Jim Fregosi, the greatest player in the young team's history, was Grichie's hero. So Bobby made up his mind right there on the highway he wanted to be a California Angel.

Jerry tried to find Harry Dalton, but he was already en route to Anaheim to set up a press conference for Rudi and myself. Jerry did catch Walter Shannon before he left Providence. Dalton got word from Shannon the moment he landed in California, turned right around and flew back to Rhode Island. Grichie's deal was struck.

And we had all been afraid teams would not want free agents.

Mr. Autry's motives were clear. The Angels had never won anything but the general disrespect of the more-established teams. So The Cowboy sought to purchase respectability. And the expectations of the fans did go sky-high within a seventy-two-hour period. Finally, Orange County residents figured, they no longer had to live in the shadow of the Dodgers.

The Angels, playing the moment for everything it was worth, flew Rudi, Grichie, and myself into Anaheim for a joint press conference. It was grand, but very strange and unsettling, too. We stood in Mr. Autry's box high above the Big A field. Only there was no field. Instead there were mounds and mounds of dirt, some as high as three-story buildings. The city of Anaheim, owner of the Big A, was running one of its off-season, rent-a-field extravaganzas. That week's guest was a traveling motor-cross show.

I couldn't believe it. Why would they let anyone do that to such a marvelous field? Somehow I could not envision the O'Malleys allowing any pile of dirt larger than a pitching mound to soil the beauty of Dodger Stadium. All I could think that entire day was that Mr. Autry would have to spend another $5 million to get the field ready so his new millionaires would have a place to play.

After dealing with Charlie Finley, Mr. Autry seemed like a gentle Santa Claus in a cowboy hat. He was a legend in the entertainment industry, a rebel years before in Hollywood's own version of the free-agent wars, when he bucked the studio system and prevailed. He went on to make his fortune buying and selling radio and television stations.

From the beginning I felt from him a genuine affection. He loved his baseball players. He had suffered a great deal since the early days of the Angels, watched as his team was treated as a doormat. That hurt him because he cared so much. So, in the winter of '76, he gambled, hoping that by signing big-money players used to winning, he could change that bad luck. And among Rudi, Grich, and myself, there were nine division titles. Rudi had played on Oakland's three world championship teams. So it was no wonder that the press conference was more like a festival for Mr. Autry than a routine question-and-answer session.

There were more television cameras and reporters than I remembered around the Orioles during the '74 playoffs. We were presented as the three saviors who were going to lead the way to the promised land.

I started feeling less like a free-agent superstar and more like a guy who had a helluva lot to prove. And it was only December. I'm sure the other guys felt the same way. In our hearts, we were thinking we were about to be paid like superstars, so we had to perform like superstars and earn every cent of that $5.2 million. I wish someone had slapped some sense into us right then and there, told us there was no such thing as a million-dollar hit, let alone 200 to 250 such hits in one season. It would have made life a lot easier.

As soon as we arrived we felt the burden of not being the Dodgers. Why the Angels wanted to be Dodger clones was beyond me, but the emulation never ended. The mentality was to do it the Dodger way. I never realized before just how much influence the Dodgers had in Anaheim. Red Patterson, the Angels' vice-president, grew up in the Dodgers' organization. Buzzie Bavasi, who would soon displace Harry Dalton as general manager, did, too. With all that Dodger Blue bleeding around me, I instantly began to hate the mere mention of that team.

The Dodgers were all Hollywood. The Angels? We were little Hollywood. Mr. Autry was our big movie-star connection, but he was about the only star who cared about us. The rest of the celebrities, like Frank Sinatra and Cary Grant, went to Dodger Stadium.

The Angels had such an inferiority complex they actually attached importance to spring-training games—their big Freeway Series linking Anaheim and Los Angeles at the end of each exhibition season. I'd never seen anything like that buildup and never thought I would again. Unfortunately, I did a few years later when I saw George Steinbrenner dictating lineups for Mets–Yankees or Yankees–Red Sox spring-training games.

To the Angels the Freeway Series was deadly serious, as if to admit it was as close to a World Series as they would get.

Each preseason, the two teams played three games, with home-field advantage alternating. That was okay, I guess. At least it got us home a good deal ahead of the regular season.

One thing that never alternated, though, was the Freeway Series banquet. It was always in LA. The Angels had to travel thirty miles by bus for the privilege of sitting on the same dais as the Dodgers. My feeling was that it was an awfully long way to go to be compared to the great Dodgers. Standing off-stage waiting to be introduced was an education in itself. My first year I listened in disbelief as Dodgers manager Tommy Lasorda told our second baseman, Jerry Remy, he could not play on his team. Then he told Nolan Ryan that if he were in the National League he would have to beware because even the best pitchers gave up at least 3 runs a game to his team. Then he told Nolan he probably could not pitch for the Dodgers. Tommy seemed to be joking, but I didn't think it was funny. Neither did Nolan. He takes pitching very seriously. And, in my mind, Nolan could pitch for anyone he damned well pleased.

We were seated on the dais, alternating, Dodger, Angel, Dodger, Angel. Directly in front of the table at which I sat was Dodgers right-fielder Reggie Smith. He sat through the whole dinner reading a book, not speaking to the Angels around him. His whole attitude was "don't bother me or else." That sealed my opinion of Dodger arrogance, from Smith to Ron Cey to Davey Lopes. I came from a league where players treated each other as equals. Throughout the entire evening only one Dodger acted like a gentleman—Steve Garvey, naturally, the guy disliked by most of his teammates. That night I lost my appetite for dining with Dodgers. I went back in 1978, was on my way in 1979 when I reached a fork in the road. One freeway would take me to Newport Beach where I lived and the other to Los Angeles. I said to myself, *No more* and turned onto the ramp marked Newport Beach.

Buzzie wanted to fine me $500. The next day I told Buzzie he could go right ahead, but I also told him that I wouldn't ever change my mind because I didn't feel it was right to get hammered on all the time by comedians and emcees. The Angels were always the butt of jokes, not the Dodgers. My days as a straight man and subject of ridicule were over. Surprisingly, Buzzie said he did not blame me. Even his Dodger-blue blood boiled. He never asked for the fine money. Eventually Buzzie saw to it that the Dodgers came to Anaheim every other year for the banquet.

But the coming of age for the Angels was still far off in 1977. In my first season in Southern California, the Angels were second-class citizens. Sadly, a lot of that was brought on by some of the Angels themselves. I soon found out that, for the first time, I was on a team that did not have a major-league attitude.

There was a laid-back Southern California atmosphere that was amazing. Win or lose, it did not seem to matter to some of those guys. I had seen that attitude from the other side for years. When I was with the Orioles, an Angels' pitcher named Tom Murphy was legendary. He was called "Murph the Surf" because he'd always come to the park wearing swimming trunks, a T-shirt, and sandals. When I saw Murph from a distance I couldn't believe he was a ballplayer. It was as if he was telling everyone that he'd just come to work for a little while and that he'd put his sandals and swim trunks back on as soon as he could and go back to the beach.

"Murph the Surf" was long gone by the time I signed with the Angels, but that laid-back feeling still existed. And I did not like it at all.

That loose atmosphere could have been fixed if the Angels had a strong manager. We did not. We had Norm Sherry.

The first time I saw Norm Sherry's brand of discipline I was shocked. I was still with the Athletics in 1976 and Oakland had Sherry's pitcher, Frank Tanana, in trouble. I was on second, another runner was on third. With first base open, Sherry had held up four fingers, indicating he wanted the next hitter, Nate Colbert, intentionally walked. Tanana looked at Sherry and shook his head, "No." It went back and forth that way for a half a minute until Sherry popped out of the dugout and stalked to the mound.

Tanana wasn't scared. He was stubborn and he had no intention of walking Colbert. Standing out at second, I could hear him saying how he wasn't going to walk "an old man." He didn't care if Colbert heard, which showed he had no respect for a veteran. It also showed Tanana had no respect for the manager and, therefore, Sherry had no control over his players. It almost seemed as if he was begging Tanana to follow orders. Eventually, Tanana gave in.

Sherry and the Angels had not changed by 1977. There was a general feeling that everything was out of control, even in spring training. We had five open fields at the Angels' complex in Holtsville, Arizona, and, from day one, Norm could not get a handle on it all. Sherry was just not stern enough or tough enough as a manager, a first for me. Another first occurred halfway through the season. I watched as a manager was fired.

That move did not make things go any smoother for the Angels. Sherry was replaced by Dave Garcia, a guy who had been around for a long time as a coach, but whom time seemed to have passed by. The players did not respect Garcia any more than they had Sherry, so discipline remained nonexistent.

I'd never been on a club where the managers were so lightly regarded. It was disconcerting and weird.

That '77 Angels team did have consummate professionals, veterans who knew how to play, like Bobby Bonds, Tanana, Dave LaRoche, Ken Brett. And they had Nolan, the most professional of all. There were long-time Angels regulars who were gamers. Davey Chalk, a little guy from Texas, had a lot of heart. But when I arrived Davey was the Angels' number-three hitter and that was indicative of the team's condition. Chalky, try as he might, was no Don Mattingly. Our captain was a guy named Jerry Remy, a tough little second baseman. But Remy could not command the attention of an entire clubhouse, like a Frank Robinson.

So the anarchy continued. Nobody epitomized the lack of discipline more than Freddy Kuhaulua. Freddy and Ken Brett were once sent ahead of the team, from Boston to New York, because they were supposed to pitch in a doubleheader at Yankee Stadium in September 1977. The idea was to get them some rest, which seemed like a good call because the remainder of the team got fogged in and could not fly to New York until game day. By the time we landed, there was only enough time to take the bus right to the stadium and walk in with the fans. I was thinking what a good move it was to have got the pitchers to New York. I was wrong.

Kuhaulua and Brett had gone out on the town, with Freddy leading the way and Brett trying to keep Freddy on a leash to make sure they got back to the hotel at a decent hour. He failed. Freddy met these two girls, wound up losing his wallet and all his money. They spent the night trying to get the money back. We were relying on these guys. And we got swept, wiped out. Thurman Munson hit one pitch into the upper deck in left. Reggie Jackson hit another into the upper deck in right. It was a nightmare.

Rudi, Grich, and I had never been associated with a losing team and did not accept it. We could not drop a game and then go to the beach to watch the sun set. I figured that was why Mr. Autry had brought us in. What Mr. Autry's money could not buy, however, was assurance the three of us would always be around.

By June 1977, both Bobby and Joe were gone.

15

THE LONGEST SEASON

ON June 26, 1977, I led off a game against the Rangers' Nelson Briles and hit a ball into the left-field bleachers at Anaheim Stadium. Two batters later, Briles came up and in with a pitch on Joe Rudi. Joe threw his arm up to protect his face and the ball broke his left hand. Joe, who had driven in 53 runs in 64 games, was gone for the season.

That happened seventeen days after Bobby Grich had undergone back surgery to repair an injury he suffered while lifting an air conditioner right before spring training. He had only lasted 52 games.

I wanted to be a California Angel, but I wanted nothing to do with that organization's history. I knew that it was viewed as a jinxed team. Horrible things always seemed to happen. In earlier days, Angels players died or were severely injured in car crashes. Shortstop Mike Miley, an All-American the Angels had lured from Louisiana State, where he was touted as the top quarterback in the country, was killed in an accident. Pitcher Minnie Rojas was paralyzed from the neck down as the result of another auto accident.

And pitcher Dick Wantz pitched just one inning before he died of a brain tumor in 1965.

Rudi was beginning to think he was jinxed, too, he had suffered so many injuries. He moped around with his hand in a cast. Mr. Autry looked upon Joe as an adopted son. He knew Joe was special to the players, too. So Mr. Autry called a clubhouse meeting. He had the Angels' equipment manager, Mickey Shishido, arrange all the chairs in rows like church pews. It seemed like a very solemn occasion—until The Cowboy spoke. He told us he was aware that we had just lost our best player and that the team had started to slip a little. But, Mr. Autry said, life is full of disappointments, bad timing, and rotten luck. Then he turned to Rudi and told him, "You did not deserve that, just like the one time I had gonorrhea . . . I did not deserve that, either."

We all cracked up. The Cowboy was trying to tell us there was still reason to laugh. That might have been the last laugh the 1977 Angels enjoyed.

When Joe went down the Angels were 2 games out of first place. After he got hurt we staggered, losing 8 of ten games to fall 11 behind the first-place White Sox. Sherry was fired July 10. By July 21 we were a pitiful 42–46. The Angels fans turned on the only millionaire still in uniform.

Me.

I had not helped my own cause by going through my annual 0–for–April ritual. May was not much better, with a .149 average, 1 home run, and 6 RBI in thirty-one days. Just when I had started to find my pulse, Rudi and Grich went down. In the horrible months that followed I kept thinking back on my first meeting with Angels writers during spring training and how I'd told them that the normal pressures of big money would not occur because there were three free agents, not just one. "Pressure is what you create in your mind," I had said. "Pressure is the guy on the unemployment line with two kids and mortgage payments."

But there *was* pressure, the ridiculous kind I put on myself. By July, I wasn't trying to earn my $1.6 million on every swing. I was trying to earn the entire $5.2 million Mr. Autry was paying Rudi, Grich, and me. With each failure, the fans at Anaheim Stadium let me have it.

It got so bad that first-base coach Del Crandall started booing me while we were still in the clubhouse. He just wanted to prepare me for my daily trouncing. I did not find it funny, his boos or those of the 20,000 to 30,000 angry Angels fans who came out to the Big A every night, apparently just to make my life pure hell.

Jimmy Reese, Babe Ruth's former roommate and one of the kindest men I'd ever met, made it easier just by being there. He was a coach, but he was also a friend, someone I could talk to. He never had a bad word to say about anyone. He could put things in perspective. He never let me get too down or worse, feel sorry for myself.

In interview after interview, Rudi and Grich begged the fans for tolerance. Harry Dalton was there for me, too, pointing out that I was on pace to equal my career-high in home runs. Their support was not enough. And the abuse worsened when Sherry, very popular with Angels fans, bitterly told the press upon his firing: "I couldn't hit for Baylor."

Sorry, but I could not manage for Norm. Or miraculously cure Rudi or Grich, or sore-armed pitchers like Gary Ross or Paul Hartzell. Sorry, Norm, I just could not do it.

Dave Garcia, who replaced Sherry as manager, also asked for the fans' understanding. "Because of the salary, people expect more," Garcia told reporters. "I don't expect Don Baylor to hit twice as much as he did in the past just because of his contract. If he does what he's done in the past he'll be worth it. I'm not trying to defend him, but the people are being unfair."

But the abuse continued, even more so when the fans realized I would not react on the field. I never pleaded for mercy or cried in the press. But I hurt inside. And it went beyond me. I stopped bringing Donny to the ballpark because of the hostility. It's impossible to explain to a four-year-old why 20,000 to 30,000 people seem to hate his dad's guts. I was trying to give a hundred percent every day, but the fans did not understand or accept that as enough.

At first the hostility stunned me. I had always heard about the laid-back fans of Southern California. They were laid back, all right. Laid back and waiting for me. The Angels fans had lost their favorite target, Alex Johnson. I took his place.

I never went into the stands after the cruelest, most hostile fans. Nor did I ever make an obscene gesture, the way Garry Templeton did in St. Louis, or start ripping the fans in the media. They were paying to see me have a good day. The more I tried to give that to them, the more I failed. I told reporters, over and over, "I'm going to be gentleman enough to take my punishment."

In my mind, the reporters divided into two camps, the fair ones and the hatchet guys. One local columnist, Glenn White, wrote: "Don Baylor is indeed worth a million bucks or so. That is, he is if an ice cream cone sells for $2 million. . . . He should have been given a ticket to leave town. A one-way ticket, if you please."

I started to withdraw. On July 25, after I hit 2 home runs in the Seattle Kingdome and ended the night with 6 RBI, I set a personal record: dressed and gone fifteen seconds after the last out. Garcia told angry reporters he would talk to me about my attitude.

I had a great deal of respect for some of the writers, including Tracy Ringolsby of the *Long Beach Independent Press Telegram,* Ross Newhan and columnist Jimmy Murray, both of the *Los Angeles Times.* TV broadcasters Jim Hill of KABC and Ed Arnold of KTLA also went out of their way to be fair. But that year, I was torn up emotionally and sometimes I figured if I didn't have anything good to say, it was better to say nothing. I hadn't cried when I was going bad, so why should I gloat after a couple of good games? Besides, I owed some of those guys—like Glenn White—nothing.

Three days after my breakout in the Kingdome, I hit the first grand slam of my career in a game at the Oakland Coliseum. In my first 89 games I'd driven in 37 runs. In the course of 3 games in that stretch I'd driven in 11.

I knew I was back. And there was absolutely no doubt in my mind why. When Garcia became manager he brought in a new hitting coach—Frank Robinson.

Frank made an extraordinary effort to help me. He lived thirty-four, forty miles away. He'd get to Anaheim by three P.M. for seven-thirty games just so we could work. The first thing Frank did was knock some sense into me. Frank hammered away at my beliefs that I could carry a team all by myself, that I could earn millions of dollars on every swing.

Frank used video equipment to dissect my swing. After every at-bat we'd talk. He had an unreal ability for figuring out how pitchers were going to try to set me up. He wanted me to lower my hands and not square up at the plate. He saw what I did not, that I had drifted back toward my Carl Yastrzemski hands-held-high stance. Frank wanted those hands back down around the letters to take advantage of my power.

When Frank arrived on July 10 my average was hovering in the .220's; a month later I had added 18 points. In one 13-game stretch, I put together 17 RBI and 6 home runs.

When the bat started coming around, I started to try to figure out how I had gotten so fouled up in the first place. I placed a lot of blame on attitude—mine. The day I signed I was under the impression I would be the Angels' left fielder. When the Angels signed Joe twenty-four hours later I knew I'd be shoved into the DH spot. The Angels had Tony Solaita at first base, Bruce Bochte in centerfield, and Bobby Bonds in right field. There was no position left for me.

The situation might not have been as hard to swallow if I hadn't believed Sherry when he told me that I had a chance to win the centerfield job. I was even put on a new throwing program to try to learn to throw more with my body and legs than my arm. Pitcher Mark Clear told me I never followed through because of poor mechanics. There I was, relearning, of all things, how to throw a baseball. In my mind, it was worth it. I was going to be the Angels' centerfielder.

It was a ruse. Sherry turned center over to Bochte, a converted first baseman. I was going to DH. I was scared I would rip a hamstring trying to steal bases after sitting on the bench for three innings at a time. I multiplied the inactivity by six years and wondered what my value would be by 1983 if I was considered half a player in 1977.

By May, my head was completely screwed up. I kept thinking about how I'd taken less money, how I could have gone to the Rangers where I surely would have played first base, how I probably would have gone if I'd known the Angels were going to put Rudi in left and me in the DH spot. I considered requesting a trade to Texas and almost did in July. I wrestled with that, but then thought about my word to Mr. Autry. I owed him a full season.

By August, the outfield position was taken away from me for good. Garcia volunteered to put a stationary bike in the clubhouse, runway, dugout, or wherever, if my concern was staying loose. But no more outfield. He made his point in the newspapers and sent Frank to tell me. When reporters came to me, I simply said that I would go along with Dave and Frank because the team was still in a pennant race and we had a chance to win.

But we did not win. The Angels still finished fifth, 28 games behind the division-winning Royals.

That December, facing the second year of DHing, playing for fans who seemed to hate me, I decided to have Jerry request a trade, preferably to the Rangers. By then, Harry was out of power and Buzzie Bavasi was in. Buzzie talked to Texas but he wanted no part of the only deal the Rangers were willing to make. Texas had offered pitcher Bert Blyleven, first baseman Willie Horton, outfielder Tom Grieve, and pitcher Tommy Boggs. The Rangers not only sought me, but also Nolan Ryan, who was on the verge of playing out his option. Buzzie demanded more, namely an everyday player, like third baseman Toby Harrah or second baseman Bump Wills.

The deal never was worked out by spring. I was glad it wasn't. It had taken a long winter to develop emotional callouses. But, in time, I realized I still wanted to be a California Angel. There was some good in 1977. Harry was correct. I equaled my career-high in home runs, with 25. I drove in 75 runs, stole 26 bases, and wound up hitting .251. I had played through some injuries, including a hamstring pull, but I had been determined that one of Mr. Autry's free agents would finish the season, no matter what. I did. And I had survived.

In many ways, the lessons of 1977 would carry over into the following year.

The Angels were getting better; we could sense it. There was an infusion of new players, such as Lyman Bostock. And there was a new manager, Jim Fregosi.

Fregosi replaced Garcia in May 1978 in a strange changing of the guard. One day I looked in the paper at the Pirates box score and saw "E: Fregosi, 2." The next day he was released. Two days later, he was our manager.

Grichie was ecstatic. Fregosi was his childhood hero. Their friendship almost ended before it started, though, because of Grichie's roving eye. Grichie, as usual, was checking out the stands the first day Jimmy arrived in Anaheim. He spotted a pretty blonde sitting in the section where the players' free-pass seats were located. Grichie sent a note to her, introducing himself and asking for a date. The note came back: "I'd like to, but I'm married to the manager."

I thought Grichie was going to die. There he was, finally playing for his hero, and he'd got caught hustling Fregosi's wife. Luckily, Fregosi had a sense of humor.

Jimmy was an Angels' legend. He was signed as an eighteen-year-old, played for ten seasons, and held many of the team's offensive records. It took Jimmy a decade to compile a franchise-record 115 home runs. The first time I peeked at the record book I knew I could catch him at least in that category, which I did, in six years. By the time I left the Angels I had hit 141. But records are not why I had a soft spot in my heart for Jim Fregosi. Soon after he arrived I realized I finally had a manager who would tell me the truth about my role.

Garcia had me boxed into the DH job again, but would not say if it was permanent or what. The June 15 trading deadline was about ten days away when Jimmy arrived and I was seriously considering pursuing a trade again because of Garcia. I no longer believed anything he said to me. And Frank was gone; dismissed after the '77 season despite a promise of a job.

When Fregosi arrived he called me into the visiting manager's office in Baltimore and laid it out for me. He knew I wanted to play left field every day or I wanted out. He said, "I don't want anybody here who doesn't want to be here. I'll do what I can to trade you."

"That's not the problem," I said. "I want to be here, but I also want to play." I told him that I was really bothered by the label that the Angels wanted to attach to me. He had come from another league, inherited Garcia's old formulas, had not given me a look.

Jimmy said he understood and we struck a deal. He would use me in the outfield, first base, or whatever, take that hard look, but would make no promises other than he would do what was best for the team. He said that if I saw myself penciled in as the designated hitter it was because he felt, for that day, it was the best alignment possible. I was to live with that or go through with the trade request. I told him I could live with it as long as I felt I was given a fair shot.

Fregosi and I were friends from that point on. He put me in the field, but also used me as a DH, 102 of 158 games. But this time I could live with it because there were no lies, "contests" for openings that never existed.

I thought about 1977 and '78 years later, about the transition to designated hitter, which I knew would never be reversed. I will never agree with some critics who believe it is selfish to want to be a complete player or to want to play every day. In Jim Fregosi, I felt I had found a manager who understood the way I felt and did not hold it against me for just wanting to play. Most importantly, Jimmy made the transition easier for me by instilling a leadership quality. He showed me I could be an asset, whether I played the outfield, first base, or served as DH. Jim Fregosi helped me find a peace within myself.

16

LYMAN

THE Angels were playing the White Sox in Comiskey. We were down to our last out. Lyman Bostock, Mr. Autry's latest million-dollar free agent, stepped in to face Lerrin LaGrow.

The tying run was in scoring position. Lyman, flirting with .300, was one of our hottest hitters. He could not poke the ball through that time. He grounded out. It was one of the few poor at-bats he had in the second half.

The date was September 28, 1978. The last embers of another near-miss season were just about to die out. The Angels were still fighting to avoid being mathematically eliminated. That fate was just three days away, though. The knowledge did not keep Lyman from slashing away. He was a perfectionist. Nobody liked making the twenty-seventh out of a game. Lyman hated it more than most, especially when it happened at Comiskey Park. He had grown up practically next door, in Gary, Indiana, and, as usual, half that city was there to see him play.

I was in the on-deck circle when Lyman stormed by and into the clubhouse ranting and raving. He showered and dressed in record time. And veterans know enough to leave other veterans alone. Lyman would see LaGrow again. And .300 hitters always get their revenge. So when Lyman walked by I did not say a thing. I did not know there would be no next time for him.

That night Rudi took me to one of his favorite restaurants, Eli's, in downtown Chicago. The food was good, so was the company. Our third-base coach, John McNamara, was there with friends and sent over drinks. Joe and I visited the piano bar for a while and then walked back to the hotel. It was a pleasant fall night, with just a nip in the air to remind us the off-season was approaching. Joe and I talked about 1979 and how there would be enough talent to finally get Mr. Autry to the Series.

It was about eleven-thirty when I got back to my room. My phone was ringing. It was my wife, calling from California.

"Lyman's been shot, somewhere in Gary, Indiana," she said. She had heard the news on the radio.

I went numb. Lyman had just made the last out. He was supposed to hit tomorrow, in the third spot, with me right behind him. Nobody gets shot in baseball. Nobody.

I ran next door to Rudi's room. By the time I got there his phone was ringing. Rettenmund was in the hallway; he'd gotten a call, too. So was Davey Chalk. Word spread up and down the floor, where most of the team was quartered.

I heard my phone ring again. It was Buzzie calling from Anaheim.

"Lyman has been shot," he said. "Pass it on."

"We're on our way to Gary," I said. "We're trying to find out where he is."

There was a long pause.

"Don't go," Buzzie said. "There's nothing you can do. Lyman's got over a hundred pellets in his head."

Lyman had been hit with a shotgun blast at close range. There was no hope.

I walked out into the hallway and told four or five other players. We all collapsed right there.

McNamara returned from the restaurant and when we told him the news he nearly went into a state of shock. Then he went to his room and started making calls to find out where Lyman was. Calls started coming in from reporters. I'd never hung up on a reporter before but that night the intrusion was too much. The phones were needed and we really didn't know more than the writers did.

Then shortly after one A.M., we got the call no one wanted. Lyman had passed away. Some players started to cry. I know I did. So did Joe. The two of us were probably closer to Lyman than anyone.

Joe believes in God, just as I do. But when Joe asked me, "It's God's will that it happened, isn't it?" I did not know the answer. There would be no answers to such questions that night.

We all sat in that hallway. Hotel guests walked by, stepped over and around us, but we didn't care. Hours passed. Finally Joe and I were the only ones left.

"Can you sleep?" Joe asked.

I shook my head. So we stayed. And cried some more, talked some more, too. About anything, everything. But mostly about Lyman.

Both Joe and I felt a special kinship with Lyman because his first season as an Angel had been as painful as ours had the year before. Mr. Autry had dipped back into the free-agent market and signed Lyman to a five-year, $2.25-million contract. The economics of the time enabled Lyman's contract to instantly make our windfalls look small. But that was okay. He was the kind of professional that our lineup needed, one of the last missing links.

Lyman had finished second to his Twins teammate, Rod Carew, in the batting race the year before. He wanted to prove he was even better than that. Prove it to himself and to the Twins. A lot of the black guys left Calvin Griffith's team feeling that way.

Lyman was a pure hitter. He knew that, we all knew it. But he started out trying to earn every cent of his contract on each swing. He wanted to carry the club. Just like I tried to do in '77. Lyman couldn't do it, either.

I never had an April as ugly as Lyman's. Fans booed him mercilessly because all they ever saw him do was hit into double plays.

He had to dream about those double plays. I tried to help, talked to him a lot. "Just try to block it out of your mind," I would tell Lyman. "Don't worry about the contract. You can't live up to that money all at once. Everyone knows you can hit. Guys in this clubhouse know. Don't ever worry about them."

And the guys did know. Everybody liked Lyman because he was a good-natured guy. He kept us laughing and was always talking. He had so many words spilling out of him that Kenny Brett nicknamed him "Abdul Jibber-Jabber."

Still, I knew Lyman was hurting inside. Guilt ate at him. He had let someone talk him into posing for *The Sporting News* wearing sunglasses with white dollar signs painted on the lens. If I could have I would have talked him out of it; the year before, Rudi, Grich, and I had posed for *The Sporting News* cover with our hands dipping into saddle bags full of money, a play on the millions The Cowboy was paying us. I'd felt uncomfortable about that photo, and there had been three of us to bear the brunt. I couldn't imagine doing what Lyman did. If people were not aware he was making a lot of money before that, they knew it then. So the notoriety was there from the start.

When he started out so badly, Lyman went to Mr. Autry and tried to return his April salary. Lyman's offer was unheard of for a player. Fortunately, Mr. Autry rejected it. A contract was a contract to Mr. Autry. He was a man of his word. He also proved he loved his players. Not liked— loved.

Lyman's offer was well intentioned. But the story leaked and the nuts really came out, "volunteering" to take the money off his hands.

Lyman starting pulling out of it in mid-May. Suddenly he was as hot as he had been cold. He fisted bloopers over the infield. Line drives, which were caught before, started dropping in for hits. Suddenly he was sizzling. Two hits a game, 4 hits, 3 hits, 2 hits, 1 hit, 3 hits. It just went on and on. It was amazing and fun to watch. No team had a clue as to how to defense him. It was almost like watching Carew. It was uncanny.

The fans started warming to Lyman. When he just kept hitting, the rest of us jumped on for the ride. And we started to win. Win with little things, big things, home runs, sacrifice bunts. Suddenly, the California Angels were a very good ballclub.

Lyman and I became good friends. We came from different organizations and different backgrounds, but we had the same values. Lyman didn't come from a winning tradition, but he wanted to win. He had seen a lot of mediocrity in Minnesota, felt like he had been used and underpaid. When he said good-bye to Griffith and hello to Mr. Autry, he said he felt like he'd gone from being a boy to a man. He respected The Cowboy because Mr. Autry respected him. It wasn't the money with Lyman. Production and being professional were the most important things to him. When he stepped into the batter's box he was all business. Abdul Jibber-Jabber and all that other stuff was gone. It was time to hit.

Joe and I sat in the hallway for hours. It was the longest night I've ever spent. Finally, at about four o'clock in the morning, Joe said we had to try to get some rest. There was a day game that Sunday and we had to leave for the ballpark in less than six hours. I walked to an all-night drugstore to get some aspirin because my head hurt so bad I couldn't think of laying it on a pillow.

Six hours later I was on the team bus headed for Comiskey. It was the quietest ride of our lives. Everyone was reading newspapers, trying to find out more about Lyman. Details were still sketchy at first. We later learned that Lyman had gone to a dinner party in Gary with his uncle, Ed Turner, and two women. One woman, Barbara Smith, was a childhood friend of Lyman's. The other, Joan Hawkins, was Barbara Smith's sister. According to police reports, Leonard Smith, the estranged husband of Barbara Smith, started stalking the foursome by auto. When Lyman's uncle pulled up at a traffic light, Leonard Smith pulled alongside and fired a shotgun into the backseat where his wife sat. She was hit by one pellet. Lyman, sitting next to her, caught almost the full force of the blast in his face. Three hours later, Lyman was dead.

Leonard Smith was tried twice for first-degree murder. The first trial ended in a hung jury. The second jury found him innocent by reason of insanity. Smith was institutionalized for seven months. He was freed just twenty-two months after Lyman died. The outcry was tremendous. That case helped push Indiana to change its judicial system to allow those found mentally impaired to also be found guilty and sentenced to jail.

When we arrived at Comiskey there were cameras and reporters everywhere. Lyman's locker was already empty, his belongings in a duffel bag. Only the name plate over his locker remained.

The finality of it all was devastating. When a photographer came in and started shooting the empty locker, it was just too much. I grabbed the guy and led him out the clubhouse door. I didn't physically abuse him, maybe even saved his life because the other guys started to go crazy, screaming and yelling at him.

Chapel was canceled. Max Patkin, the clown prince of baseball, had been scheduled to perform that afternoon, but he came in and told us he would not out of respect for Lyman. Jim Fregosi, who looked as if he had aged a hundred years, canceled batting practice. Francisco Barrios, the White Sox pitcher, was the farthest thing from our minds.

I ran sprints with Rudi and Grich. My legs felt heavier than they'd ever felt before. My head was still pounding. I didn't want to play and needed to play at the same time. In my first at-bat I hit the ball off the upper deck in left field, my 24th home run of the season. The Angels equipment manager, Mickey Shishido, took me aside and said, "That was for Lyman, you did that for Lyman." Mickey did not have to tell me. I knew. But it didn't seem enough. All I could think about was Lyman's last at-bat, how maybe if he had gotten that one hit things might have been different somehow, some way. But he had not been there to drive in Sunday. He was gone, wiped out of the lineup, off the face of the earth.

Following the longest day of my career came the longest overnight flight home. That Monday was an off-day. I knew Lyman's wife and mother would fly in that day, with the body. I wanted to be there at the airport, believing a lot of guys would be there, too. No one else showed, though. I never found out why. I watched as Lyman's wife, Yuovene, disembarked, bringing home her husband of less than two years.

Yuovene saw me and walked over. She was really broken up, could not go on. She asked that I go to the cargo area where a hearse was waiting and claim Lyman's body. My heart said no. I was not prepared, not yet, not so soon, even though I knew the casket was sealed. But I told Yuovene I would. Fortunately, one of his cousins volunteered to claim the body.

I thought it could not get any worse. On Tuesday it did. I was in the clubhouse when Buzzie Bavasi called downstairs and asked if I would come to his office. When I got there Buzzie started ranting and raving. "Son of bitch" this and "son of a bitch" that. I did not understand what was going on until Buzzie told me that Lyman's agent, Abdul-Jalil, had called within hours of the accident requesting money from Lyman's paycheck, supposedly for some unfinished business deals that Lyman's wife was not aware of. Buzzie was incensed, having already given Lyman a check to cover the agent's fee—$145,000—and he stood there vowing not to pay out another dime to anyone but Lyman's widow. I was angry, too. Lyman was not even buried yet.

Buzzie told me right then and there that he would never, ever deal with Abdul-Jalil again and I should go tell that to Abdul-Jalil's other clients on the team: Ron Jackson, Ken Landreaux, and Danny Goodwin.

I went down and called the three guys over and delivered the message. I told them about the request for money Abdul-Jalil supposedly had made. I did not tell the amount, which Buzzie told me was in the thousands of dollars. "Buzzie didn't think it was time to do that," I said. "So he does not want to deal with this agent at all."

The three did not react, so I left it at that. The next day I got a mailgram from Abdul-Jalil informing me that he intended to sue for $1 million for defamation of character.

I was not afraid, just angry at Jackson, Landreaux, and Goodwin. Lyman was supposed to be their friend, yet they saw nothing wrong with Abdul-Jalil's action. Defamation of character?

I did question his character. I did so even more when I found out a few days later Lyman had no will, leaving the way open for the state of California to get paid before Lyman's widow. Then I learned that Abdul-Jalil had rejected the club's request that Lyman take out an insurance policy instead of the club. If he had done so, the benefits would have gone to his wife, tax-free. Instead the beneficiary was the club and Lyman's widow then received the money as taxable income. What would have cost Lyman about $11,000 wound up costing his widow about $500,000 in taxes.

No, I did not care for Abdul-Jalil's character at all.

On Thursday Lyman was buried in Los Angeles. The team was bused to the church. Ken Brett gave the eulogy. Nolan also spoke. Kenny, who has a way with words, concentrated on the lighthearted side of Lyman. Listening to Kenny talk about the man he nicknamed Abdul Jibber-Jabber brought back the good memories. He even made some of us smile through our tears. At the cemetery, as I walked up the hill with Nolan, I saw Abdul-Jalil. I wanted to drop him right there, take out all the fury I was feeling on him. But that was not the time nor the place. He acknowledged my presence and I did likewise. That was it. I never saw him again until last summer. He was in the computer business and out of the player-agent field. That was fine with me.

Abdul-Jalil never sued.

Every year I play at least six games in Chicago. The feelings are always bittersweet. One of my uncles died suddenly in Texas while I played a game there. Yogi was fired by Steinbrenner there and, on that day, I saw Yankees cry. But every time I walk into Comiskey Park I think of Lyman most of all. Looking back, I wish I had said that one last thing to him before he walked out of that clubhouse forever.

17

CONTROLLED AGGRESSION

I ONCE read an article in which the Dodgers' Steve Garvey said he got even with headhunters through controlled aggression.

Instead of charging pitchers and risking ejection and injury he killed them with his bat. Garv figured that he batted between .600 and .700 in at-bats immediately after he was knocked down or hit by pitches. Once he went 6–for–6 with 3 home runs.

Frank was like that, too. Some teams fined pitchers if they knocked Frank down because it fired him up so much.

I decided very early on to try to go that route.

A year after I took Reggie Cleveland deep at Fenway he tried to take my head off the first time I faced him in Boston in 1976. I know Cleveland threw at me. I had hit him hard all through the minors. The home run off the transformer in '75 incensed him. So, on June 8, 1976, he came up and in with a pitch right under my chin. I stepped out of the box, thinking that if I go after him I'm out of the game. I never want to give up at-bats in Fenway. So I thought, *Key down. You want this guy and you want him bad.* Cleveland ran the count to 2–0. I pulled the next pitch foul and into our dugout. I said to myself, *Back off. Don't go crazy here.*

I drove Cleveland's next pitch toward the top of the Green Monster. I just knew it was out, so I started running toward first by way of the Red Sox dugout, screaming at Cleveland all the way. I called him every name imaginable, words I surely did not learn in church. There was only one thing wrong. I didn't control my aggression long enough. The ball hit off the top of the wall. I was so busy yelling I forgot to run all-out. I barely made it to first base, the longest, most humiliating single of my life. Carl Yastrzemski stood on first, his glove held over his face. He was laughing so hard I thought he was going to cry. "You thought that was out of here," he cackled.

I learned two lessons that day. First, never yap at a pitcher when you think you've hit a home run. And, number two, the wall giveth and the wall taketh away.

I would score from first on a Joe Rudi double that day, as the A's defeated the Red Sox. It did not seem like enough.

By the time my California Angels years came along, I'd already developed another theory, Controlled Aggression II. If you were the fiercer aggressor, you could frighten the opposition into not hurting you or your teammates. Call that kind of player an enforcer or whatever, but everyone knows who they are. Dusty Baker and Bill Madlock were notorious in the National League. As for me, American League pitchers began to get the idea that I was just a little too unpredictable to take lightly.

In 1976, when Red Sox right-hander Dick Pole hit me, I charged the mound. That September Royals right-hander Dennis Leonard hit me square in the back after Sal Bando had hit a home run on a 3–0 pitch. Leonard never even looked at the catcher for a sign. He just drilled me. I started toward Leonard, but umpire Bill Haller jumped right in and walked me to first base. As soon as Haller went back to the plate, I took off for the mound. Leonard, rubbing up a new ball, never saw me coming until I was in full charge. He finally glanced at me and it looked like his life was flashing in front of his eyes. He ran—right toward our dugout. Gene Tenace and Claudell Washington nailed him before I could. If they hadn't I probably would have been suspended for maiming a pitcher.

A brawl broke out. The only guy who said I hurt him was George Brett. A bunch of Royals had me by the arms and were pulling me away from the fight. I got my left arm free and when I did, I accidentally hit him in the chin. George told me later I almost sprained his back I hit him so hard. How that could happen by hitting a guy in the chin I'll never know.

All kinds of skirmishes broke out that day. That's when the fun usually began, when the Royals and the A's declared war.

Incidents like that prove to a team that it is united. That A's team could not be intimidated. And after Leonard hit me, Oakland scored 3 or 4 runs in the inning.

One thing I learned that season was that if you made the first move, you'd better back it up. I saw one player who didn't.

Bert Campaneris started a brawl using a relay throw to low-bridge the baserunner, Indians third baseman Buddy Bell. Campy had been hit by a pitch the night before and was still fuming. He didn't care that the Indians had some heavy armor. Frank was player-manager of Cleveland. Big Boog Powell was the first baseman. You could tell Campy was plotting something. With Bell on first and Powell at the plate, he told Garner he'd take the play at second on a grounder. Phil thought it was a bit strange, but said okay.

Boog hit a grounder. Campy took the relay throw. then, instead of throwing down from under, he came across the top. I was waiting at first for the throw, but it never came. He hit Buddy right in the face above the eye. I knew instantly it was intentional. Campy had thrown overhand, right toward the ground where Bell was sliding. Then he jumped on Bell and started throwing punches. Boog Powell started toward second. He ran so fast he slid into the pile of bodies and turned his ankle. Boog was out a couple of weeks.

Frank was furious. Not only did he lose his first baseman, but he had watched Campy bean one of his young stars a day after Campy had spiked pitcher Jim Kern while sliding into home plate. Frank told reporters the Indians would get Campy. The next day Campy asked me to translate Frank's quotes. Campy listened, then shrugged and said, "Me don't care."

A week before we were to return to Cleveland, Campy was standing around the infield during batting practice at Tiger Stadium. Claudell Washington threw a ball toward the infield and accidentally hit Campy right between his shoulder blades. Campy went down like he was shot. He told Chuck Tanner he could not play. And he didn't. Not in Detroit. And not in Cleveland.

To this day Frank believes Campy ducked the Indians. He thought Campy started something he was afraid to finish. I am inclined to agree.

If I have a reputation for trying to protect my teammates, I owe it to a couple of incidents that occurred when I was with the Angels.

In 1978, when Lyman got hot, pitchers started going after him. Lyman tolerated the headhunters for a while. Finally in a game against the Royals, Lyman said enough is enough.

Al Hrabosky, a left-hander who called himself "The Mad Hungarian," was on the mound that particular day. It was the late innings, Hrabosky's show time. He had gone behind the mound to do the little psyche job he was so famous for, acting like a bull ready to charge, snorting and smashing the ball into his glove. The fans loved it. I thought it was stupid. After going through the whole bit, he faced rookie Carney Lansford. Carney "psyched" the ball all the way to the grassy knoll behind the left-field fence at Royals Stadium. The ball just sat out there like a nine-iron chip shot. It was beautiful.

Hrabosky was still fuming when Lyman stepped in. Before I even knelt down in the on-deck circle, Hrabosky threw the best knockdown pitch I've ever seen. The pitch was right at Lyman's head and when he ducked the ball went between his head and helmet, which had flown off.

Lyman charged Hrabosky and all hell broke loose. Benches and both bullpens cleared. I was out there swinging, feeling like I was back in Clarksville. Hrabosky had tried to hurt a friend. I have never minded getting hit in the shoulder or back and believe brushbacks are part of the game. But I hate headhunters. Bells go off and I just lose it. So I wanted Hrabosky. Not to hold him, grab him, or push him, but to hurt him.

By the time I got there, Bostock had Hrabosky around the waist and they were rolling on the ground. Bodies started to pile up on the mound. I jumped in head-first but the only part of Hrabosky I could get to was his back. So I started pounding him as hard as I could. While I was pounding on Hrabosky, Royals manager Whitey Herzog was yelling in my ear, "Donnie, Donnie, let him go. Don't hurt him. He's our pitcher!" Davey Chalk, our starting third baseman, told me it sounded like I was beating on a big bass drum.

Finally, the brawl broke up. Nobody was ejected, so Lyman got his bat and stepped back in. I went back to the on-deck circle, dead-tired, and tried to figure out how I was going to hit. I was hoping Lyman would have a good, long at-bat. Unfortunately, Lyman still wanted Hrabosky. He looked at Hrabosky. Hrabosky looked at him. And they charged each other. Here we go again. Lyman tackled Hrabosky and in a moment it seemed like a hundred guys were rolling around the mound again. That time all I could reach was Hrabosky's face. I got my fingers in his left eye and squeezed. I often wonder if he's got a tic there.

Looking back, I wish Hrabosky was as good a headhunter as I once considered him to be. I wish he had hit Lyman, not hurting him bad but just enough to cause Lyman to miss some games. Or I wish that Lyman had kept fighting so much the league would have suspended him. Because that was the trip prior to the one that took us to Chicago and to Lyman's death.

The pitcher I thought was the most dangerous was John Denny.

Denny had a reputation as a headhunter by the time he arrived in Cleveland from the National League in 1980. When I saw his act I understood why. With Hrabosky it was part theater. Denny really appeared to be a menace, his eyes dilated and rolling. I saw the signs of a crazy man out there. He hit me once in the head that season. In a follow-up game, I stepped in against him with the bases loaded shortly after the beaning. I wanted to hurt him bad, only in Garvey's way. I slammed a double. When I pulled into second I saw the most beautiful sight in the world. Denny was rolling on the ground behind third base. He had run over to back up the throw and twisted his ankle. Our whole bench screamed and howled when the Indians came and carted Denny away. He missed about two weeks.

In 1981, Denny hit Dan Ford in the back. The whole team charged him at once because we knew an intentional hit-by-pitch when we saw one. It did not help Denny at all that the black guys on the team felt Denny singled us out for knockdowns. So Juan Beniquez, Rod Carew, and I shot out of the dugout like the gun had gone off in the hundred-yard dash. We drilled him. That brawl lasted for a good ten minutes.

That was the good part of the afternoon. The bad part came after the brawl ended. I was walking back to the dugout, past Denny's teammate, Rick Waits. He made the mistake of jokingly saying he was looking for me, like he wanted to fight. I knocked him to the ground with one punch. I still feel bad about that. I got kicked out of the game. Denny did not and wound up beating us. That's when Gene Mauch, by then the Angels' manager, told me, "You should have hurt Denny so he could not have finished the game." He was joking. I think.

Denny doesn't pitch anymore, but he's the one guy I'll never forgive or forget. If I see him again, even at a church picnic, it would take everything I have in me not to drill him.

It took some time for me to get that angry again. But it did happen, in 1985, when I was with the Yankees. Steve Crawford and Al Nipper of the Red Sox both hit me with pitches in one game, in the shoulder. I'd had my fill of Red Sox pitchers throwing at me. From Reggie Cleveland to Dick Pole to Al Nipper. It seemed that was their club policy. After that game at Yankee Stadium, the media came over to ask about the Yankees' loss. I was still seething about Crawford and Nipper, so it just sort of spilled out, my threat against the entire Boston pitching staff, their infielders, everyone in a Red Sox uniform.

I never raised my voice much above a whisper. I did not throw anything, curse, or go crazy. I just stated that a Red Sox pitcher should never throw at my head again—or else. A couple of New York reporters told me later it was one of the most frightening displays they'd ever seen. And they wrote it that way.

The message got through. The next night, my teammates Dave Righetti and Bob Shirley were out in the bullpen. Nipper called out to them from the adjoining visitors bullpen and asked what my problem was and why I thought they were trying to throw at me.

"All I know is that you better not throw at him again," Shirley said. "He's serious. He could hurt you guys."

When I was traded to Boston the next year, Nipper and Crawford were among the first guys to come over. Rather timidly, I thought. "No hard feelings," Crawford said, extending his hand.

No hard feelings. Right. Don't try to hurt me, I won't try to hurt you.

I never minded being hit by pitches that were not aimed at my head, with one exception: I did not like being hit anywhere by illegal pitches.

Everyone knew that Billy Martin's staff in Oakland threw spitters. No one ever caught them, but everyone knew. Those guys can't comb their hair with their pitching hands, that's how badly throwing the spitter ruined their arms. Anyway, one day in Anaheim in 1982, I fouled a ball off against Matt Keough. I know that's a great time for a pitcher to get saliva on his pitching hand, when everybody's watching the foul ball. I didn't watch the ball that day. I watched Keough. And darned if he didn't go right to his mouth. I shook my head and yelled, "No, no, no," and called for the ball. The umpire threw the new ball out of the game. Not Keough, though.

Later, I put Keough and Mike Norris on notice. "If you hit me with a legal pitch, I can understand it. But if you hit me with an illegal pitch I'm not going to say anything to the umpire. I'm going to come out there and break you in half. That pitch is illegal and you can't throw it to me or at me." Keough and Norris both said they'd never throw spitters to me again. They never did.

Some hit-by-pitch incidents are comical. In 1972, I got 10 straight hits off Andy Messersmith of the Angels. The next time I faced him he hit me in the middle of the back. He came at me and for a moment I thought he wanted to fight. But Andy just wanted to tell me there were no hard feelings. "You've got to admit it," Andy said. "It's about time. And, hey, can't you just rub it a little bit? It's very depressing if you don't."

Sorry, Andy, but that's just never been my style. Only once did I ever try to rub away the pain. That was in 1972, when Nolan Ryan hit me and nearly broke my wrist. Ryan's Express can make anyone wince.

I've always believed pitchers much preferred to hit me than to have me hit their pitches. Some guys I just tormented. Like Ken Kravec of the White Sox. Ken had good stuff, but his natural motion brought the ball into my zone. In 1978, I hit a Kravec pitch over the scoreboard and the players' parking lot in Anaheim. The ball bounced off the base of the Big A sign, about 480 feet away. In 1979, I hit a Kravec pitch off the back wall of the upper deck at Comiskey just a whisker from the roof. Next time up I singled up the middle. The third time up he asked the umpire for a new ball and walked toward the plate to receive it. I thought maybe he wanted to get real close to better aim it at my head. But Kravec just blurted, "Where do you want this one? Because wherever I throw it you're going to hit it."

I had to step out of the box, I was laughing so hard.

For the most part, when it came to confrontations, pitchers were on my mind. One of my more bitter feuds, though, was with a manager.

In 1979, Tony La Russa, a guy fresh out of law school and running the Chicago White Sox, came into my life in a very irritating way. On May 27 Chicago left-hander Rich Hinton ran the ball up and in on me. I ran Hinton's next pitch into the lower deck at Comiskey Park. Next time up I took another pitch by Hinton into the upper deck. Hinton dusted the next batter and both benches emptied. Chicago's Alan Bannister also went down. Things got ugly in a hurry. La Russa was out there in the middle of everything, a brash little street fighter from Tampa, half-Italian, half-Spanish, and all red-ass.

He saw me and shouted, "What are you doing out here? You're only a DH, a part-time player, anyway."

If he hadn't been wearing glasses I would have smashed him in the face. I had not liked him before that because he was always on the field, arguing or talking to his catcher, Carlton Fisk, the human rain delay. Between La Russa and Fisk, a guy could watch the first two innings, go to the movies, and then come back and catch the eighth and ninth.

After La Russa insulted me I screamed at him every time he left the dugout. "Little rookie manager, get off the field!" I'd yell. I took his insult very personally. I had eight years in the big leagues. He had maybe two weeks.

La Russa didn't intimidate me and I didn't intimidate him, either. I know he lost his mind that day because he was trying to protect his players. That's fine. He was willing to pay the price, if need be, and he knew there was nothing in the rule book that said a manager is exempt from getting punched in the face. He also knew there could be other prices to pay. I hit 5 home runs off his pitchers and drove in 18 runs; the Chicago White Sox staff kept me in the big leagues in 1979, helped me win the MVP award.

La Russa and I went at it verbally for years. Every time he stepped out of the dugout it would start. Finally, in 1984, La Russa and I agreed to call a truce. By the winter of 1985, he was actively trying to acquire me from the Yankees. Three years later, Tony was managing the A's and talked me into signing with Oakland. The relationship always remained interesting. At least when I played for him, his pitchers couldn't throw at me anymore.

Sometimes, my most frightening enemy was myself. By the late 1970s, I was not as wild and crazy as I had been in Baltimore. I was trying to control my temper, not so much on the field as off. I tried never to slam equipment in front of fans or the other team. But I could let loose in the tunnel, splintering bats, pounding walls, rattling water coolers and dugout johns. One close call in 1979, however, stopped me from ever letting go of my bat again.

I'd made an out in a game to continue one of my few slumps that season. I went up in the tunnel behind the dugout at Anaheim Stadium and blindly threw the bat as hard as I could. The bat bounced off the wall just as Nolan Ryan walked out of the clubhouse. The bat nearly decapitated Nolan. There I was, still trying to get to my first World Series and I almost killed our best pitcher. It was the last time I ever fired a bat at anything but a pitch. That is, unless I was absolutely sure it was just me and the bat, one-on-one.

I never liked the idea of hurting anyone. I play hard, but clean, on the bases. So I never gave an infielder reason to go at me. Only one ever did.

In a game against Texas in 1973, third baseman Len Randle blocked my path as I ran from first to third even though he did not have the ball. So I hit him in the chest with my forearm to knock him out of the way. Lenny threw down his glove and went into a karate stance and started to kick and chop at the air. I'm thinking, *Okay, let's go,* but Lenny kept backpedaling, to second base and onto the outfield grass. I stalked him for a few moments but finally lost interest. Some fight.

For the most part, on the bases there was always an obvious grudging respect. Don Zimmer, the manager of the Red Sox when I was in California, compared my base-running style to that of his former Dodgers teammate, Jackie Robinson. Zim said I was the best in the league. His shortstop, Rick Burleson, agreed.

Burleson told writer Peter Gammons the players he considered the most dangerous in the league, who could get to second quickly and slide hard, were George Brett, Hal McRae, Al Bumbry, and Ron LeFlore. But, he told Gammons, "Baylor's probably the toughest of them all."

18

SEEKING HIGHER GROUND

ON the next-to-the-last day of 1978, I was sitting on 97 RBI when I stepped in to hit against Larrin LaGrow of the White Sox. The bases were loaded with two outs. Every player's goal—100 RBI—was within reach, but time was running out.

LaGrow threw a fastball and I pulled the ball down the left-field line. It was a sure double, good for 3 RBI, or so I thought. The fence in that corner of Anaheim Stadium is only waist-high, so when the ball bounced on top of the wall it just rolled over into the stands. It was a double all right. A ground-rule double. Ken Landreaux, running from first base, had to go back to third. My 100 RBI became 99. And stayed there.

The 1978 season had been my finest, but the last two games left me hungry. All winter long I thought about 100 and 35. Those numbers almost became an obsession. People remember 35 and 100, not 34 and 99.

The way I figured, no one really cared about those near-miss numbers besides me and my closest friends.

I knew I was on the verge of reaching another level, one reserved for guys like Jim Rice and Eddie Murray and Mike Schmidt. I felt I had matured as a power hitter. In 1977 I hit a career-high 25 home runs. Then, in 1978, I passed the 30-home run mark. Frank's lessons rang in my head. I found myself looking for pitches thrown to my power, from the middle of the plate, in. Not only did I better read the situations where pitchers would have to come in, on 2–0, 3–0, 3–1 counts, but once they did, I knew what to do, knew how to turn on the ball and drive it. I also knew better numbers were attainable.

Somewhere, the dream of 100 RBI and 35 home runs, grew into a dream of winning the league's Most Valuable Player award. I figured, why not? My 1978 stats had earned a seventh-place finish in balloting among the Baseball Writer's Association of America members. I wanted to be up at the top. I had watched Boston's Rice go for it all in 1978, competing against the Yankees' untouchable left-hander, Ron Guidry, who was 25–3 that season. Rice's numbers just kept going up and up and up and the rest of the hitters watched in awe. Rice wound up hitting 46 home runs and driving in 139 runs, phenomenal numbers, standards to shoot for. Rice was where I wanted to be.

To get to that higher level would mean rehabilitating my shoulder, strengthening my legs and arms. I threw myself into training, making it a full-time commitment, hardly ever missing a day. For the first time I discovered long-distance running. There was something peaceful about running for miles at a time along the Pacific coast. It gave me time to think about my career, about my life. I was alone by then. My marriage was over; my wife and son were living in Austin while I remained in our house in San Juan Capistrano, California. I had nothing but time on my hands. I spent it working.

I ran in the mornings, played golf with LaRoche and Tanana in the early afternoon, then worked out at the stadium. It was a dedication I'd never felt before. I was determined to put the bad Aprils behind me, determined to step forward in the clubhouse and on the field.

I was driven. It did not matter what my schedule was. I had to keep working out. While driving to Texas for the holidays, I was out in the middle of New Mexico, at one of those pit stops between here and there, a place where you spend the night only when you're just too tired to keep going. Before the sun came up, I was out on the high desert running. It was pitch-dark, freezing, so cold I got an earache unlike any I had before or after, at least until the 1987 World Series in frozen St. Louis. But I kept running, my ears aching, struggling to breathe. All the while I was thinking about a hundred things—all of them RBI. That's what kept me going, through the holidays and on into spring training.

By the time I reported to camp in Palm Springs I was in the best physical shape of my life. My regimen improved even more because of the presence of a healthy Joe Rudi and our latest free agent, Rod Carew.

Both Joe and I roomed at the Gene Autry Hotel near the new Angels complex and we became closer than ever before. When Joe and I were not at the ballpark, we were messing around with his ham radio. We talked to people all over the world at night and were having a pretty good time until Harry Dalton heard of our setup. He was none-too-pleased that we were stringing antennae wire from off the roof of the hotel to the golf course next door. Harry shut us down; I guess he was afraid Joe or I would fall and break a leg, or worse.

Every morning, at seven, Joe and I had already eaten breakfast and were on our way to the batting cages. The thing that killed us was that Rod Carew always arrived ahead of us. Rodney didn't go to hit; he was working on his bunting. There he was, a seven-time batting champion, out there all by himself two hours before players had to be in uniform, just dropping bunts down the third-base line.

While Rodney worked on his calling card in the cage, Joe and I would run laps. The outfield grass was always still wet with dew. The only sounds were our breathing and Rodney hitting the ball. It was peaceful there, the most beautiful place in the world to train. I hadn't felt that at peace with the game in a long time. I could not wait for the 1979 season to begin; the feeling that something great awaited was so strong.

My paramount goal was to be ready for April and its evil twin, May. Other months, like July, August, and September, had kept me in the big leagues. April and May always tried to boot me out. To me, having a truly great year meant avoiding another awful start. In a personal triumph, I did more than that. I did not have a big home-run month but, for the first time in my career, I hit over .300 in April.

By late April, I began to feel that not only was a good year possible, but a great one. On April 21, everything seemed especially connected, the will, the desire, the effort, the training. Before our game, against the visiting Athletics, I had been out in the batting cage next to the left-field bullpen. Fans were hanging over the wall watching. There were no taunts; the fans had come around to my side the year before. On that day there was just a sort of quiet curiosity and no interruptions. I felt real locked in on my swing and the fans seemed to sense that.

It was one of those particularly hot California days, but still I wanted the extra work. The bat just felt too good in my hands to put down.

When the game started, Bob Lacey, the A's left-hander, threw me a little slider, down and in. The pitch looked just like the balls I had seen in batting practice. Big and fat, as if it were sitting there on a tee, begging to be hit. Almost every pitch looked that way. I crushed a first-inning grand slam. The ball landed right on the netting covering that batting cage where all those fans had been watching me less than two hours before. I usually do not watch my home runs, but I stood there for a few seconds, mostly thinking about the hard work that day and all the days before, how maybe it could all translate into something really big.

The challenges were growing, with more breaking balls being thrown, more teams openly daring me to beat their best. More often than not, in those first two months, I accepted the challenges and won.

Bob Lemon gambled that I could not in a game against the Yankees on April 30 in Anaheim. The Angels and Yankees were tied, 1–all, with one out in the bottom of the ninth. We had runners on first and third when Rodney walked to the plate. Thurman Munson looked at Rodney and said, "You aren't going to get a chance to hit." Incredibly, with first base occupied, the Yankees walked Rodney intentionally to pitch to the cleanup hitter who stood just 1 RBI away from establishing a new league record for RBI in April. Me. I lined a game-winning single into left. It was RBI number 28, an AL record for the month of April that stood until 1988, when Dave Winfield tied a major-league record by driving in 29 for the Yankees.

After April I felt as if I had conquered the world. May was even better. I drove in 23 runs, hit 8 doubles, and 7 home runs to earn the American League Player of the Month award.

On June 1, Rick Wise of the Indians served up a 2-run home run in my first at-bat and I figured that was a sign that another of my least favorite months was about to be conquered. Unfortunately, that was not the case. I seemed to go all the way to my birthday, June 28, without another RBI. Only a big push at the end of June got me into double figures—11 whole RBI.

I hadn't lost my stroke. I'd lost the strength in my left hand and I could not turn my wrist. Something was wrong. X-rays showed no breaks, though. The diagnosis: I had an inflamed tendon in my wrist.

For weeks, trainer Rick Smith treated the hand and wrist with an electro-galvanizer stimulator. I had to submerge my hand and wrist in ice water while the stimulator sent electronic pulses through the water. I did that for twenty minutes a day for almost a month in an effort to restore flexibility, but my hand just did not respond. My average started to suffer and the pain grew worse. I wouldn't come out of the lineup, though, and tried to get on any way that I could, dropping in flare hits here and there. By the end of June, I was in a devastating 0–for–27 slump.

Merv Rettenmund, a clubhouse wit who harassed me from Baltimore to California, saw the injury was eating away at me. I sat slumped in my chair in the visitor's clubhouse in Arlington, when he sent Donny over to me with questions only a six-year-old could have asked and lived to tell about.

"Dad," Donny said, "will you ever get another hit?"

Merv and the other guys cracked up. I guess I would have, too, except I knew I couldn't answer the question, seriously or otherwise. My hand and wrist were so weak I could barely hold the bat.

19

MOST VALUABLE DREAMS

BY the last week of June, I knew all my hard work and preparation for 1979 were in jeopardy because of my wrist.

I had tendinitis, a recurring ailment I'd suffered since 1973. My worst fear was that I was about to suffer the same sort of power failure that had crippled me in 1976, when I had a broken hand. I knew I had to do something.

Dr. Robert Kerlan, team doctor of the Los Angeles Lakers, was in Texas that week, so the Angels arranged an appointment. He reconfirmed that I had tendinitis and decided to give me a shot of cortisone. When the first needle filled with Novocaine pierced the inflamed area I wanted to jump right out of the chair. My wrist started to swell. Then came a numbing sensation. The next injection was the cortisone.

Cortisone won't do any good if it doesn't reach the inflammation, so you just pray it hits the right spot. Dr. Kerlan did and it felt like a miracle.

After the injection he marked it with a ballpoint pen so that it could easily be found in case another injection was needed. That season I had three injections altogether. By June 29, my hand and wrist felt a lot better and so did my swing.

I had played through the pain. Most importantly, I played, period. It was not the first time I would be injured that season. I separated my shoulder trying to make a diving catch in a game in which Nolan was trying for a no-hitter. I played through a pulled hamstring and a badly jammed thumb. When the season ended, it would show I played all 162, something no other Angel player managed to do.

In a series in Texas I faced off against Ferguson Jenkins. Fergy and I had a silent battle going, one which had started the year before. I had once hit one of his sliders into the left-centerfield bleachers in Texas. Jenkins took exception, did not think I should be able to pull a breaking ball that was down and away, did not even think I should have been leaning over the plate in the first place. So, the next time I face him, he threw one under my chin. That was okay. He was from the old school. So was I. He could only scare me if I let him. Jenkins knocked me down again that day in Arlington. Then I doubled. And then homered. It was a nice birthday present to myself.

On July 1, in the last of 3 games in Kansas City, with my parents watching, I greeted Paul Splittorff with a 2-run home run in the first inning. As I rounded third and shook Bobby Knoop's hand, I shouted at him, "Welcome, July!" Bobby, our third-base coach, started to laugh. He was starting to get used to my visits. The next time up I hit another home run, this one against Marty Pattin. I wound up with 4 RBI that day, 13 altogether in the first 4 games of the month to go with 5 home runs.

I was starting to believe that I couldn't do anything wrong, if I stayed healthy. On the Fourth of July, I faced A's reliever Dave Heaverlo in the eighth with a man on. Heaverlo, a stocky guy with a shaved head, stood on the mound peering into his dugout at A's Manager Jim Marshall. Heaverlo started nodding and then turned to face me. I figured Marshall had signaled him not to give me anything to hit. It didn't matter. Moments later, Heaverlo was walking off the field; I'd hit the first pitch over the left-centerfield wall at the Big A.

In the middle of that month, the whole game paused for the All-Star break. I'd never given the game much thought until 1978. That was the first time I felt I really belonged. It was also the first time I felt genuinely snubbed. Billy Martin, then manager of the Yankees, decided he was going to take some guy named Dwight Evans from Boston as a last-minute replacement for injured Carl Yastrzemski. It's been many years since that summer. To this day, I ask Dwight and Billy Martin one question. How could you keep a guy with 20 home runs and 50 RBI off the team and choose a guy who had about 15 home runs and 22 RBI, or whatever Dwight had at the time? Billy said he wanted defense and Dwight's the best right fielder I've ever seen. Dwight has become my best friend; still, a slight is a slight. I'm not a person that holds grudges, but I never forget.

I had no such problem in 1979. Bob Lemon, who replaced Martin at the end of 1978 and managed the Yankees to a world championship, got to choose the American League All-Stars not voted into the game by the fans. He chose me. Lem had been a constant at Anaheim Stadium the season before, when he served as the Yankees' West Coast scout. I always went out of my way to say hello because he had a good reputation as a man and as a player. It meant a lot to me when Lem chose me because of his baseball background. The fans were not about to choose me. They didn't recognize the California Angels, with one exception. Rod Carew led all players with a total of 3.9 million votes. But Rodney was injured and had not played since June 1. When the vote totals were announced not only hadn't I missed a game, but I led the major leagues in RBI, with 80, and was tied for second in the league in home runs, with 21.

I finished fourteenth among American League outfielders.

I did not understand the fans' logic at all. Neither could a lot of players. More than 300 of us signed petitions that year requesting the vote be returned to the players, coaches, and managers. It never was. The one consolation is that the *New York Times* ran a survey in which players voted on their All-Star choices. And my peers and teammates voted for Jim Rice and Fred Lynn of the Red Sox and Don Baylor, a vote that really flattered me.

Rodney could not play, so Lem moved Carl Yastrzemski—one of the three outfielders voted in by the fans—to first base. His outfield subs were Reggie, Steve Kemp of the White Sox, and Don Baylor. Lem again chose me and batted me third in the lineup he sent out against Phillies left-hander Steve Carlton.

More than 60,000 fans jammed the Seattle Kingdome. I'd never seen that many people in the place. There was hardly any air and what little there was was stagnant. I didn't think the dome could get any hotter or more uncomfortable.

I wouldn't have changed places with anyone in the world.

I couldn't shake the feeling that someone was going to walk up and demand what I was doing there with all those All-Stars. I was kind of asking myself the same thing as I watched Jim Rice and Dave Parker, Pete Rose and Reggie milling around. Then Rose, of all people, reminded me why I was there. He walked over and said, "You have twenty-three home runs and eighty-five RBI at the All-Star break. That's unheard of." Finally, I felt I belonged, thanks to somebody named Pete Rose.

Steve Carlton's reputation was enormous. My first test came in the first inning. George Brett was on first with two outs. I had heard about Carlton's slider, said to myself, *How good could it be? I've faced Ron Guidry and no one's slider could have been better than Guidry's was in 1978.*

Carlton drove the count to 3–2. I was still looking for that slider. Finally, he threw the "legend." I fouled it off and he threw another. I fouled it off again and he threw it again. Carlton threw five in a row, down and in, and I fouled off five. Poor Brett was dying, having run on each 3–2 pitch. Then Carlton threw one more slider. By then I'd seen it enough, knew not to chase it down in the dirt, knew where the break was.

I hit the ball on the sweet part of the bat, pulled it down into the left-field corner for an RBI double. Next time up, I got a single. I grounded out in my next at-bat. My fourth and final at-bat came against a big, tall right-hander from Cincinnati named Mike LaCoss, whose ball runs back in on right-handers. I figured one more hit would give me a shot at the MVP. I lined out to short. Lee Mazzilli of the Mets came up with a pinch-hit home run and a bases-loaded walk to lead the Nationals to a 7–6 victory. Dave Parker won the MVP, for hitting a home run and throwing out two baserunners. Close, but no cigar. Still, it was a game I'll never forget, my first and last All-Star Game.

It was about then that I had to do some growing up not only as a player, but as a man and father as well. The divorce was being processed, but very slowly. There were still the trappings of a marriage, at least publicly. I believe I allowed it to continue so things would be easier for Donny. There was a tremendous amount of guilt and fear on my part because I love him very much. That special bond we had was being stretched, across 2000 miles, between two parents who were separating. There was a threat, maybe imaginary, maybe not, to that relationship. I felt I might not be able to see Donny if I didn't see my wife, too. That last part became difficult to accept because I was not in love. And because, that season, there was someone else in my life, someone else I cared about a great deal, Becky Giles.

Becky worked for United Airlines in Los Angeles.

I would run up to Los Angeles as often as I could, after games, on weekends to see Becky. Even though I was legally separated, I still felt guilty, so I kept the relationship in the background.

It all came to a head at the All-Star break. When Lem chose me to go to the game, my wife decided to be Mrs. Baylor again, at least publicly. She invited herself to Seattle to be with Donny and me. Becky had planned to go, too, but could not. She was extremely hurt and I realized the double life had to end.

How to end it was the tough decision. Taking that one last step took its toll. The pressures did not show in the box scores or when I was at the plate. But inside I wondered if I could go through that and play ball well all summer. Divorce scared me. I had watched Grichie go through a divorce in 1974. He was going to the plate and taking balls right down the middle of the plate. You could tell his mind was not there. I kept telling myself that I would not let it affect me. I would fight to stay locked into the game. It did affect me, though, in a strange, frightening way.

Every time I'd get near the park I would get severe migraines. No doubt they were stress-related because the only time they'd hit me was at the stadium. I would think about baseball there, but I would also think about divorce, about the pages and pages of documents, the community property statutes. It was too much of everything jammed in my head and I paid the price, every day.

By the time batting practice ended I would have such tremendous pressure and pain behind my eyes, the trainer would have to put ice towels across my face and behind the back of my neck. I'd lie on the training table and pray that the pounding would go away. I'd play through it, get in my car. Then, nothing. No migraine, no nothing.

That happened for five consecutive days before the All-Star Game. I took every type of pill imaginable, but I knew the pain was psychological in origin. The wrist was physical, something cortisone could cure. The doctors had no cure for what was going on in my head. You'd like to think you're immune, that you can't hurt emotionally. That summer I realized the easy part was on the field.

I could hit in the bottom of the ninth with two outs. I could stand in against anybody's fastball. I was finding it painfully difficult to stand up to the reality that my life was changing so drastically. Neither baseball nor the divorce was life and death. But what was happening off the field was not a game.

So I had to do something. The pretense had hurt too many people. Finally, I just signed all the documents needed to end the marriage. I had to let Becky know there would be no more hiding. Let her know it did not matter to me what people thought. It did not matter if people wanted to pass judgment on the broken marriage or on interracial dating. Becky is white. So what if some people had trouble with that? The most important thing is that Becky and I had no trouble with it, then or now.

That winter, when the All-Star teams toured Japan for a series of exhibitions, I took Becky. The closet door was open for good. Eventually I made her my wife.

After the 1979 All-Star Game, it was time to get back to the races for the pennant, and the MVP.

After I busted out in the first week of July, I never looked back. I hit 11 home runs in July, drove in a team-record 34 runs. I was grinding it out and, by the first week of August, was on the verge of that magical 100. We went into Oakland and one of the starters was Paul Mitchell, the pitcher I was traded with by the Orioles to the A's three years before. I did not dislike Paul, but something in me wanted that 100th RBI to come against him. I thought that would be poetic justice. I needed 3 RBI against Mitchell in the opener, though, and only managed to get 1. So I had to look to the next A's starter, Matt Keough.

I found the plateau when Keough threw me a curveball, which I hit for a 2-run home run. Three digits. One-zero-zero.

The only questions then were, Where to go from there and would reaching 100 be good enough? The answer was maybe not. If Pete Rose was impressed with my numbers, I was also impressed by the numbers being posted by Ken Singleton of the Orioles and Jim Rice and Fred Lynn of the Red Sox. We were all in the same neighborhood at the break, with Freddy about 15 RBI behind me. Then he went into Detroit one afternoon and drove in 10 runs by hitting 3 home runs and a triple. Ten RBI, just like that. I couldn't believe it. After holding the RBI lead practically all season, I started hearing footsteps. Singleton, a switch-hitter, was coming at me from both sides of the plate. I needed a big game. I got it on August 25 in Toronto's Exhibition Stadium.

That day, on a whim, I passed up batting practice. I was running sprints with Nolan when I told him I just didn't feel like taking BP. Toronto left-hander Balor Moore came out throwing at about 90, 91. Then he tried to come in with a fastball and missed. I turned on the ball and hit it for a first-inning grand slam. It was as hard and as far as I can ever remember hitting a ball in that park. It hit off the facing of the wall holding up the roof over the left-field bleachers. The seagulls up on the roof took flight to get out of the way. In my second at-bat that day I hit a 3-run home run, off right-hander Jackson Todd. In my third at-bat I hit an RBI double into the left-field corner. Three at-bats, 8 RBI. I was beginning to scare myself a little.

We romped and stomped. I wound up with 8 RBI in seven at-bats. That came about eight or nine days after Freddy Lynn dropped the ten-spot on me. He was probably thinking, *Oh, no, Groove dropped eight on me.*

Those were my last RBI for August, giving me 22. Twenty-one more would follow in September. My 139th, and last, RBI came in my 162nd game, on my 36th home run. I needed every digit because Singleton finished with 35 homers and 111 RBI, Lynn with 39 and 122, Rice with 39 and 130.

It had been a dream season. I led the league with 120 runs, hit .296, and counted 33 doubles among my 186 hits. I played all but one inning. I had started with 5 RBI in my first 4 games and never looked back. Jim Fregosi started me in left field ninety-seven times, once at first base and only sixty-five times as DH, a vote of confidence in my fielding I never overlooked nor will I ever forget. Even if it was only important to me, I felt I disproved a label I'd always considered a backhanded compliment—that Don Baylor was the best half-player in the major leagues.

I had won over the critics—those in uniform, the stands, and the press boxes. No longer did anyone question whether the $1.6 million had gone to waste. In an era of $800,000-a-year salaries, I made $160,000 in 1979. Suddenly Don Baylor had become the biggest bargain in baseball.

The fans, especially, responded and their warmth and affection erased all the hurt left over from 1977. There was a special kinship, a kind of mutual understanding that we all had persevered and the payoff was at hand. All that summer, one fan often displayed a three-foot banner in left field. Written in big white, block letters on a navy-blue background was one word—"GROOVE." Every time I saw the sign, I'd wave to the fan, whose name I never knew. I never got to thank him. But I noticed and remember, still, because it is the only sign a fan ever made for me.

Setting goals, then attaining them, had given me tremendous satisfaction. I had put together MVP numbers. By September, though, there was a more important race to think about—the pennant race.

For the first time I really felt the Angels were ready to win.

We had a lot of self-starters, like Nolan, shortstop Dickie Thon, Grichie, Rod Carew. We had a lot of strong personalities, a lot of guys who were leaders. But, for the first time in my career, I did not feel overshadowed by anyone. I felt I could step out front and I did.

20

STEPPING OUT FRONT

THE California Angels clubhouse was not mine, alone. But, in 1979, I felt a strength there I'd never known before.

That feeling might never have occurred if I had depended on things like salary scale. I had been a headline for all of one day when Rudi signed. Then came Grich, Bostock, Carew, and, in the seasons after 1979, Freddy Lynn and last, but certain never least, Reggie.

My first inclination, in 1977, was to not step out front. If I did, I figured, the longtime Angels, like Nolan or Jerry Remy, might say I was full of crap and ignore the whole thing. Besides, 1977 was a horror show. I'd just struggled to keep my own sanity.

But by 1978, I felt comfortable enough to call a team meeting for the first time in my career. The Angels were in a pennant race and I felt I had put up numbers that gave me the right to assume a more prominent position. When I did I sensed I had everyone's attention and respect.

Sure, there were guys on that team making $450,000 a year and I was making $160,000. I had no official awards. But those things were not important to me. The bottom line was to come out of that clubhouse, come off the field every day like winners. That happened in 1978. It had never happened to the Angels before. They had always been the Red Sox of the West. Taking off in twenty-five different cabs. And, in Southern California, there were twenty-five different freeways to get them to twenty-five different beaches. There just was never anyone willing to pull them together.

Rudi had the heart to lead, but injuries were killing him and his will to fight back was slowly being drained. Carew was more a self-starter than a starter of other players. Nolan is a strong figure, but I always felt he purposely held back because he is a pitcher. Remy had been a force, a scrappy little guy, the team captain. But he was traded to Boston in 1978. No one seemed willing to replace him. So I did. No one ever said, "You're lying" or "You're out of line." If they had, I might have cleared the room. That's how sure I was that it was time.

After eight years in the majors, the expectations I had not only of myself, but of my teammates, suddenly seemed very clear. I'm the type that goes in hard at second. I expect the guy hitting behind me or ahead of me to do the same.

I knew what the standards were because I finally realized what being a leader is all about. He's not the guy with the loudest voice or the most press clippings. In Southern California, Dodgers bat boys get more ink than California Angels All-Stars. A leader isn't the kind of guy who goes around smiling when the team loses because he went 4–for–4. He isn't the kind to mope if he's 0–for–4 and the team wins. Instead, he pats guys on the back for playing well or consoles the guy who just might have had an even worse day than he did. In my mind, you lead by running out ground balls, by breaking up double plays, by being out there every day.

I felt I had earned the right to express myself along those lines. Still, timing and circumstance mean everything. I have never forced myself into a clubhouse if the manager did not want me there. When I sense there is a hesitancy, I pull back. That happened in Minnesota in 1987. I was there for six weeks and a complete stranger to Tom Kelly, a rookie manager who was a year younger than I. Kelly sent signals he had no intentions of calling on my leadership qualities. So I backed off. To do otherwise would defeat everything I believe in. The whole idea is to make it easier for the manager, not to go behind his back. I never wanted a manager to think I was after his job. As I got older I could see where a manager close to my age might fear that. I believe that's why Kelly kept his distance. But if I'm a player, I'm a player. I don't want any other job until the bat goes into the trophy case.

Fregosi understood that. In later years, so did Yogi Berra and John McNamara, Gene Mauch, too. Yogi and Mac asked me to start kangaroo courts in New York and Boston, respectively, to instill discipline. Gene never gagged me in his clubhouse. And it was just that. *His* clubhouse. I was no threat to him or anyone else who could not be threatened. But if it made Tom Kelly more comfortable that I sat at my locker, read my newspaper, kept my mouth shut, and DH'd against lefthanders, fine. And that's what I did.

In 1979, with Jim Fregosi's blessing, I pushed ahead. First, I had to make sure I was doing the things I demanded of everyone else. I had to hustle on and off the field, play from first pitch to last. I knew I could do that. I also knew that Jimmy knew. He never worried that I would pull up lame just to get a day off. He knew I would not come to the park hung over or burn myself out. I had one steady girl and I did not take her from bar to bar.

Jimmy also knew I expected to play every day. I told Jimmy in spring training he could take 162 lineup cards, mark "Baylor" on each one, and I'd be there for him. Jimmy rewarded that desire by not only putting me in there, but by batting me fourth. In my mind, the cleanup man, above all others, is in scoring position when he steps to the plate. He hits with a lot of men on base. He has to produce two-out hits, early and late. He cannot leave it up to someone else. That's the way I felt, both on and off the field. Fregosi never said I was wrong. Neither did Nolan, Grichie, Carew, nor Rudi. Their endorsements were good enough for me.

When I started to call meetings in 1978, guys knew it had to be serious. By 1979, I sensed I had the entire team. I don't know if I made anyone play any harder. But I believed that baseball was no longer just a four-hour-a-day job in Anaheim. When we walked on the field, we did so with confidence. Not arrogance. There was just more of a feeling that we could play with any team, if we played *as* a team. The majority of those meetings were to reinforce that feeling. Once I told the guys how the Orioles had gotten together in 1974 because some of the veterans were upset over a newspaper article about the team. It was just riddled with "I" and "me" references. It cannot be that way on a winning team.

Sometimes it's hard to throw that selfish part out. I also knew, from personal experience, that sometimes you have to swallow your pride, give up the field to a stronger arm if you believe that's what is best for the team.

The meetings were not about ridicule. If a player needed to be knocked into line, an open meeting wasn't the place to do it. The meetings had more to do with keeping twenty-five guys, including myself, on course.

Sometimes you have to do more than read a team's pulse. Sometimes you have to speed it up or slow it down. I never understood why veterans on the 1988 Orioles didn't call a meeting when they were in the process of losing a record 21 straight games at the start of the season. No one on the '74 Orioles would have let that slide go on without trying to do something. I truly believe that such inaction would never have occurred on any team for which I played. Not as long as I was able to walk, talk, and breathe. I can't say that the 1988 Orioles would have lost one less game if I had been there. I do know I would have tried to bring that team together, tried to turn the losing attitude around. I would have pointed out the mistakes, starting with my own. I probably would have thrown a chair, punched a wall, or taken a bat to a water cooler. something, anything to snap the lethargy. And I know one person who would have welcomed it. Because it must have killed Frank Robinson, the manager, there was no one like Frank Robinson, the player, on the 1988 Orioles.

I could lose it if a clubhouse needed to be cleared. The day about twenty reporters asked our pitcher, Chris Knapp, if he felt he choked after a brutal loss to the Royals in 1979, I exercised the unstated authority. "You, you and you, everybody, get the fuck out of here right now," I said, pointing to the reporters. I said to Knapp, "Go into the trainer's room. You don't have to answer these questions."

Knapp was like a lot of our pitchers. Unlike Nolan and Tanana, he was never going to win a Cy Young award. But he was trying his best and he and a lot of other guys with heart had us in first place. We needed Knapp. And he did not need negative thoughts planted by reporters.

As a player, you're more likely to know if a teammate's susceptible to words like "choke." You'll also know if there's dissent, if there's an "I-hate-the-manager" corner forming. There are some things coaches and managers are sometimes too distant from or distracted to realize.

The manager is too busy trying to put the best players out there. That doesn't mean others cannot pay the unhappy players some attention. Just as I recognize the "I-don't-care,-I'm-playing" section of the bench or the "I-want-to-play-so-I'll-cozy-up-to-the-manager" section, I recognize that far corner when I see it. I was born down there, because of Billy DeMars.

A lot of veterans don't realize it, but that is where you find a lot of Latin players, feeling a loneliness most of us will never understand. Luis Polonia, a real hard-working kid from the Dominican Republic, showed me he was dying to learn when we were teammates in Oakland in 1988. So we talked a lot of baseball. Halfway through the season Luis told me I was the first veteran to ever talk to him or to Stanley Javier, another kid from the Dominican. Luis said that in 1987, his rookie season, no one, coaches or teammates, really took time to explain anything to him in slow, deliberate English. Luis taught himself to speak English so he could play here. The fact that no one was willing to return his commitment is unforgivable.

I was once a scared kid, too. Every player was once. But some forget where they came from. To me, if a player recognizes that such a corner exists, but ignores it, that's worse than being a cancer on the team. It doesn't cost anything to put your arm around a kid and say, "You have a job to do and when you get a chance, just do it."

I know doing that sort of thing doesn't necessarily work for all veterans. That's okay. I have to do what makes me comfortable. Talking to Luis Polonia, becoming a player rep and later the American League rep in the Players Association, organizing chapel, forming "65 Roses" clubs, all make me comfortable.

I believe that's a major part of why the '79 season was most valuable to me, because I had helped make a difference off the field, too. The Angels and I had come of age together. My teammates realized that. The year before, we had all latched onto Lyman. In 1979, the Angels latched onto me.

21

ANGELS COME OF AGE

ROD Carew had a habit that became a dilemma for the 1979 California Angels.

Whenever Rodney batted with men on first and second in no-out situations, he bunted, gladly taking the infield hit or the sacrifice. Jim Fregosi wanted more from a lifetime .333 hitter, like a healthy cut and an occasional RBI.

It baffled Jimmy. Other people, too. Hitting coach Deron Johnson had one question to suit all situations—"What's the action here?" Pretty soon, he would ask me that each time Rodney bunted. "I don't know," I said. "But if he wants to leave them out there, I'll drive them in."

I thought the whole thing was kind of funny. I credited Rodney with getting me off to a good start in the RBI column that season because of his generosity. He would bunt, I'd get 2 RBI, and then he'd do it again. Along the way Rodney would get his 1–for–3. That's how you end up a lifetime .333 hitter. It wasn't exactly what most people envisioned in a number-three hitter, though.

It went that way for about a month or so. Then Jimmy moved Rodney to the top of the order in place of Brian Downing. That really ticked off Rodney. He and Fregosi had a cool relationship to begin with, supposedly because of a hard slide Rodney put on Bobby Knoop years before, which resulted in a pretty serious spiking. That same Bobby Knoop was California's third-base coach, and Jim Fregosi's best friend. Rumor always had it that Fregosi had put a $500 bounty on Rodney's head after the Knoop incident, which occurred in the early 1970s. Half a decade later, Rodney was playing for the guy. And Rodney, the 1978 league MVP, felt like he had been demoted by Fregosi, especially after Jimmy made a couple of statements that he moved Rodney to get him out of the way.

Rodney and Fregosi never pretended to be friends.

But the beauty of that relationship, of the whole team, was that everything worked. Jim didn't have many rules. He wanted us to show up at the park on time, stand on the top step of the dugout when the national anthem was played. And play hard all the time. I never had any problems with those three things. Not many of the guys did.

There was never any doubt where Jim was coming from. And I felt that he, as much as any of the million-dollar free agents, was one of the last missing ingredients. I had learned a lot in the two previous seasons, grown up, and reshaped my expectations and beliefs. I had not realized it would take more than just one or two players to turn that around. Neither had the fans. They wanted to win in the worst way, too. And they were paying their money to see free agents with saddle bags filled with money do that winning. But we needed more than big names. We needed some continuity. And we needed to believe in the manager, in ourselves, in the organization.

I feel Jim Fregosi instilled that belief on all those levels. He knew how the frustrated veterans felt. He had been there through the doormat years and absolutely hated it. When you're a competitor losing is unacceptable, no matter how often it happens. You go home with it every day and every night and it just kills you. I knew right off that Jimmy wanted to change all that and it made me want to play even harder for him.

Jim Fregosi demanded dedication. And he battled from the start to assure every one of us gave that every day. He had hurt Rodney's feelings when he moved him up in the order, but he knew it had to be done. We all knew it. And Jimmy was not finished there.

After Rodney vacated the number-three spot, Jimmy gave it to another refugee from Minnesota, Danny Ford, who had been acquired the previous December for Danny Goodwin and Ron Jackson. (Yes, Buzzie made good on his promise and eventually traded Landreaux, too, but not until 1980.)

Danny Ford instantly became Fregosi's biggest project. Known as "Disco

Dan," even the nickname spoke volumes about Danny Ford's personality. Disco had a lot of talent, but he made most managers crazy. It seemed that only Gene Mauch, his manager in Minnesota, knew the right amount of stroking and thumping it took to get Danny to play consistently. Deserved or not, Disco had the reputation of being a hot dog and a dog at the same time. He'd shown that the year before when he cost the Twins a home run because of his antics. He was running from first when Jose Morales hit a home run. There had been a man on second, so Danny ran real slow. By the time he got to third, Disco decided he would turn around and face the guy running behind him. Well, Morales passed Danny and lost his home run. Instead of the tying run scoring, the Twins were still behind. They eventually lost.

Jimmy knew all about Disco Danny Ford. And he wanted to keep that guy in check. Fregosi wasn't a drill instructor. He went out of his way to make things loose and fun. He also let us know, in no uncertain terms, that we were going to get our work in, and on time. When Fregosi said practice began at ten, he meant ten. That was tough for Disco because he was used to coming in on his own schedule, on his own spaceship. Jimmy understood, sort of. He had just retired as a player, was still young and rebellious himself. But Jimmy also knew he had to rule the clubhouse or lose it. So he rode Danny. And Danny responded. He got there on time, even if he had to arrive on the fly, buttoning his pants, buckling his belt, tucking in his uniform.

Both Danny and Carew got me going a couple of times because they brought Twins baseball with them and it started clashing with Orioles baseball, Oakland A's baseball, and all the other styles piling up in Mr. Autry's menagerie. Twins, it seems, were taught to fake stealing bases. Lyman had done it the year before. Bluff, bluff, bluff. Now there were two of them out there, bouncing around, but not going anywhere. When I hit, I am never surprised to see a guy running; that movement didn't distract me. But, for some reason, I was distracted when the ex-Twins didn't run.

I started taking pitches every time they'd bluff. Good pitches. My reasoning was that I would rather drive in a man from second base than from first or third rather than second. But those guys wouldn't run. Disco pulled that one day on second and I took a breaking pitch because he broke into the visual plane where I usually picked up the ball. It was a strike. After the inning I pulled Disco aside and said, "That's it. When you're on second, stay right there. Don't move. I will drive you in. Tell Rodney, too."

Danny thought it was funny. He was having a blast. When he moved into the number-three spot he took off, hitting home runs, dropping in

The 1966 Stephen F. Austin High School Baseball team, Austin, Texas. I'm fifth from the left, back row. Coach Frank Seale is at far right.

Austin's young outfielder getting ready to hit.

Hitting for Rochester in 1970, when I was Co-Minor League Player of the Year. (ROCHESTER DEMOCRAT AND CHRONICLE)

Three prospects on the Rochester Red Wings: Roger Freed, myself, and Bobby Grich. (ROCHESTER DEMOCRAT AND CHRONICLE)

Baby Birds: I'm flanked by Roric Harrison (left) and my friend Bobby Grich. (BALTIMORE ORIOLES)

Frank Robinson, my model as a young player on the Orioles. (BALTIMORE ORIOLES)

Orioles' Hall-of-Famer Brooks Robinson scores behind me. (BALTIMORE ORIOLES)

Sharing a laugh with Frank Robinson, then the San Francisco Giants manager, in 1982. (SUSAN RAGAN)

Two examples of aggression: controlled, on a hard slide to the plate . . . (JOE BARNET/VISUAL IMAGES)

. . . and uncontrolled, in a brawl after Cleveland pitcher John Denny threw at a batter. Denny is on the bottom of the pile; Juan Beniquez got to him first, and I'm second from the bottom. (SUSAN RAGAN)

Meeting President Richard Nixon in 1979; Angels' owner Gene Autry looks on. (CALIFORNIA ANGELS)

The California Angels fielded four American League Most Valuable Players: Fred Lynn, myself, Reggie Jackson, and Rod Carew. (CALIFORNIA ANGELS)

Angels' All-Stars in 1979: Brian Downing, Nolan Ryan, myself, Mark Clear, Rod Carew, and Bobby Grich. (CALIFORNIA ANGELS)

Following through on a home-run cut. (CALIFORNIA ANGELS)

Taking a lead off first base with the New York Yankees. (SUSAN RAGAN)

A grand slam: being greeted at the plate by fellow Yankees Butch Wynegar, Don Mattingly, and Dave Winfield.

Some good friends on the Yankees that have lasted: Dave Winfield...
(SUSAN GRAYSON)

Ken Griffey...(ARLENE SCHULMAN)

and the Niekro brothers, Phil and Joe.
(NEW YORK YANKEES)

In the Boston Red Sox
dugout with close friend
Dwight Evans (center).

Preparing to hit with the
Red Sox...

And doing it: a grand slam over the Green Monster at Fenway in April
1986.

Meeting President Ronald Reagan with Boston's ace, Roger Clemens. (OFFICIAL WHITE HOUSE PHOTOGRAPH)

Out at the plate: a close call with the Minnesota Twins in the 1987 World Series against the St. Louis Cardinals. (MINNESOTA TWINS)

Enjoying the Twins' victory parade with my wife, Rebecca.

Celebrating my first World Championship: on the field with my son Don, Jr., (right of center), Joe Niekro, Tim Laudner, Kirby Puckett, Jeff Reardon, Al Newman, and Tom Nieto.
(MINNESOTA TWINS)

Family and friends:
with my son Don, Jr.,
and my father George
Baylor.

With my mother, Lillian Baylor, and my sister Connie.

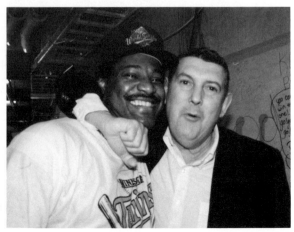

Celebrating with my
high school baseball
coach and friend,
Frank Seale, after the
1987 World Series.

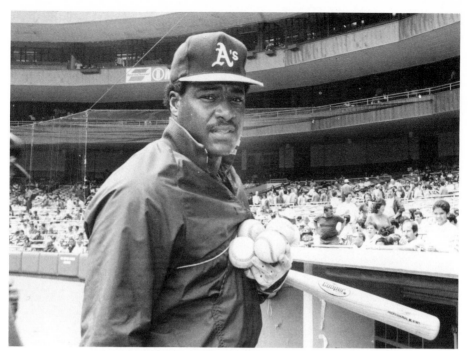

After batting practice with the Oakland Athletics. (SUSAN GRAYSON)

The A's sluggers: Dave Parker, Jose Canseco, Mark McGwire, and Don Baylor. (MICHAEL ZAGARIS)

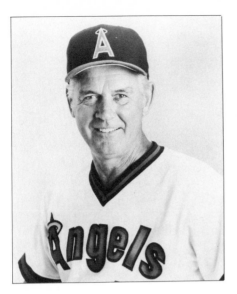

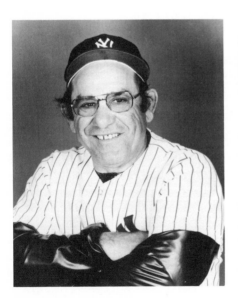

A few of the managers I've played for: (*Clockwise from top left*) Gene Mauch (CALIFORNIA ANGELS), Earl Weaver (BALTIMORE ORIOLES), Billy Martin, and Yogi Berra (BOTH NEW YORK YANKEES).

some big hits. He wound up with 101 RBI. That gave the Angels 240 RBI from the numbers three and four spots alone.

Even though Rodney sulked a bit, he still hit .318. And though he might not have been the terror Fregosi wanted, Rodney was still the most consistent hitter I've ever seen, more so than three other great ones I have played alongside; Wade Boggs, Don Mattingly, and Kirby Puckett.

Rodney showed me why he was special from day one. Mattingly takes off in July, other guys in May or June. Rodney was ready for the season by the exhibition opener in the first week of March. After just two weeks he didn't have anywhere else to go. He was maxed out, getting 2, 3 hits every day while the rest of us were just trying to get two or three good swings.

Left-handed pitchers could make Rodney look bad on breaking balls. But nasty left-handers, like Ted Higuera or Mark Langston, can tie up Boggs or Mattingly, too. One thing Rodney could do that maybe only Boggs can equal is wait and wait on a pitch and then flick it foul. Carew could hit the "bastard pitches," but, more importantly, he could foul those balls off until the pitcher had to throw Rodney's pitch. Then, forget it. Base hit.

Carew was also in a class by himself as a bunter. I don't care if the infielders were right on top of him, Rodney would still drop a bunt so softly you'd swear he rolled the ball out there and then ordered it to stop.

Rodney once did something I never saw before or have seen since. He was batting against our club in 1977 with Twins runners on second and third. Since Rod was batting about .410 at the time, an intentional walk was ordered. With the count 3–0, Carew swung at ball four and fouled it off. Then he did the same thing on the next "ball four," daring our pitchers to throw strikes. Finally, he accepted the walk.

It was awesome. So was Rodney in 1977, when he hit .388 and won the MVP.

He was not the MVP in 1979, but he was still Carew, still dangerous. He and Lansford sat atop our lineup and scored 192 runs collectively.

Rudi hit fifth until injuries took him out for good. Downing, a strong, young catcher who would eventually become the Angels' all-time home-run leader, moved up to fifth and wound up with 75 RBI. Grichie, our number-eight hitter, drove in 101 runs and hit 30 home runs. We scared pitchers to death.

It was not just a four- or five-man offense, either. To win, you need depth. The greatest example of that depth came when Rodney went down with a hand injury. Willie Mays Aikens took over first base and contributed immensely.

Willie fascinated us. He was bilingual and could speak Spanish fluently. He could not speak English fluently, however, even though it is his native tongue. Willie stuttered when he spoke his own language. Willie wasn't shy about it. He liked to speak out at team meetings and tried mightily. He did so once and tried to explain what the younger players saw as their roles. At least I think that's what he was going to say. But he got nervous and started stammering badly. I felt bad for him, but didn't know what to say. Grichie did, though. He jumped up and said, "Time out. Time out. Write it down, Willie. We don't have all day."

Everybody cracked up, including Willie. That's when I told him he should be a quarterback because of all the linemen he could draw offsides on fourth-and-one. He laughed again. And he fought that stutter. He knew TV guys avoided him. He wasn't comfortable with them, either. But one day he went on the air, live. He was proud of himself, afterward, telling me he used thirty minutes of air time to do a thirty-second spot. He was a good kid. Maybe it was all too hard, though. Maybe that's why, years later, Willie got caught in that drug scandal in Kansas City, which cost him jail time and, I believe, his career. That was a real shame, a worse affliction than any speech impediment. But, in 1979, Willie hit 21 home runs and drove in 81 runs in just 116 games.

Our lineup produced runs early and late. Big first innings were not uncommon. Unfortunately, we knew we might give up 2 or 3, too. Our pitchers compiled a 4.34 ERA, alarming for a contender. But we scored 866 runs, the most by a team in fifteen years. The fact that I led the league in both RBI and runs scored was indicative of just how much we pounded the ball.

Right before the 1979 All-Star break we were playing the Yankees, still the team for all contenders to measure themselves against. More than 43,000 fans, suddenly fervent believers, turned out for each of the three games. That was as full as the Big A could get until the stadium was expanded in 1985.

That Friday night game, on July 13, belonged to Nolan. It was being broadcast back East, so it had to start at five-twenty P.M., Pacific Coast Time. I would not have wanted to face Nolan, at sunset, not with his throwing out of the shadows at about 150 miles per hour. Sure enough, Nolan pitched a thing of beauty. Mickey Rivers, Thurman Munson, Willie Randolph, Jim Spencer, Bucky Dent, Chris Chambliss, they were all overmatched. It was no contest.

Nolan had a no-hitter going into the eighth. Spencer hit a ball to Rick Miller in centerfield, a knee-high line drive. Rick tried to make a diving catch, but failed. The ball hit off the heel of his glove for an error. From the fans' reaction, I didn't know if we were in Anaheim or Yankee Stadium. I figured there must have been a lot of transplanted New Yorkers in that crowd. Anyway, the fans were booing and looking up into the press box, where the official scorer was sitting. What they did not know was that Nolan had an incentive clause in his contract for no-hitters.

Dick Miller, a writer for the *Los Angeles Herald Examiner,* was the official scorer. Not only did he have 43,000 fans on him, but Buzzie came over and started haranguing him, too.

Down on the field, Munson and Reggie kept the fans going by standing on the top step of the visitor's dugout waving a towel at Miller. Reggie was shouting, "That's a hit! That's a hit!"

In the ninth inning, Reggie led off and hit a clean single back through the middle, right between Nolan Ryan's legs. If it had been Jim Palmer or Tanana or Mike Boddicker on the mound, the ball would have been fielded, but still, that was a hit. Reggie was running to first base, looking up at the press box and pointing to Miller, and shouting, *"That's* a hit!"

It was crazy and it was fun. A near no-hitter. Home runs. Great pitching. And, most of all, a pennant race. That may have been old hat to the Yankees, but not the Angels. This time the first-place berth in question was not in the American League East, but the American League West. This time it was the Angels who were holding onto first place as they entered the last weekend of the first half with a 1-game lead over the Rangers. The Yankees were floundering. They had lost Goose Gossage, their heart and number-one stopper, in April. He had ripped his thumb while horsing around with Cliff Johnson. Their "wrestling match" cost New York a division. But that July, there was still a magic about the Yankees. It made the series electric. Nolan didn't get his no-hitter, instead settling for a 1-hit, 9-strikeout gem and a 6–1 victory.

Suddenly, the California Angels could not wait to get to the ballpark. Not only were we confident, we were a little cocky. We were a few days away from sending six players to the All-Star Game, we were holding back the Royals. And we wanted the Yankees real bad. No more surfboards, no more swimming trunks. Finally, baseball was the only thing.

In the second game of that series, Yankees left-hander Tommy John had us down, 6–0, going into the sixth inning. With the All-Star break coming up, Lem decided to get some work in for Gossage, who had just come off the disabled list two days before. So they brought him into the game in the sixth when John got into trouble. By the time Gossage got out of the sixth the Yankeess' lead was cut to 4. By the time Gossage got out of the eighth the Yankees' lead was 2. He had served up home runs to me and to Rudi, back-to-back. The Yankees got 1 run back in the top of the ninth; still, the fans were going wild. A Southern California crowd actually stayed to see the end of a game, stayed to see Gossage take on the Angels one more time.

Goose was seething. There was no one like Goose when he got that angry. No one scowled the way he did. No one's Fu Manchu mustache looked as menacing. His eyes were barely visible, he pulled his hat so low. By the ninth inning. Goose was psyched out of his mind. You could almost hear him growling as he blew away the first two batters. It seemed like the distance between the mound and home plate was getting shorter and shorter, Goose was throwing that hard. Nobody wanted to hit off the guy when he was in a good mood. And Goose wasn't in a good mood at that moment.

He got Carney Lansford down to one strike, then Carney punched through a single. Then Disco Danny Ford reached, putting it on me again. Gossage was really fuming. I know he must have looked at me and thought, *There's that SOB who began my troubles in the first place.* And even though I had hit a home run off the guy, I had to fight the urge to tiptoe back in there because Goose has been known to throw a couple on the screen to let you know what he thinks of you and your livelihood. So I stepped in thinking, *Get on the back line and give yourself as much room, as much time, as you can.* My thinking was pretty basic after that. First ball, fastball. Because Goose was going to try to blow me away.

To this day I could not tell you if the first pitch he threw was high, low, inside or outside. All I know is that it was in my zone. And when I hit it I knew I got it good. The ball stayed on a straight line headed right for the foul pole. It hit about three-quarters of the way up.

Three-run home run. Game tied.

The whole place went crazy. It was as if the Angels had won the seventh game of the World Series. I mean, it was awesome, one of the greatest feelings I've ever experienced in my career, one of the most memorable home runs I've ever hit. It was show time and it had come right on time. I had taken their best and I turned it around, with a mammoth home run.

Gossage was gone. Ron Davis came in on a day he figured he had off. The stopper had not stopped us, so Gossage's setup man had to try. Davis could not, eventually losing when Merv Rettenmund doubled in the winning run in the twelfth inning.

The Angels were one game away from a sweep, one victory away from carrying a lead into the All-Star break. All we had to do was beat Guidry. He was no longer a 25–3 pitcher, but he was still brilliant. That bright Sunday in Anaheim, Guidry did not exactly shut us down, but the only guy who hit him was Grich, who had doubled in a couple runs and drove in a third. By the bottom of the ninth it was Yankees 4, Grichie 3. Guidry got two outs and, with one on, faced Bobby again. Grichie hit a ball to right-center field. During the day the ball travels a lot better than it does at night because of a little jet stream that could carry it about ten feet farther.

Grichie's power wasn't to right-center. But when he hit that ball, it rode that jet stream right over the fence. Two-run home run. Game, set, match to the Angels.

There it was, the sweep of the great Yankees. I've been in five playoffs and three World Series since that weekend. But, without a doubt, those three games were the most thrilling I've played in.

It took more than just runs and brilliant performances by Nolan Ryan to win. It took a special mix. And we had that. Jim remained pretty sensitive to everyone, molded all the different attitudes into a real cohesive unit. The 1979 Angels were as close a team as I'd played with since the 1974 Orioles. And we had finally learned to win the big games. If we had lost the third game to the Yankees, the Rangers could have pulled into a first-place tie with us in the American League West. Instead, they lost on the last day before the All-Star break, giving the Angels a 2-game lead going into the second half. After that, there was really no stopping us, a message the speakers blasted every day at Anaheim Stadium. The 1979 Pirates had "We are Faam-a-lee" by Sister Sledge played every day at Three Rivers Stadium to celebrate their march to the National League East championship. The '79 Angels had "Ain't No Stopping Us, Now," by McFadden & Whitehead, a Top-Forty rhythm-and-blues single.

Every time the song boomed out, I listened, especially to the first two lines, "Ain't no stopping us, now. We're in the groove." And we were—I was—all through that very special summer.

By season's end, the Angels had 88 victories, a 3-game margin over the Royals, and, for the first time ever, an American League West title.

22

BROKEN BONES, BROKEN DREAMS

IF the Texas Rangers, instead of the Kansas City Royals, had finished second to the Angels in the American League West in 1979, then Jim Barr would not have taken a swing at a plastic toilet seat marked "A Royal Flush" in a local watering hole. He would not have broken the little finger on his pitching hand. The Angels would not have been pitching-short going into the 1979 American League Championship Series when good pitching had been sparse to begin with.

That one ominous sign was obscured for a while by the good times, the incredible joy of winning the division. The good memories, like snapshots, still seemed so fresh.

- Frank Tanana covering first base to make the last out of our division-clinching victory over the Texas Rangers.
- Tanana, our league's answer to Sandy Koufax for so long until his

arm gave out, winning on guts and guile all that year, leaping straight in the air to begin the celebration. Frank quickly engulfed by the fans who flooded the field, the first-non-Dodgers victory celebration ever for Southern California.

- Gene Autry, soaked with champagne in the Angels clubhouse, his years of patient waiting finally over.

- President Nixon, one of the biggest baseball fans in the area, inviting the entire team to his compound in nearby San Clemente to salute Gene Autry's triumph.

- My carefully wrapping up a Seiko clock modeled after my Player of the Month gift from the league. I wanted to present it to President Nixon for all the kindness and consideration he'd shown me during my days in Anaheim.

- The Secret Service not-so-carefully unwrapping that package at the gate. The package wasn't even ticking since batteries were not included, but I thought they might dismantle the clock. Fortunately, they only dismantled the package.

- Going through the receiving line and handing the President and Mrs. Nixon that jumbled mass and saying, somewhat sheepishly, "It really did look nice."

It had. But that didn't mean a thing once it was all unraveled. I guess it was a sign of things to come.

The Angels, too, having looked so good all season, unraveled. It should not all be laid on Jim Barr. He could not win a pennant for us on his own. That real toilet seat, which Barr thought was made of papier-mâché, did not pitch an inning or go hitless in the postseason. But the accident was a bad sign. As it turned out, our pennant hopes were made of papier-mâché.

We went against the still-strong, very experienced Orioles in the playoffs with a very young staff, with the exception of Nolan.

Nolan pitched well enough to keep us in Game One against my old friend, Jim Palmer. We went into the tenth tied at 3—all. John Montague, who had relieved Nolan in the eighth, got into trouble in the bottom of the tenth, putting two men on. He needed one out, got to 0—2 against John Lowenstein, who was reduced to pinch-hitting because of a sprained ankle. Montague threw a forkball, a pitch that soon would be called the split-fingered fastball, the rage of the eighties. Montague's pitch didn't do anything. It just hung there. And Brother Lo, swinging on one good leg, sliced an opposite-field home run just inside the left-field foul pole. It was vintage Orioles. Winning with pitching, defense, and a 3-run home run that went over the 309-sign, or "three-oh-ten," as the Orioles used to say of their favorite home-run alley in Memorial Stadium.

The next night, we scored once in the first inning, then watched as the Orioles scored 9 by the fourth inning. We started back against Mike Flanagan as Danny Ford hit his second home run in two games. My RBI single off Don Stanhouse in the eighth made it 9–5; a sacrifice fly that same inning made it interesting. Stanhouse, the Orioles' stopper, was called "Full Pack" because of all the cigarettes Earl would puff watching him dance in and out of trouble. Earl probably went through five packs in the ninth. Stanhouse issued a walk, then a pinch-hit double to Willie Davis, a former Dodger trying to avenge LA's loss to Baltimore in the '66 World Series. A grounder and a single by Lansford made it 9–8. Ford singled with two outs and we wound up with runners on second and third. Earl gambled, ordering Stanhouse to load the bases by intentionally walking me. Earl won. Brian Downing grounded out to end the game.

We were down 0–2 in a best-of-five series, making for a long flight to Anaheim. The Angels' traveling party, including Mr. Autry, the front office, broadcasters and writers, were scattered around the chartered airliner. Most of the players were at the rear of the plane when a commotion broke out up front.

I was sitting three-quarters of the way back on the stretch DC-8 when I heard yelling. Don Drysdale and Fregosi were going at it.

Drysdale, the six-foot-six ex-Dodger, was then an Angels broadcaster. "Big D" had been one of the most intimidating pitchers of his time. You could have cut off his right hand and he still would have tried to pitch with his left. Don was a competitor. Staring at our shambles of a staff, Big D did not hold the same opinion of Jim Barr. Barr had won 10 games that season, saved 5 others. He wasn't Cy Young, but he just might have helped prevent the fiasco in Memorial Stadium. Drysdale thought so. So there he was, right in Jimmy's face, screaming that Barr was gutless because he wouldn't pitch.

Fregosi started to defend Barr and push Drysdale. By the time I got to the front they were rolling in the aisle. Jimmy was on top of Drysdale and had him by the throat. Bobby Knoop and I grabbed Jimmy. It took everything we had to pull them apart. Drysdale jumped up and started criticizing Barr again. Fregosi was going crazy trying to get past Knoop and me.

That's when Buzzie took over. "Don, go sit in your seat and stay there," he yelled at Drysdale, like a teacher sending an unruly student to the corner. Darned if Drysdale didn't sit down.

I knew Drysdale was depressed, like a lot of people on that plane. I also knew why he is a Hall of Famer. I'd just witnessed the pride and the toughness. He couldn't understand Barr. At that moment, looking at the competitor in Drysdale, I could not understand Barr, either. Barr should have wanted to go out there even if the bone was showing. He had an opportunity to get to the next level, the World Series. Under any other circumstance, Lowenstein would have been his guy to face. But Barr hadn't asked for the ball. And Fregosi had not asked him to take it.

Game Three could have been the first and last playoff game seen by Angels fans. Dennis Martinez held us to 7 hits and 2 runs in the first eight innings, one coming on my home run. Frank Tanana had allowed Baltimore 2 runs in five innings before giving way to Don Aase, who allowed a third Orioles run. We were down to our final two outs when Rodney doubled. Earl turned to Stanhouse for the third time in three games. "Full Pack" walked Downing. Grichie then lined to center. The crowd went wild, even though we all knew it was an easy out. But it was not. Bumbry could not hear the crack of the bat, but broke back because he was thinking a big, strong guy would drive the ball. Grichie had hit a chip shot. By the time Bumbry realized he was playing too deep, it was too late. He could not recover in time. The ball dropped in and the game was tied. Larry Harlow, who was playing left in place of the injured Rudi, ended an 0–for–7 slump by looping a game-winning double down the left-field line. We didn't beat the heck out of them, but we beat them.

It just delayed the inevitable because "The Magician"—Scott McGregor—awaited us in Game Four. We hit Scottie hard. Bullets were flying everywhere, except out of range of Scottie's fielders. Houdini was playing on the Orioles that day. We went into the fifth trailing, 3–0. That's when the pennant was lost. We had loaded the bases with one out and it seemed Scottie had run out of magic. Shortstop Jim Anderson stepped in as more than 43,000 fans went crazy. Anderson turned on McGregor's second pitch and hit a vicious one-hopper down the left-field line. There was no way that ball should have been caught. But Doug DeCinces, diving to his right, stopped it, scrambled to third ahead of the runner, then threw on to first for the double play. Later, Belanger told reporters he had seen that same play hundreds of times, but by a different third baseman. So had I. Brooks must have been proud.

After that, the Orioles might as well have thrown a McGregor glove out there, that's how easily we went, losing, 8–0, as Scottie completed a six-hitter.

As the last out was made I sat and watched the American League champion Orioles mob McGregor on the mound. I envied and admired my old friends. I knew the Orioles were good; so were we. But pennant winners are more than good. They are ready to win. The '79 Angels still were not there. Most painful of all, I realized I was not. I had just 3 hits in 16 at-bats, only 2 RBI.

Everything I had trained for, had accomplished, felt like it had just been wiped off the face of the earth. One hundred and thirty-nine RBI and 36 home runs—so what? From that point on, it's, "What did you do in the playoffs?" And I had hit .180 or something ridiculous like that. I know one player cannot carry a whole team. But the Angels had counted on me all season to get the big hit, to drive in the big run, to send a pitcher's best pitch off the foul pole or out of the park. That stopped when the regular season stopped. And the Angels stopped with me.

So, as I sat there, I didn't want to know about All-Star games in Japan, MVP votes, Player of the Year awards. All I wanted to know was how you crack this World Series thing. How do you get there? I still did not know. There was still something missing.

The pain soon wore away. And, in time, the good memories slowly overtook the bad. Nineteen seventy-nine had begun with tremendous commitment, which paid off in a division title. There was still more to come.

On November 19, I flew all day and night from Japan to Los Angeles after completing the tour with the major-league All-Stars. Ken Singleton was on that flight, too. We kidded each other about our MVP hopes, wondered why it was our misfortune to choose the same season in which to have career years. The winner was on that plane, neither of us doubted that.

The next morning I awoke at six A.M. I had to catch a flight to Austin. It was Donny's birthday and I promised him I would be there to help him celebrate. I knew the award already had been announced in New York, so as I drove to the airport I was fiddling with the radio trying to learn who'd won. I found one announcer who was talking about the award. All he was saying was "Ken Singleton" this, "Ken Singleton" that. So I switched to the Angels' flagship station, Gene Autry's KMPC. The disc jockey said he wanted to dedicate a song, "You Are My Special Angel," to Don Baylor because I had just been named the American League Most Valuable Player.

I almost drove my car off the road.

Members of the Baseball Writer's Association of America had voted me first on 20 of 28 possible ballots. Singleton, my closest competition, had received three first-place votes. For only the third time, a player from the American League West had won. For the first time it was a California Angel. I'd always known it took incredible credentials for a player west of Kansas City and south of Oakland to catch the eye of the national press. You have to convince the East Coast media you deserve consideration by throwing impressive numbers at them for an entire season. The writers had been convinced.

I knew the Angels wanted to set up press conferences, TV spots, the whole bit that day. But I had an appointment with a seven-year-old in Texas. I landed at the same little airport in Austin I had flown from in 1967. There were all kinds of media, TV cameras, politicians. The Baby Bird had come home an MVP.

The banquet circuit beckoned for the first time. Suddenly a player from Anaheim was wanted on every dais.

National League co-MVP Willie Stargell, AL Cy Young winner Mike Flanagan, and I were among the nominees for the Hitchcock Award and attended the banquet in Rochester, New York. This prestigious award is presented to the athlete of the year and the nominees are drawn from all sports. Frank Robinson was honored for his 1966 MVP season, winning the award when it used to be the Hitchcock Belt, a diamond- and ruby-studded treasure worth about $50,000. By 1979, cost dictated the Hitchcock Award be Steuben crystal, still a beautiful trophy to behold. As Mike, Stargell, and I watched, the Hitchcock was awarded to Scott Hamilton, the diminutive figure skater and Olympic Gold Medal winner.

Mike and Stargell and I just kept staring at each other in total disbelief. The home runs, the strikeouts, the RBI, all down the tubes. A five-foot-tall figure skater was the athlete of the year.

There were others to be won, though, including the *Sporting News* Player of the Year. In January came the big one, the presentation of the MVP at the banquet held by the New York chapter of the Baseball Writer's Association of America. To me, it was the big show. Broadway. Not Hollywood, not shuffling off to Buffalo. That banquet was the place to be and I was being honored by the most knowledgeable baseball writers in America.

I savored the MVP victory all winter, thought about the dedication that had led to such rewards. It was also a winter of hard work. I would reach for even higher goals, including the one that still eluded me, the World Series. It was back to the same training regimen.

At the end of March, the Angels' board of directors voted to give me a $50,000 bonus for winning the MVP. Buzzie also suggested that Jerry and I put into writing a formal request that the team reconsider its policy and give Bavasi the power to negotiate a contract extension.

But other things were changing. Nolan Ryan, who had been feuding with Buzzie over money for two years, played out his option and signed with Houston. There were 15 victories, 10, 12 strikeouts a game, gone. Buzzie said he could get two pitchers who could replace Nolan's victories for the same money Nolan wanted. Buzzie did not understand. They might equal the win total, but they could not replace the pitcher, the wear and tear he saved the bullpen, the fear he put in the opposition. He was the only pitcher in the majors capable of pitching a no-hitter any time he took the mound. I did not know it at the time, but Buzzie's tough stance would be repeated with me. The talk of a contract extension was just that. My relationship with Buzzie deteriorated from that point.

When Buzzie traded Aikens to Kansas City for Al Cowens, I thought we had traded away our only left-handed power. Little did I know that was the good news compared to what 1980 had in store for the Angels.

We lost Brian Downing after just 9 games when Rickey Henderson of the A's slid into him at home plate and broke Brian's ankle. Dan Ford was in and out of the lineup because of a sore right knee; he played only 65 games. Joe Rudi was again felled, this time by an Achilles' tendon injury.

In the first month of the 1980 season I checked by swing on a breaking pitch thrown by the Indians' Victor Cruz. The ball hit the knob of the bat, not me. Still, I felt as if someone had just shot a bullet into my left wrist. I played for a month or so thinking that the pain would go away, just like it had in '79. The pain stayed this time. It was confounding. X-rays were taken before games, after games, but the doctors could find nothing.

In a series in Anaheim that May, Aurelio Lopez—Detroit's "Señor Smoke"—threw a pitch I usually deposit in the seats—a pitch I make my living on, in spring training, July, anytime. I swung and my ring finger and pinkie flew off the bat handle. I could hardly hang onto the bat. The ball died on the warning track. The next day, Tigers pitcher Dave Tobik hit my left hand with a pitch; I fell and jammed the wrist. I couldn't sleep that night because of the throbbing. The next day I told Jimmy it was time to get a healthy body in there. I could no longer hold the bat, let alone grip it.

That evening I watched from the bench for the first time in 237 games. In my heart I knew I'd been absent for a long time before that game. I had not hit a home run in 1980, not in spring training, or in 92 regular-season at-bats. After 26 games I had just 12 RBI. I knew something was terribly wrong.

The team left for a road trip the next day. I did not go along. The latest cortisone shot had not helped, so I drove up to Orthopedic Hospital in Los Angeles to see Dr. Charles Ashworth, a renowned hand specialist. The X-ray method he used photographed from the top of my palm down through my wrist. My fingers had to be stretched back in order to fix the angle. I could not do that myself, the pain was so severe, so the nurses used elastic bands to tie my fingers back.

There was a fracture, big enough to drive a truck through, Dr. Ashworth said. A small bone called the hamate had had its tiny hook end severed off completely. The Angels' orthopedic surgeon, Dr. Lewis Yocum, said it was an injury that plagued power-hitters who roll their wrists while hitting. The severed portion of the bone had to be removed. Dr. Ashworth said I should go home and think it over. I knew if I left I would not come back. I checked into the hospital. Surgery was performed the next day.

Fregosi had lost Ford, Rudi, Downing, and me. The Angels plummeted in the standings. Jimmy tried to pull a lineup together, but he could not find a winning formula. Soon he was suffering from a severe stomach disorder. I watched helplessly and wondered if the team would break his heart or just give him ulcers.

I tried to offer moral support. But it's always been my belief that if you don't play you don't really have a right to speak out. How can I say, "Hey, we can hit this guy," if I'm no longer a part of the "we"? I stayed home when the team traveled. Jogging was out; the risk of infection caused by perspiration was too great, so I took long walks, usually listening to the games on a transistor radio. Once, at a home game, I sat in the stands because being in uniform only increased my helpless feeling. The Angels got into a brawl with the Rangers. I wanted to climb the railing to help. Not being out there killed me.

About the only thing that kept me sane was the constant reminder that life was a lot harsher for other people. I had a broken bone, that's all. I wish I could say the same for the kids I visited in the hospitals in my newfound free time that summer. They were my "65 Roses" kids who were afflicted with cystic fibrosis. I knew their fates. Right before I boarded the plane to go to Japan the previous fall, I had spent part of the day at Children's Hospital in Orange County with two gravely ill children suffering from CF. I missed my original flight, but I was glad I did. The little girl died before I returned to the United States. The little boy died soon after.

When I held onto other kids with CF that summer of '79, I did so with one good arm, one bad one. But the wrist would heal. It would not kill me.

Donny was with me the day the cast was removed. My wrist had atrophied in six weeks. The doctors prescribed hand-squeezing exercises with a nerf ball and, they warned, I was not to work with any weights over ten pounds. When we got to the park, Fregosi asked Donny what the doctors had said; he didn't trust me to tell him the truth. It did not matter what he thought or what the doctors had said. I exercised at night, lifting as much weight as the wrist could take. When the surgeons cut the wrist open on May 13, they said I would miss eight to ten weeks. I was back in the lineup by June 26.

The day I returned the Angels were in the cellar, 17 games out. They had lost 19 of 22. The bad old days were back. The Angels were a dead team just waiting to be beaten.

My second day back I called a players'-only meeting. This time I would not rule out the term "riot act."

I told my teammates I did not think the season was lost. If any of them felt differently, I advised them to go home and stop wasting our time. "I don't want to keep going out there with guys who are willing to be humiliated," I said.

In my mind, if we had to lose we could either do it with our tails between our legs or clinging to the other team's throats. If the effort was there, we had no reason to be ashamed. But we had to at least try.

The snap never did come back to my wrist that season. Then, late in September in a game in New York, I chased a ball hit by Bobby Brown into the left-field corner. The walls at Yankee Stadium are padded, but the covering stops about six inches from the ground. After that, it's pure concrete. When I crashed into the wall, the two largest toes on my right foot hit the concrete and broke. I limped after the ball and finally got it back into the infield by the time Brown reached third. I spent the rest of the night at NYU Medical Center with the rest of the Saturday-night crowd—victims of muggings, knifings, gun shots, overdoses. My only thoughts were, *Get me out of here!* By the next day I was out, on crutches and jetting back to California. The 1980 season was over for me. I had played only 90 games, hit only 5 home runs. I drove in 51 runs, 88 fewer than the year before.

The Angels lost 95 games that season and finished sixth, 31 games behind the first-place Royals. But there was a different feel in the second half. We still lost far too many games, but at least the Angels revived their enthusiasm. I swear we did.

23

MONEY TALKS, PLAYERS WALK

"WHAT'S Don doing in that picture with the two hitters?"

The words jumped off the page at me as I sat in a restaurant eating lunch on April 16, 1981.

Buzzie, joking around the day before, had made the statement when he saw a program cover featuring Rod Carew, Freddy Lynn, and me. Buzzie thought it was funny. John Hall, his one-man audience, must have thought it was newsworthy because he ran it in his column in the *Orange County Register* the very next day.

There was absolutely nothing funny about those words to me. The day they were printed I stormed into Buzzie's office. I told him if that's what he thought of me, then he must not want me on the team. So I retired. Quit. Went to the clubhouse, packed my belongings, and left.

An hour later, I was still fuming. Just to do something, I went to wash my car, but all I could think about was Buzzie and the relationship that had gone downhill so drastically that I stood there with a sponge in my hand actually thinking of ending my career.

It was going sour for many reasons, every one of them having to do with good faith.

Ever since I had won the MVP, the Angels talked about how valuable I was in their lineup, in the clubhouse. I had played through injuries in 1977 and 1979. The doctors figured the fracture in my left wrist that was discovered in 1980 probably was there through the second part of 1979.

I had watched in silence as the team acquired more and more free agents, Brian Downing and I used to joke that all that was between us and the bottom of the pile was minimum-wage rookies. There were Angels making two, three times what I made.

I made $160,000 in my MVP season and was to make the same amount in 1980. Jim Rice's salary for 1980 was $500,000, Dave Parker's $1 million, Pete Rose's $850,000, Mike Schmidt's $560,000. Lee Mazzilli, a third-year player for the Mets, stood to make $350,000. The Giants had just signed part-time infielder Rennie Stennett to a five-year, $2-million deal. The Cardinals were paying a singles-hitting shortstop, Garry Templeton, $600,000.

The structure of free agency had changed. It did so within twenty-four hours of my signing, when Rudi came in at a higher price. Then came Grichie, Lyman, Carew. But I never squawked. I never asked to renegotiate. To me, a deal is a deal. It was the Angels who suggested Jerry and I formally request the MVP bonus and the extension. They even changed the team's policy, which previously did not allow extensions, so that we could negotiate. That's when I thought that I could be brought up to the same level with other players in my category. In March 1980 I asked for a three-year extension at salaries of $800,000, $900,000, and $1 million. I also asked for an extension-signing bonus to be portioned out over the remaining years of the original contract so that I might come up to parity with hitters in my category.

I wanted to stay. I'd had my fill of moving. I loved the California lifestyle. But I knew what I wanted in the way of compensation, too. I wasn't going to back down from Buzzie or his reputation. And Buzzie had a reputation for being tough at the table, brutal with guys who were trying to get better contracts.

Ron Fairly used to tell how Buzzie, as general manager of the Dodgers, would insist he was among the highest-paid players on that team. Fairly found out later he wasn't in the top fifteen out of twenty-five.

When Nolan Ryan's son was hit by a car, Nolan returned to Anaheim, missing the final days of a road trip. The team requested he give his meal money back. And Buzzie set team policy.

Harry Dalton used to make sure Jimmy Reese had good tires and free oil service on his car because Jimmy commuted every day from his home in the Westwood section of Los Angeles. Jimmy was in his seventies, not under the jurisdiction of the players' pension fund. So Harry just did that one little something. That ended when Buzzie took over.

Even though Buzzie was a "baseball man," he seemed to be building all these love-hate relationships. He wanted to turn the clock back to the '50s and '60s. He didn't understand, could not accept the new financial realities of the game.

That's the personality I faced. I'm convinced to this day that if I'd had to deal with Harry or Mr. Autry I'd still be a California Angel. When you sign with a team, a guy like Harry has a lot to do with it. When he is pushed aside, the ballgame changes. And Harry had been pushed aside. I had to deal with Buzzie. And we were fine, until the broken wrist. That's when all talk of working out an extension ended.

By the end of the 1980 season, Buzzie was openly talking about not wanting to trade me. All the same he kept bringing up trades. The arrival of Jason Thompson, a first baseman with no position because of Carew, gave the Angels a ready replacement. My no-trade clauses had expired at the end of 1979 and the 10–5 veto rights belonging to all players would not apply until the end of the 1981 season.

I set a time limit. Throughout the second half of 1980, I stated that the longer it took, the higher the price to get my signature. When the stalemate continued into 1981, I had Jerry inform the Angels that if there was no extension by the end of that season, there would be no negotiations during the 1982 season. I had seen what that double duty had done to Nolan. I would not let a salary dispute interfere with my play.

That's when Buzzie and I came to a parting of the ways that would eventually lead me out of Anaheim.

By spring training of 1981, Buzzie was openly critical and sarcastic. He thought it was funny to ask reporters, "Who's going to play left field?" when he knew I was out there breaking my back trying to show Jimmy I could handle it.

Then, on April 1 of that season, Buzzie traded Jason Thompson to the Pirates for catcher Ed Ott, sealing my fate; I became the full-time DH. When reporters asked me about the deal, I answered that like all trades, it would have to be evaluated at the end of the season and that some of the team was disappointed at the loss of Thompson. "You never know about these things," I said.

Buzzie went crazy. He accused me of slamming new teammates. So he told reporters, "If Baylor could play left field, we wouldn't have had to trade Jason. We couldn't DH them both and Rod Carew is our first baseman . . . I don't care what players think. They're paid to play baseball, not discuss trades."

I was stunned. I didn't know what Buzzie wanted of me any longer. It was me he'd called when Lyman died. As the player rep, I was the one who Buzzie called upon to show the team's financial accounts to when the '81 strike hung over spring training. Buzzie had a way of stroking me in public, telling the media I was the only American Leaguer who played like a National Leaguer, like his beloved Dodgers. Then to slam me like that, I just could not understand.

The day Buzzie questioned my hitting ability I'd hit bottom, anyway. My left wrist still was not at full strength and, in a new scare, bones in my left hand and fingers were inexplicably causing excruciating pain.

So there was Buzzie, in all his wisdom and compassion, kicking me when I was down, when I was wondering if more bones were broken, when I was trying to play through more pain and survive a 2–for–27 start.

Maybe I was paranoid, but I think not. Before Buzzie's slam on April 16, Peter Gammons of the *Boston Globe* had written a column for *The Sporting News* criticizing Bavasi for making me "the whipping boy for the team's dismal flop of 1980." Gammons also ripped into Buzzie for renegotiating the contracts of Fred Lynn, Rick Burleson, and Butch Hobson, among others, while ignoring my requests for an extension. Ross Newhan for the *Los Angeles Times* quoted an anonymous teammate as saying, "Buzzie has shown a remarkable lack of sensitivity involving Don. His remarks have been as tasteless as his timing has been poor."

The only thing that drew me back to Anaheim Stadium after Buzzie's latest attack was a belief that I owed Jim Fregosi an explanation.

I went to see Jim in his office. For a half an hour, we talked about sensitivities and loyalty. It was an emotional meeting. I know Jimmy was shocked at my level of frustration. I did not want to leave baseball, but I did not know if the Angels wanted me anymore and the thought that 1979 had meant nothing shattered me. Jimmy said that what Buzzie said in newspapers meant nothing to him. He told me I *did* mean a lot to him, and to his team. He needed me and said that was all that should count. He asked me to put the uniform on for him—no one else but him.

I still was uncertain, so at first I sat in the weight room trying to collect my thoughts. That's when my teammates came in to ask me to return. One by one they came; Grichie, Carew, Danny Ford. Mike Witt, our pitcher that day, told reporters, "I need him. Maybe I could beg him to come back." And Mike did put in a heartfelt plea.

I felt horrible. I was reminded of how we all felt when Chris Knapp jumped the team for two weeks in the middle of the 1979 pennant race. That had left a bad taste in my mouth. In my heart, I knew I could not do the same thing.

Then Gene Mauch arrived. He was serving as a special consultant to the team at the time. Gene told me that "Little people do little things and big people do big things. You are not a little person."

I un-retired. I was still shaken, though, and Jimmy kept me out of the lineup and the press away. Buzzie must have figured he was in real danger of losing me because he called down to the visitor's clubhouse and asked Billy Martin, then the manager of the Athletics, to talk to me. Right before the game, Billy spotted me sitting on the railing in our dugout and sent a message asking me to meet him in the tunnel. I did. Billy was wearing his Oakland A's hat, and on the very tip he had a little crucifix. Out of respect for him and that crucifix, I listened. Billy told me to just keep playing baseball the way I knew how. He didn't tell me to make up with Buzzie, though. He told me to tell Buzzie to shove it and maybe I would be traded— to the A's.

Buzzie had friends all over baseball.

By the end of April, I was 4-for-65 with 2 RBI. The first RBI had come in the Angels' eighteenth game, on a home run, only my sixth since 1979. That same night I lined into a triple play, indicative of how the little bits of good in my life were easily obscured by the bad. My mechanics were completely screwed up because of my overcompensating for my injured wrist, bad habits by then a year old. I'd step in thinking about where my hands and feet were. Nothing was natural anymore.

But it started coming back, ever so slowly. By June 12, I think I had shown Buzzie and the critics. I was hitting .187, but I led the team with 33 RBI and 7 game-winners.

It was not enough to save Jimmy. By mid-May, Jimmy stopped shaving and looked haggard. Mr. Autry no longer came into the clubhouse to talk to his "favorite sons," which is what he called us. We knew Jimmy was gone if we didn't win, every day. Jimmy was no longer easygoing, but as tense as the team, waiting for his adopted "father" to fire him. When we fell to 22- 25, Mr. Autry did. Gene Mauch was named manager.

Thirteen days later, on June 12, the Major League Baseball Players Association went on strike.

It was a dark, dark day for baseball. As a member of the negotiating team, I knew the issues and the lengths the Association was willing to go in order to keep the owners from turning back the clock. The owners wanted to regain the control arbitrator Peter Seitz had taken away when he declared McNally and Messersmith free agents. The emancipated players liked the freedom, the new salary structure. The game was thriving. We did not see any reason to go back to the bad old days of complete restraint.

The sticking point was compensation. The owners wanted to water down free agency by attaching significant levels of direct compensation, such as plucking another player from the purchasing team's roster, thereby discouraging ventures into the market. Such concepts had killed free agency in other sports. The union, represented by Marvin Miller, viewed significant, direct compensation at such levels as an absolutely nonnegotiable issue.

The Association had taken similar stands on arbitration and the funding of the pension plan, insisting management continue to contribute one-third of its television revenues to the player fund. The owners capitulated on both issues before a proposed strike date in May 1980. The compensation debate was tabled at that time. When that lone issue could not be settled by June 1981 and the owners imposed direct compensation, the players responded by calling the strike.

To this day Bowie Kuhn says the players underestimated the owners' resolve. In my mind, the owners underestimated the players' resolve. The owners figured the players would miss one paycheck and come crawling back.

From day one, fans were incensed. Some tried to sue to have the games resumed. Players and management were denying them their right to their favorite entertainment. Well, it was our right to make a living, too. We weren't viewed as Hormel Meat plant workers or any other union with the basic right to strike. We were viewed as rich thieves stealing a part of the American heritage.

We *were* well paid. But we gambled that the 650 major leaguers, as a specially skilled group, could demand a fairer share of the millions the owners were reaping. You can't take someone out of a meat-packing plant or auto factory and put him against a Tom Seaver or a Steve Carlton. The owners knew that. They could not ask that of minor leaguers. The public would not stand for scab baseball. We felt our talents were such that it was worth the risk to protect the free market. That's why we were on strike. That's what every fan, who had the right to move from job to job, did not understand.

Ray Grebey was hired by the owners to negotiate. As a player representative who sat in on the negotiations throughout that summer, I got to see Grebey up close and personal. I can only speak for myself, but my dislike for Grebey was instant and complete.

Grebey was a labor gunslinger with a history of overseeing protracted strikes. Grebey had negotiated for General Electric in a long, bitter strike that lasted more than a year. Mark Belanger, a MLBPA pension representative, had a special dislike for Grebey. His mother was one of the strikers at GE.

From the start, Grebey looked upon Marvin, MLBPA general counsel Donald Fehr, and the players with absolute disdain. Everything he said dripped with sarcasm, arrogance. Grebey's tactics were so distasteful that Marvin refused to be photographed shaking hands with him when the strike finally ended. In contrast, when the two-day strike of 1985 was over, the negotiating parties shared a magnum of champagne, which I supplied. Donald Fehr insisted that the management negotiators, by then headed by former American League President Lee MacPhail, partake. There would have been no such offer if Grebey had still been associated with management.

I believe Grebey's presence in 1981 indicated owners felt overmatched by Miller. As the Association's executive director, Miller was a powerful, persuasive negotiator and labor leader. He was totally committed to making the Association the strongest in professional sports. Marvin was the moving force behind free agency, arbitration, and, subsequently, a stronger salary base. The owners may have hated these ideas, but there was always the sense they felt a grudging respect for Marvin.

Marvin treated players with the utmost respect, kept members a well-informed, viable force. He insisted that players be part of the talks, something Grebey detested. That made it possible for leaders to spread the word throughout the game. And those leaders were among the highest-paid players. When Reggie Jackson, Bob Boone, Doug DeCinces, Tom Seaver, Dan Quisenberry, Steve Rogers, Belanger, Phil and Joe Niekro, Phil Garner, Buck Martinez, and Don Baylor, among others, stepped out front, it made it easier for all the players to pull together. I believe the fact that baseball "superstars" have always been out front separates the MLBPA from the NFL Players Association, a union that has consistently struggled to make gains.

The owners had strike insurance, $50 million worth, courtesty of Lloyd's of London, to cover a period of forty-nine days. The speculation was that if the clubs actually collected the full amount, some franchises could actually make more money by not playing baseball.

The union had no insurance. So even before the owners' policy came to light, everyone had been warned that the strike could be long, ugly, and costly. Have interest in new investments? Put if off a year, the players were advised. Save money. Be wise.

We were also cautioned to take care of what we said. To show weakness could cost everyone money. I winced when Mike Schmidt was quoted as saying he could not afford to strike. Joe Jones, who had to get up at six o'clock in the morning to punch a clock, didn't want to hear that. We did not need those types of headlines.

Soon some of our fears became reality. Some guys wanted to settle quickly, though not on management's terms—the only terms available. But after about ten days, the owners' first dividend kicked in. Trench warfare had begun. Grebey stonewalled at every turn, looking for complete capitulation or else. Some guys had been working out, but the enthusiasm for that soon died. The union did not want the workouts anyway, partly out of fear players might injure themselves. The union also wanted management to know that the longer the strike lasted, the longer the parks would be closed even after a settlement, because players would have to work themselves back into shape (when the strike did end, it took about ten days before the season resumed).

Players started to scatter, heading to their winter homes or going on vacation. That caused many to lose their taste for union meetings.

Even though there were less than ten players who opposed the strike in a poll taken by Marvin the previous spring, grumbling grew louder. The dissent became public.

There was almost a settlement after the first month, but the owners read quotes attributed to Davey Lopes that the strike should be ended and that others, such as Jim Palmer and Reggie Smith, were having second thoughts. So management jerked the settlement off the table, believing the players were about to crumble. I heard that management negotiators were wagering as to the day we would capitulate.

Word got back to the membership of that fiasco. In one regional union meeting attended by players from teams all over California, shouting matches broke out in discussions about the Lopes quotes. Dissidents were told to keep their mouths shut because they could hurt the cause if the owners misinterpreted what they said. It took about two weeks to convince management that the players were not about to fold.

Then it came to light that some players were being paid because they had guaranteed contracts that did not make exceptions for strikes. There were about 10 players with such clauses, including Garvey, Pete Rose, and Tommy John.

Then there were the guys who were disabled and argued that technically they were not on strike because they were not playing because they were injured. Grichie was one of the disabled guys who wanted to be paid. He was out with a broken hand. Though Marvin and Donald Fehr had qualms about some players being paid while most were not, the union did push for payments to continue to the disabled and the players with the strike-proof contracts because the primary interest was in imposing as many additional costs on management during the strike as possible.

I can only speak for myself, but I was disappointed in all the players who took the money or tried to, through arbitration. I was sitting in an airplane seat, flying to New York and Chicago, trying to negotiate for the players. In my mind, the only thing those players were worried about was getting paid. I had a big problem with that. I felt the players had to stay together, period. Either you're a part of it or you are not. I respected Marvin and Donald and all the union stands for. Our opinions differed on that one issue. I feel the same way about Grichie. We are friends to this day, but our philosophies clashed on that one point.

When the fear increased that the entire year could be lost, some players stated they would sell their homes and move in with in-laws before they gave in. I was prepared to start selling off some of my holdings if the strike reached September or October. I had planned well enough, but alimony payments started coming out of my savings and I had to consider the worst-case scenario.

I spent most of the summer traveling to negotiating sessions or working out. For the first time since I was a high-school kid I had the Fourth of July off. All I wanted was to be in a ballpark that day instead of barbecuing at home with Donny.

The strike ended one day after the owners' insurance ran out. The owners settled for what they could have had several weeks before.

The players made small concessions on compenation, allowing teams that lost free agents in certain classifications to draft from a pool of unprotected players. One major player was affected, when the Mets left Tom Seaver unprotected and he was picked up by the White Sox. Other than that, the concession proved to be so minor that four years later, the owners conceded their "victory" meant nothing. During the negotiations of 1985 they voluntarily scrapped compensation at the professional level.

The players had preserved free agency and the direct result was significantly higher salaries, up from an average of $185,000 in 1981 to more than double that by 1985. We had won. But, in the end, so much was lost by baseball as a whole. Seven hundred and thirteen games were permanently wiped off the calendar. Ballparks had been padlocked from June 12 until August 10. Players forfeited money, at an average rate of $1,000 per day.

Perhaps most significantly, the game lost a certain innocence.

The public did not forgive either side for bringing real-life disputes into what they wanted to remain a pastoral pastime. We went back to hostile crowds, a split-season that filled the record books with asterisks. And players, management, and fans alike were left with a tremendous sense of loss.

I thought it would take a long, long time to heal the wounds. I was wrong. All it took was four good division races in 1982, three of which were decided on the final weekend of the season. It seems the game is greater than the sum total of its parts and can and does survive us all.

24

THE IMPORTANCE OF BEING REGGIE

WHEN Joe Rudi, Bobby Grich, and I were introduced to the media in Southern California, it was a small ripple on the Richter Scale compared to the coming of Reggie Jackson.

By 1982, Gene Autry had signaled he was ready to make his last stand. With Fred Lynn already in the fold for one season, and Carew, Grichie, Burleson, and myself old hands at battling windmills, Mr. Autry bought into the market for one more big name—Reginald Martinez Jackson.

Reggie always seemed one step ahead of me. In Oakland, in New York, in All-Star games, always in fame. Our paths, which had crossed so many times, finally had intertwined.

Reggie had always fascinated me. From the time I played alongside him in Santurce, Puerto Rico, to the moment he walked into that news conference in Anaheim.

As a kid playing in Puerto Rico in 1970, I wanted to listen to everything

Frank had to say about finding my power zone and using it wisely. My mind said listen, but my heart followed my eyes, which were riveted on Reggie's gut-busting, from-the-heels swing. Frank had hit a lot of home runs—in his day. Reggie was hitting his home runs in my day. And that swing, and the 47 home runs it had cranked out the year before, mesmerized me.

In 1977, when I was with the Angels and he was with the Yankees, I was window-shopping on Fifth Avenue on a trip into New York. I saw a wall of people moving toward me—a real New York City celebrity ruckus. The commotion was caused by Reggie. Cab drivers were honking, guys in business suits were acting like little kids at their first major-league ballgame, trying to just get near the guy.

Reggie was on a first-name basis with a city of eight million people. How many ballplayers could say that? It was awesome. It was even more amazing to me that Reggie saw me watching him and stopped the parade. So I walked over to him and we chatted. People probably figured I was an athlete, too, because of my build. But I had a feeling of total obscurity, especially after Reggie moved off in one direction, followed by his adoring public, and I walked off in the other, alone.

In my mind, that was a vivid example of the importance of not only being a Yankee, but of being Reggie. I really didn't know who was better off, the guy who could go unnoticed and window-shop or the guy who was always starting a parade.

Right from the start, there were Angels who took a huge step back from Reggie, intimidated by and not trusting the Jackson persona. In spring training it seemed Reggie was out there alone. Despite the falling out with Buzzie and a growing sense I was playing my last season as a California Angel, I tried to remain cognizant of things like that. Players expected the first move to come from me. Even guys on other teams looked for that. The year before, when Freddy Lynn arrived, Cecil Cooper of the Brewers said to me, "You've got to make Freddy play."

I had to make Freddy play? He was making ten times what I was making and I do believe someone else was managing the Angels. But I knew where Cecil was coming from. So, when Reggie arrived, I made a quick decision that someone had to make him feel like he was a part of the club. So I did.

I asked Reggie if he had a place to stay. It was a little thing but "Jack" jumped at it. We became roommates. We palled around all through spring training, Reggie delighted in showing me the finer aspects of Arizona, a state he knew well, having attended Arizona State. Tempe was just a short drive from Casa Grande, the Angels' training site in 1982. Jack was still the Big Man on Campus. It seemed like one of the places he really felt comfortable. Or as comfortable as Reggie could feel.

The idea of making Reggie feel at ease and the idea of feeling at ease with Reggie were often mutually exclusive. Having dinner every night with Reggie was a chore. No matter how obscure the restaurant, Reggie could not go unnoticed. People would come over to the table and ask for autographs, or, I should say, *his* autograph. Usually it was right in mid-bite. Reggie did not handle that well at all. There were scenes. Many scenes. I was just waiting for the last supper, when someone would whip out a six-gun and slaughter us. Reggie could be that rude and boorish.

It happened everywhere, in Arizona and in Palm Springs, when the Angels moved camp in the second half of the exhibition season. I wish I could say it was a pattern that was linked to preseason jitters. It was not. That was just Jack. No matter how good the situation on the field, walking into a restaurant with him was like walking into a minefield.

The worst incident occurred after the Angels clinched the division. Reggie came right to me and said, "Where are we going to celebrate?" My first thought was *As far away from Anaheim and those familiar with Reggie Jackson as possible.*

So I thought of a Chinese restaurant down the coast in La Jolla called The Mandarin, where the owner had always treated me very well.

Reggie decided he was going to drive the whole party, which included Becky and me, Angels catcher Joe Ferguson, Joe's date, and Reggie's date. So Jack showed up with his white Rolls-Royce. Real inconspicuous for a guy who hated to be noticed.

I had informed the restaurant that a party of six was coming. So they knew to expect at least one ballplayer. When they saw Reggie it was like Chinese new year. The restaurant was jammed to begin with, but when he walked in, it was like Moses parting the Red Sea. The patrons just moved out of the way. Everybody knows Reggie.

The waiters started falling all over themselves. Tables had already been set up off to the side to ensure as much privacy as possible. But the maitre d' had gone to the trouble of having a large placard made congratulating "The American League West Champions."

That was mistake number one when it came to dealing with Reggie: showing kindness.

Reggie looked at the sign, said, "Get this shit off the table," took the sign and fired it to the floor. I looked at Becky, who appeared about ready to die. I thought to myself, *Uh-oh, here we go.* Becky and I just kicked at the sign to get it under the table before the maitre d' saw what had happened.

The owner, figuring he knew the real specialties of the house, had arranged an order of delicacies for us. A nice gesture, I thought. Reggie spent the rest of the evening moaning about not being able to order for himself.

There was still the chef to be insulted. The Mandarin specializes in duck, has quite a reputation for that dish. The chef is well known in Southern California and comes to prepare the duck in person only when he considers the guests worthy of his presence. Well, he came to our table with his chef's hat on, ready to go the whole nine yards. He was going to slice and dice. Then he made the fatal mistake. He said, "Mr. Jackson, sir, can I have a picture taken with you while I'm slicing the duck?"

Reggie looked at the guy and said, "Am I paying for this meal or not? If I'm paying for this meal, no, you can't have a picture."

I was ready to disappear. I said, "Hey, Jack, let's just take the picture instead of drawing a whole bunch of attention."

He refused. At that point I was willing to tell him anything to calm him down. I was going to pay for the meal, even buy him the restaurant if he'd just stop being a jerk and show the man a little respect. I didn't have to intercede, though. The owner of the restaurant came over and said, "Mr. Jackson, we're going to comp everybody here, so whatever you want, fine."

Suddenly, Reggie wanted to pose with everyone. And, incredibly, the chef still wanted that photo taken.

There we were, supposedly celebrating a championship and I couldn't taste my food. My guard was up, ready to run interference.

The employees were placated by now. That left the rest of the people in the place to worry about. All hundred of them.

Sure enough, while Reggie was eating, three or four women came over to the table and asked him for an autograph. I was praying to God not to let Reggie start. God must have been busy at that moment.

Reggie said, "I don't have a pen."

One of the women answered, "I have one here."

He replied, "Well, I don't want to sign. Can't you see I'm having dinner?"

Reggie said it in such a way that things immediately turned hostile. The women became indignant, especially after Reggie grabbed the pen and fired it at them saying, "I'm not signing, period . . . Get away from my table."

With that, the women practically crawled away, embarrassed.

I'd had it. "Please, let's finish our dinner and get out of here," I said in the tone that usually let Reggie know show time was over.

We ate without further incident.

I don't know if Reggie had a good time or not. I know I didn't. You wanted to be able to have a good time with Jack, but the problem was that you just could not hide him anywhere. If he wasn't harassing patrons he was harassing me, stealing food from my plate and everyone else's. That night I didn't care if I ever dined with Reggie again.

The next day, Reggie sat next to me in the clubhouse looking depressed. I thought maybe he felt bad about his behavior. But all he said was, "Somebody keyed my car last night."

"What are you talking about?" I asked.

"Somebody keyed my car . . . You know, took a key and scratched my car all the way down one side while we were in the restaurant."

There couldn't have been many suspects. Just every person Reggie had managed to insult. Dozens, at the most.

Reggie taught me one valuable lesson. Never drive Reggie to dinner. Let him drive. Who can afford a new paint job after every meal?

Those situations were embarrassing, for everyone involved. No one likes being insulted by a jerk, being in the company of a jerk. Deep down, I don't believe Reggie liked being Reggie at times like that. I just don't believe he ever knew how to handle the attention. Don't get me wrong. He craved attention, but a certain kind. Reggie is insecure and people bothered him when he wasn't where he felt comfortable. He loved the attention standing at home plate. The batter's box was his own little world. He could get lost there, would have stayed there forever if baseball had let him. Reggie was also at home in front of the media. But not in public, where he was exposed to, well, just plain people. The more crowded it got, the crazier it could make him. It was like watching the walls close in on a claustrophobic.

There was another Reggie who hated to be ignored, though. Rodney could make Reggie angry by chiding him. He could make him crazy by pretending Reggie did not exist.

The only other place Reggie seemed comfortable was around his cars. His collectibles were like children to him. He knew each one's history, who owned it, when the last ring job or oil change was performed.

I could put up with Reggie's many sides because I got to see all of them, which is rare because he doesn't let many people get close.

Reggie lived with me for the first month and a half of the season. Here's a guy I figured was going to show me something about conditioning I did not know. He's a big guy, rippling with muscles. I wanted to know what the regimen was. It was quite simple. Stay in, watch television, eat cookies, candy, pretzels, any kind of junk he could get his hands on. The guy used to scream at me because I didn't have that stuff around the house. I said, "Jack, I don't eat those things so I don't buy them."

One thing I truly admired about him is that he knows baseball. I mean the history. Not like kids today, like the Twins' Dan Gladden, who didn't know Dwight Evans is a Gold Glove winner. He only won about nine, Dan. Reggie honored his sport by knowing everything there was to know, so much so that we called him "Stat Man." Reggie can tell you the dates Joe DiMaggio's streak started and ended. He could tell you how many home runs Mickey Mantle hit or where he, himself, stood on the list, where Mike Schmidt and the other current guys stood, too. Reggie took that stuff seriously.

Reggie also took himself seriously. And that ego spilled into the clubhouse with the subtlety of a California mud slide. To some guys it was about as welcome. Not that it was all Reggie's fault. The Angels had a lot of millionaires and egos to match the dollars. You couldn't take a swing without hitting an MVP, batting champ, or home-run king.

There were personality clashes. I can't count how many of them revolved around Reggie. And I can't count the number of times I wound up in the middle, trying to keep everybody from killing each other. Most of the arguments were good-natured. That could not be said of Reggie's war with Rodney.

Carew and Reggie were always putting themselves on a pedestal and there just wasn't room for both. Rodney never got used to being taken for granted by basically everybody in the game. I think Reggie embodied everything Rodney resented about the game's "superstar" club to which he never was given full membership.

Rodney was hard to figure at times, but Reggie's presence made him withdraw even more. Rodney was real sensitive that way. When we toured Japan in the winter of 1979 he bolted the tour and flew home because Pete Rose got more attention and endorsements. Reggie was just another big name obscuring his own. It made it tough on everyone. Reggie being Reggie did not help.

The clash usually began when Reggie called Rodney "an intermittent shower." "Intermittent," as in spraying the ball around the field, here and there. "But I'm thunder," Reggie would add. Rodney liked the "thunder" line about as much as Thurman Munson had liked Reggie's "straw that stirs the drink" remark in New York. Which is to say, not at all.

Rodney would fire back, "How many batting titles have you won?" That would get it going in the clubhouse, with all kinds of egging on from the sidelines.

One day Rodney, DeCinces, Grichie, Bob Boone, Reggie, and myself were all in the trainer's room—listening to Reggie, of course. "I have this many home runs, and I hit this many in the playoffs . . . How many did you hit in the World Series?" On and on.

Finally, DeCinces says, "How about the 'So' column?"

Reggie looked at him kind of funny, so Doug said, "You know, the one on the back of your bubblegum card they have for strikeouts. The 'So' column. S . . . O . . ."

I thought Carew was going to fall off the training table, he was laughing so hard. Dougie had done what almost every third party tried to do that season—break the tension between Jack and Rodney.

Rodney and Reggie never came to blows. If they had, I think I'd take Rodney. Reggie would take off his shirt and flex his muscles and show his guns and Rodney never backed down. He was the one who would say, "If you want to go, let's go." Rodney knew karate. He was also just a bit crazy. Yes, I would have taken Rodney.

Rodney was not alone in having a problem with some of Jack's "bigger-than-life" buildup. Guys ragged Reggie all the time about his attendance clause. Fifty cents a head if the crowd was above a certain figure. There was some resentment there. I thought it was funny in a way, my sense of humor becoming more and more perverse. I figured if the Angels drew fans it meant *we* were doing it. It would also mean Reggie just might make more money from his fifty-cent-per-head deal than I did in salary.

The situation never threatened the team. Not with "The General" running that club. Gene Mauch knew how to take care of his so-called superstars. He paid Rodney the attention he needed; Freddy, too. As for Reggie, he let him be himself as long as it did not interfere with the team. It seldom did.

I know people find it hard to believe, but Reggie and I got through an entire season without coming to blows. It perplexes me to this day why people assume Reggie and I fought after the Angels lost the 1982 playoffs to the Brewers and that I had given him the infamous black eye he has always claimed occurred when he walked into a door.

I never hit Reggie. I spent the last gloomy night in Milwaukee with my father and son, first at a restaurant, then at the hotel. Not until the next day, when I was paying my hotel bill, did I find out Reggie was hurt. I saw the Angels' trainer, Rick Smith, leading Reggie out the door and Reggie had a towel over his eye. They were on their way to the hospital. I just assumed he had a recurring problem with cinders in his eye from the next-to-last playoff game. I went to the airport and sat with the rest of the team in our chartered plane on the runway waiting for our wounded hero.

The story I heard was that Reggie had ventured out after the last game with Joe Ferguson. Rumor has it that Reggie finally ran into someone or a group of someones who didn't appreciate his act. Supposedly, somebody said something about the Angels. Jack answered back and that somebody smoked him in the eye.

When Reggie walked on the plane, his eye was patched up. Fergy, acting like a seeing-eye dog, led Reggie to the back of the plane. It was quite poignant. Until Rodney stood up and said, "Hey, Reggie, that's the way you played all year." Reggie, just looking for a little sympathy, didn't say anything. On the last day of 1982, he had finally run out of comebacks for Carew.

Our relationship was much smoother. Reggie never got in my face in any serious fashion. And I never got in his. Something kept him from polishing his barbs on me the way he'd do with everyone else. He knew how much Rodney could be pushed and therefore knew when to back off. He could not read my degree of insanity. So he never tested it.

I left Reggie alone for the most part, too. The only thing I rode him about was his conduct in public. On the field there was never a need to get on him. In fact, I wish there were more like him. Reggie could rise to the occasion or he could strike out with anybody in baseball. But Reggie made everyone stay in his or her seat when he hit. There were no runs to the beer stands or the restrooms. Or the clubhouse.

Once in a game in Seattle, Reggie had struck out four times. His fifth at-bat came with the bases loaded. Rene Lachemann, the manager of the Mariners at the time, looked toward our dugout and nodded his head as if he's saying to himself, *Yup, I'm going to get Vande Berg out of the bullpen.* Ed Vande Berg is a left-hander and Reggie is left-handed. I'm on-deck, a right-handed hitter Lach knows will pounce on Vande Berg if he fails to get Reggie. It was a moot point. Reggie crushed a grand slam. Later, he said, "I don't know if I had a good day or a bad day." A "golden sombrero"— four strikeouts—and a grand slam in one game will do that to you.

Reggie's temper was fierce. I had to hold him back when he tried to take a Gatorade cooler to the mound while going after Gaylord Perry. He wanted to "suggest" Gaylord dip the ball in the cooler as long as he was going to load up the ball and throw a spitter. I hated to see Jack get too angry because he usually ended up hurting himself, punching walls and slamming bats. But Reggie was a professional. He never took a bad at-bat out to the field with him. The grounder he didn't run out hasn't been hit yet.

That wasn't false hustle. Reggie never cheated anyone who paid his salary. Reggie made other guys play harder. You had to because here's a guy who's bigger than life and he was grinding it out. The feeling became, if *he* didn't do it, *I'd* do it. No one felt he had to take a backseat, but everybody appreciated the fact that Reggie played hard.

The thing that surprised me most was that Jack was the most insecure player I knew. Despite all his accomplishments, it amazed me how much reassurance he needed that everything was all right, that he was all right. In 1982, I had my usual horror-show April, only this time it was multiplied by two. He also had a wretched month, and I wound up trying to push myself and him, too, feeling more pain about his .200 than about mine. When he started to flourish the other Reggie came back.

Reggie needed 1982 and the Angels. The years with Steinbrenner's Yankees had taken a toll. With Gene Autry, there was no more ridicule, finger-pointing. Billy Martin was only a bad memory for him. The media in California was not into feeding off Reggie or fueling his ego. It was almost like R & R for him.

But New York still could get his juices flowing. Steinbrenner had run him out of town. Reggie was primed by the time he returned for his first visit to Yankee Stadium. I could have sat for a thousand years and never thought of an entry like the one Reggie made. I'm not talking about the game-winning home run he hit off Ron Guidry, which gave birth to the now-famous "Steinbrenner sucks" chant. I'm talking about Reggie's first step onto the field, timed to occur at exactly 6:44 P.M. Not 6:43 or 6:45. It was "44" on the nose as No. 44 played games with the clock at Yankee Stadium. What a master.

When he finally did walk down the tunnel and onto the field, he did so on a carpet of towels laid out by Rodney. Even Carew could appreciate good Reggie Jackson theater when he saw it.

Reggie and I played together for only one season. And it was something to behold. I had a very good year, with 24 home runs and 93 RBI. Reggie had *the* year, though, the perfect answer to Steinbrenner. He hit a league-high 39 home runs. He drove in 101 runs. He wound up in the playoffs; Steinbrenner's Yankees did not. In 1986, I would follow much the same path after an unfriendly exit from New York. It was another time I gladly followed in Jack's footsteps.

The 1982 season would be my last with the Angels. Reggie stayed on through 1986, for Mr. Autry's third and last division title in his free-agent era. After that, Reggie returned to Oakland for one final season in the city where it all began for him. Released at the end of 1987, Reggie never signed with another club, though the stories of a return to New York or a foray into Japan were rampant throughout 1988.

I joined the A's after Reggie left. I saw him a lot in '88. He paid regular visits to Jose Canseco and Mark McGwire, two kids who worship at his feet. I only hope for them they can bring the dedication to their individual games Reggie gave to his, on every swing, from the first to the last. They should remember the private moments, too, when Reggie lets them inside. They are rare and to be cherished. I know I will remember.

During the 1977 World Series between New York and Los Angeles, I sat in the stands at Dodger Stadium with Donny, my father, my uncle, and a friend. Our seats were at the rail near the right-field foul pole. And I was still an Angel, on the outside looking in at the big show.

Reggie spotted me. He didn't just wave. He came over and started talking. It was not just chitchat. It was one ballplayer talking baseball with another.

"I'm swinging good," he said, trying to explain away what was becoming a 1–for–3 struggle against Tommy John. "It doesn't look like it, but I'm swinging good and I'm going to take somebody deep and . . ."

That was Reggie, always talking about taking somebody deep. But darned if he didn't do it the next game and again in the game after that. It was only a prelude to the night Mr. October was born. In the sixth and final game of that Series, Reggie stepped onto the game's biggest stage and hit 3 home runs. Reggie—there's never been another quite like him.

25

THE RED SOX OF THE WEST

THERE was a growing belief that the Angels were becoming the Red Sox of the West, a team beset with bad luck, broken hearts, and an unshakable history of failure. Mr. Autry had tried to win by spending millions. Now, he was turning the stable over to one of the game's toughest tacticians and taskmasters—Gene Mauch.

The team was his to mold, his to control. He was "The Little General," famous for his clubhouse tirades, his demolition of food tables, his intolerance of mediocrity. He was one of the winningest, most respected managers of our era.

Gene held a meeting with us in Comiskey Park as soon as he took over in May 1981. It was a rainy, miserable day. Everyone was down because Jimmy Fregosi had needed us to save his job and we did not get it done. So we sat, waiting for a legendary manager to show us how to win.

Gene, clad in long johns, called the meeting to order. All I could think was, *This is it, the dean, the guy everyone talks about.*

Gene, very solemn, very forthright, told us he'd been brought in by Mr. Autry to win, that he expected to do so.

Gene went over the rules, told us what he expected us to do to get untracked. Then he asked for any input from the floor. The quiet was deafening.

Somebody had to say something. So I cleared my throat and said, "Gene, I have one question. Can you tell us, once the game is over, will the food be on the floor or will it be on the table?"

Everybody fell out, including Gene.

"Yeah, well, I used to do that," he said. "We'll see . . . Depends on how mad you guys make me."

The 1981 season wasn't meant to work for Gene any more than it had been for Jimmy. The next season was a different story, though, because of Reggie and a return to health by almost everyone, including me. And, for the first time since 1979, the Angels did have that winning feeling. And Gene was in control.

Gene took the game home with him, wanted his players to have that same intensity. Gene would often look through you, even if you were the only two on the elevator. It wasn't anything personal. He was either replaying that night's game in his mind or he was already up to the third inning of the next night's game, maybe even a game two weeks away.

With Gene as manager, you could learn something new every day. Some guys act like they invented the game. Gene may well have written the rule book. Once in a lifetime, probably, catcher Mike Heath acted on instinct and tried to stop a ball by snaring it with his mask. The umpires did not object, Mauch did. He was the only person on the field who not only knew that was illegal, but also knew the ramifications. He had the umpires reverse the play and the runners returned to their original bases.

Gene was the first manager I ever saw since high school make an outfielder play as a fifth infielder when the winning run was on third. He did that once against the Angels when he managed the Twins. He brought in the outfielder and then ordered his pitcher, Davey Johnson, to issue an intentional walk to load the bases to set up forceouts at all bases. Johnson went into his windup, caught a cleat in the pitching rubber, and threw the ball halfway up the screen, allowing the winning run to score. All Gene could say and keep a straight face was, "I had everybody positioned right, except I didn't have anybody up there on the screen."

Gene maneuvered the team well, if a bit conservatively. The lineup of Downing, Carew, Jackson, Lynn, Baylor, DeCinces, Grich, Tim Foli, and

Bob Boone—well, it could hurt people. And it did. Five guys hit 20 or more home runs; Grichie hit 19. Five guys drove in 80 or more runs. The Angels' pitching was still a problem. Mike Witt, a twenty-one-year-old kid, was still learning to pitch. Our big winners were Geoff Zahn, with 18 victories, and Ken Forsch, with 13. From there, it was pitching by committee. Right before September, the team caught a break.

Back in New York, George Steinbrenner was having one of his infamous feuds, this time with left-hander Tommy John. Even though the Yankees were also in a pennant race, they traded John to the Angels. John won 4 games in September. We needed each one. California finished with 93 victories, 3 more than the Kansas City Royals. The American League West was ours.

Everything said that the California Angels should have defeated the Milwaukee Brewers in the playoffs. Especially after we went up, 2–0, in the best-of-five series. We didn't. That's when we all became believers in the theory once put forth by the late New York columnist, Dick Young, that "Gene Mauch was put on this earth to suffer." Because we were all about to witness just how real and agonizing Gene Mauch's heartbreaks were.

The first two games had been a dream. I never felt more relaxed. There was more tension getting ready for the trip to the park, what with scrambling for tickets, sixty-mile round-trip jaunts to the Los Angeles airport to pick up relatives and all. After that, I needed R & R and the comfort of a playoff game. Reggie was relaxed, too, clowning around about what we were going to do to "Cartwell." It took a couple of seconds to figure out he was talking about Brewers left-hander Mike Caldwell.

Any concern about my stroke disappeared after one swing, when I hit a first-inning sacrifice fly. By the third inning, Tommy John trailed, 3–1, but Grichie singled in 1 run and I tripled in 2 more in the bottom of the inning to give T. J. the lead. An inning later, I singled in 2 more runs against a little bulldog of a pitcher, Jim Slaton. We won, 8–3. My 5 RBI matched the single-game playoff record.

When I hit the triple, the ball just ticked off the top of the wall in right-center. I'd never hit a home run to right of centerfield, something Gene always took pains to point out. He kidded me constantly, promised to buy me a car if I found the range to the opposite field. The triple scared Gene to death. The first thing he said to me after "congratulations" was that playoff home runs would not count against the bet. As of 1988, I still had not hit that home run, but I'll always know where to find Gene if I do.

The hot feeling you can get at the plate can grow cold quickly. Pete Vuckovich shut me down in Game Two. But that was okay. We won, 4–2, behind Bruce Kison, who threw a five-hitter.

We were rocking and rolling. All we needed was one victory. We had to go to Milwaukee to get it.

Mr. Autry was so certain we had it won he ordered a DC-10, one of the bigger jets, to take the team not only to Milwaukee but on to either St. Louis or Atlanta for the Series. We all packed for a week. Becky did not even go to Milwaukee. She just planned to meet me in the National League host city.

The Brewers won Game Three, jumping out to a 5-run lead against Geoff Zahn and Mike Witt. Then Milwaukee held on, behind Don Sutton and Pete "Big Foot" Ladd, for a 5–3 victory. The extent of my day: a double in 3 at-bats. I'd driven in 1 run with that hit, but Reggie, trying to go from first to third, was thrown out, a rally killer. Reggie came up off the bag holding his face; he'd gotten gravel in his eyes when he hit the ground hard and when Paul Molitor came up with the tag. When Reggie hit the dirt with that less-than-graceful slide, the fans went crazy.

Weirdness was setting in.

Ken Forsch, our number-four starter, following John, Kison, and Zahn, was our second-winningest pitcher. No doubt in my mind, Forsch was one of our better pitchers, a veteran of more than a dozen years in the majors. But he never even warmed up. Why? No one knows. Gene Mauch's not the type of guy who invites you over and asks you politely to critique his moves. But you can't keep yourself from thinking. And I thought, *This can't be. Must be a reason.*

There was. Gene wanted to start Tommy John in Game Four, on three days' rest. A lot of guys started to think about 1964, when Gene Mauch got stuck on two pitchers—Jim Bunning and Chris Short—and the Phillies lost a 6.5-game lead with two weeks to go partly because of a pair of valiant, but tired arms. I tried not to make comparisons. *Nah,* I thought. *If anybody knows what he's doing, Gene knows.*

It was miserable and rainy when Game Four began. The wind was blowing straight in, a bad sign for all the hard hitters on the Angels and Brewers. But "Harvey's Wallbangers," as Harvey Kuenn's Brewers were called, didn't need wind-blown home runs to rout T. J. He did not survive the fourth inning, allowing 6 runs on 4 hits and 5 walks. Tommy John never walks people, period. But it was obvious the real Tommy John was not out there that day.

By the end of four innings, the Brewers led, 6–0. In the eighth we trailed, 7–1, when Haas loaded the bases. I stepped in, having had only 1 hit since Game One. One mistake on Moose Haas's part was all I asked. He made it, throwing a slider out over the plate. I drove it through the teeth of the wind and into the left-centerfield stands. We were back in it, for all of half an inning, until Dave Goltz gave up 2 runs. Brewers 9, Angels 5. Series tied, just like that.

The old dreads started coming back. Freddy Lynn was 8–for–14. I'd driven in 10 runs. Still, we were 2–2. We'd given a great team and a great baseball town momentum. Sure, there was another way to look at it. Reggie and Rodney weren't hitting, our pitching was a mess, and still we could win it all. That was the attitude I wanted us to have before Game Five. Instead, I felt tension, in Gene, in twenty-five players, in Mr. Autry.

We jumped out 2–1, then 3–1, thanks, in part, to 3 more hits and 2 RBI by Freddy. Ben Oglivie, back in the Brewers lineup, despite sore ribs, got one back with a home run off Kison in the fifth. One run separated the teams going into the seventh. Luis Sanchez, who had relieved Kison, retired his first batter. Then Charlie Moore blooped a ball over the mound toward a diving Grich. Second-base umpire Al Clark ruled Grichie caught the ball, but home-plate umpire Don Denkinger overruled him. A Jim Gantner single, an out, and then a walk to league MVP Robin Yount loaded the bases. In stepped Cecil Cooper, 2–for–19, hitless in 9 at-bats, but a .313 hitter during the season and a tough out from the left side of the plate.

Gene had left-hander Andy Hassler ready. Everyone in the American League knew Hassler terrorized left-handed hitters. No less than George Brett had told Andy that by way of a compliment earlier that season. "Andy," Brett said, "you're making me look so bad, I'm not going to swing. You might strike me out looking, but I'm not swinging." That's how tough Hassler could be.

Gene never made the move. He visited the mound, but did not remove Sanchez. Cecil was probably the most surprised man in the park, aside from about twenty or so Angels. I was thinking, *That's it? This is nonsense. Gene must have something up his sleeve.*

He did. A hunch that a control pitcher like Sanchez was better than a wild sidewinder like Hassler. Cooper proved him wrong, singling in 2 runs.

The Brewers won, 4–3. In the end, Reggie was kneeling in the on-deck circle when Peter Ladd got Rodney for the final out. Mr. October's magic could not overcome the hexes on Mr. Autry and Gene Mauch.

Gene may be the most knowledgeable manager I've ever played for and is definitely one of the finest people in the game. But he also did not take chances. He played it safe, played "little ball"—sacrificing, not running the bases—and made "defensive" decisions ripe for second-guessing. If you want to put a team away you go with the guy who can get the strikeout or pop-up. That was Hassler. As if to underline that point, the fates set up the exact scenario in the first game of 1983. The only difference was that Gene had resigned and John McNamara was the manager. Mac, looking at Cooper in a bases-loaded situation, gave Hassler the ball. Cooper grounded out. Game over. Time to second-guess, again.

Gene knew everything about how to win. But in 1964 and 1982 Gene did not know the one ingredient needed to get to the Series. Gene retired in March 1988 because of ill health. By that winter, though, he was contemplating a comeback. If he ever returns, I hope he can win it all and kill the demons. My wishes also extend to the Angels. Gene Autry spent and spent trying to make the team into champions. But, through 1988, he was still searching for his first World Series. The Angels may have surpassed Boston in frustration. In 1986, Gene and the Angels lost yet another playoff, this time to the Red Sox, helping Boston end its own World Series drought. I witnessed Gene's pain that time from the other side of the field.

I sat in the trainer's room at County Stadium for a long time, thinking about that final loss of 1982, thinking about Freddy's .600 average, my record-tying 10 RBI. I also thought about how three Brewers pitchers limited me to 1 single in 4 at-bats that day. It was such an empty feeling. Four playoffs, four losses, a new "record." It hurt.

Donny was sitting there, too, fighting back tears. He was nine years old, just a kid. He didn't know what it was really about, but he looked as if his world had ended. I realized that if he was ever to learn about winning, he'd also have to learn about losing—in his life and mine. I would, too.

I had not been able to go and congratulate the Orioles in 1979. Too many old memories had kept me away from their victorious clubhouse. In 1982, though, I knew it was time to be a professional. It was time to show Donny you could lose and still do the right thing. So we walked to the Brewers clubhouse together, to wish the American League champions luck in the World Series.

All through that October, I had tried not to think about free agency. I could not fathom leaving the Angels. But I had no contract nor any indication Buzzie would negotiate in good faith. One of the writers covering the team reminded me that not many people even realized that the playoffs might have been my last stand as an Angel. After all, he said, Steve Garvey was also on the verge of free agency and everyone was too busy wondering what the Dodgers, not the Angels, would do. I just smiled. Some things, it seemed, would never change in Southern California. "Garvey's an institution," I told the writer. "I'm just a player."

A player who was about to move on, again.

I didn't want to. But there was a principle at stake. I had stood by my original contract like a man. I wanted a show of appreciation for that and for the good years I'd given to the team and the community. At the end of that October, I asked the Angels for a $6-million, five-year contract. Buzzie said that was too much and offered $3 million for five years.

Funny, he never thought $400,000 a year was too much to pay sore-armed Bill Travers, who spent two years charting pitches and bowling. Shortstop Rick Burleson, a guy with a big heart but bad rotator cuff, never got to give the Angels a return on his salary of about $900,000 a year. Buzzie never made a serious attempt to extend my contract, but extended others'. I never said a word about the inequities, about how I played with broken bones for a lot less. Now Buzzie not only wanted to pay me less than Carew, Lynn, and Jackson. He wanted to continue paying me $300,000 less than Burleson, who probably would never play again. Buzzie must have figured I had no self-worth at all.

Jerry and I sought a compromise, offering to pare down the $1.2 million-per-year request to $875,000. Buzzie would not give in. It was still "take a hike" if I did not accept the $3 million by November 9, the team's self-imposed deadline.

My teammates wanted me to return. Reggie and Carew kept calling. John McNamara, who replaced Mauch on November 8, pleaded with Buzzie and gave interview after interview saying how much he wanted me on his team. I heard the pleas but I had to make my own decisions.

I sat in my living room in Newport Beach as the deadline approached. Jimmy Hill, a local sportscaster, came over to do a live interview in which I made an emotional plea for a settlement. Buzzie never picked up the phone. The next day the Angels passed me over and drafted former Royals DH Hal McRae.

It was over. And it hurt more than I ever let anyone know.

PART

3

26

NEW YORK, NEW YORK

ALL through the summer of 1982 I had listened to Reggie's tales of the "Bronx Zoo." I can't count the number of times Jack said, "That is a living hell, playing in New York."

When Tommy John arrived in California at season's end, it became a chorus of two, as both ex-Yankees told mindboggling stories of baseball's most famous three-ring circus. Reggie, wondering if I was considering going to New York and wanting to share his experiences, I'm sure, left message after message for me all over Southern California.

I did not return his calls.

It was nothing personal. I appreciated Jack's concern. I also had to make up my own mind. I was a big boy, could live with the consequences of any action I took.

Steinbrenner's rule did not scare me. I'm not a troublemaker. I just put my uniform on and do my job. I'll take criticism if I deserve it and go on from there. I may have been an unknown from the other coast in the eyes of many New Yorkers. And maybe I was about to step into a clubhouse full of big-name players. That was no problem for me, either. I respected Goose Gossage, Dave Winfield, Willie Randolph, Graig Nettles, Ron Guidry, and Ken Griffey. I also knew I could fit in with them, just as I had with some pretty impressive players in California. Although I was wary of the media, I knew I had survived the worst sort of coverage in 1977. The press no longer scared me.

I briefly considered a couple of other teams. Milwaukee, at the urging of their general manager and my friend, Harry Dalton, contended. Baltimore showed a cursory interest. But the Yankees pushed the hardest. In the end, my decision was fairly easy. I'd got a second chance at free agency, a second chance to sign with the Yankees. I didn't want to pass it up again. It was time to go to New York. The Yankees wanted to win. And they wanted me.

On December 2, one day after I was formally introduced to the New York media as George Steinbrenner's latest free-agent acquisition, I sat in a suite at the Plaza Hotel and signed a four-year, $3.7-million contract. That pact included signing bonus, salary and deferred payments, and an $875,000 option for a fifth year, which the team could buy out for $375,000. With one stroke of the pen, the Yankees made me their twelfth free agent signed for over a million dollars. And I stepped into a salary structure that made me the highest-paid Yankee after Winfield, Griffey, and Guidry.

The Yankees contract more than doubled what I had earned in the half-dozen seasons I played in California. It was also about $1.5 million less than what I'd asked of the Angels, which infuriated Buzzie. What he never understood was that my demands on the Angels had to do with a need for a show of appreciation. Other teams could win me over for less.

Before I even signed, I got a taste of the power of the press and the strange relationship between New York newspapers and Steinbrenner. On November 30, one day before the scheduled news conference at Yankee Stadium, I received a phone call at my home in Newport Beach, California, from Bill Madden of the *New York Daily News*. He had all the terms of the agreement and wanted a few comments. How he found out about the deal or even where I was living I'll never know. I assumed his information came from the Yankees. So I gave him a few quotes. It became a huge back-page story in the tabloid. Steinbrenner got wind of it before the December 1 edition of the *News* even hit the streets. He was fuming. He threatened to pull the deal off the table. The pending signing was not leaked by Jerry or myself, but that didn't matter to Steinbrenner. It seemed like it took forever for him to calm down.

I was still a little stunned at Steinbrenner's reaction by the time I arrived in New York in the early-morning hours of December. So I went out to buy the newspapers. I wanted to see what Madden had written. In one short walk, I ran into guys who were delivering newspapers, guys at the corner stands, passersby. And many of them recognized me, wanted to wish me luck, said they hoped I could help the Yankees get back on the winning side. I could not believe it. One back-page headline and Don Baylor was recognizable in New York City.

I realized more than ever that once you put on the Yankees pinstripes, you put on instant fame. I was about to play for the number-one team in the country, in all of sports. Everyone knows that "NY" insignia. All over the world people know that means the New York Yankees. When people see an Angels hat, they associate it with something different, Disneyland, Southern California beaches, but not winning and tradition. I had won an MVP there and still could not get on an even footing with the Dodgers. Signing with the Yankees gave me more visibility in one day then I'd got in six seasons in Anaheim.

I liked the reception. I came in with a positive attitude and fans and media returned the feeling. If I played every day, I was going to give them a good effort and do a good job.

When I was introduced to the press at Yankee Stadium, I put on the Yankees cap and it seemed like a million strobe lights flashed. The media crush was unlike any I'd ever seen. It dwarfed even Reggie's gala news conference the year before. It amazed me that I could draw that much attention. It was flattering and more than a bit frightening. Players from other cities were intimidated by what we considered the tough, hard, relentless press corps of New York, which we perceived could make or break a player and would do so at will. I found the opposite to be true. I found the writers who covered the Yankees to be among the most professional in the country.

The standout, in my mind, is Murray Chass of the *New York Times.* Murray covers the labor scene unlike any reporter I know and he's always been fair, honest, and thorough. Murray is not owned by anyone, in management or labor. Of all the reporters I've met, he's probably the one that I will miss the most when I leave the game. Then there's Moss Klein of the *Newark Star Ledger.* I don't agree with everything Moss writes, but he's man enough to stand up for what he believes. In 1986, after I was traded to Boston, Moss wrote a strong column in *The Sporting News* about what he felt were Red Sox shortcomings, a column that I made sure found its way to the clubhouse bulletin board. When we visited New York for the first time, a lot of guys were laying for Moss. We were in first place and the guys wanted to rub it in. The problem was a lot of the Red Sox didn't know Moss by sight. So, as soon as he walked in the clubhouse, I did my duty. "Wade Boggs, this is Moss Klein . . . Dwight, this is Moss Klein . . ." The guys jumped on Moss pretty good, but he took it in good humor. He also didn't back down. Dwight respects Moss to this day because he did not hide.

Murray and Moss are not alone. Mike Martinez of the *New York Times,* Tom Pedulla of Westchester Rockland Newspapers, Marty Noble of *Newsday,* and Claire Smith of the *Hartford Courant* all covered the Yankees during the three years I played in New York. I found them to be honest writers who didn't try to force their opinions on anyone. Dave Anderson and George Vescey of the *Times* are special because both understood the power they held as columnists and used it fairly. Mike Lupica of the *Daily News* never backed down from anyone, especially Billy Martin or George Steinbrenner. He also didn't automatically hammer guys who were in the Yankees' doghouse. That was appreciated.

I'm not saying the media was perfect, just as all players aren't perfect. There were writers there who did Steinbrenner's bidding, then hid until the clamor died down. Just like there are players who hide after a loss or a bad game. But, for the most part, I found the New York media acted fairly and treated players with respect.

On January 11, Steinbrenner relieved Clyde King of his managerial duties and brought in Billy Martin. It was my first experience with a Yankees' managerial move and I had not even played an inning yet. For Billy, it was his third go-round and he was usually the focus of Reggie's worst horror stories. But Martin's resurfacing in New York did not bother me. I would have signed whether he was manager or not. Besides, I did not have a problem with the idea of playing for Billy Martin. He had always stood out in my mind as one of the best, right up there with Earl. His Yankees teams of the seventies were awesome, like well-oiled machines. I felt I was the kind of player Billy liked, hard-nosed and aggressive. Billy had a reputation for being a players' manager. He was known to be fair, making decisions on ability and not based on skin color. I had no problem with Billy coming in at all.

Billy was not the one guarding the bottom line, anyway. I knew I would have to answer to the main man, "The Boss." I vowed to stay away from trouble with Steinbrenner, to keep my mouth shut and just do my job. I figured Steinbrenner could not have any problem with that. I also knew that, if any criticism started, I could take it. I knew I would have the respect of the players, if I did my job. That was the respect that counted. Playing in New York would not change that basic belief in myself.

So I felt I understood Steinbrenner's Yankees, New York City, and all it entailed. I had been wined and dined, provided first-class accommodations and limousines. The same celebrity treatment accorded every free agent the Yankees ever signed.

It did not take long to realize what many Yankees, including Reggie and Tommy John, had learned the hard way. Once you sign, you are no longer treated like a celebrity. You are treated like a piece of trash.

27

BILLY AND THE BOSS

MY first feeling in spring training with the Yankees was that I was being watched.

Every morning, before the dew dried on the field at the team complex in Fort Lauderdale, The Boss was there, in a navy-blue windbreaker, his military-school upbringing obvious in every step he took. Steinbrenner was always on the prowl, on the field, in the clubhouse, huddling with Billy. And watching, always watching.

When we were on the field, George would stand by the chain-link fence or sit in the dugout and watch us run, probably to make sure we ran until we almost dropped. I figured he would jump the fence and start running with us just to make sure we ran every single lap.

The only warm feeling you got came from the Florida sun.

We arrived early, about mid-February, about seventy or so players, more than I'd ever seen in one spring-training complex. The Boss had seventy guys there early, but not the one he wanted. Dave Winfield chose not to report until the official start of spring training, March 1. Steinbrenner was not a happy man.

Right before the team was to leave Florida, Steinbrenner called a meeting in Tampa, where we had traveled to play the Reds. He told us he was paying $800,000 for charters because he was tired of hearing beefs about the travel accommodations. So, he said, "I expect you guys to win."

The charter I expected, since the Yankees were known to do everything first-class, so I just laughed off the speech as preseason jitters. After all, the guy did want to win. As long as they stayed out of my little cubicle, I figured, things would be okay. Nobody could mess with your head if you didn't let them.

Steinbrenner closed the meeting by telling us that if everything went well we would not hear from him until the All-Star break. Three months before the break, The Boss was back. He blew into Texas on May 1 and herded the entire team into an incredibly hot visiting-manager's office for an eighteen-minute meeting. We were struggling and Steinbrenner, showing his temper, told the media, "I can lose like this with the kids from Columbus."

The next thing we knew, curfew checks began, as if grown men were college kids away from home for the first time. Just because we had not won the pennant by May 1.

There it was, that relentless Yankees' pressure to win every game. I thought I had seen everything when George made his charter-airplane speech. I hadn't. Billy had not been under pressure to win every spring-training game. Yogi Berra would be two springs later. Most Yankees managers are, because spring training in Yankee land is unlike anything in all of baseball.

George is obsessed with winning, even in the spring. Especially if the Yankees are playing one of the teams that makes George crazy. Like the Mets. The Yankees never play the Mets during the season, so George put the pressure on to win exhibition games, made the Mets–Yankees contests like the World Series. It was the Freeway Series nightmare all over again, only worse. No Angel or Dodger ever lost his starting job because of an error in those games. Casualties of the Yankees–Met rivalry were legendary. A kid pitcher named Mike Griffin saw his dream of a Yankees career die with one bad spring-training outing against the Mets in 1981. A year later, Tucker Ashford committed an error against the Mets and he was sent down, never to return again.

That same kind of spring-training overkill carried over to games against the Red Sox and to any game being televised back in the New York area.

One such television game was jeopardized by a rainstorm. The field at Fort Lauderdale was flooded, but George would not give up the broadcast.

Instead, he hired helicopters to come in and blow-dry the field with their rotor blades. George directed the choppers in a scene straight out of *Apocalypse Now.*

I couldn't believe he put himself that close to tons and tons of rotating blades. I couldn't respect George for that. He was trying to ready a field that was iffy at best. Then he ordered his prime-time lineup out there, just for television. If a Don Mattingly, Dave Winfield, or Ken Griffey had ripped up a leg, would it have been worth it? If it was September and we were down by a game, that would have been different. I would have been out there right beside him. But not for an exhibition game.

That sort of zealousness would have been funny if it hadn't had a serious edge. Everything about the Yankees was deadly serious. It was like they hung a sign atop Yankee Stadium that said, "No fun allowed." Players were made to feel that their kids were not welcome. Most clubs encouraged the idea of family, allowing sons to take the field during early batting practice with their fathers and shag fly balls. Not at Yankee Stadium. I found that out when I was with the Angels. I brought Donny to the park about five hours before the game. We were in the visitor's bullpen playing catch. Suddenly, a stadium security guard approached us and said players' kids weren't allowed on the field. After I pointed out that Donny wasn't on the field, the guard persisted and finally said Donny would have to leave because Steinbrenner had a standing edict about kids.

Not my kid. I was a major-league ballplayer in a major-league ballpark. Donny was not a criminal, just a little kid tossing a ball with his dad. I said to the guard, "You tell George to come and tell me himself." The guard turned and walked away. I kept on tossing the ball with Donny.

Once I became a Yankee, I saw vindictiveness permeate the organization, something I'd never seen before. If a guy didn't execute, punishment drills were ordered. Players would be out at three o'clock for a night game, practicing their bunting or fielding or taking ricochets off the wall.

In 1983, that always "unnamed" authority mandated that we had to work out on every scheduled day-off until we were in first place. One day we had to fly on an off-day to Milwaukee after a night game in New York. We were ordered to work out at the stadium before departing on a thirty-minute bus trip to Newark Airport, meaning a start time of about seven A.M. That was punishment, pure and simple. Billy apparently agreed. He pushed back the workout to that afternoon in Milwaukee and made it voluntary. That goodwill gesture nearly cost him his job.

A lot of times, the only way players could retaliate or blow off steam was to go public in the press. Or rail at fans, the press, or the front office. The media was sometimes viewed as the enemy because Steinbrenner, the front office, or the manager would rip players and the negative messages often showed up in print. The next day fans would be hollering those headlines at the players. That especially galled Goose Gossage. One day, in 1982, Goose had read and heard enough. And he ripped the fans, the reporters, and Steinbrenner in perhaps the most famous tirade ever to come out of the Bronx Zoo.

"This cock-sucking place is a fucking joke," Goose ranted as reporters' tape recorders whirred. "The way they boo fucking everybody. . . . And all you mothers with a fucking pen and a fucking tape recorder, you can fucking turn it on and take it upstairs . . . to the Fat Man. Okay? Because I'm fucking sick of the negative, fucking bullshit. You got that?"

Goose's tirade went on from there as he defended teammates such as Ken Griffey and let off a lot of steam. The ironic thing was that his outburst came after Goose had saved both games of a doubleheader. The pressures of having to save games didn't get to Goose that day. The pressures of being a Yankee did. And he showed the frustration and bitterness many Yankees felt. And guys popped off regularly. I'd never seen that before, where both sides used the papers to get even. I had been taught that was not the way to go. But I also saw how feelings had to be vented or things would explode, especially with guys as volatile as Gossage, Lou Piniella, Rudy May, or Billy. George knew which buttons to push and those guys would push back.

Dave Winfield showed he'd stand up when he took The Boss to court in a dispute over funding of Winfield's nonprofit, charitable foundation. This occurred three times, 1982, 1985, and 1988. The most recent escapade resulted in a countersuit filed by Steinbrenner. Charges and countercharges involving misuse of funds and failure to contribute promised donations made the feud between the two all the nastier. Still, Dave refused to cut and run; in 1988, Dave rejected an attempt to be traded away from the Yankees by Steinbrenner.

In 1985, Steinbrenner and Winfield went at it in front of the entire team. Right before the two-day strike, Steinbrenner came into the clubhouse to persuade players to voluntarily sign up for Commissioner Peter Ueberroth's drug-testing program. Ueberroth, not getting anywhere with the Association, had asked club officials to speak to the players. Most teams sent in their general managers. Steinbrenner led his own foray. He told us he'd stand right there at the urinals and test along with us.

Then he started to hand out the commissioner's forms. Winfield stood up and objected. He was the Yankees' player rep to the MLBPA and as such, he said, he was the only person who could give players that sort of material.

Steinbrenner answered he wouldn't be the rep for long, that he would get rid of Dave. Dave, protected by a 10–5 clause that took effect that year, shot right back that he couldn't be traded. They stood there going back and forth in front of GM Clyde King, Billy Martin, the coaches, about eight team vice-presidents, and all the players. Finally, Steinbrenner just put the forms on a table and said he expected each of us to call him with an answer. Winfield threw the forms in the trash as soon as Steinbrenner left. The next day Steinbrenner called Winfield to his office and demanded to know which team he wanted to be traded to. Winfield told us later he just laughed and walked out.

George raged against everyone, not just players. He once fired a parking-lot attendant at Fort Lauderdale Stadium because the poor kid forgot to leave a set of keys in a car blocking Steinbrenner's Cadillac. He once hurled angry words at Bobby Meacham's wife because her entrance into that parking lot caused Steinbrenner's wife to slow her car and Steinbrenner rammed his half of their matching his-and-her Cadillacs into Mrs. Steinbrenner's.

In one of the more incredible displays of 1983, Steinbrenner and American League President Lee MacPhail waged the "night of dueling memos" in late May. The incident involved George's incessant complaints about umpires. George had slammed Derryl Cousins and John Shulock in a statement and intimated that MacPhail agreed that the two umpires had blown calls. He'd threatened to sue Cousins after Cousins suggested George, as owner of a shipbuilding firm, should go somewhere and play with his boats. MacPhail, having already suspended Billy once that season for dirt-kicking incidents, had had enough. He suspended Steinbrenner for a week, the first time the league ever took such an action against an owner.

George's actions in 1983, from publishing a media guide with a cover depicting Billy kicking dirt on an umpire to constant run-ins with MacPhail, eventually led to another first—a $250,000 fine assessed by Commissioner Bowie Kuhn. George is an amazing man, constantly ticking away, threatening to explode at anyone at any time. Never, it seems, is he more volatile than when Billy Martin is around. It was just my luck to arrive for round three in their very strange love-hate relationship.

At the start of 1983, Billy Martin struck me as a pretty strong guy, not yet self-obsessed or caught up in his television image of "Brawling Billy," which grew out of his "I-didn't-punch-that-doggie" beer commercial. Billy Martin was into one thing in 1983, the New York Yankees. Sometimes, though, I think you can want to win too badly.

Billy could not take losing. That applied to individual games as well as the entire season. Managing the Yankees was the most important thing in his life. When things did not go well, Billy began to fray around the edges. And the conflicts started.

We didn't get through the first game before I witnessed Billy's first serious rhubarb with umpires. We didn't get through April before seeing him suspended by the league for kicking dirt on umpires. It was the first of two suspensions that season.

On May 15, Billy threatened to throw Henry Hecht of the *New York Post* into the whirlpool. Billy was incensed that the contents of a closed-door meeting appeared almost word-for-word in an article written by Hecht. Billy called another meeting and, for the first time in my life, I witnessed a manager invite the media, including Henry. And he lit into Henry, calling him a "little scrounge" and threatening to dunk him if Henry ever entered his office again. Billy told the players he could not keep us from speaking to Henry, but that he would have no respect for us or deal with us if we cooperated with Hecht. Henry gave it right back to Billy, in front of the players, then walked around laughing and joking and shaking hands with guys right in front of Billy's coaches.

May's antics also included a run-in Billy had with a bar patron in California in which bullpen coach Dom Scala interceded. Authorities later cleared Billy of any wrongdoing. It was a rare off-the-field victory for Billy that season.

In June, Billy lost a big one. He defied George and made the mandatory workout voluntary. When only three guys showed up, George went crazy. It did not help that Billy missed the workout himself because he had arrived in Milwaukee on a later flight with a female companion. His troubles worsened when Steinbrenner learned that Billy had carried on a running conversation with his friend during one of the games, passing notes from the dugout to the stands.

On June 17, George struck, firing Art Fowler, Billy's pitching coach and closest friend on his staff. Billy was livid. He stormed around, slammed doors, and walled himself up in his office. Steinbrenner also made it public that he was considering firing Billy, but finally chose not to. That turned it up another notch. The very next day Billy, reacting in kind, gave George real cause to carry out his threat. Billy got into another clubhouse incident. A pollster from the *New York Times* named Deborah Henschel accused Billy of using extreme profanity against her. Steinbrenner issued not one, but two apologies. At first The Boss said that if anyone said such things to his daughter, he'd get a gun and shoot the guy. Then, in a reversal, Steinbrenner exonerated Martin, citing a lack of witnesses for the prosecution.

It was another typical day in George and Billy's zoo.

Players were not only provided with bizarre theater. Unfortunately, we, too, often were on the receiving end of Billy's tirades. He was under so much pressure, he would take it out on the team.

Billy never said a word to me and treated most veterans with respect. But, as the team's regular DH, I was on the bench more often than not, watching Billy's tactics with other players. Some bothered me tremendously. I couldn't pretend not to see other guys hurt by his constant criticism and his second-guessing of the pitch selection.

The pitch selection was a conflict that would flare between Billy, his pitchers and catchers. Billy was his own pitching coach, even when his buddy, Fowler, was there. When Fowler was fired, Billy became even more protective of this role. Billy's constant second-guessing had not happened when Thurman Munson was alive. I know because I saw how Thurman dealt with Billy. I was on-deck for the Angels once when Billy tried to call a pitch while Thurman was catching. Thurman pointed to Billy and growled, "This is my game." That was that. But Thurman died in 1979. And no other catcher had come along to stand up to Billy. Rick Cerone didn't. Butch Wynegar didn't, although Butch would yell back occasionally. Mostly, though, Billy rode roughshod over everyone. And he would second-guess almost every pitcher but the most veteran, like Ron Guidry.

The tension did not end once Billy walked off the pitcher's mound.

Martin had always been known as a perfect manager for young players. I did not see that in 1983. Instead, Billy would air out kids in front of the whole team. It was the first time I'd ever been around that sort of hostility toward kids. Earl never did that. He would criticize, but it was constructive. Chuck Tanner put his arm around you if you made a mistake to explain what you did wrong. Even if you wanted to pull away you couldn't, he was so strong. Gene Mauch was an authoritarian, but fair.

What Billy did was not constructive, but detrimental. Billy intimidated kids like shortstops Bobby Meacham and Andre Robertson, almost to the point where they couldn't field ground balls. What team needed a player to slip into a state of shock, then take the field? But you could see that happening. Bobby Meacham was criticized to the point where he couldn't make routine plays. He would go out there knowing that if he threw another one away, he was either going down to the minors or would have to take extra grounders the next day.

It was not just Billy who fostered that intimidating atmosphere. There was a trickle-down effect from the front office that helped put Billy on edge. There was a feeling in the organization that Yankees should be perfect. But the times no longer allowed players to stay in the minors for six years and come up as ready-made major leaguers. The Yankees knew they had to teach, but tried to do that through intimidation. Theirs was not a learning process, but a screaming-and-yelling process. And that's a shame. Because the Yankees' real tradition is winning through sound fundamentals. Fielding a routine ground ball, making the routine plays. It's not screaming and hollering.

Gene Michael, who was a coach off and on during my years in New York, worked well with infielders. So did Don Zimmer. Jeff Torborg tutored pitchers and catchers endlessly. But a lot of what the coaches did could be undone in one screaming session. Or by a demotion.

In 1984, in the first week of the season, Bobby Meacham committed an error. The next day, his name plate was removed, his locker emptied of his possessions. In his place sat Keith Smith, a kid called up from the minors, equipped with a uniform, even a freshly stenciled name plate. Bobby Meacham had been erased, shipped not to Triple A, but all the way down to Double A.

Yogi Berra, our manager by then, was devastated. So were the players. For once in a rare turn, Yogi wouldn't talk to the media. That didn't stop the players, including myself. "The kid works hard, that's why guys feel bad," I told reporters. "Some other guys come up here and feel the world owes them. Meacham knew his role and tried to fulfill it the best way that he could."

Other teams, unlike the Yankees, seemed to understand that treating an error like a felony was not the way to go about teaching kids. The Yankees didn't understand anything except the way it used to be. And no one's past looked more perfect than the Yankees'. Especially to ex-Yankees. Phil Rizzuto, a former Yankees shortstop, who announces on the team's television broadcasts, would innocently comment that a player should have used two hands instead of one to catch a ball. Next thing you know, George is hammering that point, Billy's hammering that point, and the player is getting hammered, period.

Neither coaches nor players were spared, even if the screw-up was Billy's fault. He had an intricate system of signs, some of which he would forget. One such sign called for a squeeze when he leaned on the dugout post in Tiger Stadium. Billy forgot about that, leaned away, and then went crazy when Zim dutifully relayed the sign to Ken Griffey at the plate. Grif was hitting about .500 that week, so Billy took the bat out of the hands of his hottest hitter. He laid into Zim in front of the entire team, a real embarrassment to a man who's given so much to the game. It never got better between them. Zim helped our infielders a lot with defensive positioning, his specialty. When Billy brought in another coach, Lee Walls, to take Fowler's place as his best buddy, Zim withdrew even further because Walls was waving towels at infielders and outfielders, moving them all over the place. Zim went to the other end of the bench for a drink of water and stayed for three months. He resigned at the end of the season.

Billy also had a pitchout sign linked to a scratch of his nose. Billy's nose itched one day, so he kept scratching and poor Butch Wynegar kept calling pitchouts. It was incredible. Butch wasn't spared Billy's wrath, either.

Even guys extremely loyal to Billy were singed. Matt Keough, one of Billy's pitchers from Oakland who pitched complete games until their arms practically fell off, came to New York to try to pitch and to try to save Billy's thin pitching staff. Matt struggled for about 10 starts, which ticked off Billy because he'd campaigned to get Matt. Keough was to start against his old team when Billy informed the media he would not stay with Matt long, especially if he put Rickey Henderson on. Keough warmed up for the game and Bob Shirley warmed up right beside him. Keough walked Henderson and faced just two more batters. Shirley relieved the kid in the first inning.

I felt bad for Keough because he was one of Billy's big boosters. Keough always told guys how Billy took care of his Oakland players. He couldn't say no if you asked him for a favor, like a day off or permission to travel on your own instead of with the team in order to visit family, Keough said. That's the Billy he knew. That guy didn't manage the Yankees in 1983, though.

Billy treated me well in comparison to some of my teammates. He still amazed me as a manager. With "Billy ball," the unpredictable was the rule. In one game against the A's, Billy batted me cleanup—and had me bunt, not once but twice. The second bunt was a suicide squeeze. Ironically, it came against Keough, who was soon to join the zoo. As an Athletic, he did not pretend to understand. "What's going on?" Keough asked me later, trying not to laugh. "Why are you bunting, the way you hit me?" I couldn't give him a straight answer, so I just shrugged and said, "I don't know. All I do is read the signs."

While I was learning about Billy, he was learning about me, too. When he sent Zim around to get each player's list of three or four pitchers he preferred not to face, I handed Zim a blank sheet. Billy told me later that my stats indicated I should have written down some names. I said, "I'm not ducking anybody." He accepted that.

We had no problems that year. I never had to put up with a screaming session. But, as I watched Billy deride other guys while they were out on the field, I couldn't help but wonder what he said about me when I was not nearby. I knew I was giving a hundred percent, but so were others and that didn't buy them reprieves. So, I decided if you can't trust 'em, don't join 'em. I drifted to the other end of the bench, too. I talked to Billy's targets a lot. You can't put your arm around a fielder or pitcher who's just had his head handed to him, but you can let him know he's not alone. The way I figured it, I had to live with those guys. Just because the first year was going well for me, didn't mean I could just take my hits and ignore the rest. I just felt players shouldn't be treated that way. Players shouldn't be pampered, either. But I always heard Billy's players adored him. That feeling was nonexistent with the majority of players by 1983.

28

WHAT A STICKY MESS

IF the 1983 Yankees had just had to coexist with Billy and George we might have made it. But the Yankees could not overcome the big three—Billy, George, and Pine Tar.

The final barrier was a typical Yankees distraction, the sort I'd always heard about, and never really believed until I witnessed it up close and personal.

Halfway through the season, Graig Nettles and Don Zimmer had noticed that George Brett of the Royals was using a bat that had pine tar spread too far up the handle, an illegality umpires hardly ever notice or enforce. Billy tucked away that information and lay in wait for the hitter who, above all others, tormented the Yankees.

On July 24, Billy found his moment. Brett stepped in with one on and two outs in the ninth and the Royals trailing by 1 run. Brett faced Goose Gossage. It was two of the game's best, two long-time adversaries staging another awesome battle in absolute show time.

Goose threw a 94-mph fastball. Brett swung late and hit a mammoth foul ball down the left-field line. Two pitches later, Brett turned on another fastball, but this time he did not swing late. As hitters say, he turned the dial up from about three to about nine and drilled Gossage's pitch into the right-field bleachers to put the Royals ahead, 5–4.

Billy and Zimmer pounced on the umpires, Billy protesting, "That bat's illegal." Amazing as it may seem, the umpires actually agreed with Billy and overturned the home run, ruled Brett out. Game over. The Yankees were awarded a 4–3 victory. Brett lost his mind and had to be restrained by teammates and umpires.

Billy was ecstatic. So was Nettles, who took credit for Goose's "victory." I didn't know what to think. I hadn't been happy to see Brett hit the home run; it had cost me a potential game-winning RBI I'd driven in with a triple. But we also had the bottom of the ninth to try to turn the loss into a victory. I wanted to feel a part of that "victory," but my heart wasn't in it. It didn't feel like a victory, just an ugly win with an asterisk.

The umpires said we won, but a guy had just gone one-on-one with our best reliever and beaten the Goose with his bat, only to lose his home run on a technicality. Say what you want about the rule, but pine tar did not help that ball out of the stadium. Brett did that all by himself. All pine tar does is help a hitter get a better grip on his bat. Infielders use it in their gloves, pitchers use it on rainy days. Still, it is considered an illegal substance. During the 1988 National League Championship Series, the Mets suspected the Dodgers' Jay Howell of having pine tar on his glove during an appearance in Los Angeles, then had him checked on a messy, cold day at Shea Stadium. The umpires found the substance and threw Howell and his glove out of the game. Bart Giamatti, then National League president, using the technicality, suspended Howell for two of the remaining LCS games. Pine tar didn't help Howell in Los Angeles; he lost the game to New York. And I wonder if the Mets would have preferred that Howell lost control of one of his pitches while pitching in the rain at Shea and hit Mookie Wilson or Len Dykstra in the head. I'm sure my buddy Davey Johnson wanted Howell rousted and maybe warned or shook up. I know Davey. I don't think he wanted to beat the Dodgers by using a technicality that cost Los Angeles a player.

Technicalities shouldn't win ballgames. Players should.

Four days after Brett had his home run taken away, the league president, Lee MacPhail, reversed the umpires' decision and ordered the game resumed on August 18, with the Royals' 5–4 lead restored.

For a half a month, the team fretted over the decision. Fans sued to halt the game's resumption on the bizarre basis that rescheduling it on a school day would deprive kids of an opportunity to attend. Steinbrenner scheduled an afternoon game, but the earliest start he could get approved was six P.M. So he protested on behalf of "campers" who would not be able to attend. That was the weirdest twist of all, since I'd never seen a camper near Yankee Stadium in my life. No one had any idea of what Steinbrenner was talking about. It turned out he wanted to bus in kids from summer camps, a nice gesture in the middle of sheer insanity.

From the vantage point of our fishbowl, it seemed like the whole world was spinning out of control.

As the league rep, I huddled with Dave Winfield, the team rep, to consider asking the players to possibly forfeit the game. Our initial thinking was that it seemed pointless to go through the farce of bringing the Royals all the way back to New York and put us through a circus just to play one and a third innings. The resumption was scheduled for what was a much-needed day-off from the craziness. We did not forfeit, though. We were still in a pennant race and we could not afford to rule out a possible ninth-inning comeback, even if it was a month delayed. We left the decision to management. And they awaited the outcome of all the legal action.

The courtroom scenes and lawsuits added a surreal air, especially when noted attorney Roy Cohn was engaged by the Yankees to act as defense. Technically, the team fought the injunction sought by the fans, but argued for it in spirit. The Yankees "won." We had to play. The surreal atmosphere turned tragic the morning of August 18. About twelve hours before the Pine Tar game was to be finished, Andre Robertson had a near-fatal car crash. Andre was critically injured, suffering a broken neck. His companion, a friend visiting from Texas, also suffered critical injuries and was paralyzed for life. Andre never played again that season and never regained his once-promising form.

The game was played that afternoon in an incredibly somber atmosphere. We were wondering if a teammate was dying, playing in front of enough reporters to fill the press box, but only about 1200 fans, not enough to fill one section of the stadium. We were also playing for a manager who was so despondent he'd locked himself in the lounge, which was probably for the best considering how many "targets" with press passes were walking around.

That day I truly felt sorry for Billy, he was so tormented. I also felt anger. The season was getting away from us because we had spent too much time fretting over the damned Pine Tar game. It was an adversity, but we didn't have to be waylaid by it. We were, though. When MacPhail reversed the Royals' defeat on July 28, his decision subtracted a game from our victory column and knocked us from first place to second, one-half game behind the Orioles. From that point to when the game finally ended on August 18, the team lost 13 of 22 to fall 3.5 games back. We were trailing not only the first-place Brewers, but also the Orioles, Tigers, and Blue Jays.

We were better than that. Still, we could not stop the free-fall. Little things became huge media events. Dave Winfield threw a ball at a sea gull to chase it off the field at Exhibition Stadium, not knowing the bird was ill. Instead of scaring it, Winnie accidentally killed the bird. Toronto police arrested him. It took a half a season, but the Yankees had an international incident.

Steve Kemp, the other big hitter George had plucked from the free-agent market, was walking in the outfield one day during batting practice, not paying attention. A ball hit by Omar Moreno struck Kemper in the face, shattering his cheek bone and damaging his eyesight forever. Kemper, jinxed all year, was just coming back from an early-season shoulder injury suffered when he, Jerry Mumphrey, and Willie Randolph collided chasing a ball in blustery Exhibition Stadium. Kemper steamrolled the other two guys because he had cotton in his ears to ward off the wind. He broke Mump's toe, nearly killed Willie, and wound up causing the first-known ban of cotton from a major-league clubhouse.

Always, little things turned into big things with the Yankees.

Billy couldn't stop any of that from overwhelming the team. He should have told us to put the stupidity of the season behind us, to not let events control our destiny. But Billy couldn't even put that stuff behind himself.

That's when I realized events could seize control of Billy. He wasn't immune to the craziness, but was more vulnerable than anyone. Mere losses took a phenomenal toll on him emotionally and physically. I feared that season would kill him.

No matter how smoothly the game goes, baseball is hard on Billy. He starts a season in the best of health, as George liked to say, tanned and rested. Halfway through, he looks like death. The stress and his lifestyle leave him haggard.

That year, George knocked on his office door three or four times and walked away, believing Billy had not arrived. Billy was in there, asleep or sick or whatever. Quite a few times we had no lineup until an hour before the game. That made it difficult to organize batting practice, since you take practice swings in the cage according to who's playing and where you're scheduled to hit in the batting order. A lot of times Jeff Torborg would sneak into Billy's office to get the lineup. Or else we would hit in groups of threes based on the previous night's lineup.

I don't know why Billy was sleeping at the ballpark. It wasn't any of my business. And I didn't go in there to see if he was inebriated. He was just in there, asleep, as far as I was concerned. Sometimes food would be sent in, or the trainers would go in and give him vitamin supplements because Billy could not eat. Whether he drank too much or not wasn't my concern because he never found me in a bar to accost me. And I never saw him drunk on the field or in the clubhouse, never saw him take a drink in between innings. I didn't see it, wasn't looking for it. There were other problems, though.

On July 4, the day the leagues paused for the three-day All-Star break, Billy entered a hospital to be treated for internal bleeding. On December 16, when Martin heard the news that Yogi Berra was to replace him as manager, he was in a hospital bed in Minnesota. He was again to undergo surgery for internal bleeding. George cited health as one of the reasons Billy was being "elevated" to the position of front-office consultant.

At no time in 1983 could I get used to the firestorms that swirled around Billy and George. Every time something bizarre would happen, Ron Guidry would just laugh and tell me to sit tight because things would get better.

Guidry was right, not only about that season but the years to follow. Billy alone didn't make the Bronx Zoo a zoo. But I think Billy embodies what has gone wrong with Yankee baseball in the eighties. When it was just baseball, Billy was so sharp, just like the team. When he was left alone and could just be Billy Martin, the manager, he was great to play for, actually a joy to be around. He put the best lineup he could on the field everyday, wanted to win as badly as anyone I've ever seen. But that desire could not keep away the demons or make him invulnerable to his personal troubles, or the pressures only George can bring to bear. The same can be said of the team.

The Yankees hardly ever lose a division because the winning team is better. In my mind, the Yankees mostly always beat themselves. Other teams count on that. And, sure enough, enough problems to derail the strongest team crept into our clubhouse all season long. Billy was like every Yankees manager I've ever known in this decade. Each one says the clubhouse is his, not Steinbrenner's. But they are eventually worn down. Billy was no different. At the start of the season he was ready to fight for what he believed in, would constantly say that we were a good team, that we would win in spite of everything else. And we would have won if it hadn't been for the "everything else." Even though we finished third, 7 games behind the division-winning Orioles, I'll always believe we were the better team. It wasn't much to hold onto, but at least we knew we were good. And we had all survived, perhaps the most incredible feat of all.

29

PRIDE OF THE YANKEES

THE Angels were playing a game at Yankee Stadium in 1982 in which New York first baseman Davey Collins attempted to field a bunt. He bobbled the ball several times before giving up on the play altogether.

The Yankee fans went crazy, booing and screaming.

After the game I went to the weight room to work out. The only other person there was Collins. He was crying his eyes out. He was petrified, a real mess, another Steinbrenner "millionaire" being worn down by the constant pressure to be perfect.

When you're in Little League you cry if you don't get a bunt down or if a coach yells at you. I didn't think major leaguers cried. I found out differently in New York.

Collins and Ken Griffey had come over from Cincinnati that year, charged with infusing the Yankees with some of that Big Red Machine success. Davey also was given $800,000, which the financial times dictated the market could bear. But Davey was bearing singles and stolen bases and that's about it. All the money in the world couldn't make him into another Mickey Mantle and he was being vilified for that.

I sat and talked with Davey for a while because he was a former Angels teammate and friend. Speaking from experience, I tried to tell him about the futility of trying to earn a million dollars on each swing, how he just had to relax. By the time I left, Davey had stopped crying, but he still had a dazed look on his face.

Davey was traded to Toronto before the 1983 season. Others with that same blank stare took his place. Toby Harrah. Omar Moreno. Eddie Whitson. Matt Keough. Butch Wynegar. Some guys can handle New York, some can't. I'll never look down on the ones who can't. Only guys who have been there really know what those long Junes and Julys, Augusts and Septembers with Steinbrenner's Yankees are like. In 1983, I got my first taste of those long marches and learned a great deal about how I would cope. I also learned about how others coped and marveled at how much stamina and professionalism permeated that clubhouse. Many teammates stick out in my mind, the following the most:

Dave Winfield

No one I played alongside of in New York was as mentally tough as Dave Winfield. In my mind, he epitomized professionalism under the most trying of circumstances.

I admire his magnetism, and ability to handle the BS that has come his way ever since the '81 World Series, when he was scapegoated for getting just 1 hit in 22 at-bats against the Dodgers. You could see the pride, the ability. No matter how bad the feuding with Steinbrenner got, Dave never stopped giving the Yankees 150 percent every single day.

Dave has met every attack and just keeps putting up Hall of Fame numbers, something I know his teammates and players throughout the game recognize and appreciate.

It probably took a full season before Dave Winfield and I became close friends. There was definitely a feeling-out period. I was curious about him and he was probably curious about both Steve Kemp and me, about whether he'd have more big names thrown in his face. It did not help when Steinbrenner told reporters, "I have two cannons to put around Winfield," as if Dave was in dire need of protection. Dave already had the legend of Reggie haunting him. He did not need that.

When Dave and I did become close, I felt it was something special because he gives friendship so sparingly. He is not standoffish. I believe he is just weary of being let down. Dave has been burned by teammates, in both San Diego and New York, guys who probably resented a six-foot-six black man making $22 million. He got no such feelings from me. I was just sorry he didn't get $44 million. Every dollar earned takes players up to another level. And he has never cheated anyone out of one cent. I think Dave pulled back from some guys for other reasons, too. He gets hammered by the owner for everything he says or does. He was painted as a selfish player when he was going head-to-head with Don Mattingly for the batting title in 1984. No matter what, he just couldn't win. And more often than not, Winnie was left to hang all by himself.

I couldn't help but think that the organization and the fans sided with Mattingly over Winfield in 1984. That was unfair. Mattingly and Winfield are both Yankees. Both are special because they play the game hard. Both represent so much that is positive in the game. Donnie is a home-grown Yankee and one of the hardest workers I've ever seen in uniform. That season, he represented the Yankees' future and represented it well. Dave is out there every day, fighting for kids and the community. How many players have actually written a book about drug abuse and worked hand-in-hand with the federal government on antidrug projects? Dave has written such a book and does such work, year in, year out. He is an asset to baseball, something the Yankees have never acknowledged. Donnie would learn in later years about the abuse that always comes with a $2-million-a-year contract. In 1984, though, that torment was strictly reserved for Dave because Donnie was still a kid making one-tenth of what Dave earned. Dave had another strike against him. Not only did he make about $1.5 million that year, but he is a black man who made $1.5 million. That was unacceptable to far too many people.

The divisiveness never spilled over into the clubhouse. Sure, some of the younger guys who played with Donnie in the minors were in his corner. And some of the veterans who knew that another such year might not ever come Dave's way were pulling for him. But no one rooted against either one.

I don't think management could say the same.

The organization wanted Mattingly to win, period. That stunned me. It wasn't Mattingly vs. Boggs or Mattingly vs. Brett. It should have been a great rivalry. Instead it was a repeat of the good-guy, bad-guy syndrome that marred the Mantle–Maris home run race in 1961. And it took a serious emotional toll on Dave. On the final day, Mattingly got a standing ovation. Winfield wasn't nearly as well received. That was disgraceful.

To their credit, both Dave and Donnie handled the outside distractions with class and dignity. Donnie praised Dave often for his gentlemanly approach to the race and the consideration and respect he paid to a younger,

less-experienced player. When Don edged Dave on the last day, .343 to
.340, thanks to a 4–for–5 performance, there was no loser, only two
winners. Dave did not stick around to talk to the media after the final game,
leaving the spotlight all to Mattingly. The truth is, he was also too torn up
over the loss. Too much had happened to soil what should have been a
banner day for both players.

For three years I watched Winnie take it and take it without really
answering back. In the spring of 1988, he did, in his autobiography,
Winfield: A Player's Life.

Steinbrenner, not treated kindly in that book, went after Dave like never
before. And all hell broke loose.

Winfield wrote that Willie Randolph had once commented that blacks
could be considered good Yankees but not true Yankees. Winnie never
directly quoted Willie, but said that such a conversation took place. Willie
came out with a statement saying his confidence had been betrayed and that
his words were taken out of context. Steinbrenner used that as a pretext to
try to isolate Dave in the clubhouse and to force Dave to accept a trade. A
lot of people are afraid of the truth. Ken Griffey is not. Neither am I. Grif
and I knew that what Dave wrote was true. And we both publicly backed
him.

I did not side with Dave Winfield and against Willie Randolph. I think
Willie probably shied away from the truth because of the pressures of just
trying to survive. He was still in New York. Grif and I were not. Whether I
was or not, though, I believe I would not have let Winnie hang. I told the
truth as I knew it. So did Grif.

I don't ever remember using the exact words that blacks couldn't be "true
Yankees." I know that conversations along those lines took place. I know all
four of us were there. Mostly, the conversations were humorous. We would
tease each other about how we did not expect to be invited back for Old
Timer's games because we hardly ever saw former Yankees who are black
other than Roy White attend those events. We also joked about how we
would never have a "day" like the Yankees gave Lou Piniella, Bobby Murcer,
Phil Rizzuto, and Billy Martin.

I can't speak for anyone other than myself. But I know part of my intent
was to try to ease some pain and anger. I was just trying to understand.
Why did it have to be that way for Winnie and some of the others, especially
the black players? I wanted to know what a "true Yankee" was. What are
the connotations? I didn't know what the rules were. I still don't.

How do black guys buy into that "tradition"? Keep your mouth shut and
go along? I couldn't do that. Neither could Winnie or Grif. If that's what
you figure you've got to do, fine. Both Willie and Ron Guidry made it

through a decade by not making waves. They kept their good standing and didn't have their heads knocked off. That probably also assured longevity and titles as cocaptains. I have absolutely no problem with that. They're both good people, good friends.

Winfield being Winfield doesn't make Dave a bad guy, though. Grif played hard every day. So did I. Not one of us ever asked for a "day" or wants one. I believe all we ever asked for was a little respect. All we ever got was slammed to the mat if we so much as said a word in dissent. Being black, we couldn't help notice that when white guys would say something similar, the response was, "Oh, that's frustration speaking" or "He's a competitor." In my years there it seemed the only major exception to that rule was Steve Kemp; he got hammered so much the guys teased him that the Yankees must have mistakenly thought he was black.

That's what our conversations were about, the funny ones and the ones that hurt too much to laugh. I spoke on those subjects. We all did. Grif knows that. So does Winnie. And so does Willie.

Winnie survived that crisis and wound up hitting .322 with 25 home runs and 107 RBI in 1988, his response to all the garbage that had been heaped on him. "True" Yankee or not, Dave Winfield is truly awesome.

Don Mattingly

Since I have played alongside Wade Boggs, Don Mattingly, and Rod Carew, there's always a call to compare. Those three are the best hitters I've ever seen and I wouldn't know which order to put them in because they all do different things so well. But of the three, Donnie is more of a damage guy than Boggs is or Rodney was. Donnie's more like Brett, a guy who will drive in the big run, collect the extra-base hit, and pull the ball over the right-field wall. He doesn't possess the Boggs art of making contact. Nobody does. He is not as consistent as Carew. But as far as keeping the average up there and driving in runs, Mattingly is tops.

Watching Donnie grow as a player was one of the fun parts of being a Yankee. Donnie thrives because he has great instincts and learns quickly. He learned to pull the ball in one season of winter ball and has been a home-run threat ever since. He has great hand-eye coordination and does every single thing a hitter must do to hit .350. He locks out distractions as well as any player I've seen, a good attribute to have in New York. He deserves his status as a Gold Glove first baseman and his reputation as a hard worker. Donnie doesn't have the bursts of speed on the bases, like Rickey Henderson, or the aggressiveness of a Winfield, who is always a first-to-third threat. But if Donnie could do those things he'd be perfect and there are no perfect players.

Off the field, Donnie's learned some lessons the hard way and still has some more to learn. He tried to have it both ways by attempting to appease Steinbrenner and the Players Association. The most notable example: In 1986, Donnie said he wanted to explore the possibility of taking more of a lead in the Association. Then he listened to Steinbrenner's warning that the Yankees had no intention of paying a player $2 million a year, so he asked for $1.975 million in arbitration. He could have asked for $2.5 million and won, since he was the only player that year to earn perfect ratings in all categories used to measure a player's worth in arbitration hearings.

As it turned out, Steinbrenner ended up signing Donnie to a $2-million-a-year contract the next season.

Both Donnie and Wade Boggs need to understand that, as two of the top five players in the game, everything they do contractually has a trickle-down effect on other players' negotiations. That may be uncomfortable, but other top players, including Tom Seaver, Ted Simmons, Brooks Robinson, Reggie, Mark Belanger, and myself, have taken stances to make the association stronger. Over 600 players sacrificed fifty days' pay in 1981 to assure that Donnie had the right to arbitration. If the top guys in Donnie's generation forget all the guys coming after them, the union will fall apart.

Donnie and I never agreed on that issue, until the winter of 1988. That's when he addressed the executive board of the Players Association, during our winter meetings. Donnie said he was beginning to understand the importance of his role in the union and his obligation to other players. Only time will tell how deeply Donnie's newfound commitment runs. Whatever happens, though, it won't erase the friendship we share or the memories I have of watching Donnie grow into the great player that he is.

Ron Guidry

Ron Guidry is a lot like Dave Winfield. He does not give friendship easily, either, but once he does it's for life. It probably took three years before we reached that point. Ron Guidry was worth the wait.

I've been a fan of Ron's for a long time because of his competitiveness on the mound. When I first saw Ron Guidry pitch, my initial thought was, "How can this little guy throw so hard?" But he just kept coming at the league and got better and better. In 1978 he was Cy Everything. He struck out 18 Angels in one game, was 25–3 and absolutely untouchable. The Yankees caught "Louisiana Lightning" in a bottle and ran with it. Ron

Guidry was as instrumental in the Yankees' return to respectability in the seventies as any other player.

Guidry is not just an excellent pitcher. He is as fine an athlete as you'll find on any team. From 1982 through 1986, he won five Gold Gloves. He could easily play centerfield and can run with anyone. "Gator" catches line drives that would kill other pitchers or drive them into centerfield or to the showers. He covers first as well as any pitcher, too.

The most surprising thing about Gator is how quiet he is. I don't think he's shy. He is a man of few words, but when he speaks, people listen. Not that he's standoffish; he has friends all over that clubhouse, especially pitchers. He also provided leadership in his own way, by taking the ball every fourth or fifth day, going out there, throwing strikes and giving the Yankees quality innings.

Goose Gossage

The snarling, tenacious Goose Gossage was well known to me long before we became teammates. I respected his game, admired his style so much I would push the back line of the batter's box to its outer limits just to try to get an edge against his 96-mph fastball. He was as close to a football player in a baseball uniform as anyone in the game, a guy who oozed intensity and never, ever accepted losing.

Goose may have been a growling, intimidating force on the mound, but the truth is he's a big teddy bear. I never personally witnessed Goose wrecking a hotel, but I believe every story of his escapades to be true. Goose just loves to have fun.

By 1983, things were not too much fun for Goose. He watched friends like Rudy May and Bob Shirley sent to Billy's doghouse. Goose and George Frazier became a two-man bullpen and Goose went crazy because he didn't know if he was the long man, short man, or middle man. Goose, Shirley, Dave Righetti, and Rudy's attitude became: just do your job and don't kill the manager.

A lot of people figured Goose just spouted off when he said baseball stopped being fun when Steinbrenner apologized for losing the 1981 World Series. Goose wasn't kidding. At the end of 1983, Goose declared free agency and said he would entertain offers from any club except the Yankees.

Graig Nettles

Graig was the Yankees' captain when I played in New York. At that point in my career, I didn't need a captain to lean on. A lot of guys did. I soon learned that just because you have the title doesn't mean you're a captain.

I had a good relationship with him, did not begrudge him that title. He put in a lot of quality years there and gave the team tremendous moments at third base. The captaincy was truly special to him given that only Lou Gehrig, Thurman Munson, and Graig had held the position since 1935. But Graig took to his corner locker and turned it into an apartment, equipped with lounge chair, coffeemaker, stereo. It didn't say "Keep out," but guys didn't drift over to him and he didn't come out too often. Graig disappeared quickly after games, thus his nickname, "Puff." There were guys there who needed someone of his stature to pay them a little attention, to maybe take away the sting of a Martin temper tantrum. For some reason, Graig didn't. And sometimes his sarcasm hurt as much as Billy's. Maybe I'm wrong, but that was just not my idea of what being a captain is all about.

Ken Griffey

The first time I met Grif it felt like we had known each other for years. He makes you laugh, he makes any and all players feel welcome. He's a natural force in the clubhouse, on the field, a teacher and friend. I enjoyed every day that I spent with Grif, except the days that he hurt and I hurt.

I think we were two of a kind, players who never got a lot of credit for just being who we were. Grif joked around a lot, kept Winnie and me in stitches. Deep down, though, he probably needed to feel needed more than either of us.

Grif had two simple rules: don't mess with him and don't mess with his family. Billy learned that in 1983, when Grif was about ready to kill him for yelling at Grif's sons after a loss. Ken Jr., Craig Griffey, and Donny were playing in the tunnels behind the dugout, something players' and coaches' kids have done for years. Grif felt that if Billy had a problem with his kids he should have talked to him. Billy tiptoed real lightly around Grif after that, especially when it was reported that Grif demanded a trade partly because of that incident. Grif was so angry he sent his kids home to Cincinnati for the rest of that summer. Grif gets a real kick out of how Billy was quoted as saying how much fun Ken Jr. was to have around the stadium. Junior became baseball's number-one draft choice in the nation in 1986.

The Yankees kept Grif until 1986 even though he was unhappy. He was just too good to give away. Grif's the only left-handed hitter I've ever seen platooned against left-handers because he could handle them when other left-handed hitters, like Omar Moreno and Dan Pasqua, could not.

Grif is a lot like me in that he never forgives or forgets. A kid pitcher for

Toronto named Matt Williams learned that the hard way. Williams had beaten us in his debut in Toronto. "The Yankees are beatable," Williams told reporters. "I got Baylor. I got Nettles. Shoot, I got everyone at least once." Williams faced us at Yankee Stadium a week later. He worked his way into a bases-loaded jam with Griffey due up. I was next. We were standing in the on-deck circle when Grif turned and said he had never hit a grand slam. "Grif," I said, "do me a favor. Just leave me two, okay?"

Grif hit Williams's third pitch 415 feet into the right-field bleachers. He left me nothing. I had to settle for a solo home run, which knocked Williams out of the game.

That's Grif, in all deference to Mike Easler and Don Mattingly, my "Hit Man," my "Hired Assassin." And most of all, my friend.

Willie Randolph

I might never have dinner with Willie Randolph again, maybe never carry on another conversation with him. And that's a shame because I still consider him a friend. What happened in the spring of 1988 because of the Winfield controversy may be something he'll never forgive or forget, but I know that no one ever wanted to hurt him. I hope Willie knows I would have done the same for him if he had been in Dave's position because that's what friends do for friends.

I have a tremendous amount of respect for Willie. He's extremely dedicated to the team, his family, and the community. He was the serious guy in our foursome, the target of most of Grif's good-natured needling. He's seen a lot, suffered a lot, too. I bet he's lost track of the number of guys, including myself, who came to New York, made a lot more than he did, and then moved on, leaving Willie to break in new teammates, take scared kids under his wing.

Guys like Willie and Guidry are survivors. Graig Nettles, Goose, Reggie were a little more outspoken and maybe that's part of the reason why they were gone long before Willie. Willie and Guidry, they just did their jobs and rolled with the punches. That's okay. If it's not your nature to speak out, don't change character and pretend.

The funny thing is that I always felt Willie wanted to speak out, but was afraid to be himself for fear he would not be able to stay. He had only played for one major-league team, except for a few games with Pittsburgh in his rookie year. He had spent the bulk of his career playing in the city where he was raised. Those ties were so strong, Willie never did anything to jeopardize his position.

The Yankeess never appreciated Willie and, in the winter of 1988, showed how little Willie's loyalty meant to them. Willie was a free agent, but wanted to remain in New York. Instead of re-signing him and allowing him to finish out his career in New York, the Yankees chose to sign free agent Steve Sax, a former Dodger. They did so without informing Willie that he was no longer in their plans. Willie was stunned. He learned from the media that Sax was signed, ironically, on Thanksgiving Eve. Willie then found a new home, signing with the Dodgers in November 1988.

Willie's Yankees days are over. He had always been underrated and underpaid in New York even though he clearly made the Yankees a better team every single time he stepped on the field. Other players and other teams always knew that. I often wondered if Willie did. I hope so. He is one of the best. The Dodgers are lucky to have him.

Dave Righetti

I don't know if the Yankees have had a finer young pitcher than Dave Righetti in years. Rags is a tremendous athlete, a real hard worker.

One of my fondest memories of that season is Dave's Fourth of July no-hitter against the Red Sox. The twenty-seventh and final out may have been his toughest—a strikeout of Wade Boggs. I was proud to have hit a solo home run that day against John Tudor to help Dave win. You always want to contribute in some way to a no-hitter and my contribution as DH could only be with the bat. Well, maybe in one other way, too. The day before, Rags was sitting on the dugout steps in the 94-degree heat, watching batting practice. I went up to him and said, "Rags, you're young and wise. Why don't you get off this bench, go inside and relax? You might need that energy tomorrow." He went to the clubhouse.

Rags was well on his way to becoming a fine starter when Goose left. He was told the team needed him in the bullpen. Rags took one for the team and became one of the league's finest relievers.

Rags doesn't breathe fire like Goose. You hardly ever get two words out of him, he's so quiet. He needs encouragement and a pat on the back. Once he gets that, he'll throw the ball through a wall for you. He's loyal, something I hope the Yankees appreciate. Even when he couldn't get his contract incentives adjusted to his reliever's role, he never cried. He showed a lot of class and did his job. Dave Righetti could play on my team any time.

Don Baylor

When I hit my first home run as a Yankee, Yogi Berra jumped out of the coach's box so fast to shake my hand he startled me. I'd never shaken hands with a first-base coach before, let alone Yogi Berra. I soon learned that was Yogi's tradition. Therefore, it was Yankees tradition.

Pete Sheehy, the Yankees' clubhouse man since 1927, used to tell me that Joe DiMaggio was the best player he ever saw. When you've handed uniforms to Lou Gehrig, Babe Ruth, DiMaggio, Yogi Berra, Roger Maris, Mickey Mantle, and Whitey Ford, you can make that statement. I hung on every word Pete said, from the day he handed me my first Yankees uniform until he died in August 1985.

Before the 1983 Old Timer's Game, I walked into the clubhouse and saw DiMaggio and Whitey Ford putting on the pinstripes. Lefty Gomez sat at my locker trying on my spikes. Bill Dickey, who shares the retired No. 8 with Yogi, came over and started chatting. I grabbed my uniform and said, "Move in, guys." After all, they were the legends. And I was in awe.

Every day presented a new lesson in Yankees tradition, a tradition that runs deep, a tradition I wanted to be a part of.

As a right-handed hitter setting out to earn a living in Yankee Stadium, I had some proving to do because of the "death valleys" in left- and right-center. Just remembering a 430-foot fly ball I hit to left-center the year before off Ron Guidry gave me nightmares. I could still see Jerry Mumphrey tracking down the line drive and hear Gator laughing. I admired Dave Winfield because he was so strong and had enough leverage in that six-foot-six frame to hit the ball out at any point. I've hit some home runs to straight-away center, but I knew that, in order to survive, I had to find the wall in left-center or aim for the very small, short porch in left. I had to force the count deep in search of pitches from the middle of the plate in, pitches that I could pull. In my efforts, I flirted with the left-field line a lot, probably killed some fans on the other side of that pole in the upper deck. If they had moved the "fair" line just a little more to the left, I would probably be challenging Hank Aaron's home run record right now.

I worked hard at making the adjustment; it paid off. I hit 10 of my 21 home runs at The Stadium. I also found the gaps and led the team in doubles, with 33. I had 85 RBI in 144 games and, for the first time ever, hit over .300, finishing at .303. It was all good enough to win the Silver Bat award for designated hitters.

I had not stepped into that clubhouse at the start of 1983 and said, "Hey, I'm here to lead you." I just wanted to do my job, earn the kind of respect I had for the people who were already there.

I believe I did.

30

YOGI AND PHIL

WHEN a team trails by 10.5 games on April 30, 20 games by June 20, goes on to win 87 games, but still places a distant third, there's not much to look back upon fondly. That was the fate of the 1984 Yankees, one of many teams bulldozed by Sparky Anderson's runaway Tigers, who won 35 of their first 40 races to end the season early.

That year did have two saving graces, however.

On December 16, 1983, George Steinbrenner had "shifted" an ailing Billy Martin to the front office and handed the team over to Lawrence Peter Berra. I was no longer staring at legends carved in bronze and hanging along Monument Row in centerfield. I was playing for one. I was playing for Yogi.

Then, on January 6, 1984, the Yankees signed Philip Henry Niekro, one of the most exceptional people this game has ever produced.

When Yogi took over, a lot of players welcomed the change. No more hollering, no more screaming, no more intimidation. Just total respect, given by and returned to a man who was revered just for being Yogi.

If you cannot play for Yogi you cannot play for anyone. He treated us like men. He never hid when a tough decision had to be made. If he had to sit a player or send him to the minors, Yogi would call the guy into his office and tell him face-to-face. Yogi didn't believe in using coaches as messengers, a welcome change from Billy Martin's mode of operation. Halfway through the season, when the Tigers had pretty much put us away, the organization decided to look at some younger players, such as Brian Dayett, Stanley Javier, Vic Mata, and Mike Pagliarulo. So a lot of veterans spent more and more time on the bench. I played in only 134 games, Grif in 120. Toby Harrah and Oscar Gamble each played less than 100. Nettles did not even make it out of spring training. Feuding and fussing with Steinbrenner, he was traded to San Diego the day the Yankees left Florida. Soon to disappear from the roster was Lou Piniella, who retired midway through June to become the hitting coach. Roy Smalley was traded halfway through the season.

None of the veterans who lost at-bats or jobs were happy, but no one hammered Yogi. The attitude was if that's the way Yogi feels, fine. You knew he was being honest, you could see that it hurt him to have to tell a veteran he would have to sit a day, let alone a week. You could tell he really cared about his players. What a difference. With Billy, there were rarely explanations. It was like, "Why should I bother, you're only a player." Yogi felt guys with ten, fifteen years in the bigs deserved at least a conversation, even if it took only a minute of his time. And hearing it from Yogi made it almost painless.

Yogi didn't use a caste system, either. Yogi never missed a day talking to every player, one through twenty-five. He's like your grandfather or favorite uncle. He is very easy to talk to, laughs and jokes all the time. He tells stories unlike anyone else because he's, well, Yogi.

He told me that once, when he was in a slump, his manager, the legendary Casey Stengel, told him to hold his hands this way, his bat that way, position his feet thusly, and on and on. Finally, after Yogi struck out twice, he told Casey, "I can't hit and think at the same time."

There it was, my first Yogi-ism. And it made sense. When you're hitting you can't think too much. If you do, you're not going to relax. Yogi's statement made as much sense as another of his, that Steve McQueen "must have made that movie before he died." Of course he did. It's perfectly logical. So is Yogi.

Yogi is a rock, as strong emotionally as any man I've ever met. But he could be hurt. In 1985, when Dale Berra was acquired by the Yankees from Pittsburgh, Yogi became the first man since Connie Mack to manage his own son. Yogi also suffered the misfortune of having to wait for the verdict that Commissioner Peter Ueberroth was scheduled to hand down that spring to players who were involved in the Pittsburgh drug scandals. Dale was one of those players.

Dale and most of the others were ordered to pay hefty fines, perform lengthy community-service work, and undergo random drug testing.

I never had a lot of tolerance for the players who used drugs. I even demanded a public apology from one—Juan Bonilla of the Padres—when he was quoted as saying every major leaguer had either snorted a line of cocaine or smoked a marijuana joint. Bonilla had slandered not only me, but countless other clean players. I had a serious problem with that and "followers" like Dale, who made drug dealers rich, dealers who try to sell dope to kids. Maybe even my kid.

I have compassion for the guys who have tried to straighten out. I have even more compassion for Yogi Berra and others who are hurt by the drug abusers. And Yogi was devastated when he realized Dale had lied to him. Yogi deserved better. Dale was fortunate, though, because Yogi never deserted him, never stopped loving that kid.

Perhaps the most amazing thing about Yogi was his stubborn refusal to transfer the pressure he was under from day one to his players. And Yogi was under pressure in 1984 because the Yankees were not allowed to watch another team win 35 of 40 without responding in kind.

Yogi did not rush out and build a doghouse, air-conditioned or otherwise. He maintained his even-handedness even though the minds that thought it was such a stroke of genius to bring in Yogi started backpedaling by June.

The most ridiculous charge to come out of the Yankees' front office was that Yogi was too easygoing. That was considered a weakness. What the Yankees never understood was that players stayed in line because of Yogi. No one ran up and down the halls or tore up hotels. There was no misconduct on airplanes. We respected him too much to do those things. Yogi set a high standard for himself and his players. He was no threat to citizens in a bar because he didn't hang out in bars.

There was also an undercurrent that some management people looked down on Yogi because they did not think he was intelligent. Yogi could not have excelled as a player and a catcher in his brilliant Hall of Fame career or become a self-made millionaire if he was dumb. He does not use the King's English, but he spoke well enough to teach us many new things about baseball.

The constant pleasure of Yogi's company that season was augmented by the presence of a new teammate—Knucksie.

Unlike a lot of pitchers of his stature, Phil Niekro did not have an aura of royalty about him. He is one of the nicest, wittiest, most down-to-earth people to ever put on a uniform.

Phil signed with the Yankees after he was released by the Braves, the only team for which he had ever pitched. What Knucksie brought into the clubhouse was truly special.

Every player accepted him immediately and, in a short time, loved him immensely. No matter how many years a guy had in, Phil had more, so the general feeling was that we were all privileged to play alongside him, not the other way around.

Phil had about fifteen to twenty years of aches and pains stored in his body, probably one million miles logged, nearly 5000 innings pitched before he arrived in New York. He had seen everything in our era, a lot of things before it, too. Phil knew about the split-fingered fastball when it was just a plain old forkball. He was around before Boeing 757s, luxury buses, all-night room service, and designated hitters. Phil made all the adjustments over the years, except maybe to modern music. He will forever be stuck on polkas. He used to scour phone books during road trips in search of Polish-American clubs so he could dance the nights away.

He spent many years in the minors because the Braves' catchers were reluctant to be on the receiving end of his knuckleball. Labeled because of his special pitch and introduced in the era of Gibson, Koufax, Marichal, and McDowell, Phil survived all the hard throwers, the strikeout kings.

On April Fool's Day in 1984, Phil turned forty-four. Some of the opposing hitters he faced had not yet been born when he threw his first major-league pitch. He didn't look much like a pitcher, more like a coach. But I never said, "What's this guy doing here?" Phil would reach the 3000-strikeout milestone that season and win his 300th game the following year. The man could pitch. He was a Hall of Famer just postponing the vote for a while and you had to admire his fight-back spirit. And Phil showed the Braves by winning 16 games for the Yankees in 1984. He ranked among the league leaders in ERA, winning percentage, and victories.

Phil figures he was told that he was too old to pitch for about the last fifteen years of his career. But he had one of those freak-of-nature pitches that drove hitters crazy, screwed up batting strokes, and just kept the victories coming.

After Knucksie threw certain pitches he would do a little jump-step and reach toward the plate with his glove hand. That was pretty animated for Phil, so I was curious about what it meant. He said he'd instinctively do that when he threw the read good knuckleball because he just knew it would not be hit. The reach toward the plate was a "throw-it-back-to-me" gesture to the catcher. Of course, when the knuckler was dancing, Phil had no more idea where the ball was going than the catcher or hitter did. Fittingly, his

3000 strikeout, against the Rangers' Larry Parrish, wound up at the backstop.

Phil had a strong but gentle way in the clubhouse. He looked after Eddie Whitson, who was following the same path as Davey Collins and other big-money guys who could not handle New York. If Whitson lost a game, Phil would go over to him and sometimes talk, sometimes just sit there until he was sure Eddie was okay.

That was just a part of his caring nature. I never saw Phil yell at a teammate or glare at a fielder after an error. Usually, he would go out of his way to pat the guy on the back.

Perhaps the most poignant battle I ever saw was Phil's push for number 300, which lasted for 5 excruciating starts from early September to October 6, 1985. Phil's back was killing him. Sometimes cramps would temporarily paralyze his pitching hand in its knuckleball grip, a frightening sight. Trainer Gene Monahan would massage Phil's hand and arm until the cramps subsided. Then Phil would take the ball and keep pitching.

During his drive to number 300, Phil's father was critically ill. Phil and his "little" brother, Joe, also in his forties and pitching for the Yankees by September of that season, flew home to Ohio as often as possible between starts. That was possible because both were knuckleballers and they did not have as rigid a running regimen as other pitchers. But the mental strain was tremendous. You have to have strong minds and hearts to perform under such circumstances. Phil and Joe both showed a lot of courage during that month.

Phil also had to host an ever-increasing media horde before and after each attempt at 300. It was a terrible strain, but he handled it with dignity and patience.

We all marveled at how he coped. And I never saw players try so hard to get a teammate a milestone. Maybe we tried too hard. We scored just 9 runs in Phil's four failed attempts. All those games were heartbreaking, but none more so than a loss in Detroit on September 18. That was the night Billy sent left-handed-hitting Mike Pagliarulo to bat right-handed for the first time in his career. Billy had many right-handed pinch-hitters available to send against Tigers left-hander Mickey Mahler, but stuck with Pags because he had seen Pags take batting practice right-handed once.

I wondered what was going on. If it had been Whitey Ford going for his 300th, would Billy have done that? Winfield and I thought maybe it was a trick play. The only trick played was on Pags. And Phil. Mahler, who had intentionally walked me moments before, struck out Pags on three pitches to get out of a two-out, two-on jam. Phil lost, 5–2. Phil didn't complain, even though it was costing him a fortune to fly his family from city to city so they could be with him when he finally won.

On October 6, 1985, Phil took the mound in our final game of the season. He knew that his number-one goal of reaching his first World Series had died the day before when the Blue Jays defeated us and clinched the division.

Phil was disappointed, but he was also a competitor. He still wanted number 300. He wanted Toronto. And he wanted to prove he was a legitimate pitcher, not just a man hanging on because of a trick pitch.

For eight and two-thirds innings, Phil did not throw one knuckleball. And he did not allow a run. With one on and two out in the ninth, Phil faced his old Braves teammate, Jeff Burroughs. After an impromptu mound visit by Joe, Phil thought about the last out and about the pitch that had got him through the first 299 victories. So he took the butterfly out of his back pocket and threw three of the darnedest knucklers to strike out Burroughs. Phil had an 8–0 shutout and his 300th victory. As soon as he walked off the field he learned his father had been removed from intensive care.

Machismo stops players from acknowledging the emotions of such moments, showing genuine appreciation. But after watching Phil in that month of triumph and near-tragedy, I had to do something more than just savor the moment. For the first time in my life, I gave another player a gift, a crystal baseball, engraved with his stats, to commemorate Phil's milestone.

Phil also won 16 games in 1985. That winter, the Yankees signed both Niekros as free agents. Then the Yankees released Phil on March 28, 1986, just before the season was about to begin. Joe was devastated. Phil walked into the office of GM Woody Woodward and handed him his uniform. He told Woodward the Yankees would never find anyone who wanted to win more than he did. He was right. Phil signed with the Indians and won 11 games for the fifth-place team. He pitched more innings than any Yankee and won more games than all but one.

At the start of that 1986 season, Phil and Joe, Bob Grich, Jose Cruz, and I ranked as the players with the most service who'd never reached a World Series. When I finally made it that October, Phil sent me a bottle of Dom Perignon inscribed, "When you win, raise a toast on me and somewhere I will toast you, too." That bottle remains unopened, a cherished gift that sits beside an autographed hat Phil gave me the day he won his 300th and a baseball he signed a year later.

The ball is inscribed: "Special friends are God-sent. I thank Him for you."

The feeling will always be mutual.

31

COURT'S IN SESSION

NOT even Connie Mack could have forestalled
the calamity of 1984. When you lose a Goose Gossage, have to make a Dave
Righetti a reliever, when your roster turns over constantly and when the
Tigers win 35 of 40, well, it gives a team very little to hold onto.

Yogi constantly sought ways to ease the soberness of that lost season. One
day he asked if I would start a kangaroo court. Yogi did not see such a court
as an infringement on his authority. He was like Earl. He wanted the players
to help each other and recapture the purpose of why we were playing. He
saw how badly we were struggling. He never wanted us to feel we had
nothing left to achieve. He felt the court would put the emphasis back on
execution. And he also wanted to inject a little levity to break the boredom
and frustration.

Such a court would have been out of the question in 1983. Nettles was
still there and it would have been in his jurisdiction to start a court if he
wished. Graig did not wish. In 1984, Graig was gone. There were no toes
to be stepped on or feelings to be hurt. Guidry, Randolph, Winfield,

Righetti, and Rick Cerone, the holdovers from the Yankees' pennant winner, did not object. So Yogi posed the idea and asked me to sleep on it. I did not have to. I jumped at the opportunity. Frank's gavel had finally been passed on. Court was in session again.

My first decision was to make Phil Niekro a one-man Supreme Court. Frank Robinson never answered to a higher authority, but I just took it upon myself to say Phil's word would outrank mine. To appeal any fine I assessed, players had to go to Phil. Lose and the fine automatically doubled. To my knowledge, Phil was implacable. He never overturned a verdict. He was the man most responsible for building a rich war chest for our season-ending "kangaroo-court" party.

The offenses were easy to avoid. All players had to do was execute.

If you batted with a man on first or second and less than two outs, you either got the guy over or it was five bucks. To do less is giving away an at-bat. Do that just once and it can mean the difference between 99 and 100 RBI. Do it fifteen times and it can mean the difference between first and second place.

Fraternization also cost five dollars. Two minutes, no longer, were allotted to ask a friend on another team about the wife and kids. Friendship might cloud your judgment when you're sliding in at second or if you have to come up and in with a 95-mph fastball.

Pitchers were fined for allowing 0–2 base hits, the severity of the penalty depending on the situation. My fines were usually in the five-dollar range. When Phil surrendered a grand slam to Ken Phelps on an 0–2 pitch, though, the fine was one hundred dollars—twenty-five for each base. I hated to do that and Phil hated to pay. But he hated the idea of the grand slam even more. He was a veteran. He knew better. He dropped a hundred dollars on my chair.

That was the first of only two hundred-dollar fines I ever issued. The second was levied against Steve Lyons two years later when we were both with the Red Sox. In a game against Milwaukee, Brewers pitcher Mark Clear faced Wade Boggs with two out and two on in the ninth in a game we trailed by 3. Lyons, called "Psycho" because of his bizarre base-running habits, stood on second. Marty Barrett was on first. Boggs had 3 hits already and we liked the chances of a fourth. But that's when Barrett told Lyons that Clear had a big leg kick, so he should take off on Clear's first move. Someone forgot to tell Marty that Clear had changed his delivery and had canned the high leg kick. He got the ball to the plate, the catcher fired on to third, and Lyons was an easy out. That was it. Game over.

John McNamara, Boston's manager, was livid.

He grabbed Lyons and said, "Who is the best hitter in baseball?"

"Wade Boggs," Lyons answered.

"Then who the hell do you think was hitting?" Mac yelled. Then he told me he would double whatever fine was given Lyons in the Red Sox kangaroo court. When I said $100, Mac said that was not enough. He fined Lyons $250.

The Yankees' answer to Lyons was Bobby Meacham.

Meach once hit a home run down in Texas with Wynegar on second and Randolph on first. I could see from the bench that the ball was gone, but Willie went back to first to tag up. Meach, running with his head down, passed Willie. Instead of the 3-run home run, he had to settle for a most-embarrassing 2-run single and an automatic out. We lost by 1 run.

Even in grade-school kick-ball, you always watch the guy in front of you. When I slapped Meach with a fine, he said his high-school coach always told him to run with his head down. "Yeah," I said, "but he didn't tell you to run with it up your rear end."

Meach paid thirty-two dollars for being caught off base when Rickey Henderson lined into a triple play. Henderson and Billy Sample—the other runner trapped off—each paid sixteen dollars. Bobby got doubled up because he appealed and, naturally, he lost.

Not even I could bring myself to deepen Meach's pain by fining him when he was thrown out at home plate in a game against Chicago in 1985. Bobby, trying to score from second on a Rickey Henderson double, stumbled, then, still trying to reach home, ran through a stop sign flashed by third-base coach Gene Michael. Dale Berra, running from first, actually pushed Meacham to try to speed him along. He should have worried about himself. He also ran past a very startled Michael. Not only did the relay arrive in time for Carlton Fisk to tag Meacham. He got Berra, too. Henderson hit a 430-foot double and wound up hitting into a double play because Berra and Meacham were both tagged out at home. The next day the *New York Times* diagrammed the play, like it was a successful end-around in the Super Bowl. It was unbelievable. Too incredible to take money from those guys. Besides, I'm sure Steinbrenner more than took care of them in that department.

Joe Cowley lived in my fine book, the pitchers' answer to Meacham. Joe seemed to live to make stupid 0–2 pitches. He also got docked for walking batters when he had more than a 2-run lead. That fine doubled if he or any pitcher committed the infraction from the seventh inning on. If Cowley got to the seventh he usually ended up in the book—and the Yankees' doghouse.

Rickey Henderson may have got one of the more peculiar fines. In 1985, Rickey got a little carried away about his pending homecoming and bragged that when the team arrived in Oakland, "two-thirds of the fans will be there to see Rickey, two-thirds to see Billy, and two-thirds to see the Yankees."

That was six-thirds. We would have needed two ballparks. That odd mathematical figuring cost Rickey twenty-five dollars.

There were players you simply could not count on to screw up. Righetti was by far the toughest target. He didn't make many mistakes pitching. And he never fraternized. How could he? We could hardly get two words out of him.

Mattingly hardly made mistakes, either, but we gladly took five dollars when he tried to turn a double play with two outs.

There were fines that might as well have not existed. I never had to assess a fine because a player did not run hard in an effort to break up a double play. When I started the court in Boston in 1986, I pointed that out to hitting coach Walt Hriniak. He kind of smiled and said it wasn't because that never happened. "Guys never went hard into second all the time until you came here," he said. "Just your reputation made them want to play the same way." That was nice. That hustle saved my Red Sox teammates some money.

Fining and collecting are two different art forms. Winfield, the highest-paid Yankee, might as well have been the poorest. Come collection day he was always pleading poverty because he refused to carry any more cash then he needed to get across the George Washington Bridge and back to his home in New Jersey. The only thing you could do was use the threat Dave feared most—a double penalty. Dave impressed with his ingenuity, though. One day he pleaded poverty because he'd forgotten his wallet. He'd even had to talk his way across the bridge to get to the ballpark, he said. Then, to solidify the story, he asked for a loan so he could get home. Not a buck, not a five-spot. He asked for a hundred dollars. "How many times are you going to cross the bridge, Winnie, that you need a hundred?" I asked. I was not buying it at all, especially since you didn't have to pay to leave New York, only to enter.

Dave was only surpassed in stinginess by Dwight Evans of the Red Sox, who argued over every cent of his fine and then threw the money at me just as the fine was about to double. "If you have to have it, here," Dwight would snap and stomp off. It was great.

Some guys were the exact opposite. Ron Guidry knew he would give up 0–2 hits because his pitches were always around the plate. So he would just give me a hundred dollars to cover fines he knew would surely come and occasionally ask, "How much do I have left?" If the hundred ran out he would write another check.

Collection day was every Sunday at home, before the first at-bat. That was a soft-touch day. And it was always a big-cash day because teams either head out on the road or players head out to dinner with their families.

When you assess fines everybody tracks *you* looking for infractions. I played with just about every player in the American League, so the Yankees watched me like a hawk in search of a fraternization rap. They even tried to set me up, sending Reggie or Carew or Lynn or Grichie after me. I actually had to dodge my friends. And at times like that, with money on the line, it seemed like there were thousands to dodge.

I once grabbed the book and wrote myself up after an embarrassing display of hitting in Baltimore. The Yankees won, 10–0. I got the game-winner, by way of a first-inning sacrifice. I then struck out 4 of the next 5 at-bats, my first-ever "golden sombrero." I almost turned platinum, but I avoided a fifth strikeout—by grounding into a double play.

I was so mad, I didn't pay careful attention to the concrete steps leading into the dugout, slipped, and hurt my back. I went into the tunnel and smashed my bat against the wall so violently, Eddie Murray could hear the noise out at first base. He was laughing so hard he started to cry. I injured myself, shattered four bats—one for each strikeout—gave Murray the only good laugh he had all day, and made my best contact on the wall. Now, physical mistakes usually didn't cost a cent. But I fined myself fifty dollars for the four strikeouts. Like Phil, I was a veteran and knew better than to turn in a performance like that.

The next day I could laugh, but that's about all. I had hurt my back so badly, spasms set in and I was on the bench for a few days.

It was not the first, nor the last time I fined myself. Another such occasion occurred when I suffered "vapor lock" in an at-bat against the Rangers' Frank Tanana. I was looking for a fastball, got a fastball, but could not swing. I saw the pitch more than well enough. I could have counted the stitches, could read the league president's signature backward. I could do everything but swing the bat. I fined myself twenty-five.

Not that I professed to be George Washington. I fined myself if there were witnesses against me. No witnesses, no fine, as far as I was concerned. If any of my Yankees' teammates ever had a problem with that they could appeal—to Phil. And once I got to Boston there was only one court—mine. My Red Sox buddies could have appealed there. But, then, they already knew what kind of justice they would get.

32

BILLY'S BACK

‑‑‑‑‑‑‑‑‑‑‑‑‑‑‑‑‑‑‑‑‑‑‑‑
‑‑‑‑‑‑‑‑‑‑‑‑‑‑‑‑‑‑‑‑‑‑‑‑
‑‑‑‑‑‑‑‑‑‑‑‑‑‑‑‑‑‑‑‑‑‑

DURING the winter of 1984, George Steinbrenner gave Yogi Berra a vote of confidence, saying he would be the Yankees manager for the entire 1985 season.

By the time we got to spring training, the rumors that Yogi was in trouble had already begun. The tension was immense. Once again, we were being watched. Every exhibition game had to be won—or else.

Then, in the first week of April, Steinbrenner stood on the rooftop of Fenway Park and told the media that the third game of the season was "crucial" because we'd already lost the first two. He said, "Our pitchers stink but they know they stink." He talked about the danger of falling too far behind and pointed to the Tigers' 35–5 start the season before.

We had 160 games to go, more than enough, in my mind, to make up a 2-game deficit. In Steinbrenner's mind, two losses were more than enough to turn up the pressure on Yogi. We immediately started hearing a new manager was coming in. We heard we were undisciplined. We were informed, through barbs in the media, that if we really "loved" Yogi we would

◆ 235 ◆

win more, perform better for him. We heard that the vaunted Yankees' team spirit was lacking. Steinbrenner started invoking the names of Rockne, Bear Bryant, Earl Weaver. Not surprisingly, Billy Martin's name soon appeared on that list.

It was torture for Yogi and the team. One week into the season, we were all pressing. It was a replay of the Angels' situation in 1981, when every at-bat seemed to carry Jim Fregosi's fate. Four years later, I was trying to bat 1.000, for Yogi's sake.

In our game of April 28 in Chicago, my only thoughts were, *Get a hit to win,* when I stepped to the plate against Britt Burns. The game was close and we were trying to escape the city with at least one victory in three tries over a lost weekend. I hit a ball into the seats, but just foul. I then settled for 1 of my 2 singles in the game. I had driven in a run, but the home run would have made the difference, because we lost, 4–3, in the bottom of the ninth.

So there we were, with a 6–10 record, in a sixth-place tie, 4.5 games out. Still, it was only April. It was early. And Yogi had had the services of Rickey Henderson for only 6 games because Henderson had sprained an ankle in spring training. But that did not matter. Steinbrenner wanted Yogi gone.

So, before we even lost on that gray day in Chicago, Steinbrenner phoned GM Clyde King at Comiskey Park and ordered him to announce after the game that Yogi was fired.

Billy Martin was coming back.

As soon as Clyde left his hastily called closed-door meeting with Yogi, he handed out press releases to the media. Moss Klein brought his over to me. Most of the reporters hovered around my locker to get my reaction. They knew that when Yogi's job was on the line the previous summer, I'd spoken out in his favor—and against the possible return of Billy. Those statements, more in support of Yogi than anything, sparked major headlines, including one in the May 25, 1984, edition of the *New York Daily News* that read: BAYLOR! NO BILLY!

I'm sure Billy was well aware of my sentiments that previous summer, right down to a quote widely attributed to me: "If Billy comes back, then this whole team is going to have to be reshaped because a lot of guys are going to ask out. There are some players who can play for the man and some who can't . . . I don't think firing Yogi is the answer."

I hadn't changed my mind by that April afternoon in Chicago.

As I read the news release, the media awaited. But I was too angry to speak. Don Mattingly, who lockered nearby, realized something was wrong, so he asked what was going on. I handed him the release and then walked to the shower. Along the way, I kicked a trashcan across the room, a show of frustration that soon would register on Billy as a sign of rebellion. Whatever he wanted to believe was fine. My main thoughts were for Yogi. He walked around that clubhouse saying good-bye and wishing us luck. In those fifteen minutes, Yogi showed more class than had been shown him in fifteen months.

The whole situation was infuriating. I was also upset with myself. I had not got the home run that maybe would have saved Yogi, if only for another day. The maddening thing was that, for a change, April had not been a struggle for me. The day Yogi was fired I was hitting .276, almost unheard of in my own spring history. I had driven in 9 runs in the 16 games, providing two of the team's six game-winners, and, in a personal triumph, my 999th and 1,000th RBI, on a 2-run homer hit off Boston's "Oil Can" Boyd. But the individual achievement was overshadowed by yet another loss, something that occurred all too often that first month. Those losses were just killing everyone because we knew the ramifications for Yogi.

The team struggled for many reasons. The pitchers were giving up a lot of runs, 29 alone in the first three losses in Fenway at the start of the season. If Phil Niekro had not started out 3–0 that first month, heaven knows where we would have been.

We could not put together a consistent offense. But I knew we would, especially with the arrival of Henderson. He would have made a difference in the first 16 games. Of the 10 losses, 8 were by 3 runs or less. Rickey can help manufacture that many runs in a game with his speed. We saw that for the remainder of 1985, when he became, in my mind, the best player in the game. But Rickey was not there for most of Yogi's term. If he had been, I believe we would easily have been 10–6, probably better.

The trashcan was not my only target. When a TV camera crew tried to bypass the Yankees' ban on TV cameras by sneaking into the clubhouse through the rear entrance, they also got the boot from me. The guy with the microphone said he was just trying to do his job. His job wasn't to circumvent clubhouse rules and sneak in to see if he could get some tears or heartbreak for the six o'clock news. I hated being in that Chicago clubhouse. It had held nothing but bad luck for people I cared about, from Lyman to Fregosi to Yogi.

Mattingly, who was like a son to Yogi, was devastated. He showed his hurt by firing a bottle of shampoo across the room. Joe Cowley, that day's losing pitcher, sat at his locker sobbing into a towel. Dale, Yogi's son, cried, too, even though his dad told him that, as a professional, he expected Dale to keep playing just as hard for Billy.

Like I said, Yogi has a lot of class. When we took the bus to O'Hare

Airport that afternoon, we dropped Yogi off at the terminal so he could fly home to New Jersey. When he stepped off the bus, he was given an ovation. We had let him down and lost a friend.

My mind turned to Billy, who awaited the team in Texas. My opinions hadn't changed since 1983, when I'd looked for the Billy of old, but instead found a man who intimidated young players, threw others into the doghouse, and who looked beaten by the last part of the season. After Billy departed, the Yankees became a family under Yogi. Guys felt greatly for each other, felt we could win it all in 1985. That environment was the exact opposite of the one that had crippled the 1983 team. Now Billy was back. And I felt that with him, the clubhouse would once again become a place of individuals scrambling to survive.

Billy held a team meeting right away when we arrived in Arlington, ostensibly to put us at ease. He said he'd heard about our emotional display for Yogi the previous day and understood because Yogi was one of his best friends. He also said he'd heard some unspecified "things." Looking right at me, Billy said his door was always open and that, contrary to what people might think, he really was not a bad guy and really did not carry a gun. "But I can always get one," he added.

Billy kind of laughed when he said it, but I didn't think it was funny. I knew exactly what he meant. I felt he was talking directly to me. If it was a joke, it was a poor one. *Hell,* I thought, *I can get a gun, too, but I don't need one.*

Billy also introduced a new coach, former Tigers great Willie Horton. He told reporters Willie was the tranquility coach. The players translated that to mean Willie was brought in to keep Grif and me away from Billy. Willie came over to me as soon as the meeting ended and told me not to listen to that stuff, that he wasn't there to be a bodyguard. That was fine with me. But, I told Willie, I wanted to make one thing perfectly clear: I respected him as a player and a man, but if it came down to it, not he and five of his brothers could stop me if I went after Billy.

For three days, the Yankees' traveling writers hovered around me to see if I would say anything about Billy. He had told the writers that what had transpired at the end of 1983 to his return was a "dead issue." So I replied in kind, saying that I personally had never had a problem with him. I explained to reporters that I had met with Billy at the Old Timer's Game the summer before to make that clear. Most of my sentiments about the oppression others felt were accurate, but one quote attributed to me was not. I never said I couldn't play for Billy. I said I couldn't play for him, or any manager, when my name was not in the lineup. Every day that happened made me hard to live with, which is the attitude I assume managers want their players to have. I wouldn't want a guy around who didn't feel he could make a difference every day he was in the lineup.

I did not pretend that Billy and I were best friends. There was an undercurrent there. But something had to be said, for the team's sake. There were a lot of kids in that clubhouse watching to see what the veterans would say or do. We had 146 games left, a long summer, to get through. Fighting among ourselves would make it endless and unbearable. So I took Billy at his word that bygones were bygones. Yogi was gone, but there was still a pennant that could be won.

The team started to come around. Was it the change in managers? I think it was more that we had so much overwhelming talent that finally started to surface. Henderson was playing healthy and he was inspired. The report on Rickey from his days in Oakland was that he only played well for Billy. It was holding true and that was fine with us. Not that we doubted he would have done the same for Yogi. Rickey simply never had a chance. When Rickey took his rightful place at the top of the lineup, his speed and power crushed the opposition and opened up holes and gave those that followed—Randolph, Mattingly, Winfield, and myself—ample RBI opportunities. I cannot say we turned it on for Billy any more than people can claim that the 1988 Red Sox turned it off for John McNamara and then back on for Joe Morgan when they won 19 of 20 at Fenway for Morgan after he replaced Mac as manager at midseason. I think in both cases it was just a matter of the talent surfacing.

We were in a race with the Blue Jays and, through July and August, the Yankees did pull it all together. The Boss had started rumblings even before Yogi left that he wanted to find a left-handed platoon partner for me. But I did not let the threat of that interfere with what I considered my primary job—driving in runs.

On June 17, I drove in my 43rd run in 212 at-bats, giving me a ratio of an RBI every 4.69 at-bats. I ranked third in the league in RBI, second on the team to Mattingly's 45. By the All-Star break on July 14, I had 64 RBI in 270 at-bats, or one every 4.22 at-bats. Donnie led the team in RBI, but had only 5 more than I did at the break. He had 67 more at-bats and an RBI ratio of one in every 4.88 at-bats.

I was not pleased with my .237 average, but I was still getting the runs in. I had 15 home runs. With 77 games to go, I figured I was well within range of my goal to drive in 100 runs and hit 30 home runs, plateaus I had not achieved since my MVP season.

The Yankees felt differently. By that June 17 date, Billy decided to institute a platoon at DH; I was given the starts against left-handers. Grif and Dan Pasqua were to split the at-bats against right-handers. From June 17, to September 15, I started only 49 of the Yankees' 83 games.

For all intents and purposes, I had been told my full-time services were no longer needed.

I figured I must have been missing something. Maybe I was bad for the team. Maybe I was stuck on myself. Maybe it *is* selfish of a player who drives in 64 runs in 76 games to figure he's doing the job.

I wanted someone to explain why my help was no longer required. So, in the last week of August, I asked Billy why. Billy said I should ask GM Clyde King.

I've since read that Steinbrenner said I went to King without consulting Billy. I would never do that. The protocol is always to follow the chain of command. I would never break that rule, especially with Billy. I did not need for him to tell people I went behind his back.

I did not go to see Clyde right away. We were in a pennant race. But, by mid-September, when the Yankees played 4 games against the Toronto Blue Jays, I changed my mind. Toronto was the team we were chasing. We lost 3 of the games. I started in only one and got all of 8 at-bats in the series. After Billy bypassed me in a crucial situation in the September 13th game, with left-hander Gary Lavelle on the mound, I'd had enough. I took that trip upstairs, the one that Billy had approved.

I asked Clyde why I wasn't playing in the middle of a pennant race, especially considering my reputation as a good stretch-drive player. Clyde pulled out the stats and pointed to my average that, at the time, was .232. I told Clyde that average won't tell the story when it comes to run production. I pointed instead to 82 RBI and 21 home runs.

Clyde said nothing.

It was frustrating. There were no satisfactory answers to be found in his office, either. I knew I could still give the Yankees 100 if they just gave me the at-bats. But they seemed dead-set against that. I didn't even know whose lineup it was anymore. All I knew was that I could have been playing a part, but wasn't.

After Clyde "explained," I knew what I had to do. I told him that if he didn't have a place for me to play, then maybe he could find a team that needed me down the stretch. Even though the rosters were frozen for post-season on September 1 and I would not be eligible with another team, I figured I could still help a club get to the playoffs. The Yankees made it clear they did not want my help.

Clyde said he would pass my concerns on to George Steinbrenner.

My career as a Yankee had come to the beginning of its end. And it was destined to be a bitter final chapter.

33

YANKEE, GO HOME

WHILE the Yankees were in the process of losing the third game of that big September series against the Blue Jays, George Steinbrenner took a leisurely stroll through the press box.

"Where's Reggie Jackson?" Steinbrenner asked of the writers. "I need Mr. October. All I have is a Mr. May, Dave Winfield . . . I need Mr. October. Our big guns are letting us down."

The next day during the fourth and final game, Steinbrenner took another stroll past the writers and dropped a few more pearls. That day he said, "I'm not going to get on them today. The players have embarrassed themselves enough. This series has been a terrible embarrassment. If they're not embarrassed, they should take off their uniforms and walk away from our pay window."

We were not embarrassed. We were angry. That loss in the fourth game dropped us 4.5 games behind the Blue Jays. But it was only September 15. We had 20 games left, enough time to make up the deficit. But, in my mind, the pennant was lost in that week, because of Steinbrenner.

We heard of his words, read them when they were printed under sensational headlines. Steinbrenner had ripped Winfield, who was in the process of putting together a 26-home run, 114-RBI season. He had ripped Griffey, who'd spent that summer running into fences for the man, but who'd made the unpardonable mistake of going 2–for–13 against Toronto. And Steinbrenner ripped me, even though Billy had only allowed me the one start and 8 at-bats.

The hard-luck pitcher in our 3–2 loss to Lavelle on September 13 was Phil Niekro, who was making the first of his five attempts to win number 300. Grif had made a great effort to catch a ball hit by Al Oliver, but it got by him for an RBI triple, the eventual game-winner. When Steinbrenner came into the clubhouse after that loss he put his arm around Phil and walked him toward the trainer's room. While talking to Phil, he looked in the direction of Griffey, Winfield, Billy Sample, Willie, and myself and told Phil that he pitched well, but the hitters "stunk." He was not heard by the guys over in the "ghetto"—what some of the black players called the side of the room where the Yankees lockered most of the black guys, a policy most of us had never seen on other clubs. But some of our teammates, such as Don Mattingly and certainly Phil, heard Steinbrenner.

Griffey and I were both so angry we did not trust ourselves to talk to the media. Winfield and Mattingly did, though. Winfield said Steinbrenner's actions of that week were tantamount to "rattling a stick across the bars of a cage with some animals in it. . . . There's a feeling among us that you want to tell him to 'Shut up, you don't know what you're talking about.' "

Mattingly said, "You've got an owner here who likes to say things. But to belittle [players] is out of control."

The whole situation was out of control. In a moment when a little pat on the back would have done wonders, we were made to feel like convicts.

The hostility was palpable. Every other team played with twenty-four, twenty-five guys. The Yankees played with fifteen. Everyone else was in the doghouse. And it's bullshit if Billy says he doesn't have one. He's got three. One's air-conditioned, one is air-conditioned with carpet, and the other is just bare minimum, nothing.

Bob Shirley was in the doghouse with no floors, no nothing. Every manager needed a whipping boy and Billy had Shirley. Bob was a spot starter and left-handed setup man. Not only could he give a team a lot of innings, but a lot of heart. What Shirley could not give Billy was perfection. So his occasional failures landed Shirley in the worst doghouse of all and he'd be banished for weeks at a time. He never lost his sense of humor or his desire to take the ball again, though—something that even had to impress Billy.

I was in Billy's air-conditioned doghouse. I knew that the moment Billy did not give me the at-bat against Lavelle. Billy wanted to show me he was in charge. He knew I was unhappy. That was my punishment for saying I wanted to play. He showed me, all right . . . showed how small he could be. And he, and Steinbrenner, kept right on showing me.

I had gone to Clyde King in confidence and not run to the media. I did not want to disrupt the team by publicizing my concerns. When I found out that some reporters were aware of the meeting, because they had impeccable sources on a team that has more leaks than a sieve, I asked that they not publicize the trade request. One day after I talked to Clyde, though, both Billy and George went public. Then, later on, I would be accused of being disruptive and selfish and quitting on the team in a pennant race.

After Steinbrenner ripped the team, we lost focus. We also lost 8 straight games, from September 13 to September 20, to fall 6.5 games behind. Billy started to make strange moves, such as sending left-handed hitting Pagliarulo to the plate to hit right-handed against the Tigers. On September 21, Billy crossed paths with an angry Ed Whitson late one night in a hotel bar in Baltimore, leading to the infamous brawl at the Cross Keys Inn. Eddie, scratched from a start by Billy, was incensed because Billy had told reporters he was hurt. Eddie was not hurt and wanted the ball. He referred all questions to "Dr. Martin," then went off to drown his sorrows. He ran into Billy late that night and something snapped. By the time Eddie was through, Billy had a busted arm and some cracked ribs. From the description of the fight he was lucky to be alive because Eddie bounced Billy on his head on a concrete sidewalk outside the hotel before being subdued.

That's the incident that finally convinced me that Sparky Lyle's description of the Yankees as "the Bronx Zoo" was absolutely correct. The team was in anarchy. Billy had fought a player and almost been killed in the process. When Eddie was allowed to return to the team a couple days later, security guards were in the dugout and clubhouse to keep Billy and Eddie separated.

It wasn't baseball. It was a battle zone.

The uncontrollable, self-inflicted wounds were open, just like they had been in the Pine Tar season. From the day Steinbrenner made his "Mr. May" speech, we were done. On paper we had a chance. And we did have the Blue Jays within sight by the final series of the season in Toronto. We needed to sweep in order to tie. Suddenly Billy and George and everyone else looked for a miracle, looked for that special ingredient—heart.

The players didn't quit, but emotionally, there's only so far you can push yourself. You need someone else to help you, even if only a little bit.

Pennant races in July, August, and September should be the best times of a player's season. In New York, playing during those months was like suffering through a bad marriage and an even worse divorce. You just don't want to go to the ballpark. You don't want to read the papers. You're 2 games out of first place and all you want is the season to end.

Even if we would have forced that tie, defeated the Blue Jays, would it have satisfied a man who cannot be pleased? None of us thought so. We knew that a division title would simply mean Steinbrenner or Billy would have more opportunities to raise havoc in the playoffs or the World Series.

I've played on seven division winners, three pennant winners, and a world championship team. I was with the 1988 A's, who won 109 games. The 1985 Yankees were the best team I have ever played for that did not win it all. The fact that we finished 2 games out in spite of the distractions speaks for the talent of that team. Those guys were winners, but we were all trapped in a no-win situation.

After the last game of the season, on October 6, the team flew home from Toronto. We landed at Newark Airport and I had to wait there for Becky, who had flown into LaGuardia in order to pick up our car. As I stood outside the terminal a stretch limousine pulled up. The door opened and there sat Billy. He handed me a beer and invited me to sit with him until his driver retrieved Billy's luggage.

Billy looked horrible. He sensed that he was about to be removed from the job again. The '85 season had taken a severe physical toll on Billy. His arm was still in a cast. He never regained his health after a physician in Texas accidentally punctured his lung while administering a flu shot.

We sat and talked for a while. Billy talked about the brawl with Eddie Whitson and how he'd never had a player try to kill him before. Eddie was on his mind because, for the first time since the September 21 brawl, he and Eddie had spoken. They'd bumped into each other in the Toronto airport and had a very emotional meeting. Billy said Eddie apologized for what had happened. Billy also told me he was troubled because he was going through a difficult divorce.

Speaking from experience, I told him he should put the divorce behind him so he could get on with his life. That's about all I said. We did not talk about the season, the lost at-bats, the relationship that had started to sour in 1983 and deteriorated so badly that 1985 season. It was like it had never happened. Billy wanted only to talk about Billy.

That's when I realized I would never understand him. How could I? He probably doesn't understand himself. He tries to get everyone's sympathy, but you never know if you're dealing with Jekyll or Hyde. Players just did not know how to approach him, what to make of him. Dale Berra, whose dad told him to play hard for Billy, who listened when Billy said Yogi was his close friend, also listened when Billy stood on the top step of the dugout and screamed at him, "Where did he learn how to play baseball?" Yes, Dale had made an out on the bases. Billy probably did that a couple of times, too. And Billy knew where Dale had learned to play ball. In a home headed by a Hall of Famer—Billy's "close friend."

Sitting in that limousine, looking at that forlorn man, I felt bad for Billy. I also walked away and never looked back.

On October 17, Lou Piniella replaced Billy as manager. When a reporter phoned to ask if that would change my mind, since there was still a possibility of a trade on the table, I replied, "The manager changes, but the owner remains the same." The way I figured, Lou might want me in the lineup, but who was to say he'd have control of that decision?

Still, I did not know if the Yankees were trying to move me. After my face-to-face conversation with King on September 14 and our phone conversation later that day, we did not speak again. He never again mentioned the list of my preferred teams, in person or through intermediaries. I never mentioned it, either. That's the way things stood at the end of the season. Then I started to hear my name linked to the White Sox and a possible deal involving catcher Carlton Fisk and pitcher Britt Burns.

The longer they pursued the deal with Chicago without consulting me, the less chance there was that the White Sox would be my choice. The bottom line was that I *did* have a choice. I had a no-trade clause, which I would have to waive before the Yankees could move me. What the Yankees did not understand, I guess, is that requesting a trade and waiving a no-trade clause by signature are two different things. I never forfeited my trade-veto power. I'd worked too hard, too long to earn such a privilege to give it away in a five-minute conversation.

That misunderstanding on the Yankees' part led to the fiasco of the winter meetings that December in San Diego. I watched with interest from my New Jersey home as the Yankees pursued the deal. The Yankees beat writers in San Diego knew that the team was working on a trade it could not consummate without my cooperation. They knew the teams that I would have approved. Milwaukee because of Harry Dalton. California because of Gene Mauch. Baltimore because Earl and Frank were both back there. I would have gladly gone to Boston because John McNamara—a real supportive guy in his one year as coach in Anaheim—was by then the Red Sox manager. All of those men I trusted and respected and knew they respected me.

When Murray Chass of the *Times* and Claire Smith of the *Hartford Courant* broke the story that the Yankees–White Sox deal had this one little roadblock—me—Steinbrenner was furious. He attached a "greed" label to me. He said if the White Sox wanted me, they could work out a deal by negotiating a buy-out of the no-trade. White Sox owners Jerry Reinsdorf and Eddie Einhorn, GM Hawk Harrelson and Manager Tony La Russa, all got on a conference call with Jerry Kapstein, attorney Bob Teaff, and myself to try to sell me on Chicago.

La Russa and Harrelson were eager to have me. The two owners were more reserved and wanted to know what it would take. That was simple. I asked the White Sox to guarantee my option-year, 1987, which called for an $875,000 salary but, under the option, could have been bought out for $375,000. And I asked the Sox to extend the contract for another season after that. I wanted security; the no-trade clause was my leverage. The White Sox wanted no part of that deal, though, so the talks never reached a serious stage. And so Steinbrenner accused me of blowing up the trade.

What trade? Fisk was a free agent. The Sox had not even re-signed him and he was balking at a possible trade to the Yankees, something veterans were doing more and more.

Soon it was being written by certain columnists that I was a greedy player asking for a million dollars. Phil Pepe, a columnist for the *New York Daily News,* wrote that Roger Maris would have been ashamed of both Ed Whitson and myself for requesting trades. Roger had just passed away when that comment was written. Pepe's opinion was that Roger was a "true Yankee" and we were selfish, greedy players. Pepe wrote that I asked out in the middle of a pennant race. So did the late Dick Young, who wrote a column for the *New York Post.*

In my mind, selfish means caring about yourself and not the team. I never wanted to collect money without earning it. I didn't see that as taking a shot at Yankee tradition. I just wanted to help the Yankees win.

Shortly after Christmas, the Yankees filed a grievance against me claiming that my trade request constituted a waiver of the no-trade. A few days before the scheduled hearing in February, the Yankees dropped the grievance.

Phil Pepe and Dick Young did not play baseball. Tony Kubek did, though, for the Yankees. And he played alongside Roger Maris. When Tony wrote a book about Roger's 61-home-run season in 1961, he gave me a copy. Tony signed that book and inscribed it with his sentiments about my desire. He wrote: "You could have played on our '61 team."

That was more than good enough for me.

On March 28, a week before the start of the 1986 season, the Yankees traded me to the Red Sox for Mike Easler. It was a sad day in one sense because the Yankees made another move. Phil Niekro, coming off a second straight 16-victory season, was released. I watched my friend proudly fold his uniform, walk over to the Yankees' offices at the Fort Lauderdale complex, and hand the uniform over to new GM Woody Woodward. I saw yet another Yankee—Joe Niekro—cry. Lou Piniella looked devastated because his first duties as a rookie manager were to watch as a friend and probable Hall of Famer was released, then tell another friend and former teammate he was traded. Lou watched 16 victories and 90 RBI walk out that clubhouse door.

It was a joyous day for me. I was leaving a lot of heartbreak behind. The player some people wanted to hang the "greed" label on gladly signed a waiver of the no-trade clause without asking for or receiving one red cent.

Another door had closed. It most likely will never open again, at least during the Steinbrenner regime. There will be no Old Timer's Day invitations. I will never fit his description of a "true" Yankee. But I'll gladly accept the words of my ex-teammates. The day I was traded, Don Mattingly told the press, "Donnie has been a rock in our lineup. It's kind of scary to think of what he's going to do in Boston. I'll be kind of scared to look at the numbers at the end of the year." To be exact, the numbers would read 31 home runs and 94 RBI in 160 games. And there would be another number in that 1986 season—number one, as in the team that beat out the Yankees, as in the first of three consecutive World Series for me.

Looking back, I have no regrets about becoming a Yankee. I learned a lot, saw a lot in three years. I was treated with respect by the Yankee fans. I put on the pinstripes and felt a part of that tradition when great Yankees such as Whitey Ford, Yogi Berra, and Lefty Gomez made me feel welcome. Just being in the same room with those men filled me with a sense of wonder. In those brief moments, the Yankees mystique was alive and well.

I have only seen George Steinbrenner once since the trade. We both sat on the dais at the annual New York writers' banquet in January 1988. When I received the BBWAA chapter's "Good Guy of the Year" award I not only thanked the writers, I also thanked him for bringing me to New York. I meant that.

Still, you can say anything you want about me, George. All I know is that you can't hit for me. Pitchers would rather see you at the plate than me. That's what helped keep me going. Then, when you took the bat away, it was time to leave.

34

CARE TO SHARE A CAB, SOX?

THE 1986 Boston Red Sox did not get out of spring training before "Oil Can" Boyd threw one of his classic temper tantrums.

John McNamara asked if I could take Boyd aside and talk to him about being a major-league ballplayer. I knew immediately what the Red Sox expected of me. The day I walked into Mac's office at Winter Haven, the greeting told me everything I needed to know.

"I finally got you on my team," Mac said, a warm smile crossing his face. "I have been trying for a long time."

He had shown me in the past he respected my opinion even when I played for another team. When I was with the Yankees and Mac managed the Angels, Mac bumped into me in a restaurant in Southern California. He came over and asked me if we could talk. He wanted to know what he could do to get some of his players out of the trainer's room and into the lineup.

It shocked me when he said that guys like Rod Carew, Fred Lynn, and DeCinces were telling trainer Rick Smith they could not play. Mac's job was on the line and he felt like he was going down without his best team on the field. I told him that he would have to change his philosophy. "Put them in the lineup if you think they can play," I said, "and then let them tell you if they can't. The hardest thing for a player to do is tell a manager he can't play."

A few years later he actively campaigned to bring me to Boston, urging GM Lou Gorman to make the deal just as he had pleaded with the Angels to keep me in 1983. Buzzie Bavasi did not listen, Lou Gorman did. That was not surprising since Lou and I had known each other for years. He was a young, up-and-coming farm director for the Orioles when I played in the minor leagues.

Mac wanted me to DH every day. He also wanted me to help try to pull together a team notorious for its lack of cohesiveness. He never used the word leader or "presence." He did not have to. Asking me to talk to Oil Can spoke volumes.

I sensed that my new teammates were also looking for something more than home runs and RBI. They knew their team profile: twenty-five players going to dinner in twenty-five separate cabs. Everyone knew; those words were used in questions posed to me by reporters in the news conference the day I arrived in Winter Haven. I told the press my philosophy was simple. Twenty-five Red Sox could go to twenty-five restaurants in twenty-five different New England hamlets if they wanted. But when we put on our uniforms, there had to be a togetherness that other teams recognized and respected. The Red Sox not only had to think they could win, they had to believe it and then do it as a team. That attitude was the one I saw in the pennant-winning days in Baltimore, with Finley's A's and with the 1979 Angels.

It was well known that the Red Sox did not have that kind of enthusiasm. Perhaps New England pessimism had hung over the team for too many years. Guys like Roger Clemens, Bruce Hurst, Jim Rice, and Dwight Evans are winners. They were all still trying to find a way to make the team win. They knew no one expected them to because they were the Red Sox. So I felt my acquisition at least aroused their curiosity, if nothing else.

For about three or four days Dwight Evans kind of bided his time, watching and waiting. Finally, he worked his way across the clubhouse and said he thought it might be a good idea if I started a kangaroo court. "It might make the game a little more fun," Dwight said. "There are some guys here who don't have fun. It might also help improve fundamentals."

I knew Dwight was sincere about wanting to improve the team. He is a consummate professional, something I'd known for a long time. What I did not know is that in that very serious persona I would find my closest friend.

I needed the go-ahead of two others before I could say yes. After all, it was Mac's team. And Jim Rice was the captain. When both men approved, court was in session again. And Dwight was right. The court did inject an element of fun. And the Red Sox did become a team, one that would do all the things needed to win a division, to pull off miracle victories against Gene Mauch's Angels in the playoffs, to come within one victory of being world champions.

In that year, I would get to know all the Red Sox, through the court, through the friendships that you cannot help but build in a long, exciting pennant drive. A few I will never forget.

Dwight "Dewey" Evans

I think a lot of people shy away from Dwight Evans because he's very serious. Because he's been with the Red Sox so long, he is naturally perceived as a stereotypical Boston Red Sox superstar, distant and aloof.

From a distance Dwight can look forbidding, with those eye-black swatches painted on his face to ward off the sun's glare, with that glower and black mustache that hardly ever lifts in a smile. The last thing you expect to find is a guy with a heart the size of Texas, but that's exactly what I discovered.

Dwight Evans is one of the most caring and sensitive people I've ever met. He is also one of the most least-understood players. He's a private person for many reasons, primarily his need to focus his energies on his family due to some serious medical problems. Dwight had played only for Boston and watched as many friends just disappeared from his life. It's made it harder for him to reach out, something I fully understand, having moved on from club to club so often.

We found an immediate kinship, however. Dwight and I saw each other as equals, two guys who have been through the wars. He has survived in Boston, one of the toughest towns I have ever encountered because of cynical fans and a critical press corps. Dwight is selfless and a true competitor. He does not calculate his average at every turn, doesn't celebrate a 4–for–4 day when the team loses. And, for years he had been our league's answer to Roberto Clemente, a smooth, nearly flawless Gold Glover out in right field.

Dwight helped me through a lot. I may speak in jest about the day he gave me the Bible passages to read when I asked him if I should go after Jim Rice, but it was something we both took seriously. And when he handed me the Bible, I read it and found solace, enough to coexist with Rice even though our views on team play were diametrically opposed.

Dwight and I also discovered a common bond that goes far beyond the playing field. Both of us are physically strong. Yet we both have endured the heartaches only parents of children with medical problems can understand.

Dwight and Susan Evans have two sons and a daughter. Both boys suffer from a rare form of cancer. One son was operated on well over a dozen times in his first fifteen years. My son, Donny, was born with amblyopia, or "lazy eye," and has undergone surgery and endures countless visits to specialists around the country as we search for the best possible treatment. Every time I envision Dwight or Susan sitting in a hospital waiting room I think back on the same vigil I kept when Donny had major eye surgery at age six, about the times I had to patch a little boy's eye every day.

Dwight is an extremely caring father. And Susan Evans is, without a doubt, one of the strongest people that I've ever met. You have to be to fight through those fears year in, year out.

I've always been touched by the affection Dwight and Susan have shown Donny. It is as genuine as the affection Becky and I have for their children. Our families have shared quiet evenings together. That bond solidified during the pennant-winning season of 1986 when Dwight, Susan, Becky, and I began and ended many an evening with our special toast, "To God, good friends, and a world championship."

The fact that Becky and Susan became the best of friends made the bonds even stronger. When Dwight and I get caught up in that macho thing where it's hard to say how we really feel, we don't have to worry. Susan and Becky say it for us, even dial the phone if necessary. I'm glad they do. Because, in Dwight I know I have a very special friend, one it took a lifetime to find.

Dennis "Oil Can" Boyd

The kangaroo court added a dimension that the Red Sox could point to proudly as a measure of success. Unfortunately, the Sox had one problem the court, the manager, and even the owner could not fathom. The only person who has the slightest chance of solving the mystery of Dennis "Oil Can" Boyd is "The Can," himself.

The Can is unlike anyone I've ever met. He came from Meridian, Mississippi, as small and as southern a town as you can find. Satchel Paige lived there, used to hold Can on his knee and tell him about the old days in the Negro Leagues. When Oil Can arrived in the majors, he seemed like a reincarnation of Paige, a real countrified kid. By 1986 it was becoming apparent his million-dollar arm might not save his career because no one knew how to handle his mood swings, temper tantrums, and general inability to adapt to a society that seemed thirty years ahead of him in every way.

Oil Can derived his nickname from his beer-drinking exploits as a teenager. Beer is called "oil" in parts of the South and The Can apparently did his share for the "oil" industry. I don't know that he ever left that fun-loving kid behind. I don't believe he realized early enough why he must do so for his very survival.

As we sat and talked on a flight from Florida to Detroit, Can's hurt and confusion spilled out. He had friends on the team, but no one he could talk to. Guys picked on him, did not understand him, he said. He was always being hounded to stop his mound antics, which made Mark Fydrich's act seem sedate. When I hit against Can, I did not appreciate his actions, but I also realized that the show was real to him, helped take him to the next level as a competitor.

Boyd told me he felt isolated because of race, too. He and Rice were the only blacks on the Sox before I arrived. They might as well have been from different planets. Jimmy didn't understand Can and did not try. Rice is from the South, too, but the similarities end there. He's a very serious, urbane, but closed person. He wanted no close alliances, especially with an off-the-wall kid. And Can is just that. In one plane ride he amazed me because he could not sit still. He was so wound up he walked off that plane without his wallet. I had to lend him money just to get him through the first trip.

When I arrived in Boston, I was amazed that the word "nigger" was thrown around by white players in conversations with The Can. They teased him by using that word, supposedly in jest. Some of the guys tried it with me once, but never again after they saw the look on my face. That word will never be humorous to me. Can didn't know what to do about the teasing. And it was incessant.

By the first series of the season, Can was despondent because of all the jabs, which came mostly from other pitchers. He might have been a great target, but the Sox were going to win nothing if he was a wreck. So I spoke out, said that The Can should be left alone. Bruce Hurst and Roger Clemens and Al Nipper were always supportive. After that, more guys fell into line.

I also shut down Rangers coach Tim Foli, whose heckling of The Can got out of hand in a game in Arlington in late May. Boyd had beaned their catcher, Don Slaught, in the previous meeting in Fenway and broken Slaught's nose and cheekbone. Foli was harassing Boyd so much the crowd picked up on it. The Can wanted to go into the stands. I had to grab Can at one point and shove him into the dugout. Then I walked out to Foli and told him to shut up or I'd snap his neck.

Foli shut up.

Many of The Can's problems were of his own making.

On July 10, Tigers manager Sparky Anderson named the All-Star team. He did not choose Can, who was 11–6 with a 3.71 ERA. Can went absolutely berserk. He was ranting and raving, screaming and ripping at his uniform. I've never seen anyone that outraged. I couldn't believe what I was watching. He was the first player I ever felt like slapping because he was hysterical, like he had lost his mind.

He took off for the trainer's room with Jimmy and me right behind him. We tried to talk to him, but he looked through us as if we did not exist. I was stunned but with the other guys, it was "we've seen this before." And they had. Can tore his uniform off, put his street clothes on, and bolted. He was gone three days, during which time he was suspended indefinitely.

The Can was headed toward self-destruction.

As a condition of his reinstatement, Boyd checked into a hospital to undergo a battery of tests. He was diagnosed as suffering from hyperactivity. Medication was prescribed and it seemed to help.

When Can was permitted to return he made a tearful plea with teammates to forgive him. Dwight, Bob Stanley, and some of the others did not want to hear it anymore. They had seen Can remorseful before. As for me, the jury was still out. He would win 5 more games after his August 1 return. He was 1–1 in the playoffs, lost Game Three of the World Series. Can then saw his next scheduled start—Game Seven—taken away. Mac, using an extra day provided by a rainout, opted to go with Bruce Hurst, winner of two series games already. Can cried upon hearing the news. But that's all he did. In my mind, he had grown up a lot.

Jim Rice

When I arrived in Boston, there was certainly no grand declaration, such as "This is my clubhouse, guys, follow me."

Jim Rice was the official team captain and I respected that. That's why I asked Jim to be the sergeant-at-arms for the court, to let him know it was as much his jurisdiction as mine.

I think it worked well that one year because we were winning and Jim was locked in. I believe he relaxed because he was no longer depended on to provide all the veteran leadership. That role had been put on Jim because of his seniority and because it is not in Dwight's nature to be outspoken. Dwight was just trying to keep his mind focused on the game in light of what his family was going through. Jim wasn't comfortable with the role. He'd been burned in relationships with teammates. He was the lone black superstar for years in a city that is plagued by racial divisions. Jim pulled away from the media, from his teammates. After a while I just don't think he cared to open up to anyone.

Perhaps that's selfish, but maybe that way Jimmy assured his self-preservation. It was the only way he knew how to play and to live. That didn't always mean everybody understood.

Jim knew what coach Tommy Harper knew when Tommy brought the Winter Haven Elks Club's policy of discrimination out into the open in 1985. Tommy pointed out how white Red Sox employees were invited to use that club for years, but that blacks were not. Tommy was fired a year later, supposedly for neglecting his duties. Some players, including Dwight and Bruce Hurst, defended Tommy and felt he was being punished for the Elks Club scandal. Jim, who was Tommy's friend, said nothing. Team captains, guys with Hall of Fame numbers who carry some weight, should speak up in those situations, not crawl into a shell.

Even though Jim welcomed the diversion I caused when I first arrived, I don't know that he ever felt at ease around me. I don't think he had ever seen anyone come in and have an immediate impact before. When we were winning in 1986, things worked well. When 1987 proved to be a disappointing season for the Sox, it became harder for us to coexist, especially when Jimmy took to criticizing his teammates in front of clubhouse personnel. That bothered me, especially when he never let up. It helped fuel the negative media because Jimmy would also talk to his allies in the press, in particular Joe Giuliotti of the *Boston Herald*.

The way I figured it, if you're going to rake your teammates over on a daily basis you'd better be perfect. Jim, like most of us, suffered fall-offs in 1987. But that doesn't mean you stop trying. I feel Jim lost interest. That became obvious in a game in Anaheim. Jim had been hit by a couple pitches in previous games and was sitting out, nursing his bruises. We got into a bases-loaded situation in the top of the ninth in a game we were losing. The guys were all figuring Mac would surely use Jim as a pinch-hitter. Mac could not. Jim was already in his civilian clothes. Glenn Hoffman hit instead and made the third out.

That's when I wanted to ask Jim to step outside. A club can bear those things when it's winning, but not when it's losing. And not when it's the captain who's setting the example.

Roger Clemens

On April 29, on a cold day in Fenway Park, I had an extra-special vantage point from which to watch Roger Clemens take on the Seattle Mariners. I played first base that night. By the bottom of the second I sensed something spectacular was unfolding, Roger's stuff was that explosive. His performance reminded me of the near no-hitters I had watched Nolan throw as an Angel, performances where you know after just a few pitches that the man on the mound is pretty much untouchable. That was Clemens on that cold April night.

So I turned to first-base umpire Tim Welke and asked him to keep track of the strikeouts for me. By the end of two innings, Roger had 5 strikeouts. He was on one of those rolls only the especially gifted strikeout pitchers, such as Koufax, Gibson, and Ryan, enjoy. Sure enough, "The Rocket" wound up striking out 20 Mariners to set a major-league record.

The Mariners could not get the bats out of their holsters. They would start their swing at a fastball that seemed letter-high, but by the time it was in the catcher's mitt, the ball was shoulder-high. Phil Bradley went down four times. Ken Phelps, Ivan Calderon, and Dave Henderson wound up with hat tricks. Every time Roger would ring up another Mariner I'd look at Welke and he'd hold up another finger.

The one time I did not look at Welke was in the fourth inning when Gorman Thomas took a called-third strike, becoming Roger's ninth strike-out victim. Thomas had been given new life at the plate because, on the previous pitch, his foul ball ticked off the heel of my glove for an error. As stupid as it may seem, some reporters actually asked if I did that on purpose in order to give Roger another shot at the guy. Not in a game that was scoreless at the time. Not ever, really, even though Clemens is the kind of pitcher who has every right to turn to a fielder and say, "That's okay, I'll erase that error." On that night he did just that. And took out 19 other guys while he was at it.

It was unreal, a thing of beauty, the kind of performance hitters cannot help but tip their hats to. Roger gets my tip of the hat almost every time he goes out there.

Wade Boggs

Wade Boggs is a lot like Rod Carew in that he's a lifetime .350 hitter who will never be viewed as giving enough.

Both attract the critics because they are not damage players, but rather the consummate table-setters. Is that fair? I don't know. I do know that Wade, like Rod, gets an extraordinary amount of hits. He is as pure and scientific at the plate as anyone of his generation. But pitchers do not look at Wade as the guy to fear. You don't hear his name in the hitters' meetings, either. Guys don't sit on the bench and say they hope that guy doesn't beat them. Everyone knows Wade is a great hitter, but his name just never surfaces in those damage-control conversations the way Mattingly's, Brett's, and Kirby Puckett's do. I know it makes Wade angry. Rodney never accepted that invisible asterisk people wanted to put beside his batting titles, either.

Wade's reputation was not helped by the 1986 batting title race with Mattingly. They went into the final weekend of the season separated by a few points. The Yankees came to Fenway for a four-game showdown. Wade had a sore right hamstring and announced the day before the series he would not play. Mattingly would have needed 12 hits to catch Boggs if Boggs's average remained at .357. Donnie came close, with an incredible 8 hits in 19 at-bats to raise his average to .352. He was so tenacious I know a lot of guys were pulling for him—not against Wade, but for Donnie—because you couldn't help but appreciate his effort.

It's not for me to say whether Wade was too hurt to play or not. I know that the same thing happened again in 1988, when Kirby Puckett was chasing Boggs. Fair or not, if those things happen often enough, people start wondering. I guess that's part of the blessing and/or curse of being Wade Boggs. When people know you're that good, they'll always want a perfection that's simply inhuman.

Walter Hriniak

When you're thirty-six years old and a veteran of sixteen seasons, there's a temptation to think there's nothing more anyone can teach you about hitting. When I met Walter Hriniak I realized there were things I could learn every day.

Walter never drove in a run for any team I played on, pitched an inning, or stole a base. Yet he ranks up there with Frank as far as people who helped influence my game.

Walter was the hitting instructor with Boston for thirteen years until he left at the end of the 1988 season. Both Walter and his methods were always the center of controversy in Boston because he espouses Charlie Lau's theory of hitting and Hall of Famer Ted Williams opposes such a philosophy. Lau preached that hitters should literally use their heads as a tool by putting their head out over the plate to better see the ball. He wanted the hitter to put his head on the same plane as the flight of the ball. Ted Williams believes in perfecting the mechanics of the swing. How the hips swivel, where the rotation takes the body, from point A to point B, those are his main concerns.

There is only one Ted Williams and no one can dispute his Hall of Fame credentials. But, using their theories, Charlie and Walter have coached teams to batting titles. They were never able to make themselves into legendary hitters, but they found something that works for a lot of other guys, including George Brett and Dwight Evans.

Charlie Lau died of cancer in 1984 at age 50. Walter still works to help countless hitters improve, including me. After the 1988 season, he took his theories and dedication to Chicago, where he took over as batting instructor for the White Sox.

Walter has tremendous drive and dedication. He would arrive at a ballpark five or six hours before a game to meet any hitter's request for extra work. Even though he's got arm problems, he throws batting practice for hours, every single day.

His attention to detail was uncanny, whether it had to do with a player's mechanics or personality. On one of my first days in camp, Walter took me aside and said he could tell I knew how to pull the ball. For most guys it was a hit-or-miss proposition, Walter told me. Frank would have been pleased to know his hard work had paid off.

About a half a month into the season, Walter said that the Red Sox had never yelled at opposing pitchers until after I arrived. That struck me as funny because it had never occurred to me not to yell at pitchers. It's a form of intimidation. They may throw at me, but I yell, anyway. It was nothing personal, I'd just holler and ridicule the other teams' starters, telling them to go back and warm up. The guy could have been throwing 100 mph, it didn't matter to me. If the other team brought in their top reliever late in the game, I'd scream, "You're the guy we've been waiting for since seven-thirty." Anything to give me or my teammates an edge. Sometimes it works, sometimes it doesn't, but it's always fun. In 1988, Walter told me the Red Sox were still yelling. "You just can't shut them up," he said.

It was Walter, more than anyone else, who helped me handle Mike Witt's bastard pitch in the fifth game of the American League Championship Series. He did it by throwing me thousands of batting-practice pitches. He got me to that at-bat with an idea. "Just put your head on the ball," he would say over and over. And I'd stick my head further across the plate in order to jerk a ball I really had no right to drive, pitches like Witt's—down and away, unhittable. But I hit them. And when I did, I, too, could recognize and appreciate another teacher's hard work—Walter Hriniak's.

35

AUTUMN IN NEW YORK

ON the morning of Game Five of the 1986 American League Championship Series, I arrived at the visitor's clubhouse at Anaheim Stadium around eight, hours before the rest of the team was due.

The clubhouse was nearly deserted, but Walter Hriniak was there. It was a quiet time Walter enjoyed and one I needed. I just could not sit around a hotel room any longer. We trailed Gene Mauch's California Angels in the playoffs, 3–1, stood one loss away from having to go home. I had been at that juncture too many times, wanted to speed up time just so I'd know if a World Series berth would ever be mine.

I was eating a breakfast I really couldn't taste when Walter walked over and sat down. "This is the day we have been waiting for all year. We're down three games to one, but just so long as we have one shot left, take it," he said.

At first I just looked at him. Then I said, "Walter, you've got to be kidding."

He wasn't.

"We're gonna do our workout just like any other day," he said, dead serious. "It's the last day, but you've just got to do the same things. It's the last bullet you've got. Might as well fire it. You know Gene's over there just kind of loving it. Like 'We've got you guys, now, so do something. You have to beat me.' "

That was Walter. He had not changed his routine through all of 1986. He could not comprehend why any one of us should, either. Do what we did to get us to that point. Walter wasn't asking us to be the 1927 Yankees, just the 1986 Red Sox, which was more than good enough to win the American League East.

The Red Sox won 95 games to finish 5.5 games ahead of the Yankees. It was not as close as it seemed, considering the Yankees swept 4 straight at Fenway in the last series of the season.

Boston and New York kind of waltzed around through June, July, and August, winning on the same days, losing on the same days. On August 30, though, we stopped selling tickets for George Steinbrenner at Yankee Stadium. Roger Clemens beat Phil Niekro and the Indians, 7–3. It was his 20th victory and the first of what would be 11 straight. When the streak started we were 3.5 games up. By the time it ended we were 8.5 ahead and never were threatened again.

On September 28, we clinched at home against Toronto. I contributed to the 12–3 victory with a bases-loaded single, good for 2 RBI. It was well past August and I was on my way to a 94-RBI season. Thirty-five of those had come in April and May, months when there was proving to do in Boston and messages to send to New York. In perhaps the most satisfying game, I delivered a bases-loaded double against Brian Fisher at Yankee Stadium, in front of the man who'd said I could no longer hit right-handers. That night I heard words that were music to my ears. George Steinbrenner told reporters his "baseball" people might have been wrong in saying that Don Baylor could not do the job anymore. Later I would hear that Steinbrenner also told Massachusetts Representative and House Speaker Tip O'Neill that my bat would be dead by August. In that month I hit 7 home runs, drove in 14 runs. The night we clinched Steinbrenner called Mac to congratulate him and passed on a message to me that what he said had been misconstrued. I told Mac that I knew Steinbrenner had said it, but that was okay, too. He had given me the drive that had helped take a team to the playoffs. And we beat his team.

The playoffs started in Fenway. And the Angels overpowered us, 8–1. I had feared we would be flat after the Yankee sweep. Sure enough, we could not turn it on again, not against a pitcher like Mike Witt. He held us to 5 hits.

Game Two was important. Granted, this was the first LCS played as a best-of-seven, but no one relishes being down, 0–2, no matter how many chances you have left.

Kirk McCaskill, a young New Englander with the Angels, pitched before the home folks. I was counting on youth and nerves to work against him. We routed McCaskill and the Angels, 9–2. I got an RBI single off McCaskill, then he walked me three times after that, twice on 3–2 breaking balls. He clearly wanted no part of me. Meanwhile, Hurst pitched another complete game, stopping California on 1 earned run despite giving up 11 hits.

Even as the hits were falling in, Bruce was confident. Hurst was the best pitcher in baseball the last month of the season. He was a left-hander who had finally learned to believe in himself, a must in Fenway Park. When I faced him in previous years, he was afraid to challenge hitters. We talked a lot that year about how he had to pitch inside if he expected to win. He was more than tough enough that day. And he sent us to California with a chance.

Walking into Anaheim Stadium on October 10 for Game Three was truly a strange sensation. The fans' greeting, when the announcer said, "Number twenty-five, Don Baylor," was heartfelt and warm.

The Can was on stage that day. He did not pitch badly, but he could not match John Candelaria. The Angels left-hander gave us next-to-nothing and won, 5–3. The only real damage came against Donnie Moore, their stopper who set an ominous precedent for himself by allowing 2 runs in two innings. The Angels got a pair of unlikely home runs from shortstop Dick Schofield and centerfielder Gary Pettis. The low point of my day: getting picked off first with runners on first and second. I was so intent on staying out of a double play, I wound up right where Bob Boone wanted me—too far off the bag.

Game Four was a nightmare. We fought like crazy to get a 3–0 lead against Don Sutton and Vern Ruhle. Clemens took that lead into the ninth, about as safe a feeling as you can have. When Doug DeCinces homered and Roger gave up back-to-back singles, though, Mac figured he was tired. Clemens had started on three days' rest for the first time ever. So Mac turned to Calvin Schiraldi, our stopper. He did not stop Pettis, though, giving up an RBI double, a ball Jim Rice lost in the lights in left. Calvin intentionally walked Ruppert Jones, then struck out Grich. Calvin needed just one out and got to 1–2 in the count against Brian Downing. His next pitch hit

Brian in the ribs to force in the tying run. In the eleventh, Calvin's misery deepened when Grich doubled in the winning run.

We now trailed in the series, 3–1. The most important game of the year awaited us. The records show that the ninth-inning home run by Don Baylor made it Angels 5, Red Sox 4. Then, with two outs, Gene Mauch visited Witt and, in another move destined to be second-guessed, decided Witt was tired and replaced him with left-hander Gary Lucas. All Lucas needed was one out. All he did was throw one pitch; he hit Rich Gedman. Mauch called on Donnie Moore. The right-hander drove the count to 1–2 against Dave Henderson, then watched Hendu foul off the next two pitches. Dave then put 64,000 Angels fans into shock by hitting the next pitch into the left-field seats. The Angels, all poised on the top step of their dugout moments before, fell back on their bench and watched twenty-four Red Sox celebrate, as one, at home plate.

The game still had to be won. It was no easier for us than the Angels. California tied it at 6–all in the bottom of the ninth, on a pinch-hit single by Rob Wilfong off Joe Sambito. Soon they had the bases loaded with one out. But Steve Crawford, the unsung hero, got DeCinces on a short fly, then Grich on a jam shot to the mound.

Donnie Moore pitched into the eleventh and into trouble when he hit me with a pitch, then gave up a single to Dwight. Gedman, trying to sacrifice, bunted so well he reached on a hit. The bases were loaded for Henderson. He still had his magic. Hendu hit a sacrifice fly to drive in the winning run.

Final score, 7–6. We were going home, as united a team as I'd ever seen. Boston still trailed in the playoffs, 3–2, but there was no doubt in our minds that we were going to win. And the Angels? The look I saw on Gene Autry's face when I bumped into him on the elevator after that game told it all. They were going to lose again. No one knew it more than they did.

Games Six and Seven were no contests. We clobbered McCaskill and the Angels bullpen, 10–4, to tie the Series. Candelaria was next. We had spotted a chink in his armor in game films after Game Three. Candy tipped his pitches.

Whenever Candy would come to a set position, he would hold his glove above the belt right before he threw a fastball. If he held it below the belt it meant he was about to throw a breaking ball. He subconsciously did those two things 99.9 percent of the time. He'd only pitch from the set position, as opposed from a windup when the Sox had men on base. That was the perfect time, though, the big-money time, when two-run home runs, two-run singles would be there for the asking. Veteran guys would take such a tip from a pitcher in a heartbeat.

That day we blasted Candy for seven runs in three and two-thirds innings. The final score: 8–1.

It had all come together so quickly. I was only there seven months, but I felt such a part of it all. For the series, I was 9 for 26 with 3 doubles, 1 home run, 2 RBI, and 6 runs scored. I batted .346. It was like I'd spent my entire career with those guys. Becky and Susan, the other wives and families, were in the runway outside the clubhouse. They had been electrified by the miracle of Game Five. They were going to the Series, too, and celebrated a victory that was as much theirs as ours.

I felt nothing but joy for the Red Sox, but I also knew my dream had come true at the expense of good friends. Before Game Seven, Bobby Grich had announced he would retire after the game. Reggie now had two straight ALCS losses; Mr. October's magic was all but gone.

Then there was Gene.

Walter Hriniak told me after that game that I should never feel sorry for Gene Mauch. "If he has you down, he is going to take his foot and put it on your throat and he is going to keep you down," Walter said. Still, Gene is the only manager I ever had who sat down and wrote me a letter telling me how much I meant to his club. I felt deeply for him on that day and all the other days on which he watched his World Series dream die. He had resigned after the '82 season because the Angels said they wanted to "reevaluate" him after the ALCS loss to Milwaukee. He came back and won another division title, got one strike away. Then the demons awoke. In 1982 he was second-guessed for not making a pitching move. In 1986 he makes the move, Gary Lucas hits Gedman. The rest is history. So I did feel for Gene, along with Jimmy Reese, Grichie, Reggie, and Rod.

I also felt something else. A sense of extreme satisfaction. Years of waiting were over. The World Series, at last, was at hand. I felt a personal vindication above and beyond just having beaten the two teams that let me go. I had gained recognition in Boston for the part of my game that teams said they appreciated but seemed to fear at the same time. I had been asked to step forth for Oil Can, asked to instill a sense of team unity. I had been asked to provide big hits, too, and I had done so. It had all come together, for the Sox, for me. It was as perfect as I could have imagined.

I was going back to New York to be in the World Series. Not to the stadium that I'd hoped for, but I would take Shea and the Mets. After all, it was New York, where the World Series takes on a truly special glow. Carlos May, who played in the 1976 Reds–Yankees Series, used to talk about how wonderful the combination of baseball, autumn, and New York could be. "When the leaves turn brown and we were still around," Carlos would say, "that's what it's all about."

The clubhouse at Shea was jammed with media at the workout scheduled before Game One. Reporters who covered me at every stop along the way were there. I drew a crowd. I was in Steinbrenner's backyard and a lot of people wanted to see if I would gloat. But that was not the way I chose to go. It had taken fifteen years to get there, so I was going to enjoy every minute of it, not waste time thinking about him.

I did not start Games One or Two. For the first time the DH would be used in American League parks only during the Series. It had alternated from year to year before; it was just my luck that 1986 would have been a DH year until the rule change. Mac and I discussed pinch-hitting and decided they would be situation at-bats, not charity.

In Game One, Hurst pitched a beauty, shutting out the Mets for eight innings. When Mac needed a pinch-hitter to face right-hander Roger McDowell in the ninth he called on young Mike Greenwell, going with the lefty-righty match. He was the only pinch-hitter Mac had to use as Hurst and Schiraldi combined on a four-hitter, winning 1–0.

Game Two belonged to Clemens and Dwight Gooden, everybody's dream matchup. Sometimes dreams don't come true. Dwight Evans homered early, Dave Henderson late, and Gooden was roughed up for 6 runs in five innings. Roger did not last that long, allowing 3 runs on 5 hits and 4 walks in four and one-third innings. He struck out only 3. We had not seen the real Gooden any more than the Mets had seen the real Clemens. Gooden was one of those phenoms who come along every ten or fifteen years, a rare talent who won a Cy Young before age twenty-one. Gooden throws with pinpoint control at about 95 mph, like Roger. But the difference between Gooden and Clemens is that Dwight's fastball breaks down while Roger's takes off and explodes around the shoulders. Gooden, therefore, needs pinpoint control to win. He will have his big strikeout days, too, but mostly because hitters go fishing. He's a great pitcher, while Roger is a great strikeout pitcher. There is a difference.

We won Game Two, 9–3, thanks, in part, to Steve Crawford and Bob Stanley, who pitched four and two-thirds scoreless innings. Mac used only one pinch-hitter again. He asked if I wanted the seventh-inning at-bat. I declined. We were leading, 8–3. I did not believe that my old friend, Mets Manager Davey Johnson, would appreciate that.

We were up, 2–0. We were also playing the National League champions, a team that had won a pennant by digging deep inside against a tough Astros team. We knew there was more to the Mets than what they had showed in Shea. Maybe other people, some younger Red Sox, were thinking sweep. I was just saying let's win two of the next five.

Can was on for Game Three. He was also on for the pregame press conference and tore into the Mets. I guess they'd ticked him off by opting to skip the workout on the off-day. Can had to understand. They were National Leaguers. They could do anything they wanted.

An old teammate of the Sox, Bobby Ojeda, faced us in Game Three. He reminded me of another former Sox left-hander, a guy who got better once he left Fenway because he came to trust more in his changeup—John Tudor. My first at-bat in the World Series was a lot like my first at-bat in the majors but, at the same time, worlds apart. I was nervous that day in 1970 and still don't know what pitch Steve Hargan threw when I doubled in 2 runs for Earl Weaver. I had butterflies on October 21, too. I also had the intensity and awareness that a seasoned veteran had better possess at that point in life. Bobby Ojeda worked on me and I worked the count, showing the patience I know I didn't have back in 1970. When he tried to throw a 3–2 pitch by me, I hit it toward the Green Monster. In Shea, it would have been a home run. The wall decided to taketh away that day. The ball ticked off the top and I settled for a standup double to open the second.

That was certainly one of the few highlights of our day. The Mets romped, 7–1. Lenny Dykstra, one of the gnats who sat atop their lineup and made the Mets go, collected 4 hits, including a home run.

Our engines had stalled. Ojeda and McDowell allowed only 5 hits, shut us down in our own park. Ron Darling and a host of Mets relievers stopped us on 7 hits in Game Four and Gary Carter drove the ball over the Green Monster twice to assure a 6–2 victory. Mac gambled and inserted a fourth starter—Al Nipper—to give his big guys extra rest. Nipper pitched well, but the bullpen faltered.

We were going back to Shea, that much was certain. We needed Bruce Hurst to come through big to get us within one victory of a championship. Bruce did, pitching another complete game, beating a shaky Gooden, 4–2. The only bright spot for the Mets: four innings of 3-hit, shutout ball by Sid Fernandez, a confidence-builder that would come back to haunt us. My contribution in the final game: an RBI single in 3 at-bats, the hit that drove Gooden from the game in the fifth. In the three games in Fenway, I was 2-for-10 with an RBI. I wanted to make more of a contribution, knew I was about to become a cheerleader again. But I also knew that one victory was all we needed. And we had the best—Roger Clemens—going in Game Six.

It's over, I thought. There was no doubt in my mind.

Roger and Bobby Ojeda pitched sharply for six innings. By the top of the seventh we led, 3–2. Roger came out for a pinch-hitter in the eighth; Mac called on Greenwell again. He had other plans for me. We loaded the bases that inning against Roger McDowell. Mac saw left-hander Jesse Orosco warming in their bullpen. He told me to get ready to hit for Bill Buckner, our left-handed swinging first baseman, if he should have to face Orosco.

Davey Johnson waved Orosco in. I made my way to the clubhouse to get in my practice swings. By the time I walked back to the dugout, Buck was walking to the plate. Buck hit the first pitch on the fly to center for an easy out.

I never asked Mac what happened. I know he had a change of heart. I know he cares about his veteran players, had seen Buck play on two bad legs, two bad feet, drive in 102 runs for that team. I don't know if Buck asked to stay in. I don't know if Mac wanted him on the field for the final celebration. All I know is that the situation at-bat we had all talked about had come and gone. We had a chance to break the game open. Mac had a chance to do what he'd done in the latter part of the season. Get Buck on the bench and a healthy Dave Stapleton out at first for defense. None of those things happened. And Mac was one horrid hour away from joining Gene Mauch in the most uncomfortable position of all—a manager being second-guessed by millions.

We still led, but only by 1 run. Calvin, on a rollercoaster throughout the postseason, gave the Mets the tying run in the bottom of the eighth.

The game remained tied until the top of the tenth, when Hendu hit a solo home run off Rick Aguilera. We added another run when Marty Barrett singled in Wade Boggs. We led, 5–3. This time we knew it was over. Some Mets did, too. In the bottom of the tenth, Calvin retired Wally Backman and then Keith Hernandez. Hernandez, knowing the Mets had just lost the Series, retired to drown his sorrows in a beer. Then he watched the impossible happen.

Gary Carter, one of those veterans you never want to see at the plate with the game on the line, dumped in a single. Harmless, we thought. Kevin Mitchell, a fireplug of an infielder, followed with a pinch-hit. Calvin faced Ray Knight, another veteran you knew wouldn't kill you with the long ball but, Mac cautioned, could kill you with heart. Knight dunked a single into center. It was 5–4. Mitchell moved to third.

In came Bob Stanley. And what unfolded may be the single most damaging at-bat ever against the Boston Red Sox.

Stanley and Mookie Wilson, the Mets' mercurial left fielder, went at it for 10 pitches. Mookie fouled off a 2–1 pitch and we were one strike away. Red Sox, not Angels, stood on the top step ready to charge the mound in celebration. Mookie fouled off the next pitch. And the next. Stanley's seventh pitch wound up at the backstop and Mitchell scored, a turn that put the Red Sox on the bench in stunned disbelief. Depending on which pundits you choose to believe, it was either a wild pitch (the official scorer's ruling) or a passed ball (Stanley's friends' ruling).

Wilson still stood at the plate. Knight was now on second. Mookie fouled off yet another pitch and, incredibly, another. Stanley threw his tenth pitch to Wilson and saw it grounded to Buck. Saw Buck go down to get the ball. Saw the ball go through Buck's legs. Watched in a daze as Buck limped after the ball while Knight steamed around second to score the winning run.

During that final inning, I had walked back and forth to the clubhouse, I was so nervous. I saw a victory stand that would never be used, a draped World Series championship trophy that would never be unveiled. The Mets' message board had flashed "Congratulations, World Champion Red Sox." The champagne was on ice. We did everything right, except get the last strike.

The media used the word "choke." That's bullshit. Hendu, Barrett, Evans were all having a great Series. They didn't choke. Buck did not, either. He just did not make the routine play. If it happens in April, it's an error. If it happens in the Series, it's history. And if it happens to a Boston player, well, it's the Red Sox. The fans knew, we knew, the Mets did not beat us. We beat ourselves. I know I started to wonder about that jinx. The players may have felt something could go wrong. New Englanders seemed to know something *would* go wrong. I felt powerless to help break that spell. What could I do if I never got to grip the bat in my hands?

Game Seven awaited us. There would be no more room for mistakes. Still, we had a chance. And we had Bruce Hurst, who already had two victories and who had allowed the Mets only 2 runs in seventeen innings. Again, I liked our chances. I just wasn't as certain as I had been going into Game Six. I didn't think I'd ever be that certain of anything ever again.

Dwight and Rich Gedman both hit home runs and Wade Boggs singled in a third run to roust Ron Darling in the second inning. Darling, who had refused to speak to Dwight or me the day before at a rainout news conference, wasn't quite as high and mighty that day. Unfortunately, his replacement, Sid Fernandez, proved to be just plain mighty. He followed up his sensational Fenway performance with two and a half scoreless, hitless innings. He struck out four. And he bought the Mets time.

Bruce pitched into the sixth without allowing a run. Then the Mets struck for 3, on a 2-run, bases-loaded single by Hernandez and an RBI single by Carter. I had thought 3 runs was enough. The Mets' fight-back spirit still amazed me. They had the gnats and the guns. And they had the pitching.

Bruce was exhausted and Mac had to go to the bullpen, just as he did in Game Six when a blister stopped Clemens. He handed the ball to Calvin in the top of the seventh. Ray Knight smashed what little confidence Calvin had left by hitting a home run into the left-field pavilion, the eventual game-winner.

Some guys second-guessed the pitch. The count was 0–2 and Calvin tried to jam Knight with a fastball. I guess the thinking was that Knight wouldn't do what a Carter or a Hernandez could. He could be kept in the park. Unless he got a pitch that invited him to slam it. It happened that day.

The Mets would get 2 more runs that inning. Dwight Evans doubled in 2 against McDowell in the eighth to make it 6–5. But Orosco would shut it down right there, getting three outs, the last a groundout by me in the one pinch-hit appearance I got in the four games at Shea.

Orosco would not be touched by anyone. He was on the mound for the final out in the Mets' 8–5 victory.

The magic had disappeared two days before. The final out sealed that feeling. We had our chances, but gave a good team too many chances to win. After Game Six, we felt outnumbered and overwhelmed even though we had Bruce Hurst on the mound. We felt like the Angels must have when they came to Fenway for the final two playoff games the week before. I finally understood the severe pain Gene Mauch must have felt. One strikeout. Sometimes it's simply impossible to get.

36

AL CAMPANIS AND THE "NECESSITIES"

ONCE, before a game in Milwaukee early in April 1987, Boston General Manager Lou Gorman stood a few feet from me in the visitor's clubhouse and told a reporter that one day he wanted Don Baylor to be his assistant.

I thought, *I don't want to be Lou Gorman's assistant. I would rather be in Lou Gorman's position.*

I was having a difficult time taking seriously what was being said about me, or about any black player with managerial aspirations. Executives were scrambling to prove that there was no racism in baseball, were even revamping hiring policies.

Some, like Gorman, were well intentioned. But I did not believe everyone felt the same in 1987.

Al Campanis had proven that a few days before. The general manager of the Dodgers had "celebrated" the forty-ninth anniversary of Jackie Robinson's breaking the color barrier by telling a national television audience that blacks lack the "necessities" to hold management positions. Incredibly, Campanis backed his contention by saying blacks lack buoyancy and, for that reason, don't make good swimmers.

I knew what Campanis's statements on ABC-TV's "Nightline" represented. I've seen it my entire life. Prejudice, rampant in our society, had been brought into the open in baseball.

For many black and Latin players, expectations hit bottom. I wanted to one day manage in the majors, and eventually move on to a general manager's position. But as I sat in my hotel room in Milwaukee awaiting the Red Sox season opener, I felt a crushing depression. I watched replays of Campanis, read and reread his words.

I'd never felt more isolated or angry. I was good enough to play, but had no right to dream beyond the day I put down my bat.

Some friends said I should understand that Campanis's prejudices were ingrained during another era. He was in the minority and change was coming if I'd only be patient.

Understand? No. This man ran a major-league baseball team. He'd pillaged an entire race, had knocked the hope out of a lot of qualified guys. Who gave him the right?

Campanis inadvertently made affirmative action a hot topic. Suddenly, everybody had an opinion, from presidential candidate Jesse Jackson to NAACP President Benjamin Hooks.

Campanis was fired by the Dodgers. Commissioner Peter Ueberroth instituted an affirmative-action program as baseball scrambled to undo its institutional racism. The discrimination transcended the fact that there were no black managers or general managers. Most organizations could not point to any minorities in any significant management post. Several organizations pointed to dining-room chefs and clubhouse equipment men as significant minority hirings.

You can fire an Al Campanis, but you can't fire the feelings. They've been in baseball's fabric too long.

Everyone had excuses. Steve Fainaru of the *Hartford Courant* quoted Gorman extensively in an article on blacks in management that April. Gorman told Fainaru that, in twenty-seven years of baseball administration, he'd never been approached by a black seeking a front-office job after his playing career.

Fainaru also quoted Gorman as saying, "Maybe the black athletes that play the game are so skilled on the field they feel that is what they do the best. Maybe management has been viewed as, you know, maybe the enemy. They think it's a bad place to be. Maybe that what we do is . . . I don't want to use the term 'black magic,' but there's something of an aura about what we do."

Lou and I came up in the Orioles organization together and I consider him a friend. But sometimes I wonder if Lou knows me or any black at all when he says things like that.

Whether Campanis spurred on Ueberroth or not is something only the commissioner knows. He founded an affirmative-action committee with former Secretary of the Army Clifford Alexander and Janet Hill, of an employment counseling service, and Dr. Harry Edwards, Berkeley professor of sociology. Campanis was later named by Edwards as a special consultant.

Ueberroth is gone now, replaced in April 1989 by A. Bartlett Giamatti. He, too, must be asked: What about former players who want to work in baseball, but are denied because they are minorities?

Giamatti and the National League hopefully set a tone for fair employment by seeking out qualified candidates of all colors to replace Giamatti as NL president. The league hired former Cardinals All-Star Bill White in February 1989, making him the first black president of a major professional sports league. The league got a good, fair man in Bill White. It should also pride itself because White's hiring is the most important step management has ever taken in proving its belief in equal opportunity.

There's still a long way to go, however.

Frank Robinson is still the only black manager and Nick Levya, the only Hispanic manager. There are no minority general managers. Henry Aaron, vice-president in charge of player development for the Braves, is the lone minority at that level. Bob Watson made another inroad when he was named assistant general manager of the Astros at the end of the 1988 season.

In baseball's business end have there been measurable improvements. Alexander and Hill have helped increase the number of minority vendors, licensees, and nonmanagement front-office employees. To Ueberroth's credit, baseball opened doors for minorities and women to those parts of the game.

But what of the players?

Ueberroth placed the responsibility with Harry Edwards. Edwards wanted minority players to consider boycotting games before he joined the commissioner's office. Harry's used to boycotts. He organized the boycott by black athletes of the 1968 Olympic Games.

Boycotting major-league baseball is not in my contract. That was just one of many issues that set Harry and a lot of players, including me, at odds. Some people said that it was a mistake to make Harry Edwards an issue. Maybe. But we were asked to accept his leadership blindly. Frank Robinson, Willie Stargell, and Dave Winfield can speak for themselves and for me. Frank and Willie now do that. They, along with former pitcher Ray Burris

and former scout Ben Moore, formed the Baseball Network, an organization
of minorities with past and present ties to the game. Ueberroth recognized
the Network and it is involved in hiring strategy.

On the field, whites, blacks, Latins give society a strong working example
of the good that can be accomplished if people work together. Most white
players are unaware of the extent of discrimination at the next level. When
they are made aware they are shocked. I know Dwight was in 1987. He and
I attended a meeting called by Ueberroth during the All-Star break, my
second with the commissioner on the issue that season.

Dwight listened as former greats such as Curt Flood, Lou Brock, Billy
Williams, and Bob Gibson told how they'd wanted to stay in baseball, but
how their requests for jobs had often failed to draw responses, let alone lead
to jobs.

Dwight was stunned. Before the meeting, he told me how honored he
was to be in the same room with some of those guys, how he wished he
could have asked for autographs if he'd had a baseball. Then he listened to
the hurt, could not believe the game could not find room for such Hall of
Famers.

What Dwight didn't realize was that Campanis's words reflected baseball's
unofficial policy. We were there to hear what baseball planned to do about
it. It's been a quiet watch.

In Boston, the Red Sox constantly fight that team's image. The Red Sox
were the last team to have a black player at the major-league level. Ten years
after Jackie Robinson stepped on the field, the Red Sox finally fielded a
black, a go-slow policy attributed to the team's late owner, Tom Yawkey.
Once blacks were in, it didn't mean it was comfortable. Boston is a racially
troubled town, especially for interracial couples.

Boston is tough on black players, period. Jim Rice bore the brunt alone
for years. After experiencing Boston for two years, I understood why Jimmy
is so bitter. He never felt he had anyone to relate to or trust.

The media does not help. Rice came up to the big leagues the same year
as Fred Lynn. Both had brilliant rookie seasons. Jimmy will never believe
that the treatment they received from the media was equal. He never could
hide his anger and his reputation suffered. Did Jim Rice receive the same
publicity or endorsement opportunities as Yaz, Freddy, and Carlton Fisk? If
Boston is still a racially tense city, how could the answer to that question
have ever been yes?

In Boston, race is never far from the surface. The media raises the issue
all the time. It seemed to me that the worst writers tried to pit black against
white.

Then there is Tommy Harper. Long a Red Sox coach, he exposed the team as one that abided by and condoned discrimination. In 1985 Tommy revealed that the Elks Club of Winter Haven, Florida, invited Red Sox players and staff to use its facilities by placing invitations in lockers at the team's spring-training facility. No black was ever invited.

For years everyone, including black players, ignored it. Only when Dan Shaughnessy of the *Boston Globe* asked Harper about the policy did Tommy speak out. Tommy was fired later that year, reportedly for not fulfilling his duties as minor-league hitting instructor and Gorman's assistant.

Tommy charged discrimination. The Equal Employment Opportunity Commission for both the state and federal governments agreed and forced the Red Sox to pay Harper undisclosed damages. The team was ordered to implement an affirmative-action program.

In the year Tommy was out of baseball he worked in a garage across the street from Fenway Park. In the winter of 1987 Tommy was quoted by Mark Hyman of the *Baltimore Sun* as saying, "What the Red Sox put out on me—that I was disloyal, that I was incompetent—brought back that knot, that nauseating feeling in my stomach, like being discriminated against in the South of the 1960s." Tommy now works for the Montreal Expos.

Last season, after the Red Sox fired McNamara as manager, they actually talked of interviewing three black candidates, Bill Robinson, Billy Williams, and former Reds great Joe Morgan. It never happened because the team permanently hired interim manager, Joe Morgan, after he got the team off to a 19–1 start. That Morgan was Mac's third-base coach and, as he liked to point out, is the "White Joe Morgan." If that Morgan hadn't been an instant success I wonder if three black candidates would have had a shot, given the histories of that city and team. Gorman says yes. I believe him, as an individual. I don't know if I can say the same for the city or the team.

Boston is not alone in having to turn around the cynicism bred by its past. The Twins have never had many blacks or Latins in positions of authority, other than hitting instructor Tony Oliva. That was the legacy of former owner Calvin Griffith. He's notorious for once stating that he moved the team once known as the Senators from Washington, D.C., because Minnesota had more "hard-working white people."

There's new Twins ownership and management now. In the few months I was there, I watched GM Andy MacPhail work, got to know Twins owner Carl Pohlad. It will be interesting to see if there is a change. The jury is still out on Minnesota.

Instead of being out in front on affirmative action, the team of Jackie Robinson, the Dodgers, was revealed to be just like other major-league teams. After Campanis was fired, the team hired former pro-basketball great Tommy Hawkins as a vice-president, one of the more significant minority hirings since 1987. But mostly, the Dodgers are like everyone else. They have a black first-base coach/hitting instructor in Manny Mota, but that's about it. How many times has Mota watched coaches with less seniority move to the third-base coach's box—the stepping stone to manager? Mota and other talented baseball men, like long-time Orioles bullpen catcher Elrod Hendricks, are maybe *too* nice, waiting and hoping for miracles that never seem to come.

Then there are the Mets. In 1986, outfielder George Foster accused the team of phasing out black players. He was hounded by the media as a racist. Shortly after, he was released. People say George was paranoid, because his job was being shifted to another black, Kevin Mitchell. But after the 1986 season, Mitchell was traded to San Diego for Kevin McReynolds, who is white. Last season, the 1988 Mets had just three black players in the majors, Dwight Gooden, Darryl Strawberry, and Mookie Wilson. The crosstown Yankees started the season with twelve black and Latin players. The last time the Mets traded for a black at the major-league level was 1982, when they acquired Foster from the Reds.

Perhaps the organization that hurt me the most to watch in recent years is the Orioles. In the winter of 1987, Orioles owner Edward Bennett Williams, weak from his losing battle against cancer, called a news conference to announce that Roland Hemond, the new GM, would try to undo what he perceived as a pattern of racism.

Williams had fired GM Hank Peters and Farm Director Tom Giordano after he found out that only five of the hundred players in the Orioles' minor-league system were black. "It's hard to believe it's accidental," Williams told Hyman of the *Baltimore Sun*. Williams said he was hiring former NFL running back Calvin Hill to "deal with a deadly illness overlooked in the organization . . . I monitor my health against a deadly disease. He [Hill] will monitor the nonrecurrence of this deadly illness by never again allowing us to be insensitive to the rights of minority groups."

Williams also appointed Frank as his special assistant. Then, six games into the season, he asked Frank to take over the team when Cal Ripken Sr. was fired as manager. The Orioles also brought Don Buford into the front office. Williams died last summer, but not before he'd carried through on his policy of equal opportunity.

It's not only teams that must examine policy.

The Major League Players Association has no minorities in management other than player representatives. It took years for the Association to print the basic agreement in Spanish.

Latins are ignored by both sides. Latin players are heroes in their home countries, but when they finish playing, America forgets them. Is that what baseball really wants for great players such as Jose Cruz and Fernando Valenzuela? Latins should be able to do more for management than recruit other Latins who will come here as a cheaper source of labor to make money for major-league baseball.

No doubt, every minority group is hurt in almost every situation by the "old-boy" network. Toby Harrah, Doug Ault, Rich Dauer, John Wathan, and Mike Cubbage retire and the next thing you know they're managing in the minors and, in Wathan's case, quickly thereafter in the majors. Harrah retired after the 1986 season and was immediately named Class A manager for the Texas Rangers. Within six months he was the organization's Triple A manager. Toby's a talented, knowledgeable, dedicated guy. He was also lucky in that his former roommate from his playing days is Tom Grieve, the Rangers' GM. Blacks and Latins know it's natural that friends help friends, hire friends. But if there are no minorities in the system, is it any wonder why we're frustrated at knowing no one's there to help us? No one wants a handout, just a fair chance for all qualified candidates.

Management says be patient. They say blacks must pay their dues and be willing to accept lesser-paying jobs in the minors. Pete Rose, Bobby Valentine, and Lou Piniella were not willing, either. So they had to settle for major-league managing jobs. For Bill Robinson and Billy Williams, there's been nothing nearly as rewarding. For blacks who did pay their dues in the minors, there's hardly anything at the major-league level, no matter what.

On that rare occasion when the door does open, where is the equitable support? Instead, there is the "weight-of-the-race" pressure. When Frank became the first black manager he was practically on his own. In San Francisco, Frank's general manager, Tom Haller, made deals without informing Frank, ignored his advice. Frank wanted to keep Joe Morgan and Reggie Smith, two key players in the Giants' strong second-place finish in 1982. Haller let both go via free agency.

Maury Wills was one of only three black managers in history. He had problems that doomed him in Seattle, including a drug dependency. He could not succeed as a manager under those circumstances. That certainly was not the fault of the Mariners. Maury will probably never work in an important capacity in baseball again. What makes the Wills situation even more tragic is that critics view it as a setback for an entire race, say Wills is living proof that blacks do not have the "necessities." If that sounds like an overstatement, remember Campanis ran a major-league franchise.

That stereotyping is unacceptable. Unless every white is made to take responsibility for Billy Martin's off-field actions, then no one should have to answer for Maury Wills but Maury Wills.

It's 1989. It's time the stereotypes, the "plantation" mentality, the discrimination disappeared.

Owners, general managers, league officials should have understood long ago that players want to stay on because they love the game. No one race or ethnic group has a monopoly on that love. Frank and Brooks Robinson, Dwight and Darrell Evans, Willie Stargell, Bill White, Jesus Alou, Phil Niekro, Elrod Hendricks all had the "necessities" when some owner needed them to carry teams to division titles, pennants, World Series championships. Those "necessities" are still there when the playing stops.

Why is that so difficult to accept?

The issue of minorities in baseball has lost its urgency since the tortured summer of 1987. But the issue must never be forgotten until the fight has been won. Al Campanis made everyone aware. We need to keep it on the front burner. It's a glimmer right now, but I believe as long as one person speaks out, management will be compelled to care—and to act.

Tommy Harper took a stand, just like Curt Flood and Frank Robinson before him. Just like Jackie Robinson did over forty years ago. No one should ever have to go into the breach alone again. Hopefully, there will always be a chorus hitting back against discrimination.

I know Ueberroth pushed the game in the right direction, whether for expedient reasons or not. He may have wondered why I kept hammering at him when he kept showing numbers that indicated positive movement in 1987 and again the next year. I thought he did a good job, as did others. But if everyone agrees publicly, who will be left to push the system to keep working harder? If Peter Ueberroth picked up the paper just once and said, "What does that Baylor SOB want?" maybe it landed a spur or planted a seed that one day resulted in one door opening somewhere. If so, even if I'm viewed as the lone "radical," it's worth it. I know I cannot stop speaking out.

Some friends caution me not to criticize too loudly because I might be out there all alone, might be considered too radical and denied a job. I want to work in baseball after I finish playing. I want to have a say in a game that has given me so much. I also have to be true to myself.

I believe there are people who understand the issue and me. In 1987, Kansas City General Manager John Schuerholz offered me a one-year player's contract and then a front-office position starting in 1989. I wasn't ready to limit my playing days to one season, which is why I chose to sign with Oakland. But I'll always remember that John Schuerholz made the offer. At least one executive believed this one man has the necessities.

37

TAKING THE WORLD
SERIOUS

WHEN John McNamara called the Red Sox to-
gether on the first day of spring training in 1987 to order his players to stop
the sniping, I knew we were in trouble.

Mac was right. We had just completed our winter of discontent, when
the Red Sox lost their proudest possession of 1986—our sense of togetherness. I had never been in a Series before, so I did not know how most teams
took winning or losing it. From everything I witnessed I could not imagine
many teams took it as hard as the Red Sox.

Bitter questions and second-guessing flared and never went away.

Was it a passed ball or a wild pitch? That dispute, played out in the
media and helped along by Bob Stanley and Rich Gedman, threatened to
turn two friends and their families into the Hatfields and McCoys.

Bill Buckner, who had in one play put an indelible black mark on a long,
successful career, withdrew. Replays would not let him, or Boston Red Sox

♦ 276 ♦

fans, forget. Buck had to see Mookie Wilson in his dreams. And those dreams all had to be nightmares.

Roger Clemens was upset by reports that he'd asked out of Game Six because of a blister rather than being removed by Mac. Mac would also listen to criticisms not only for leaving Buck in the game in the fateful tenth inning of Game Six, but for not using me as a pinch-hitter against Orosco.

Then there was the dispute over the World Series financial shares. As is customary in baseball, the team gathered before the playoffs began to figure out postseason shares. We decided not to include the grounds crew at Fenway Park. The reasons were simple. We were always treated as outcasts in our own ballpark. We could not get the field for extra hitting when we wanted, saw the smallest requests treated with disdain. The last straw came in the final series of the season. Don Mattingly was fighting for a batting title and came to Fenway hoping for the courtesy of using the field. The grounds crew said there was a threat of rain and never removed the tarpaulin. Storm clouds gathered somewhere over Florida and Mattingly, the Yankees, and the team going into the postseason were denied use of the field. Players all agreed that enough was enough. Procedure calls for shares to be determined by vote and majority rules, period. Throughout the winter, however, critics surfaced everywhere, mainly Joe Giuliotti of the *Herald,* whose articles were fueled by comments from Bob Stanley and Jim Rice. The "shares" controversy became the news story of the off-season.

To make matters worse, Becky was devastated. She had caught pennant fever as early as May. I used to tease her, asking how she could possibly last the entire season. All I had to do is look at Becky and she'd say, "one strike away." It did not help that Boston newspapers and television stations rehashed the final two losses almost daily. It didn't seem like Boston could let go. We could not, either. After a couple of weeks I made a decision. We had to get away. So we left Boston and got lost for a few weeks in the wine country of California. Never was a vacation so needed.

By late December we finally let go permanently. It happened shortly after our return from California. Dwight and Susan Evans came over to watch tapes of the playoffs, which they had not recorded. We watched and watched. Soon the Series tapes were on. And a funny thing happened. The four of us, for the first time, watched the highlights from Games Six and Seven. There were tears, but a lot of laughs, too. But, most importantly, we watched. Then we put it behind us.

The team could not do the same. By the end of April, the Boston Red Sox were in sixth place, 9.5 games out. By mid-July the deficit reached 15.5 games. The season was over, as far as the front office was concerned. The decision was made: let the turnover begin.

Buck was released on July 23. Glenn Hoffman was traded in mid-August. Hendu, who saw his job given over to a slick young centerfielder named Ellis Burks, was sent to the Giants by the end of that month.

The Red Sox also promoted Sam Horn from Pawtucket and started looking at him as a future first baseman. With Greenwell moving closer and closer to a full-time position in the outfield, it appeared that Jim Rice was reluctantly heading for the DH position. And I knew that meant I would be heading elsewhere.

I did not fight it. I talked to Mac and then to Lou Gorman. I wanted to know if a move was coming, or if the Sox still had plans for me. A youth movement was certainly underway, something Gorman did not deny. The discussion was amicable, my decision was clear-cut. After all, there were pennant races, even if the Sox were not in one.

Then a funny thing happened. There suddenly was a great deal of support all over for the Red Sox to make such a move. I don't know if you could call it a campaign, but writers I'd known for years started writing again about the leadership factor. And more and more, those articles pointed me in one direction: to the Minnesota Twins, a team in a three-way battle with Oakland and Kansas City in the American League West.

By the end of August, Twins GM Andy MacPhail and Lou Gorman were hammering out the details of a trade, trying to figure out who would be responsible for the $1.4 million in deferred payments the Red Sox had inherited from the Yankees. The negotiations went down to the final hours before the September 1 deadline permanently sealed postseason rosters, but Lou and Andy got it done right before midnight. The Red Sox were scheduled to play a series starting in Minneapolis on September 1, so it was a matter of going to the visitor's clubhouse, packing my belongings, and taking the long walk to the other side of the Metrodome.

Saying good-bye to yet more friends was not easy, particularly when it came to Dwight. But we all had learned long ago that business is business. I walked out one clubhouse door and into another world. My 1987 season was about to begin.

When I walked into the Twins clubhouse the first person to greet me was Steve Carlton, a pitcher one step away from the Hall of Fame. I was overwhelmed by that gesture, which surely had to be difficult for him. The previous week I had hit a grand slam in Fenway off him, not knowing that it had sealed his fate and mine. When the trade was made the Twins dropped Steve from the twenty-four-man roster of players eligible for the postseason, but kept him on the forty-man roster. Yet as soon as I walked in he walked up to me, shook my hand, and said, "It's good to have you over here." It was the first of many gestures that would assure that the two months I was about to spend in Minnesota would be among the most rewarding of my career.

After shaking hands with Carlton, I walked into the manager's office to officially meet Tom Kelly. He was my eleventh major-league manager, but the first one who was younger than I was. He had to look upon me as an unknown quantity, just as I did him. The only thing I knew about Kelly was that he was just one month away from leading a team to the playoffs in what was his first full season as manager. His team may have been just above .500, but he had done everything well enough to have them in first place.

I told Tom right off that I knew that the Twins had gotten into first place without me and all I wanted to do was help keep them there. He welcomed that, said that I could expect to DH against left-handers and be ready to pinch-hit at any time. Randy Bush was to have the right-handed DH at-bats.

It was somewhat difficult to accept playing part-time, but it was a lot easier to accept that job on a contender. I told Tom I would do my best in whatever role he gave me.

I had a lot of catching up to do. The Twins players made that easy. I was especially happy to be reunited with Roy Smalley, the Twins's backup shortstop and the son of Gene Mauch's sister. I had known Roy since my Angels days because of Gene. We became friends when we were on the All-Stars's tour of Japan in 1979. That friendship grew during the Yankees years, when Roy and I shared many stories about Gene as well as a love of fine restaurants and fine wines. Soon after Steve Carlton greeted me, he was followed in short order by Bert Blyleven and Joe Niekro. That was about 750 victories among the three of them, so their welcome meant a lot. Joe Niekro and George Frazier were once Yankee teammates of mine, so those friendships also helped make the transition easier. I had one other ex-teammate in that clubhouse, Tom Brunansky, who played his rookie season with the 1981 Angels.

By 1987, Bruno was one of the Twins' game-breakers. Bruno, Kirby Puckett, Kent Hrbek, and Gary Gaetti combined power, enthusiasm, and an intensity that made them one of the more feared quartets in the league.

Kirby Puckett never let a hand go by he didn't want to shake. He's one of the most outgoing players in the league, without an arrogant bone in his body. Not only is he an offensive machine, but he's a great defensive centerfielder. He plays off the pliable plastic Metrodome fence like it's a trampoline, and has made over-the-wall catches there an art form. Puck's down times at the plate last for three or four at-bats at the most, while other players might go three or four days without a healthy swing. He's as dangerous as Mattingly at the plate and just as much fun to watch.

Hrbek is a talented first baseman whose main ambition in life, I soon learned, was to be a professional wrestler. He reminded me of Boog Powell, a gentle giant, quiet and friendly at the same time. He was the leader on that team and with good reason. Players who are respected both for their game as well as for their attitude usually are. Gary Gaetti is the Twins' Mr. Intensity, a player who can ignite a whole team, as I would soon learn in the playoffs against the Tigers. He is gifted with a glove as well and up until that season was one of the league's best-kept secrets.

Twins shortstop Greg Gagne and I had never met, but it seemed we'd known each other for years. He was a student of Walter Hriniak, too. Greg and I spent a lot of time at the batting cage, talking hitting. Greg couldn't get enough. Even during games he'd come over after each at-bat to discuss technique. You can't help but like that kind of enthusiasm.

There were other Twins I quickly came to appreciate. For years I had heard of Jeff "The Terminator" Reardon, once the National League's answer to Goose Gossage. Jeff was just as advertised, a serious professional who understood the nature of his job as well as any short reliever I've ever known. He reminds me of Dennis Eckersley, who saved 45 games for the A's in 1988. Both knew when their moments were at hand, and were rarely unprepared. Reardon never hesitated to take the ball, even in the Metrodome, with its reachable seats and strange indoor air currents that help hold up the Teflon roof.

Another pitcher who has no fear of the Dome is Frankie "Sweet Music" Viola. He's come an amazingly long way since he first arrived as a nervous, high-strung left-hander in 1982. By 1987, Frankie had but one equal from the left side—Bruce Hurst. Frankie was a pleasure to be around because of his enthusiasm. I don't know if he's ever had a down day. He was one of the Twins who made it fun to come to the ballpark.

Bert Blyleven and I had been teammates in one sense for years. He has long been a "65 Roses" chapter chairman, as have Roy Smalley and Brunansky. I also felt a kinship with "Little Knucksie," Joe Niekro, who was approaching his twentieth year in the majors and still searching for his first World Series. The day I arrived his big brother and best friend, Phil, was released by the Blue Jays. Joe and Phil held out hope to the end that the Twins might acquire Phil so the two could go to their first Series together. Joe knew by September that would not happen and he was down. But he came around. And even though he wound up as the odd-man-out in the postseason pitching plans, he did not hang his head. When he finally got his World Series berth, he said it belonged to Phil just as much as it did to him.

By season's end, the Twins had won only 85 games. But it was enough to win the American League West, edging the A's. And it was enough to enrapture an entire city, a love affair between fans and team I'd never seen before.

The fans believed, but they were about the only ones outside of us who did. The experts gave Minnesota no chance against the AL East champion Tigers for many reasons, including our 29–52 road record and our inability to beat the Tigers during the regular season. The Tigers, winners of 98 games, were stocked with many pennant-race veterans and were only four years removed from their last world championship.

But the whole world had underestimated two things: the Twins' confidence in their own abilities and the power of Metrodome magic.

Minnesota simply dominated at home that season. I'd never seen a team with such a split personality. The Twins loved the Dome so much, many would arrive by midday for seven-thirty P.M. games. There were always batting-practice sessions going on and seemingly an endless supply of coaches who just loved to throw BP. I soon found myself drifting to the park earlier and earlier, growing accustomed to the lighting under the cream-colored roof, the distances to the seats behind the plexiglass wall in left. By October I actually started to like the place. But then again, I'd like any park I got to play in during that month, because it could mean only one thing—another postseason berth.

The ALCS started in the Dome. Game One belonged to Frankie and Doyle Alexander, a well-traveled veteran with a penchant for winning. The Tigers had plucked Doyle from Atlanta in August and hitched onto him and his 9–0 run through the league. I did not start that game and knew Sparky Anderson did not have many left-handers. But his main man out of the pen was Willie Hernandez, a lefty with a Cy Young to his name and a reputation for excelling in October.

Hernandez and I were destined to meet, that much I knew. We did in the eighth inning of Game One in a situation both of us were paid to excel in. The bases were loaded in a game tied at 5–5. Sparky turned to Hernandez after his right-handed stopper, Mike Henneman, walked the bases full with one out. Over 53,000 fans were going berserk by the time Tom Kelly called Randy Bush back and sent me to the plate.

I don't know if the playoffs were becoming routine, but I did not feel nervous at all. It was more like another day at the office. I blocked out the fans, concentrated solely on what I had to do.

I knew Hernandez would come at me with fastballs. Sure enough, he did on the first pitch. I fouled it straight back. I just missed that pitch. I knew as soon as I had swung, that was the pitch that I wanted, my grand-slam pitch. I did not think I would see it again. I did, though, on a 2–2 count.

This time I was fully prepared and pulled the ball through the left side for an RBI single, the game-winner in our 8–5 victory.

It was just 1 at-bat, but stood for so much. I had known for a month the Twins were looking for exactly such an at-bat, if even in just one game. The timing could not have been more perfect. For the base hit not only got the team off to the 1–0 ALCS lead, it set a tone, showed that the Twins could not only beat the Tigers, but beat their best. The satisfaction was tremendous.

I would mostly watch the rest of the ALCS from the bench, getting just one start, against my old Angels' teammate, Frank Tanana. That did not dampen the feeling that something special was unfolding as I watched teammate after teammate excel against a reeling Tigers club.

Bert Blyleven was not untouchable in Game Two, but he was just slightly better than right-hander Jack Morris. Bert won, 6–3, benefiting from 2-RBI days from pesky Dan Gladden and Tim Laudner, a quiet young catcher with a thirst for learning that matched Gagne's.

We would come within five outs of stunning the Tigers in their park. But "The Terminator" could not keep Pat Sheridan from reaching the short porch in the upper deck in right, a 2-run home run that provided the margin of victory in a 7–6 Tigers win in Game Three.

Reardon is the kind of guy who wants the ball the very next day after a blown save. Kelly gave it to Jeff in Game Four and this time he helped put a 5–3 victory in the books. Our offense that day was spearheaded by Puckett and Gagne, who both homered. One more victory and the improbable World Series berth would be ours, a Series gained by, of all things, victories on the road. We asked Blyleven to get us there and he did. Bert allowed 3 runs in five innings, but benefited from big days at the plate by Gladden and Bruno. Gladden drove in 2 runs with 3 hits. Bruno homered, doubled, and drove in 3. In the five games Bruno was 7–for–17 with 4 doubles, 2 home runs, and 9 RBI, one shy of my LCS record. I couldn't have been happier because I felt as if I'd watched Bruno come of age after years of hard work.

The Twins were going to the World Series, one of the most stunning upsets in league championship play.

There it was, a second straight World Series, something I'd never dared dream of as little as two months before. It had taken over a decade and a half to reach my first series. Eleven months later I was back. Dwight marveled at it all. He pointed out a bit enviously that it had taken him eleven years to get back after his Series debut in 1975.

I felt a tremendous sense of accomplishment. I'd had only 5 at-bats, but I had made a contribution, paid a dividend with one swing. I looked forward to the Series knowing that this time home-field advantage rested with the American League. The DH would be involved in the first two games for sure and the sixth and seventh, if necessary. If it went the distance again there would be no more cheerleading; I'd be hitting.

Minnesota fans, without a title of any sort since 1970, showed their appreciation in a way I'll never forget. When the team returned home from Detroit, we were told about 4,000 or 5,000 fans had come to the Dome to watch the fifth game on the DiamondVision screen. The club wanted everyone to step on the field, wave for a few minutes, and then we could go home. No one objected, but I know everyone wanted to make it just that, a few minutes. We were all tired and emotionally spent. We were also totally unprepared for what awaited us.

As the team buses made their way from the airport to the stadium, we saw fans lining the highways and streets. Signs hung from overpasses. Cars drove alongside, horns honking. When we stepped from the buses onto the loading dock at the Dome we heard a deafening roar. The Dome was filled with over 55,000 fans. And they stood in the aisles, down the ramps, covered every inch of the stands. And they cheered and cheered, for a solid twenty-five, thirty minutes.

We were overwhelmed, especially the long-time Twins who'd played in the bad days when 6,000 people comprised a good crowd. Some guys, like Gaetti and Puckett, were in tears. It was the most unbelievable show of affection for a team I'd ever seen.

I had been there only a few weeks, but over the course of the next two weeks I could not walk anywhere in Minneapolis without people recognizing me, wanting to just come up and say welcome and congratulations. The town not only had Series fever, it had "homer-hanky" fever, a phenomenon started as a lark by the local newspaper. Soon, the white hankies were everywhere, especially in the Dome, where the fluttering sea of white dazzled us. I even saw women wearing dresses made of the things. At first the hankies were give-aways. By the first game they were collector's items.

As Game One against the National League champion Cardinals approached, I thought about the opposition. Whitey Herzog was bringing a pitching staff with left-handers in key roles, including starters Joe Magrane and John Tudor. I knew I would get my at-bats.

Magrane, a rookie, opened Game One. I'd never seen him before. We all had to rely on scouting reports. The 10–1 final shows we did our homework well. I singled in my first at-bat, 1 of 4 hits Magrane would give up in three-plus innings. He was gone by the fourth, routed in an inning in which we scored seven times. The big blow was a grand slam by Gladden. And

Frank Viola, close to invincible at home, pitched eight innings and allowed just 1 run for his first-ever Series victory.

The fourth inning was proving to be magical for us. In Game Two we scored 6 more runs in that inning. Two came on a homer by Randy Bush against Cardinals right-hander Danny Cox. Bert Blyleven took on the Cardinals and pitched just well enough to get Kelly closer to Reardon. Juan Berenguer, the thorn in the Tigers' side in the playoffs, allowed 2 runs, but Reardon pitched a scoreless ninth to close out an 8–4 victory.

The Twins had played four home games in the postseason and won them all. We left for St. Louis believing our motto, "There's no place like Dome." That could not have been truer. Because that other road-weary Twins team showed up as soon as we crossed the state line.

Our offense died in Busch Memorial Stadium, a park not at all conducive to home runs. A team needs rabbits to win there and Herzog had just that, in Vince Coleman, Ozzie Smith, and Willie McGee.

For six innings Tudor gave us next to nothing. But he trailed, 1–0, because Les Straker pitched what had to be the most inspired six innings of his career. Lester had never gone further in a game, however. Kelly, refusing to go against the game plan that had got him that far, turned the ball over to the bullpen. Berenguer again was roughed up, this time for 3 runs. That was enough for Tudor, who combined with big Todd Worrell on a five-hitter. The Cardinals won, 3–1, ran the bases with abandon, and put on the display of "Whitey ball" their fans had been waiting for.

Frankie took the ball in Game Four, our best hope at stopping any sort of emotional surge by St. Louis. But Frankie was like the rest of the team that day: a different pitcher away from home. He carried a 1–1 tie into the fourth and he watched as Tom Lawless, a man with 1 home run in 215 major-league games, hit the ball over the left-field fence for a 3-run home run. We lost that game, 7–2, and the next, 4–2, as Danny Cox, Ken Dayley, and Worrell held us to just 6 hits.

Just like that the team that had been up two games to none in the Series now stood one game away from elimination. To my amazement, though, the Twins boarded our charter almost on the verge of celebration. The reason was simple. The Twins were going home. Only the long-time residents of that Dome could fully understand just how secure a feeling that was. I started to sense it on the flight home, saw a confidence similar to that of the 1986 Red Sox when we returned from Anaheim still trailing the Angels, 3–2, but knowing deep down we would win.

By the start of Game Six I was also an absolute believer in Dome magic. By the time I arrived at the park, guys were already there, just sitting around and relaxing. There was also an intensity that had been totally absent in the three previous games.

I had not started a game in St. Louis, giving me nearly a week to key on Game Six—and left-hander John Tudor. I was more than a little familiar with him. In his years with Boston he hardly ever changed his pitching pattern against me. I knew I would see the same pitch he threw when I hit a home run off him in Dave Righetti's Fourth of July no-hitter in 1983. Inside pitches, that's what Tudor had fed me my whole career. In the first inning he served up one and I drove it into right-center for an RBI single to put us ahead, 2–1. In my next at-bat I ran afoul of an overhead speaker. A ball I popped back toward the seats behind home plate got hung up, then fell right down into Tony Pena's glove. That was my pitch. I thought I had lost my chance, that Tudor would never throw that pitch again.

He did. In the fifth inning he was in trouble, but still nursed a 2-run lead when I stepped in with Gary Gaetti on second base. Cardinals pitching coach Mike Roarke went out to talk to Tudor. I don't think he got back into the dugout before I drove Tudor's first pitch into the left-field bleachers. Just like that the game was tied. The Metrodome sound meter, which can measure the roar of jet engines, saw the needle reach its highest point as over 55,000 fans tried their best to raise the roof.

As I rounded the bases I thought of all my loved ones. Becky, Donny, my dad, my brother in the stands, my mother and sister at home in Austin. Frank Seale and his wife Anne, sat in the Dome, too. Frank had given me my first inkling that baseball was my way out of Clarksville. So many things, so many memories, it all goes through your mind at moments such as that.

The decibel level just kept getting higher, as Steve Lombardozzi singled in the go-ahead run that inning and Kent Hrbek, a home-town boy fulfilling a childhood dream, hit a sixth-inning grand slam.

I had come back to Game Six and, contributing instead of watching, helped forge a Game Seven. The feeling of catharsis was immense. I knew that twenty-three players who'd stood with me in a somber Shea Stadium clubhouse the year before would have killed to set Games Six and Seven right. The Twins were one victory away from helping me do just that.

There was absolutely no sense of foreboding going into Game Seven. Frankie Viola was on the mound for us and that was as secure a feeling as having a Hurst or Clemens out there. Herzog shocked the masses by turning the ball over to Magrane again; I never thought he'd open a way for a second straight start, not when he had right-hander Danny Cox ready to go.

I did not believe Magrane would start until he walked out of the bullpen to pitch the bottom of the first.

The Cardinals, playing without an injured Jack Clark and Terry Pendleton, showed everyone something about fortitude by jumping in front of Frankie, 2–0, in the second. Vince Coleman, known for his legs, not his arm, threw me out at home plate in the second, a very questionable call, but an out all the same. In the fifth inning with the game tied, Whitey made the move everyone suspected he would. With Gaetti in scoring position he brought in Danny Cox. Would Tom Kelly pinch-hit or let me face the right-hander? He showed his faith in me. I singled over Ozzie's head but unfortunately Coleman made a second great throw. Gaetti was out at the plate. The game remained tied at 2. But the Cardinals were just about out of their share of miracles in the Dome. In the sixth inning Cox walked the bases loaded and then watched helplessly as Greg Gagne beat out a two-out grounder for an RBI single. Gladden, capping a sensational postseason, doubled in an insurance run in the eighth. It was all Frankie Viola and Jeff Reardon needed. They combined on a six-hitter, a fitting ending to a season in which they had played such an important role.

Again I stood in a dugout as a grounder that could lead to a world championship was put into play. This time it was hit to Gary Gaetti. He had played like a Gold Glover at third all season long. This play was no different. He scooped, took aim at Hrbek at first and threw, accurate and true. With that twenty-seventh out, the Minnesota Twins had their first world championship. And I had the last piece to the most difficult puzzle of my career.

The Minnesota Twins, a team sprinkled with a handful of veterans and wonderfully enthusiastic kids, had helped welcome me into a magical season. I will forever be grateful for that. With 5 hits and 3 RBI in 13 at-bats, I truly believe I rewarded their faith in me. And, by doing so, I finally unlocked a door that had been closed for a lifetime.

38

OH, THOSE A'S

DAVE Parker, Ron Hassey, Bob Welch, and I knew exactly why we were acquired by the Oakland A's in the winter of 1987. Oakland wanted a veteran touch to complement a deep, young, and talented team. The way they figured it, a few good moments in the clubhouse, at the plate, or on the mound would help in the common goal: dethroning the defending world-champion Twins.

There wasn't much we could tell Dave Stewart, Carney Lansford, or Dennis Eckersley. But the A's had a number of talented kids up and down the roster, some of whom had struggled in the pennant stretch of 1987.

Dave Parker adopted Jose Canseco right from the start. He told Jose that he was the greatest talent he'd ever played with. In spring training, it was Parker who put the seed in Jose's head that he could become the first player ever to steal 40 bases and hit 40 home runs.

Parker was right.

Jose Canseco not only hit 42 home runs and stole 40 bases, but drove in 124 runs, scored another 120, and batted .307, as successful a season as any player could ever hope for. That effort was rewarded at season's end when Jose was unanimously voted the American League Most Valuable Player by the Baseball Writer's Association of America.

Canseco possesses the most natural ability of any player I've ever seen. Mattingly cannot run with him. Darryl Strawberry has yet to catch Canseco in run-production. And as far as raw power, who has as much? As I see it, if Jose works on his fundamentals and attitude he's going to be scary because he's about as complete a package as there ever was.

Jose has shown he can improve his game dramatically. Just look at how his batting average gets higher every year. Unfortunately, at least from what I saw in 1988, Jose's attitude can be scarier than his potential.

My first encounter with Jose was in spring training. He showed up late because he had contracted to do card-signing shows. Manager Tony La Russa was upset, but controlled. The day Jose arrived in camp, Tony had set up a mock card-show table, complete with placards, bubble-gum cards. Tony wanted to break the tension, and teach Jose a lesson. He knew the other players were not too thrilled with Jose.

Jose just laughed the whole thing off.

Some days Jose can be selfless, on others he can be one of the most selfish players I have ever seen. Once Jose learns the team things, that selfishness should melt away. Hopefully he'll realize that he's got to run to first base the way Reggie did even at age forty-two. Reggie never trotted, certainly never peeled off. Jose does. Reggie is Jose's hero. Learn from him, Jose.

Jose has a good arm, but he should take more advantage of it. He just doesn't think anybody should run on him. Jose will soon realize he had better be ready to throw a Dave Winfield out every single time.

Jose is still a kid, something of which I constantly had to remind myself. The youth combined with the pressure can get to even the most savvy youngster.

The drive to reach 40–40 took Jose out of his game in the second part of the season. He started swinging at pitches he'd laid off of most of the year. I did not envy him because everyone in the country was watching. He started swinging at pitches that were a foot inside, up and in. He would get jammed and break bat after bat, but insist that those were the pitches he'd hit for home runs earlier in the season. They were not. When Jose got into those streaks, he got frustrated and blamed others, mostly umpires.

It was obvious Jose had to make an adjustment. He had to take the pitches that were setups.

Dave Stewart, who always tracks hitters and pitchers by video in the lounge, would tell Jose whether he was swinging at balls or strikes. One day Jose asked about a swing that had cracked yet another bat. He did not believe Stew when he was told he'd swung at a ball. So I said, "Jose, that ball was not a strike. I am telling you that ball was inside."

Jose's answer to that was he would no longer shave his bat handles thin to prevent them from breaking. "Well, that's fine, Jose," I said, "but you still cannot swing at that pitch."

Jose has thrown his share of temper tantrums. He is not only goal-oriented but money-driven. Still, Jose is a nice kid, with the emphasis on "kid." He's got a lot of growing up to do. It remains to be seen how he will handle the increased attention. When he matures he will be truly awesome, as a ballplayer, teammate, and person.

Mark McGwire tries to help get his good buddy, Jose, to that level of maturity. Mark, a two-year player, went out of his way to talk to Jose about his late arrival in spring training. Mark asked me many times to have patience because deep down, Jose is a good guy. Perhaps that's the biggest difference between Mark and Jose. Mark has a big enough heart to care about a teammate and the team.

Like Jose, Mark got to be very good friends with Reggie in 1987, the year Mark set the all-time home run record for rookies, with 49. Like Jose, you can see a lot of Reggie in Mark. The potential, the power, the ability to carry a team.

Mark is the kid you want living next door. He wants everyone to like him. I don't think he has a vindictive bone in his body. He's talented. He wants to play every day. Near the end of the season, he missed about four days because of a bad back. He almost went crazy. "Remind me never to get hurt again," he said. "I don't know what to do." Some young players might have stretched that four or five days into a two-week vacation. Not Mark. It hurt him not to be in there, especially on September 20, when we clinched the division.

Mark had a tough time off the field in 1988. He had been real accessible to the media during 1987, but I think all the constant attention probably took its toll. In a way Mark was a victim of a new age. When I came up, a rookie would not dream of being the center of attention like Mark, Jose, Gooden, Strawberry, Wally Joyner. In this era of hype, first-year players have news conferences on their first trips into major-league cities. Jose and Joyner had press conferences at Yankee Stadium in the same week during their rookie season of 1986. Don Sutton, an Angels teammate of Joyner's, came into town just two victories shy of 300. There was no news conference, nothing. That's not Joyner's fault, but things are off-balance. And sometimes it hurts the kid more than the veteran.

Today's kids can be pampered and spoiled by the attention. Others can be overwhelmed. Mark remained pretty level-headed, but last season he did find out that it's not always going to be glamorous or effortless. He had a good season, with 30 home runs and 99 RBI. But it was nothing like his rookie year, when he drove in 118 runs and hit an incredible 49 home runs.

Last season was not easy for Mark personally, either. He had some off-field distractions. I could appreciate what he was going through so last summer I did a lot of talking and Mark did a lot of listening. I hope that, in some way, it helped.

With Jose and Mark, the Athletics have a nucleus that the rest of baseball envies. But Oakland had more than just Canseco and McGwire in 1988.

Dave Parker—"Parkway" to his friends—is more flamboyant than I ever will be. But make no mistake. Dave Parker teaches and leads every day he puts on a uniform.

He had a little ritual whenever the old guys started feeling surrounded by all that irrepressible youth. Whenever Dave Henderson, McGwire, or Canseco started yapping too much about monster bashes or 40-home run seasons, Dave would stand up in the middle of the lounge, a master agitator at work.

"Excuse me, but would everybody in this room who has fifty home runs please raise your hands," he'd say. Hands would go up everywhere. "Now, would everybody who has a hundred please raise your hands. One hundred-fifty? Two hundred? Two-fifty? Three hundred?"

By the time he got to up to 200, there were just two hands left. When he went over 300, only my hand remained in the air. "Parkway" wasn't finished, though. "Eck, put your hand up, you too, Welchie," he'd shout at pitchers Dennis Eckersley and Bobby Welch. "I know you guys have given up more than 300."

It was hysterical.

Parker can drown out the game's most notorious motor-mouths; he did all last summer when he outtalked Dave Henderson. When Parkway was in Pittsburgh he alienated a lot of people because he was a big, proud, boisterous black man who broke most of the rules and didn't mind flaunting his talent or wealth. I think he was probably the only ballplayer brave enough to wear a diamond earring and the only one big enough to get away with it.

He is never at a loss for words; the more outrageous the situation, the more he's on stage. In the tiny elevator that takes players, press, and executives from level to level at the Oakland Coliseum things can get downright claustrophobic. One night, Parker, Dave Henderson, and myself crowded on with a couple of New York reporters for the long ride to the top. The reporters, being just a tiny bit smaller than the average Athletic, moved to make room. One guy, Steve Buckley of the *Hartford Courant,* a nice Irish-

Catholic kid from Boston, accidentally stepped on Parker's feet. Next thing you know, Parker's booming, "Don't you know better than to step on a black man's white shoes?"

I thought that poor kid was going to die.

Players knew the feeling once Parker got going. Dave Henderson was the primary target of Dave's home-run ritual. Hendu would always say the wrong thing. Next thing you knew, "Parkway" was going off. "What have you done?" Parker would ask in that rapid-fire delivery of his. "Let me go pull the book on you. Wait, you don't have a hundred home runs yet? You've only got ninety-one? The way you talk, I thought you had more like nine hundred ninety." Not until Hendu eased into the hundred-home-run club did Parker let up.

Parkway always reminded Dennis Eckersley, Bob Welch, and all the other pitchers he used to face in the National League, of how many home runs he had hit off of them. He would tell "The Eck" how the Cubs had to redo Wrigley Field because they could not keep the ball in the ballpark when Eckersley pitched to Parker. He let everybody know he'd won a couple batting titles, would send guys off to read his bubble-gum card. "When you're done reading in about the next hour or so, get back to me," he told the A's youngsters a million times or more.

Flamboyant or not, Dave has always backed up the talk. His abilities and desire are without question. He plays hard every day. His slide into second is one of the most brazen and scary I've seen and that automatically makes him a favorite of mine.

Dave and I had a good relationship despite the awkwardness of knowing, by mid-May, that we would share the designated hitter's job. He respected what I had accomplished and I respected him. We never feuded, never talked about anything but our common goal, which was to win. He said that because we were sharing a job, we needed to be ready for certain situations. Selfishness never entered into it.

Dave Stewart was more than the number-one pitcher in the A's clubhouse. He was an agitator second only to Parker. He is also a class act and a self-effacing guy whose sense of humor has got him past some really rough times in his life.

Stew's got a sinister image, which is undeserved. It's fueled because he's imposing and fierce on the mound. Like Goose, Stew wears his hat pulled down so low you can't see his eyes. He scowls with the best of them, throws 90-plus, thus the nickname "Smoke." He has a black belt in karate, wears basic black off the field, two things that also foster a wrong impression. It's too bad that the media and fans shy away from Stew. If only they could talk to him. If only they could hear him talk.

Stew's image melts away as soon as he speaks. There's no bass in that voice. He's got a high-pitched delivery and a laugh that makes you want to say, "You've got to be kidding." That's when you see the real Stew. He's delightful, a good-hearted, gentle man who is a tremendous force on the field and in the community of Oakland, where he was raised. The word "class" applies to Stew and even that doesn't seem quite good enough.

Storm Davis has a different kind of image problem. He's the epitome of more than the guy-next-door, one of baseball's devout Christians. Being viewed as too religious can give you a bad rap; if you have a big game, don't give the guy the ball. Well, Orel Hershiser once said that just because he's a Christian doesn't mean he's a wimp. Storm is not a wimp, either. He had a rough World Series, but I would never hesitate to give Storm the ball in a big game, even the make-or-break game of the Series. I also admire Storm for what he doesn't do. He doesn't wear his religion on his sleeve. He lives God's way. He doesn't go behind anyone's back and doesn't pass judgment on guys who hold different beliefs. Maybe if more so-called 'born-again Christians' did that, there wouldn't be the mixed feelings some of those guys generate.

Carney Lansford is Mr. Intensity. He ranks in my top five base-runners when it comes to knowledge and breaking up double plays. Carney is a workaholic and an uncanny fielder. When he came up with the Angels, they tried to plant a lot of negative thoughts in his head, telling him he didn't have lateral range and needed glasses. Fortunately, Carney did not listen. Instead, he made himself into one of the brilliant third basemen of our time. He knows every inch of ground in the extremely spacious foul territory in Oakland. He knows every other park, as if he's played in each his entire career. You can't learn to be that good. It's instinctive. Carney is also good people, intelligent, caring, a guy who would walk through a wall to help a friend.

Ron Hassey was another veteran the A's signed because of the intangibles he could bring to a clubhouse. I never saw him pout even though he did not play every day. If he ever got angry, it was only at himself because he wasn't hitting or his knees gave him trouble. Most times, he's just himself, a genuinely funny guy whose influence cannot be measured in stats.

Ron's presence was definitely a positive for Terry Steinbach, the talented young catcher for the A's. He could watch and see a consummate professional call a game, see how pitchers responded. Guys put their trust in Ron and that works wonders over the course of a game and a season.

Ron and I played together in New York for a while. He is unique in that he loved the zoolike atmosphere, said it was better than watching soap operas on television. Ron also loved New York because it gave him recognition and it helped his game. As a left-handed hitter he did everything he had to in Yankee Stadium, adjusting to become a dangerous pull hitter. He found the seats in right field so often in prime-time moments, guys started calling him "The Babe." He loved it.

Ron might not ever lead the league in average, but he definitely leads in nicknames. The A's called him "Duke," because, like the hound dog on the "Beverly Hillbillies" TV show, Hass never moves. He waits for everyone to bring him things. A lot of catchers are retrievers. Ron is a nonretriever, he's so reluctant to move around. He was also called "Coach" because of his penchant for giving instructions.

The two things I'll remember more than any others about Ron is that he's a unique person, a good friend.

Another consummate professional is Dennis Eckersley. He's fierce on the mound, sometimes a little too fierce. Hitters hated Eck in his youth because of his habit of pretending to shoot his strikeout victims, as if he were a gunslinger. Dennis has toned down his act somewhat, substituting a pump of the fist for the make-believe six-shooter. But he earned the right to make that one little gesture of celebration. He saved an incredible 45 games, one shy of Dave Righetti's single-season record. He was just about untouchable all season and did put his name in the record books by recording 4 saves in four tries in the American League playoffs against the Red Sox.

Shortstop Walter Weiss was the 1988 Rookie of the Year for reasons diametrically opposed to why Canseco and McGwire won the award the previous two seasons. Walter is an impressive shortstop, with a lot of poise and grace in the field. He made the jump after just a handful of games in Triple A and played the entire season for a pennant winner, as tough a test as there is for a rookie.

Walter's a sharp kid, period. He grew up in New York and listened to the Yankees, did his homework and knows the history of the game. Walter actually knows of Curt Flood and what Curt sacrificed for other players, something a lot of kids don't ever bother to learn and recognize. Walter was a pleasure to watch, from his play to his maturity and work ethic.

In two years, I had met Walter and Greg Gagne, two youngsters who show that the new generation has its own core of dedicated players who listen, learn, and want to make themselves better major leaguers. That attitude can only make the game better.

39

BITTERSWEET SEASON

I'VE always agreed with the late Satchel Paige's philosophy, "Don't look back, something may be gaining on you." I even have the first part of that sentiment on a license plate.

I spent most of 1988 trying to live that belief. No matter how few and far between the at-bats became, I kept looking ahead. To the warm-weather months that usually brought the hits, to the stretch drive, the second season, and, finally that third season, the World Series.

The latter two goals had been attained the previous two years, a frightening regularity to some, a good-luck omen to others. I felt when I signed with the A's that they wanted more than just a good-luck charm. And they wanted more than just a veteran influence. You naturally believe that when the manager says there's a guarantee of 300 at-bats, tells the assembled media, steps right out there on a line for you.

By May we both realized he had made a promise he either could not or would not keep. Because of that a somberness fell over the 1988 season for me personally, one that lightened only for a few brief moments.

Looking back, though, I'd like to think of another promise made last winter, when I opted to sign with the A's instead of the Kansas City Royals. When Tony was still doing the selling and I was doing the buying, he said there had to be an understanding. If Dave Parker's knees could not take the pounding in the outfield or if he proved a defensive liability, Dave would share the designated-hitter's job. I had to live with that, if it should occur, Tony told me.

It did occur. And I kept my word.

Dave's problems in left field began to surface just as my bat started to come around. And the club made the switch as Tony had predicted. Dave started DHing more and more.

Maybe if I had got more hits early, Dave would have remained in left field. A typical April at the plate sealed too many people's opinions. My history of slow months followed by good ones did not seem to count that season. Perhaps a great April would not have made a difference, anyway. That I will never know.

I cannot pretend it was always easy, especially after Dave was disabled with a hand injury the first week of July, and missed over forty days. Even though I'd lost my platoon partner, I had not lost my platoon role. The at-bats still went elsewhere. In one instance Tony pulled me aside a half an hour before a game in Cleveland to tell me Jose Canseco was going to DH because he had a sore back. A start I had been given against left-hander Greg Swindell disappeared just like that. In another instance I lost a start against Milwaukee's Ted Higuera because Jose needed a day off from right field so he was going to DH. Left-handers were few and far between to begin with. By midsummer they had become pitchers other players chose to face while taking a little R & R in the designated hitter's position.

There were times when I fought the urge to say forget it, I don't want any part of this. I did go off and sulk a couple of times, but those few occasions lasted only an inning or two. There was a job to do in the clubhouse and on the bench. I had too much respect for my teammates to act selfishly while expecting more of them. The 1988 A's were a team obviously on a mission, one that would make them the best team in the game.

I wanted at-bats; the competitive part cannot help but come out. But I also knew from day one that I would not go back on my word.

Dave McKay helped a great deal, by throwing practice pitch after practice pitch. And always in the back of my mind I could hear Walter's voice saying, "You have to do your work, regardless of whether you're playing or not."

Dave Parker, who also was trying to adjust to less-than-full-time duties, would talk a lot about mental toughness, how we'd both have to dig a little deeper to get from at-bat to at-bat when they were stretched thin over weeks instead of days. The life of a swing-man was at hand.

One interested observer was Reggie Jackson, whose playing career had ended at the end of 1987. He was living in the Bay Area and visited the team often. One day in late August Jack gave me some advice. He had gone through platoons in California in 1986 and then again in 1987 with the A's. He had wanted to be a team player, so he did not express his concern about his dwindling role. Both times his cooperation led to unwanted exits at the end of the season. Reggie's concern for me was that I might be working myself into a similar position.

Reggie warned that if I did go to Tony and ask for at-bats I'd better be ready to produce. It took me two or three days to make the decision. I wanted to do it correctly, instead of on impulse.

When I did go in, Tony asked me if I were to get ten consecutive starts, would I recognize that the challenge was on? I told him that he wouldn't even need to tell me. I'd know the challenge was on when I saw my name in the lineup on the first day, the second day, the eighth, ninth, tenth day. I went into Baltimore, Boston, and New York and met the challenge, reaching base sixteen out of thirty-two times. There were some hit-by-pitches, a lot of walks, and, in Fenway and Memorial Stadium, home runs.

The starts never did reach ten, however. Dave returned from the disabled list.

But I had kept my promise. I went in, did what I had to do, challenged myself again. And it saved my peace of mind. I knew I could still play and still produce, if given an opportunity.

My strained relationship with Tony seemed to improve after we clinched. The pressure was off. The night after we won the division, I got 3 hits against the Twins in a game started by Frankie Viola, who was well on his way to a Cy Young season. The first hit off Frankie was a liner back up the middle. After the game, Tony patted me on the back and said, "You're amazing." That made me feel pretty good, after sitting for eleven days and not having seen one live pitch other than in batting practice.

Tony, who had difficulty talking to me after a period, did save one sentiment for one of his last team meetings. After we won the AL West, he wanted the players, coaches, and support staff to gather around so that he could read a list he had prepared for the occasion. He started by naming players in certain groups divided in terms of seniority. Young guys first, like Mark McGwire and Jose, Polonia, Eric Plunk, Walter, and Stanley Javier. "For the very first time you're a winner," he said. "That's so important to get rid of that monkey early. Ernie Banks's name comes up in every conversation about not winning. And it's important that you get that off your back, the sooner the better, because it becomes a burden later on."

He pointed out that Don Mattingly still had not shed that monkey after six seasons but that Walter Weiss had as a rookie. "I'm happy for him," Tony said.

Carney and Tony Phillips he praised for sticking it out through the bad years in Oakland, the many managers. He said Carney was our unofficial captain. "I'm happy for them."

Cadaret, Eck, Plunk, "I'm happy for you." Parker was supposed to be a malcontent and he'd proved them wrong, made our coaches look good, the organization look good. "I'm happy for him."

Then he came to "Baylor." Tony looked at me and said, "What can I say? This mystique about him, this presence thing, what he means to teams . . . I'm just happy we didn't screw it up. I'm happy for him."

On days like that I could see the La Russa I had heard so much about, the caring player's manager. I thought his gesture to the team was pretty awesome. I wish I could have carried that feeling over to the next day and the next.

Those moments were rare, though. And I don't know what I would have done without my wife, Becky. She made it bearable.

Becky came to every game regardless of whether I was playing or not. And the confidence she gave me was unending. I can't count the number of times she'd say, "You're playing today so I know we're going to win." That has always been her special message to me. Never was it more appreciated.

In my reduced role I hit .220, with 58 hits, 28 runs, 7 doubles, 7 home runs, and 34 RBI in 264 at-bats.

Our 104 victories was the highest in franchise history since the 1931 Philadelphia Athletics won 107. We equaled the total victories achieved by the 1984 Tigers, who started out 35–5. And we won more than any team since Earl's 1970 Orioles won 108.

Oakland's 50 road victories were tops in the major. When we clinched the division on September 20, it marked our 151st day in first place. The scares were few, even though the Twins actually won more games than they did in their championship season. But they could not catch up because we never had a real losing streak, and just kept clicking off wins. We beat the second-place Twins by 13 games. And the Twins had two more victories than the AL East champion Red Sox.

When a team is that good and then reels off four straight playoff victories, you cannot help but admire and savor some moments. The guys made it a lot more fun. Seeing kids like Luis Polonia, Stan Javier, and Walt Weiss having fun celebrating the championship reminded me of another kid in a clubhouse years ago in Baltimore. They had all pulled together and did very little to beat themselves. And they helped assure at least one veteran a seventh division championship. I have never gotten to the point where making the playoffs seems like a small accomplishment.

I knew that for a seventh time I was entering the championship series. I was also one step away from becoming the first player ever to play in three consecutive Series for three different teams. That feeling of accomplishment helped soothe a lot of raw feelings. My family gathered around me again. The leaves were turning brown and we were still around. It was getting so I'd forgot what it was to stop playing by the first week of October.

The American League Championship Series, like so many before, brought present and past together. The Boston Red Sox were taking another shot at the World Series, only won when Babe Ruth was still pitching for them.

It was a team vastly changed since it last entered postseason play in 1986.

Mac had been fired that July, never able to recover emotionally from the Series and unable to motivate the team, either. Mac was replaced by organization man Joe Morgan. Morgan, from Wapole, Massachusetts, saw Boston win 19 of its first 20 for him, then hold off the second-place Tigers. Morgan would prove to be unconventional, to say the least, pinch-hitting for Rice, Boggs, and, on the final day of the playoffs, for Dwight. It will probably take all winter for the Boston media to figure out all the subtle messages he sent in just four months.

Dwight was still Dwight, however. He rolled with the punches, including a temporary move from right field to first base. Despite the upheaval, he had one of his finest seasons ever, hitting .293, with 21 home runs and 111 RBI. I think both he and Dave Winfield each did more proving in one season than some players do in a lifetime.

Bruce Hurst, growing more dominant with each season, was 18–6, with a 13–2 record at home, unheard of for a left-hander in Fenway. Bruce, in an assignment befitting the league's best pitcher in the second half, was called on to start the playoffs against Dave Stewart. Stew pitched a five-hitter in six and a third innings. A Canseco home run came on Bruce's one major slip as we won, 2–1. Bruce allowed only 6 hits; in the first of what would be two starts, I was hitless in 3 at-bats.

I watched from the bench as Roger Clemens started Game Two, looking like the Clemens I knew so well, but whose lone mistake cost him a 2-run lead in the seventh. He allowed 3 runs, 2 on yet another Canseco home run. Rich Gedman did his best to help the Sox avoid the prospect of going to Oakland down by 2 games. He homered in the seventh off Greg Cadaret. The game wound up in the hands of the teams' respective stoppers, Dennis Eckersley and Lee Smith. Eck was the better pitcher on that day, pitching a scoreless bottom of the ninth right after Smith was roughed up for 3 hits, including Walter Weiss's RBI single in the top of the inning. Final score, 4–3.

The A's routed Mike Boddicker, 10–6, in Game Three. The ALCS seemed a blur, we were driving so quickly and assuredly toward the World Series. Bruce Hurst took the mound in Game Four, representing Boston's last stand. He again would face Stew and again come out with an "L" next to his name. But it was hard to say there was a loser in this matchup.

Stew pitched seven innings of 4-hit, 1-run ball. He struck out 5 Red Sox and his personal matchups with Dwight were the kind the good hitters and pitchers get up for. In the first Stew got Dwight to swing through strike three with the bases loaded and two out. It was the first of 2 strikeouts for Dwight, who, in quiet acknowledgment, told reporters, "I don't know if you can say some guys throw harder or not, but I would say that after facing him, when he wanted to he could put something extra on the ball."

Bruce also struck out 5, his coming in four innings. He allowed only 2 runs, but the cumulative effect of over 220 innings and a sore shoulder ended his day there. He had given up only 4 hits.

Lee Smith was asked by Morgan to keep the team close. The big right-hander did, for one inning. Then a Canseco single and stolen base, an RBI hit by McGwire pushed us up by 2 runs. With one out, Stanley Javier singled. Then little Luis Polonia coaxed out a walk. The bases were loaded. I was due up.

I knew Ron Hassey had grabbed a bat, recognized this as one of the situations where I could no longer tell what Tony's move would be. So I did not look back. I just walked to the plate. I wanted not only to get to the Series, but to help make a difference between winning and losing. I was not used to doing any less in ALCS play; when Bruce shut me down in Game One, it snapped a LCS-record twelve-game hitting streak. In Game Four, Bruce was still as tough. He caught me looking at strike three, got me on a comebacker, and then a shallow fly ball to center. I wanted that last at-bat badly. La Russa never stopped me. I stepped in and Smith threw a fastball, one of his best. I turned on it and pulled it into left-center, good enough for a sacrifice fly. It was my 17th RBI in 28 LCS games.

Afterward, as reporters asked me just how I could explain the consecutive trips to the Series, Jimmy LeFebvre, our hitting instructor, made his way through the crowd. Jimmy, soaked with champagne and a little emotional, hugged me and said, over and over, "They said you don't have the bat speed. That was a 94-mph fastball you hit."

We won, 4–1, completing the first LCS sweep since the seven-game format began in 1985. And my hat trick was complete. I know the A's probably would have won it without me. I also know I don't believe in luck. Winning at the crap table, that's luck. I know I'd tell people not to follow me there because they'd lose their shirts. So I don't believe in that at all. What I do believe is that winning doesn't just happen. The teams have to be good. And good teams have to want good players.

40

THE ODYSSEY
CONTINUES

THE 1987 Series victory with the Twins had helped rewrite my personal history in Games Six and Seven. But it was rewritten at the expense of the Cardinals.

In 1988, there was a chance to avenge the Game Six and Seven losses to the Mets, the team that beat the 1986 Red Sox. The Mets were still alive and trying to get past the Los Angeles Dodgers in the National League playoffs.

I thought about my family and friends and the 3,000-mile trek to New York, about the hostile and sometimes foul-mouthed Shea Stadium fans, about how my father, brother, and son had felt fear just walking in that park because they wore Red Sox paraphernalia. I thought about hotel hassles, crowded restaurants, and rude cabbies, traffic jams, dirty streets, and polluted air.

I wanted to go back.

I wanted the Mets, not only for myself, but for Dave Henderson, who was still by my side and also looking for a way back to Shea. Then there was Rene Lachemann, my friend and coach in Boston and now a coach with the A's. He, too, recalled standing on that top step of that dugout at Shea waiting for the celebration that never came. We all wanted back into that feud.

I stated that on several occasions to writers. And, on national television, I told NBC's Bryant Gumbel that, as the 100-game winner in the American League, it would be fitting for the A's to play the other 100-game winner, the "best team in the National League."

Well, I guess the Dodgers took exception. Tommy Lasorda and Orel Hershiser started sending "messages" through the media. "Tell Don Baylor this," "Don Baylor" that. It was like sitting up on that dais again, Angels, Dodgers, Angels, Dodgers, being straight man for Southern California's favorite sons. I thought it was funny, for about fifteen seconds.

I never slammed the Dodgers nor questioned their right to be in the Series. If they reached that final level, more power to them. I'd sat in too many clubhouses on the losers side in LCS play to ever begrudge a team its pennant victory.

Then the words I never want to hear reached me. A reporter I know said that the Dodgers' Jay Howell had jumped in, saying upon their pennant-clinching victory, "Don Baylor should apologize for being in the World Series. He's lucky to be there."

On the eve of my milestone Series, I felt I had been called a charity case. I responded. I told Bud Geracie of the *San Jose Mercury* that Howell's actions reflected the arrogance of that league that I'd had my fill of years before as a California Angel. Howell, I said, was right where he wanted to be during the playoffs—suspended, because he didn't want to pitch under pressure.

What I said was a reaction to what was said about me, as well as to the person who was doing the talking. If it were Orel Hershiser or someone else who had accomplished something, maybe I could have understood a little. But the inference came from someone who had been suspended four days earlier because of illegal use of pine tar on his glove. It is a technicality, but the rule was violated, in the eyes of the baseball establishment. Maybe it was Howell who was lucky to be there.

Geracie's paper gave the story to the *LA Times,* which put it on page one. It was silly, a lot of fuss over a guy who had not pitched in a week and a hitter three games away from a possible start. Still, it was a story. We all had to deal with it.

The day the A's arrived at Dodger Stadium for the pre-Series workout, Howell reached me in the trainer's room, very upset because of my remarks.

I told him I was very upset with his. Jay said his words were misconstrued. "You know me," he said.

"I thought I did," I answered. But there were no apologies because even though he insisted his words had been distorted, the two that were not taken out of context were "Don Baylor." He'd introduced names in reaction to an innocent comment I'd made on behalf of former Red Sox. I never mentioned a Dodger by name, let alone the Dodgers team. I told Jay I don't talk about players to the media like that, don't slam people unless I'm slammed first. When that happens, I told him, all anyone will ever get is one free shot. He'd had his.

The Dodgers did not win Game One because of my words. They won on a gutsy effort by Kirk Gibson. Unable to play, barely able to walk because of one bad hamstring and one bad knee, he pinch-hit in the bottom of the ninth with one on and two outs. And Gibson hit Dennis Eckersley's two-strike pitch into the pavilion in right field at Dodger Stadium.

For the entire postseason, the Dodgers had talked up their injuries and underdog status. The picture of Gibson limping around the bases was pure Hollywood, but it fit right in with the reputation the Dodgers were building. It worked for them and epitomized the Dodgers's ability to emotionally rise to the occasion. For five games, the A's just could not get the same kind of emotions flowing.

That might be the first time I ever felt a team counted one loss as two. We all knew who awaited us the next day, the man whose mere presence almost made it imperative to win the opener—Orel Hershiser.

The team of the year had the manager of the year, player of the year, fireman of the year, comeback player of the year, rookie of the year, and exec of the year. All we had to do was get past the pitcher of the year. The A's had the intensity to pull off such feats all season. We had beaten Saberhagen and Viola. We had beaten Greg Swindell when he was 10–0. We'd rolled through the playoffs against Clemens and Hurst, two guys who hardly ever gave up losses back-to-back. We needed to show Orel he could be beaten. Unfortunately, he's still waiting to be shown.

He was, throughout the playoffs and again in the Series, simply masterful. He shut us out, 6–0, in Game Two. I don't know that it was that close. Orel, as crafty as Nolan is wickedly fast, just danced a variety of pitches through the strike zone all night long. I pinch-hit against him in the eighth and struck out, one of his eight victims. With his shutout he ran his postseason stats to 3 runs in thirty-three and two-thirds innings. By the end of the Series he would have 2 complete-game victories and a stellar 17 strikeouts in eighteen innings. He only allowed the A's 2 earned runs. To have a pitcher like that on a roll is every manager's dream. He's the kind of imposing figure who can get into hitters' heads three days before he pitches. I know we were thinking about him coming back again in Game Five as soon as he threw his last pitch in Game Two.

Hershiser wasn't as perfect as he had been at the end of the season, when he pitched 6 shutouts and change to snap Don Drysdale's seemingly unbreakable record of fifty-eight consecutive scoreless innings. Orel was stopped at fifty-nine innings only because the season stopped on him. To me, that's a record like DiMaggio's consecutive-game hitting streak. Just attach the "can't be broken" tag . . . until the next Hershiser comes along.

Orel spoke at the news conference following Game One and was asked if he wanted to give a promised statement to Don Baylor, his response to my TV comments that he'd facetiously promised. Orel showed his class. Referring to me as Mr. Baylor, he said he'd never held anything against me and considered us teammates because we both would be on the players' negotiating team when contract talks begin in 1989. Orel also is involved in the "65 Roses" clubs and donated the car he won as Series MVP to cystic fibrosis.

Orel's right. We are on the same team in a lot of respects.

When Orel was through with us in Game Two I had a feeling we had lost our drive and focus. All year long we rose to every occasion. After that game, when I looked around I saw expressions of concern and worry. We were going home, but we did not feel as comfortable as the Twins had the year before or the Red Sox in the '86 ALCS. And those teams had stood one loss away from elimination.

Mark McGwire's ninth-inning home run off Howell in Game Three gave us a much-needed 2–1 victory. Still, it was a struggle. It was a game you knew would be won with a home run, but it was a questions of which team would get the big blow first. All the clutch-hitting was coming from the other dugout, not ours. Their emotional surges were endless. Even our victory seemed to leave us drained.

Before the start of Game Three I found out, from the media, that Tony was thinking about going with his two catchers against left-hander John Tudor. Terry Steinbach was his best hitter against left-handers and he wanted Ron Hassey to catch Bobby Welch. I was told by Tony, in a familiar refrain, that although the at-bats against John Tudor were rightfully mine, he had no choice but to use Steinbach at DH.

That topped the whole year off. I was still searching for that one big game that could make me feel a part of the team, not just an observer of a team that had won. I felt I still had to make a contribution. That game was going to be it. Because Tudor I knew. Tudor I could hit. It was show time, the World Series. Tom Kelly would not have hesitated. He didn't the year before, started me against Tudor, who was then a Cardinal. The home run, the 3 RBI in the 1987 Series spoke for themselves. The A's did not hear. The only message coming through to me was "We didn't count on you during the season or playoffs, so we won't in the Series."

The Dodgers won Game Four, 4–3. They were without injured right-fielder Mike Marshall, catcher Mike Scioscia, and Gibson, their left-fielder. The night before, they had watched a possible end to Tudor's career when a bad elbow forced him from the game. Yet they were still winning. I wondered if the word "destiny" had cropped up in Lasorda's news conference more than a couple hundred times that night.

Orel Hershiser put an end to the Series a night later, winning a sloppy game, 5–2.

The Series should have been the perfect place for our young bashers to shine. Jose had opened on such a good note, with a grand slam in Game One. Mark had our only game-winner. The two also had our only homers. And those homers were their only hits.

Jose and Mark did not swing the way they had all season. Maybe they were overmatched by Hershiser and the Dodgers staff. Or maybe they were just overwhelmed by their first World Series and all that the "third season" entails. Mark and Jose were not alone in their struggles. Other than Dave Henderson, no one really hit up to his capability. The team that led the majors in home runs only hit two in five games, the same number LA's backup outfielder, Mickey Hatcher, alone had in the Series.

The abilities of the A's hitters had been evident all season, but when the hitting stopped, so did the team. It's hard to say what happened; all I know is that I did not see the same team that had won 104 games during the season and had swept Boston in the playoffs.

Before the fifth game, Jose told reporters that, as a third-year player, he could not be expected to carry the team. That's too bad. I would have switched positions with him for just 1 at-bat to give that one more try. But all I got was 1 at-bat in five games. I know that did not qualify as a legitimate try.

After the final game, I dressed and walked across the outfield grass toward the parking lot behind the centerfield wall. There were still cameras set up in front of the dugouts, still whirring as reporters buzzed around while the Dodgers, their wives and families celebrated their championship.

By the time I got to the fence I felt nothing. No hurt, no anger. The 1988 season was over.

One frustrating week could not undo seventeen years, seven pennants, or the three consecutive World Series with three different teams, nothing any other man who ever wore the uniform could claim.

When I walked out of the Coliseum I knew I was searching again, already thinking about the next spring training, my next at-bat, my next pennant race. Maybe my search for that perfect organization is why I keep moving. After all the years of traveling, the closest thing to perfection was my first team, the Baltimore Orioles. And maybe one day I'll end up back there, like Frank says, for the long run in a second career, in baseball management.

The odyssey did not end that night in Oakland. I intend to stay in this game. It has given me so much, in memories, friendships, honors, and achievements.

I want to give something back.